Romanticism, Pragmatism
and
Deconstruction

B

Romanticism, Pragmatism and Deconstruction

Kathleen Wheeler

BLACKWELL
Oxford UK & Cambridge USA

First published 1993

Blackwell Publishers
108 Cowley Road
Oxford OX4 1JF
UK

238 Main Street
Cambridge, Massachusetts 02142
USA

British Library Cataloguing in Publication Data
A CIP catalogue record for this book is available from the British Library.

Library of Congress Cataloging-in-Publication Data
Wheeler, Kathleen M.
    Romanticism, pragmatism and deconstruction / Kathleen Wheeler.
        p.   cm.
    Includes bibliographical references and index.
    ISBN 0-631-17012-X. – ISBN 0-631-18964-5 (pbk)
    1. Romanticism.   2. Pragmatism.   3. Deconstruction.   I. Title.
PN603.W44   1993
809'.91 – dc20   92-46235
                                                                          CIP

Typeset in 10 on 12 pt Baskerville by Best-set Typesetters, Hong Kong
Printed in Great Britain by T. J. Press Ltd, Padstow, Cornwall
This book is printed on acid-free paper

To the memory of Jay Murphy

Experience seems to be the surest touchstone for everything.

Plato, *The Eighth Letter*

Contents

Preface

These movements of thought, romanticism, pragmatism, and deconstruction, could each be described as a reaction against the hegemony of both reason (narrowly conceived) and science, as the highest form of truth, which repeatedly asserted itself in the eighteenth, nineteenth, and twentieth centuries. Many subsidiary issues were involved in these debates, such as theories of language, art, criticism, and experience. In each of the three cases, philosophy and art criticism were both re-examined, as was the nature and role of imagination (or the intuitive and synthetic faculty), along with its main vehicle of expression, namely, metaphors and other figures of speech. Basic questions were also re-formulated about the goals and scope of philosophy, art, science, and religion, and central concepts such as truth, meaning, and literal language were examined, while the activities of interpretation, reading, and perception were reconsidered. What these three movements share most centrally, it can be argued, is their concern to challenge the 'tyranny of the reason' and all that such tyranny implies.

Like William Blake, they challenged the so-called triumph of science, as allegedly more true than any other discourse because 'universally successful'. They challenged the notion that neutrality and objectivity are possible in any meaningful sense, and they argued that meaningfulness is contextual. That they were often attacked for promulgating a pernicious relativism suggests a misunderstanding of their central, shared commitments. For their analyses of the illusions of objectivity, truth, and meaning, as conceptualized by other predecessors, were not examples of a pernicious relativism, but the healthy pragmatic scepticism of Plato's Socrates himself, as when he spoke of the limitations of geometry and mathematics generally:

the remnant which we said did in some sort lay hold on reality – geometry and the studies that accompany it – are, as we see, dreaming about being, but the clear waking vision of it is impossible for them as long as they leave the assumptions which they employ undisturbed and cannot give any account of them. For where the starting point is something that the reasoner does not know, and the conclusion and all that intervenes is a tissue of things not really known, what possibility is there that assent in such cases can ever be converted into true knowledge or science?[1]

That we arrive at our 'standards', whether moral, aesthetic, or scientific through accumulated and sifted experience, and from some point of view, and that they are subject to change given different points of view, further sifting, and greater accumulation, hardly implies that discrimination is no longer possible – that 'anything goes'. What is implied is a demanding moral and intellectual rigor to keep alert to the evidences of a need for reconsideration and alteration of our point of view and our standards, in the light of new experiences or new evidence. A considerable tolerance is also demanded, since alterable perspectives and standards mean that at all times we need to listen to others to ensure that we have not failed to take into account matters that could persuade us to change our standard, or to recognize that we have been inconsistent. Socrates repeatedly argued, especially in the *Sophist* and *Gorgias*, against the 'pernicious' scepticism of the Sophists, which he opposed with his pragmatic scepticism in numerous ways. For example, in the *Phaedo*, one of his hearers sums up his arguments:

I think, just as you do, Socrates, that although it is very difficult if not impossible in this life to achieve certainty about these questions, at the same time it is utterly feeble not to use every effort in testing the available theories, or to leave off before we have considered them in every way, and come to the end of our resources. It is our duty to do one of two things, either to ascertain the facts, whether by seeking instruction or by personal discovery, or, if this is impossible, to select the best and most dependable theory which human intelligence can supply, and use it as a raft to ride the seas of life – that is, assuming that we cannot make our journey with greater confidence and security by the surer means of a divine revelation.[2]

In the *Meno*, Socrates' pragmatic strain is strong throughout the dialogue, as when he stated:

I shouldn't like to take my oath on the whole story, but one thing
I am ready to fight for as long as I can, in word and act – that is, that
we shall be better, braver, and more active men if we believe it right
to look for what we don't know than if we believe there is no point
in looking because what we don't know we can never discover
(86b–c).[3]

Plato's Socrates spoke often of theories being 'as certain as anything can
be', or of being 'a reasonable contention and a belief worth
risking . . . we should use such accounts to inspire ourselves with confidence' (*Phaedo* 114d). Earlier, he argued for 'truth in so far as it is
possible for the human mind to attain it' (107b). In the *Republic* (539b–
d), he sharply distinguished sophistic and pragmatic scepticism, while in
the *Theaetetus* he clearly reaffirmed his pragmatic scepticism straight
through to the end of the dialogue, when he introduced his metaphor of
midwifery, his divine inspiration, and his categorical denial of knowledge. Socrates' own relativism – his pragmatic scepticism – enraged his
Athenian compatriots. He was condemned to death. Three of the main
accusations against such writers as Coleridge, Derrida, Blake, Shelley,
and Nietzsche included, first, destroying the morals of the youth, second, nihilism, and, finally, madness. Dewey and James have had their
assailants, but have been spared the viciousness of the other attacks, in
the main.

While there are many shared views and techniques amongst
Coleridge, Dewey, and Derrida, for example (as well as the other writers
discussed here), there are also notable and significant differences. Indeed, the differences in that crucial element – style – and that central
unifying technique – form – are so great as to create an almost
unbridgeable gulf, at first glance. The differences in the styles of
Coleridge and Derrida may be more of temperament and individuality
than of genre, *per se*. Coleridge's prose was attacked by his contemporaries in ways most characteristic of some present-day attacks on
Derrida's writings. Dewey and James, on the other hand, were thinkers
of a more abstract temperament, more familiar to philosophical writing,
albeit Dewey too was repeatedly criticized for his 'incomprehensible'
style! These major stylistic differences represent a substantial intellectual
diversity, just as William Blake, Emily Dickinson, Wallace Stevens, Sylvia
Plath, and John Donne, for example, are poets of marked individual
styles. Indeed, the diversity of style within English and German romanticism alone is itself well-known and often commented upon. This book
has, therefore, not so much emphasized the diversity amongst the writers
discussed (which is clear enough at a glance); rather, it has attended

more to the ways in which these three movements have all acted as various reactions against the extreme rationalist systems of philosophical and literary predecessors in each century. In such systems, aspects of experience were demoted to inferior status in preference to a narrow, analytic conception of human experience as based primarily upon reason, with science designated as truth about reality, and its language conceived of as pre-eminently literal and representational.

These three movements could also be said to be based firmly on Socratic anti-rationalism. Plato's Socrates repeatedly, avowedly, and demonstrably insisted upon the role of metaphor, symbol, imagery, irony – rhetoric in general – in the language of science and philosophy, and upon the role of what he called intuition, the 'divine gift', and inspiration to supplement logic and reason (understood as analytic). Knowledge and right opinion Socrates defined as dynamic, as relational, as the connections between things – not as univocal, discursive statements couched in some notionally neutral (literal) language.

The following chapters seek to set out some of the most striking common interests of these romantic, pragmatist, and deconstructionist writers. Nevertheless, respect for the stylistic peculiarities is maintained: one must not underplay the marvellous diversity and individuality of these several great artist-philosophers. An awareness of the similarities and differences is of intellectual-historical interest, but also clarifies some of the intricacies and complexities of post-structuralist theory which are still opaque today to many readers. A better understanding, through such clarification, may help to defuse some of the (at times, rather hysterical) attacks upon post-structuralism. Recent debates, moreover, between such writers as Richard Rorty and Christopher Norris, have revealed considerable differences in the interpretation of Derrida's writings. Norris is correct in insisting that deconstruction, and Derrida's 'philosophy' in particular, is not merely a form of neo-pragmatism, as Norris believed Rorty to allege. (Whether Rorty took quite such a positive position is arguable and, indeed, doubtful.) However, Norris is surely mistaken in his account as to why deconstruction and Derrida differ from James's and Dewey's pragmatism and from Rorty's neo-pragmatism. That is, Norris offered an essentialist argument which involves transcendental claims of the kind which Derrida himself criticized Heidegger for (allegedly) espousing (see The *Contest of Faculties*, Christopher Norris, 1986).

One of the most central arguments of the present book is that both deconstruction and pragmatism apparently offer very similar critiques of metaphysics and similar aesthetic and literary critiques (both of which also share, if not actually rely on, aspects of romantic theories of art and criticism). These similarities, however, mask important differences amongst romanticism, pragmatism, and deconstruction of the Derrida type. For the latter makes considerable strides forward in its revolution in style and language, and it is foremostly in its style and language that it is to be distinguished primarily from pragmatic philosophies, in particular (and their related literary theories), not by virtue of some essentialist, transcendentalist claim, as Norris alleged. It would of course be a grave error to imagine that differences in style and language are 'merely' differences in rhetoric or ornamentation, or that one might conclude that deconstruction is a species of romanticism or pragmatism, at least in its content, though differing in its style. On the contrary, style and language cannot be divided from content and ideas; style and use of certain types of language is a vital part of the content, theme, and idea. A difference in style and use of language means a difference in content, idea, and philosophic standpoint, and is a crucial expression of the living individuality of artists and philosophers.

By examining closely Dewey's and James's critiques of metaphysics, and Dewey's theory of art and aesthetics (based as it is on certain aspects of English and German Romanticism) and by looking carefully at Dewey's ideas on language, we can, however, grasp more clearly certain principles involved in any coherent 'critique of metaphysics' and any critique of conventional literary theories (theories, that is, which take for granted reading, perception, interpretation, and subject–object dualisms as in no need of analysis). Once these initial principles are more clearly grasped, it is easier to make a transition to what Derrida is 'on about'. It would be erroneous, however, to suppose that Derrida is just a flashy neo-pragmatist, simply because a thorough grasp of the insights of English and German romanticism and American pragmatism gives us a 'way in' to Derrida. Derrida probably goes further than any thinker in the last century, except perhaps Nietzsche, to break through the constraints of unconscious 'logocentrism', and to offer a style of writing that provides the means of a greater awareness of the ways in which language (or certain notions dominating language) constrains our view of objects, texts, art, reality, the world, experience, philosophy, perception, or whatever, to unnecessarily narrow conceptions which are devoid of imagination, stereotyped, and which inhibit fresh response.

After discussing the pragmatism of James and Dewey, Derrida's deconstructive project will be considered in distinction from the deconstructive projects of well-known American critics. German and English Romantic 'origins' for both pragmatism and deconstruction will be explored, with a view to further clarification. Moreover, it will be noted in particular that the extraordinarily liberating and revolutionary writings of such thinkers as, first, Nietzsche and Shelley, and, secondly, Hegel, have much in common with Derrida. Finally, in the conclusion to the book, the reaction to post-structuralist writing, which began in the early 1980s and is known paradoxically as 'the new historicism', will be examined with a view to clarifying further the importance of the Blakean bridling of a Urizenic reason which romanticism, pragmatism, and deconstruction offer, in their several, distinct ways.

Acknowledgements

My deepest gratitude is to John Wright, of Ann Arbor, Michigan, the Blake scholar, who, over two decades, patiently and lucidly discoursed on Blake, theory, language, delight, and 'a thousand things – let me see if I can give you a list – Nightingales, Poetry – on Poetical sensation – Metaphysics – Different genera and species of Dreams – Nightmare – a dream accompanied by a sense of touch – single and double touch – A dream related – First and second consciousness – Monsters – the Kraken – Mermaids – Southey believes in them – Southey's belief too much diluted – A Ghost story –'

To John Beer I owe decades of advice and encouragement, professional insight and support of a decisive kind, and, most of all, a warm friendship. Denise Degrois gave her time to converse about Coleridge and romanticism, while Pamela McCallum offered helpful insights in the earliest stages of this work ten years ago, as did Uchang Kim in the very last stages. Barbara Bauer thought through with me the intricacies of the new pragmatism, while Richard Rorty gave up an afternoon at St John's College in 1984 to clarify some aspects of Dewey's 'overcoming of the tradition'. Christopher Norris discussed deconstruction versus pragmatism one day at the English Faculty, while Christopher Johnson's fine doctoral dissertation enlightened us both about Darwin, evolution, and Derrida. Jacques Derrida answered some difficult questions on the occasion of his Honorary Degree conferral at Cambridge in June, 1992. Over the whole of this undertaking hovered a higher guiding intellect, however, by which one could almost emblem the Inventive faculty, or a writer of Genius, himself: 'he varies his course yet still glides onwards – all lines of motion are his – all beautiful, and all propulsive – . . . So varied he and of his tortuous train / Curls many a wanton wreath; yet still he proceeds and is proceeding –', namely, Samuel Taylor Coleridge.

A major portion of this book was written in 1986, in the paradisiacal surroundings of the University of California at Santa Barbara (an opportunity made possible by the late Bill Frost), where Giles Gunn also made useful comments about theory and pragmatism at lunch one day in the delightful surroundings of the Faculty Club, and again on a visit of his to Cambridge in 1987. To St John's College, Cambridge, I am indebted for various research grants which saw this work through several difficult hurdles. The librarians of the English Faculty and the Cambridge University Library deserve warm thanks for fundamental help of various kinds. To the Master and Fellows of Darwin College I am very grateful for many kinds of support. Finally, to Anne Rendell, who got this manuscript into legible typescript, I cannot express enough gratitude, since otherwise it would probably have remained an illegible scrawl to this day.

Abbreviations

S. T. COLERIDGE

Biographia

Biographia Literaria; or Biographical Sketches of my Literary Life and Opinions. With his Aesthetical Essays, ed. J. Shawcross, 2 vols, London, 1907.

CL

The Collected Letters of Samuel Taylor Coleridge, ed. E. L. Griggs, 6 vols, Oxford, 1956–71.

The Friend

The Friend. A Series of Essays in Three Volumes. To Aid in the Formation of Fixed Principles in Politics, Morals, and Religion, with Literary Amusements Interspersed, ed. Barbara E. Rooke, 2 vols. Vol. 4 of *The Collected Coleridge*. London and Princeton, 1969.

Lay Sermons

Lay Sermons (Including *The Statesman's Manual*), ed. R. J. White. Vol. 6 of *The Collected Coleridge*, London and Princeton, 1972.

Marginalia

Marginalia. Samuel Taylor Coleridge. The Collected Coleridge, ed. George Whalley and H. J. Jackson, 3 vols so far published, Princeton and London, 1980.

CN

The Notebooks of Samuel Taylor Coleridge, ed, Kathleen Coburn and M. Christensen, 4 parts in 8 vols, so far published, London and New York, 1957.

OTHER AUTHORS

WP

Nietzsche. *Will to Power*, tr. Walter Kaufmann, New York, 1968.

Daybreak

Daybreak, tr. R. J. Hollingdale, intro. M. Tanner, Cambridge, 1982.

GS

Gay Science, tr. W. Kaufmann, New York, 1974.

Part I

Romantic and Germanic
Backgrounds

1

Shelley and Nietzsche: 'Reality' as Rhetoric

Shelley's Universe of Poetry

We do not attend sufficiently to what passes within ourselves. We combine words, combined a thousand times before. In our minds we assume entire opinions; and in the expression of those opinions, entire phrases, when we would philosophize. Our whole style of expression and sentiment is infected with the tritest plagiarisms. Our words are dead, our thoughts are cold and borrowed.

Let us contemplate facts; let us, in the great study of ourselves, resolutely compel the mind to a rigid consideration of itself. We are not content with conjecture, and inductions, and syllogisms, in sciences regarding external objects. As in these, let us also, in considering the phenomena of mind, severely collect those facts which cannot be disputed. Metaphysics will thus possess this conspicuous advantage over every other science, that each student, by attentively referring to his own mind, may ascertain the authorities upon which any assertions regarding it are supported. There can thus be no deception, we ourselves being the depositaries of the evidence of the subject which we consider.

Metaphysics may be defined as an inquiry concerning those things belonging to, or connected with, the internal nature of man.

It is said that mind produces motion; and it might as well have been said, that motion produces mind.[1]

Shelley's 'Defence of poetry' constituted a radical break with eighteenth-century theories of language, encumbered as they were by impoverished notions of reason, nature, poetry, and imagination, and labouring under an unenlightened empiricism which led theorists to view language as essentially literal, discursive, and propositional. Figures of speech were viewed as an enemy to truth since, allegedly, they aroused the passions, clouded the judgement, and led the mind away from rational, universal statements. Coleridge had repeatedly complained about the poverty of such theories as expressed by numerous eighteenth-century writers,[2] seeking to locate a universe of symbol, metaphor, and poetry in immediate experience, as Blake was doing contemporaneously. Literal language, the univocal statement, and a narrow conception of reason (as *dianoia*, not *nous*), far from leading to truth, led to a 'hunger-bitten and idealess philosophy', according to Coleridge.[3] Shelley, basing himself firmly on a radical interpretation of empiricism synthesized with Socratic-Platonic elements, broke into new formulations of language as essentially and pre-eminently rhetorical, of imagination as constitutive of all experience (from the most basic acts of perception to higher cultural products) and of metaphor, not the univocal, literal statement, as the vehicle of truth. By developing Coleridge's theory of primary and secondary imagination into a theory of epistemology, Shelley arrived at the radical analogy between the way the human mind experiences and transforms the world of nature and reality, and the way artists make poems and other artifacts, thereby transforming the world of human culture. Like Coleridge, Shelley saw imagination not as the special province of the artist but as the paradigmatic form of all human mental activity. In these ways, the 'Defence of poetry' constitutes an anticipation of much of Nietzsche's writing on truth, rhetoric, language, and reality. It is, for Shelley, primarily the poet and poetry which lead to truth and knowledge, by means of the synthetic power of imagination (as opposed to the merely analytical understanding) and its vehicle, metaphor. Both imagination and metaphor are central to the composition and structure of experience, as Shelley learned by synthesizing corresponding elements of empirical and Platonic philosophy, much as Coleridge had done in the *Biographia Literaria* and certain essays of *The Friend*.[4]

Coleridge had explicitly discussed on several occasions the necessity of a reconciliation between the more useful, radical elements of empiricism (such as that experience, not tradition or dogma, must be our arbiter, and that we seek to revise experience, not discover final truths) and Platonism (which acknowledged the constructive role of mind, and emphasized synthesis over its servant, analysis).[5] Far from conceiving of imagination as the agency and metaphor as the vehicle for transcendence to some unchanging, supernatural One,[6] Shelley, like the German romantics and Coleridge, conceived of a Hegelian-Deweyan apocalyptic universe, a universe of poetry, apocalyptic because continuously evolving and in a constant state of creation. Dualisms collapsed as Shelley conceived of mind/world, subject/object, thoughts/things as mere conventions rather than independent existents passively perceived:

> Most errors of philosphers have arisen from considering the human being in a point of view too detailed and circumscribed. He is not a moral, and an intellectual, – but also, and pre-eminently, an imaginative being. His own mind is his law; his own mind is all things to him. If we would arrive at any knowledge which should be serviceable from the practical conclusions to which it leads, we ought to consider the mind of man and the universe as the great whole on which to exercise our speculations. Here, above all, verbal disputes ought to be laid aside, though this has long been their chosen field of battle. It imports little to inquire whether thought be distinct from the objects of thought. The use of the words *external* and *internal*, as applied to the establishment of this distinction, has been the symbol and the source of much dispute. This is merely an affair of words, and as the dispute deserves, to say, that when speaking of the objects of thought, we indeed only describe one of the forms of thought – or that, speaking of thought, we only apprehend one of the operations of the universal system of beings.[7]

More radically, Shelley argued that:

> The words *I, you, they*, are not signs of any actual difference subsisting between the assemblage of thoughts thus indicated ... [but are] grammatical devices invented simply for arrangement, and totally devoid of the intense and exclusive sense usually attached to them.[8]

Contrary to the claims of much critical writing on Shelley, like the German romantic ironists Shelley offered open-ended and stimulating, phenomenological speculations which make no pretence of determining transcendental being or truth. As with Coleridge, his indeterminate, visionary speculations led to a conception of both mind and the universe as genuinely organic, in the sense of continuously evolving in unpredictable and unimaginable ways. This more vital evolutionary conception of the word 'organic' or 'system' – as implying indeterminate growth and transformation as a major character of existence – relates both Coleridge and Shelley to the German Romantics and to Hegel, whose system is generally understood as an anti-system.[9] As with Shelley, the misplaced critical conception of the German Romantics (as positing an immutable, transcendent essence for which the spirit yearns)[10] has been established only by ignoring the import of the greater part of their writings, which suggest not so much traditional metaphysics as 'interminable agility' and 'continuous creation'.

Shelley's prefaces, poetry, and particularly his 'Defence of poetry' represent the culmination of an intellectual shift which gained impetus in the late eighteenth century with Blake, Coleridge, and German thinkers – including Kant – a shift based upon the influential but often poorly understood philosophies of such writers as Hume and Berkeley. Hume's Socratic scepticism had led Kant to a re-evaluation of epistemological and ontological issues, while Berkeley's radical synthesis of idealism and empiricism influenced Coleridge and Shelley decisively. This shift could be described as one from passive, associationist theories of mind to a theory of mind as constructive and creative in the composition of experience. Yet Coleridge had argued that this tension between passive and active mind theorists was evident throughout Western thought since pre-Socratic times; indeed, Western philosophy was the record of that conflict.[11] It is clear that Hume and Berkeley brought home to Kant and his contemporaries the complete inadequacy of sensationalist, associationist theories which viewed mind as passive. Yet empiricism was not rejected outright, since as Kant, Coleridge, and Shelley all realized, its emphasis upon sound method of enquiry, experiment, and experience was an indispensable element for understanding human experience. Idealism could not provide a satisfactory solution, however, since, as Dewey complained a century later, it endowed mind with world-creating powers, thereby contradicting experience and retaining the old dualism between mind and nature, though reversing their hierarchy. The retention of such traditional dualisms crippled any genuine transformation in intellectual orientation, as Blake, Shelley, and Coleridge realized.

The late eighteenth century could be described then as a transformation from dualistic thinking to thought based on relation and integration, on dynamic opposition and functional, relative differences, or, as Blake put it, on the 'marriage of heaven and hell'. While efforts to get beyond dualistic thinking can be seen as early as Hume, Berkeley, and in some less successful respects the neo-Platonists,[12] such strivings took a variety of different forms, and were often badly encumbered by an outmoded vocabulary which trapped thinkers into the very snares they were trying to escape. Dewey was, later, to argue precisely that Kant's best insights and radical innovations were obscured and even hidden from some of his readers by an inadequate, inherited vocabulary which imported the very dualisms and insinuations of transcendents which Kant sought to argue against.[13] Coleridge had similarly praised Kant for his advances in the logic, while arguing that – in the metaphysic – Kant had fallen prey to dualistic formulations which led inevitably to unwanted transcendentals like the 'manifold' and the 'noumenon'.[14] Nearly a century earlier, Berkeley had struggled to redefine the word 'idea' in order to express a Deweyan, Heideggerean synthesis of subject and object, in an effort to reject traditional dualistic accounts of experience. Like Dewey's redefinition of 'experience' as synthetic, Berkeley's effort was also misunderstood, and was interpreted as a traditional idealism, while Hume was seen as a nihilistic, instead of a Socratic, sceptic.

Shelley succeeded more, it could be argued, than Coleridge in creating a new and more adequate vocabulary for his non-dualistic, synthetic speculations. Coleridge, much like Kant, remained somewhat encumbered by confusing terms in his metaphysical meditations, though he freed himself more completely in his criticism and in his aesthetic, psychological explorations. These latter writings (The *Friend*, the *Biographia Literaria*) may have provided Shelley with the stimulus he needed to reformulate correspondences between Platonism and empiricism into a synthetic and compositional theory of experience. Coleridge, and later Hegel, had provided Shelley with a Berkeleyan solution to both overt and disguised dualisms, by radicalizing the conception of the nature of perception to show perception as itself essentially active and creative, as Berkeley had (so futilely) tried to do decades earlier. The senses do not receive passively an already constituted, independent material (however primitive) which the reason then orders, formulates, and qualifies. According to Coleridge and Shelley, the senses themselves are imbued with reason, actively producing 'material' which is itself saturated with connections and relations, as Dewey also later maintained. Coleridge was not making an idealist assumption in his theory of perception as itself the most primary, imaginative activity; nor did he adopt a semi-idealist notion that an already constituted, independent mind set up against an objective, material manifold creates the secondary nature of that manifold. He meant, as Shelley did shortly after him, that to conceive of a subject-mind outside the world constitutes the basis of a dualism which leads to specious 'philosophical problems'. Like Heidegger, he understood mind to be in and of the world, its powers congruent with, indeed one with, the powers of nature. Or, as scientists argue today, the observer is a crucial part of the observed.

Shelley's own elaboration of a theory of experience, perception, and poetry can be said to have gone beyond Coleridge's account, in Shelley's crucial and systematic emphasis, in both the prose and poetry, upon metaphor as the central focus for his speculations on language, art, and human experience. Through his focus upon metaphor as the vehicle for knowledge, whether in science, philosophy, or art, he anticipated modern philosophy of science in startling and impressive detail, not only by seeing the observing mind as part of the observation;[15] Shelley, in embracing Coleridge's account of perception and imagination, rejected earlier accounts of imagination as a merely expressive or representative faculty of already constituted perceptions. Emphasizing a more constructive and formative role for the imagination in perception and in the construction of human experience, he took Coleridge's primary/secondary imagination distinction and reinterpreted it accurately (unlike Coleridge's confused contemporaries, not to mention many later readers[16]) as Coleridge's account of the crucial analogy existing between basic perception and artistic (and poetic) creation. The poet's activity is not to be conceived of as some special, higher mental act, but as exemplary of the nature of all human mental activity. (Dewey made this analogy the very basis of his philosophy of education in *Democracy and Education*.)

This perception-creation analogy has been poorly understood even today, a difficulty well accounted for by Berkeley's idea of the 'outness prejudice', which, he explained, makes it almost impossible for the casual thinker to overcome her view of perception as essentially a passive receptivity of the world 'out there', while artistic creation is reserved for the mind of genius. Shelley realized, in part as a result of German and English romantic distinctions between symbol (or metaphor) and allegory, that metaphor – unlike allegory or fanciful images (such as Pegasus, the winged horse) – is marked by a genuine fusion, an essentially relational character which has integrity for the mind. This contrasts with the mechanical and artificial juxtapositions of the fancy, the memory, and the other mechanical, associative mental acts, which lead to allegories and other non-metaphorical tropes. Through the integral (for the mind) fusion achieved in metaphor, a unity is created which releases new and previously unimagined relations. Moreover, these new relations provide fresh, original materials for experience and for poetry. They constitute new knowledge in their metaphorical form, relating previously known elements not only to new elements, but also to new ways of experiencing or viewing experience. The field of knowledge is continuously expanding and rearranging itself as central elements are pushed to the periphery, while previously peripheral or previously unknown elements become centres and foci for knowledge (to use a metaphor of Quine's in *From a Logical Point of View*). For Shelley:

> A man, to be greatly good, must imagine intensely and comprehensively; he must put himself in the place of another and

of many others; the pains and pleasures of his species must become his own. The great instrument of moral good is the imagination; and poetry administers to the effect by acting upon the cause. Poetry enlarges the circumference of the imagination by replenishing it with thoughts of ever new delight, which have the power of attracting and assimilating to their own nature all other thoughts, and which form new intervals and interstices whose void for ever craves fresh food. Poetry strengthens the faculty which is the organ of the moral nature of man, in the same manner as exercise strengthens a limb. A poet therefore would do ill to embody his own conceptions of right and wrong, which are usually those of his place and time, in his poetical creations, which participate in neither:[17]

Shelley saw our body of knowledge, our experience, and our universe as in a continual state of renewal, not as static, immutable, and perfect – hence passively perceived. Like poetry and art, which are continually renewed and re-created, human experience and knowledge (as well as the mind, the world, and language), are constantly changing (as Dewey and James were later to argue, and Derrida, Nietzsche, and Heidegger demonstrated in their literary-philosophical hybrids). 'Mont Blanc', 'Adonais', and 'The Triumph of Life', far from being expressed yearnings for a transcendent reality, are open-ended, nascent visions never meant to offer solutions to the doubts and uncertainties that assail the mind:

> How vain it is to think that words can penetrate the mystery of our being! Rightly used they may make evident our ignorance to ourselves, and this is much . . . the solid universe of external things is 'such stuff as dreams are made of'. . . . Philosophy, impatient as it may be to build, has much work yet remaining as pioneer for the overgrowth of ages. It makes one step towards this object; it destroys error, and the roots of error. It leaves what is too often the duty of the reformer in political and ethical questions to leave, a vacancy. It reduces the mind to that freedom in which it would have acted, but for the misuse of words and signs, the instruments of its own creation.[18]

Like Coleridge, Shelley never developed a philosophical system or body of dogma which was meant to convey to his readers some world view. Even in Coleridge's late religious work, *Aids to Reflection,* the major thrust of his efforts is toward speculation on how words can be redefined and reinterpreted[19] to yield new, integral relations about religious themes of life, death, existence, time, and individuality, those great mysteries before which 'words tremble on an abyss'. Shelley, Coleridge, Blake, and the German romantics shared a desire to press upon their readers the implications for philosophy of a synthetic power of imagination and of metaphor as a direct instrument, record, and form of knowledge. For Shelley, as for many scientists today, mind and world are a *Dasein*; that is, they are intimately united: the so-called substance of experience is not some inconceivable, transempirical other, but the result of the primary activity of the power of imaginativeness – within and without – creating metaphors and relations which themselves form the substance of experience. Metaphors become the material from which higher-level cultural artifacts and institutions are created, as Nietzsche, too, argued. Human experience is understood by Shelley as the creation of myth from metaphors. Moreover, immediate experience is at the centre of the human being's imaginative world (as empiricists had argued), while the essential character of knowledge is relational (as idealists had argued), not discursive and univocal. With Nietzsche and Dewey, Shelley insisted that the mind has no knowledge whatsoever beyond what it itself is interested in, what it decides to attend to, whether for purposes of survival or pleasure. Consequently, the composition of thoughts and experiences from other thoughts and experiences, according to metaphorical relations and imaginative synthesis, has no integrity beyond what the human mind itself regards as integral. Hence, the unifying, productive activity of mind is expressive of its own evolving, apocalyptic nature. Its activity and the products of such activity, such as language, art, and culture, are not a reflection or representation of some extra-experiential, supernatural Reason, Matter, or Nature.

Metaphors Shelley understood to be syntheses by the imagination of the elements (themselves metaphors) of experience. The character of experience is itself compositional; it consists of such syntheses. For Shelley and Coleridge, to ask what is the 'real' substance or nature behind (or constituting) the basic material of experience is to postulate a non-empirical element of experience of which we have no evidence and no need, except in so far as dualistic thinking has created an 'outness prejudice' and an apparent need for such an unintelligible 'entity'. Imagination is said by Shelley (anticipating such philosophers as Nelson Goodman)[20] to transgress the usual ways of relating and sorting things: it crosses familiar categories and produces hybrid elements – new ways of interpreting and seeing the world. These hybrids disrupt and disturb already prevalent, firmly entrenched beliefs and habitual notions. Shelley termed such habitual, stereotyped ways of perceiving and thinking 'dead metaphors' – meaning words or phrases which have become signs for portions and classes of thought no longer apprehended as something synthesized by the mind – no longer a 'picture of integral thought'. When taken as a name for integral things which no longer are integrally fused for the mind, such 'dead metaphors', like dogmas in philosophy and religion, tyrannize over the mind and dictate to it what is no longer living, meaningful, or a stimulant to fresh response. Shelley argued that language is littered with clichés – with dead metaphors and stereotyped responses which pass for fresh response and original activity – while the language of genuine poets is characterized as vitally metaphorical – whether it revitalizes integral relations already known, or whether it marks or creates new relations of integrity apprehended by the mind:

> Their language is vitally metaphorical; that is, it marks the before unapprehended relations of things and perpetuates their apprehension, until the words which represent them become, through time, signs for portions or classes of thoughts instead of pictures of integral thoughts; and then if no new poets should arise to create afresh the associations which have been thus disorganized, language will be dead to all the nobler purposes of human intercourse. These similitudes or relations are finely said by Lord Bacon to be 'the same footsteps of nature impressed upon the various subjects of the world'; and he considers the faculty which perceives them as the storehouse of axioms common to all knowledge. In the infancy of society every author is necessarily a poet, because language itself is poetry; and to be a poet is to apprehend the true and the beautiful, in a word, the good which exists in the relation, subsisting, first between existence and perception, and secondly between perception and expression. Every original language near to its source is in itself the chaos of a cyclic poem: the copiousness of lexicography and the distinctions of grammar are the works of a later age, and are merely the catalogue and the form of the creations of poetry.[21]

He contrasted this vitally metaphorical language of poetry with language characterized by a mere manipulation, by the 'calculating faculty', from which no new integral, unifying relations emerge.

Shelley applied Coleridge's fancy/imagination distinction and the German romantic ironists' (and Hegel's) distinction between allegory and symbol – to account for the impoverished systems of thought which generate rationalist and empiricist, as well as neo-classicist, world views.

By relating the concept of the 'dead metaphor' to literal language, the values of eighteenth-century theorists were not only reversed; their dualisms were dissolved: the literal is itself a figure of speech, a dead metaphor; literal language is not, however, something heterogeneous from metaphor. Metaphor it is, but in its tired, familiar, worn-out phase. No duality exists between the literal and the metaphorical, but only a distinction between rhetoric in its stimulating, integral phase, and worn-out rhetoric which has lost the power to stimulate the imagination. Shelley argued that it is a major function of the poet to revitalize such worn-out language as well as to create new metaphorical forms. Or, as Coleridge had explained, language degenerates, new metaphors are assimilated into the prevailing systems of linguistic habits, and, however much new metaphors may once have disrupted those systems, eventually the disruptive relations are forgotten through familiarity and habit.[22] Signs become, as Shelley explained, the thing signified: a special, innovative way of perceiving something becomes perceived (through custom and time) as the *only* way. A new perspective or point of view becomes *the* perspective, *the* point of view.

Shelley's 'Defence of poetry' is a throughgoing rejection of dualistic thinking as exemplified by much Western philosophy (or at least by interpretations of Western philosophy). The world and the mind of humans were, for the Romantics, one continuous whole, one 'naturalistic continuity', to use Dewey's words. Or, in Heidegger's language, they are a 'Dasein'. Shelley, like Coleridge, challenged the division between perceiver and world, and argued only for a useful distinction, not a division. On numerous occasions, he decried the division between thoughts and things, arguing for a distinction only. 'The difference is merely nominal between those two classes of thought, which are vulgarly distinguished by the names of ideas and external objects' ('On life').[23] Further, Shelley explained:

> Thoughts, or ideas, or notions, call them what you will, differ from each other, not in kind, but in force. It has commonly been supposed that those distinct thoughts which affect a number of persons, at regular intervals, during the passage of a multitude of other thoughts, which are called *real* or *external objects*, are totally different in kind from those which affect only a few persons, and which recur at irregular intervals, and are usually more obscure and indistinct, such as hallucinations, dreams, and the ideas of madness. No essential distinction between any one of these ideas, or any class of them, is founded on a correct observation of the nature of things, but merely on a consideration of what thoughts

are most invariably subservient to the security and happiness of life; and if nothing more were expressed by the distinction, the philosopher might safely accommodate his language to that of the vulgar. But they pretend to assert an essential difference, which has no foundation in truth, and which suggests a narrow and false conception of universal nature, the parent of the most fatal errors in speculation. A specific difference between every thought of the mind, is, indeed, a necessary consequence of that law by which it perceives diversity and number; but a generic and essential difference is wholly arbitrary.[24]

He rejected idealism by emphasizing that the world is real for the mind, while the mind is as much a product of its own synthetic activities as is the world a product of congruent synthetic powers. Or rather, in Nietzschean terms, both world and mind are figures of speech, neither having priority over the other. Both are conceived interdependently and apocalyptically as in a constant state of becoming: mind and nature emerge. Shelley created a powerful myth of the world as a mind-made poem, and – with imagination as the agent of transformation – metaphor and myth become part of a process of mental autogenesis.[25] That is, when mind perceives things metaphorically, when it perceives one thing as if it were another, it becomes immediately, self-consciously aware of its own synthetic acts (as Coleridge put it, mind *is* act).[26] Time, however, and familiarity, disorganize these relations, and the mind takes as literal and external the very things (thoughts) which are made out of its own inner activity. Reality or nature as distinct from culture is a dead metaphor, Shelley argued, anticipating Derrida, since there is no way for mind to get beyond the metaphoric, relational, and integral syntheses which constitute the 'thought-things' of immediate experience, unless it ignores its own primary activity. Dewey argued likewise that dualistic philosophies precisely do ignore this primary activity, mistaking products of reflection for some notional primary substance.[27]

In the 'Defence of poetry' it is made clear that forgotten integral relations cannot be restored or revitalized by ratiocinative gestures, but only by imaginative acts. These forgotten relations, these dead metaphors, which constitute tradition and convention and do not resemble the realities of individual experience (a chasm which Blake demonstrated throughout his poetry), must be suspended by acts of immediate, individual synthesis. Given that immediate experience is radically metaphoric, Shelley showed that the act of perceiving-knowing and the act of poetry are one. Neither external objects, nor nature, nor the mind, nor the world are either ready-made and fully formed, nor are they created somehow out of some primary stuff. Rather, they all, as rhetorical figures, result from ways of taking experience, in one way and then in another, from one perspective and then from another. Such 'taking' is defined as the activity of making, from the radically metaphorical fabric of experience, the forms of perceiving and knowing that are figuratively called the world and the mind.

In Shelley's matrix or field theory of consciousness there is no fixed centre, no origin as Derrida would say. The centre is everywhere, and the circumference is nowhere.[28] Impressions and immediate experiences are conceived of as at the center, which can be anywhere, while the cultural, mytho-poetic principles of the world are at the notional circumference (reversing Quine's metaphorical centre-circumference image).[29] Moreover, in the field theory, metaphor creatively organizes and enlarges consciousness not by addition, as eighteenth-century empiricists often implied. As an act of transcendence (not a manifestation of transcendent reality), metaphor engenders both progressive and revolutionary modifications of the systems of relations taken for reality. Experience reflects for Shelley not the structure of some reality, then, but the structure of opinion, as Samuel Johnson had earlier argued.[30] In the 'Defence', Shelley showed that *poiēsis* is 'natural' or 'primitive' to the mind – that is, the mind's capacity for imaginative apprehension produces all our ideas and our cultural ideals, including the ideas of mind, imagination, culture, and ideals. Some metaphors may be judged to be more viable than others, either due to specified purposes, or because the mind sometimes fulfils with greater scope of integrity its expressive-constructive powers through the relations it apprehends in immediate experience. Imaginative acts transform old systems of belief; the circumference of knowledge is enlarged or the field of relations radically transfigured; and new complexes of metaphors lead to new myths. Polarities of time and eternity, mind and nature, centre and circumference, language and world are transcended as metaphoric relations constantly refigure our images of the web of being.

Like Coleridge and Dewey, Shelley argued that the human being is not merely 'a moral, and an intellectual, but also, and pre-eminently, an imaginative being. His own mind is his law' ('Speculations on metaphysics').[31] Given this pre-eminence in human nature of the imagination – which is the source of love, compassion, empathy, and all other forms of moral good – art and poetry in particular are the instrument of moral good, because they exercise this pre-eminently moral, imaginative faculty. After decrying in Blakean language the dehumanizing effects of 'an unmitigated exercise of the calculating faculty', Shelley argued that the human species has achieved far more knowledge than it knows how to put into practice; and concluded:

> We want the creative faculty to imagine that which we know; we want the generous impulse to act that which we imagine; we want the poetry of life: our calculations have outrun conception; we have eaten more than we can digest. The cultivation of those sciences which have enlarged the limits of the empire of man over the external world, has, for want of the poetical faculty, proportionally circumscribed those of the internal world.[32]

He then insisted that the cultivation of the imagination through poetry and art is essential to the progression towards a more humane society. The functions of the 'poetical faculty' he described as two-fold. First, it creates fresh materials of knowledge, and second it 'engenders in the mind a desire to reproduce and arrange [those new materials] according to a certain rhythm and order which may be called the beautiful and the good'. When the calculating faculty – analytical reasoning – is exalted 'over the direct expression of the inventive and creative faculty', then the human being, 'having enslaved the elements [through scientific advances] remains himself a slave'.[33]

Nietzsche's Universe of Rhetoric

In the *Will to Power*, published posthumously, we find scraps and fragments of Nietzsche's thinking, many of which he had incorporated into earlier publications. Yet many of the most stimulating and suggestive scraps were never taken up into Nietzsche's published writings, at least not in the pithy and knife-like tone and style of the notebook fragments. These notebooks are some of the most relevant of Nietzsche's works for readers today, as they address themselves to issues which have become dominant in late-twentieth-century literary theory, and for some philosophers as well. Between 1872, when Nietzsche published T*he Birth of Tragedy*, through *Human, All Too Human* (1878–9), *Daybreak* (1881), *The Gay Science* (1882), *Beyond Good and Evil* (1886), *Twilight of the Idols* (1889: a kind of history of philosophy), and *The Anti-Christ* (1895), scraps from *The Will to Power* are strewn throughout these texts, though much remained unpublished until the first edition of *The Will to Power* appeared in 1911. That book illustrates Nietzsche's aphoristic style, with its rejection of the notion of systems of thought and logical chains of reasoning, substituting instead rhetorical, figurative, metaphoric language, accompanied by sharp, stimulating, and disturbing jabs at the reader. With this anti-philosophical style of writing, Nietzsche sought to prevent his readers from passively acquiescing in discursive truths culled from the text or reduced into univocal propositions. He claimed that he sought not to teach his readers any dogma, any opinions, any truths: he only sought to teach his reader to think for herself. He wrote ironically of *The Will to Power* that it was 'a book of thinking, nothing more'. Nietzsche had a passion for independence of thought, and this is what he taught (as did Plato's *Dialogues*) by his fragmentary, confusing, ironic sentences and paragraphs, often arranged in a disorderly, miscellaneous fashion. His passion was for what he saw as genuine philosophy, namely 'a stimulation of the [reader's] mind into activity' (compare Coleridge's similar passion, especially in *The Friend* and *Biographia*).[34] Nietzsche also taught us to think differently from the conventional way: his texts are designed to show the reader that there are questions to ask and ways of reflecting that never occurred to one before. His fragments, then, like those of the German romantic ironists, oppose traditional philosophical order, logic, systems, style, and method, for a more literary style involving pieces that make up a 'field of energy' where any spot is the centre and nowhere is the circumference.

Both *Beyond Good and Evil* (1886) and *Twilight of the Idols* (1889) act as helpful introductions to Nietzsche, since they embody many of the ideas and styles of writing which he used throughout his short writing life. As has been recognized, he revolutionized the pace of the German language, through shortening sentences and using techniques thought previously to be appropriate only to poetry – eschewing logical argumentation for lucid metaphors and images. By using the techniques of poetry – with its condensation and self-referential style – he demanded from the reader the same close attention to his words that a poet demands. He sought to shock his reader out of passive receptivity – out of a lazy desire to let the author do the thinking for her, and into a disturbed and unsettled state of mind, as did, for example, William Blake. To arouse the reader to think was his goal, while he stated that his text sought to 'teach to read *well*. . . . Slowly, deeply, looking cautiously before and aft, with reservations, with doors left open' (*Daybreak*).[35] By unsettling and disturbing – even shocking – the reader, Nietzsche challenged our certainties, opinions, values, and beliefs about nearly everything. He showed us that the craving for order and certainty led to over-quick decisions and opinions, and showed us that to think differently we must learn to consider from more than one point of view (almost a Romantic definition of imagination). Ultimately, he noted that his main preoccupation throughout his life has been 'the truth about truth' and the pivotal relation of art to truth (constituting a rejection of eighteenth-century enlightenment emphases on science, truth *versus* art, reason *versus* imagination, and so on). New perspectives on 'truth' could be achieved by means of a new, plural style of writing and thinking, involving toying (free play) with words and concepts, to generate, playfully, figures of speech as the very life of philosophizing. That is, conventional philosophic notions about decorous language must be reversed. Instead of excluding poetic language and technique for literal truth and scientific, logical objectivity and order, philosophy should re-examine familiar language, and take responsibility for its own discourse. This means both seeing traditional philosophical discourse as rhetorical and figurative – and in need of interpretation – and it means generating more self-consciously figurative philosophical discourse. Language, in philosophizing, becomes self-conscious of its own limitations and character as rhetorical. For Nietzsche, it contained within itself a self-critical level of its own styles and modes. Thus the philosopher must be an artist; she must be able to create her language through self-conscious figuration, and not fall victim to her own metaphors as if they were literal truths, as Nietzsche believed philosophers had done in the past. Moreover, Nietzsche argued that the philosopher creating his text must be more distrustful of himself than of anyone else, as he is more likely to fall prey to the literal truth of his own beautiful productions.

One of Nietzsche's main techniques for achieving a different point of view and a new way of thinking in philosophy was to reverse the values of words and concepts. The reader must join him in the need to 'will a reversal' of all values, a revaluation of values, to joy in uncertainty, to accept disorder (as in his texts), to embrace illogicality. All traditional conclusions and beliefs must be seen as merely provisional and in need of reinterpretation, as James and Dewey, following Nietzsche, were to argue. All oppositions (contraries, for Blake) must be seen as interdependent on each other, as in Derrida's concept of 'differance'; oppositions are dissolved – not into a higher unity, though. There is no transcendent unity, no *tertium aliquid*. Opposition is itself a metaphor derived from logic and falsely transferred to things:

> If we give up the effective subject, we also give up the object upon which effects are produced. Duration, identity with itself, being are inherent neither in that which is called subject nor in that which is called object: they are complexes of events apparently durable in comparison with other complexes – e.g. through the difference in tempo of the event (rest-motion, firm-loose: opposites that do not

exist in themselves and that actually express only variations in degree that from a certain perspective appear to be opposites. There are no opposites: only from those of logic do we derive the concept of opposites – and falsely transfer to it things).[36]

Like Blake in his marriage of heaven and hell, Coleridge in his polarity metaphor, and Derrida, who 'undid' oppositions in his concept of 'differance', Nietzsche reversed values and thereby reversed or changed perspectives: new points of view reveal new values and still further perspectives and reversals. For example, good and evil are shown to be functions of each other, not realities which indicate substantive contrary essences. These two complementary values – good and evil – are reversed so that morality itself is said to be merely a special case of immorality (*WP*, 217); relatedly, Nietzsche argued that rationality is merely the familiar form of the irrational. Like Coleridge, Blake, and Shelley, he saw the life-death opposition to be an illusion as well – 'the living as merely a type of what is dead, as a very rare type' (*GS*, 168). Or, put in the Coleridgean way, matter is not dead, as he accused Descartes of assuming; it is organic and vital.[37]

Not only is death (not to mention life) an illusion, reality itself is, according to Nietzsche, an illusion – a dream; when we wake from sleep and dreaming, we wake up to the consciousness that the world around us and our own self is a fabrication of what he called the 'will to power'. Conscious life is only possible if we forget the bodily processes going on within us, the unconscious body activities of eating, breathing, excreting, digesting, and transforming our cells all the time. We must repress, or 'forget', our bodily life if it is not totally to overwhelm us. If we are to achieve that dream of consciousness, we must block out most of our bodily experience. Our nervous system – evolved into unbelievable complexity – leads to a transformation of Dionysiac, physical, bodily, and vital processes into Apollonic images and conscious forms, an account elaborated early in *The Birth of Tragedy*. The 'will to power' is Nietzsche's phrase for this transformation, but it is also at the centre of many of his texts, and means many things, relating his ideas to a Shelleyan dynamic field of forces rather than a system. He described the 'will to power' as appropriation, taking over, or 'making like' – as in eating we take a substance unlike the body and turn it into our bodies. This basic physical process of appropriation translates *via* the nervous system into various stimuli which lead to images and sensations and ideas. Hence Nietzsche argued that all knowledge is bodily, not spiritual or intelligential – not distinct from the physical and sensuous, but its manifestation through transformation. He asked, 'is not philosophy merely an interpretation of the body and a misunderstanding of it?' The will to power can only manifest itself, Nietzsche argued (in a Deweyan language), in oppositions, against resistance – hence it seeks resistance and appropriates it into itself.[38] Nietzsche then explained that our most sacred ideals and truths are the mere 'judgments of our muscles'. The process of assimilation (of food, air, and so on) becomes – upon repression of the bodily experience, through nervous system ideation – the very process of the discovery of knowledge or interpretation of the world which consciousness then sets up as separate from the body, as spirituality, or mentality, through forgetting its own natural experience.

For Nietzsche, this will to power – appropriation and conquest – involves 'making like' – that is, overcoming difference. He argued that this is also the character of rhetorical figuration itself – of the linguistic act of making figures of speech. This linguistic act, the figurative drive, is, he claimed, the fundamental human drive. The will to knowledge is the instinct for appropriation and making like out of difference. Figuration is itself a process of incessant deciphering of figures into other figures, of signs into other signs – of interpretation itself, which is analogous to appropriation at the physical level of eating. Nietzsche argued that categories of figuration masquerade as categories of Reality, of Truth, of Essence, when they are merely one of many different possible interpretations or points of view.[39] As Shelley insisted, because the human body and mind resists chaos, because there is something at enmity with nothingness, it imposes its own perspective forms of beauty, truth, wisdom, and pattern. Yet these forms are merely aesthetic anthropomorphisms, and not traits or characteristics of some notional reality. The process of knowledge for Nietzsche is a process of incessant appropriation, figuration, deciphering, or interpretation. It is not a disclosure of truth about the thing-in-itself or a manifestation or view of *the* Thing, *the* Reality, or Being. As in the eating of food, figuration involves fitting new material into old schemes, 'making like', what is new.

Figuration and metaphor-making is the 'originary process' of what the intellect presents as truth itself. Nietzsche explained: 'Each time the creator [of metaphors] leaps completely out of one sphere right into the midst of an entirely different one.' Truth is 'an army of metaphors, metonomies, anthropomorphisms. . . . Truths are illusions of which one has forgotten that they *are* illusions', just as for Shelley 'dead metaphors' give the illusion of a literal language. Nietzsche cautioned us, however, against falling into the idealist error of a fantasy about the mind as somehow above or behind figuration. Like the world, like the body, like truth, the mind or knowing subject is also a result of figuration and of interpretation. I, you, we, she are merely grammatical devices; grammatical custom adds a 'doer' to every deed. But Nietzsche argued that the will to power is not a process of a pre-existent subject; it is not an individual activity (compare Heidegger, who wrote that language speaks, not humans).[40] The will to power exists as a process, as an effect, not as a being. It is not under the control of a conscious subject, but is unconscious. This constitutes a questioning of the assumed certitude of consciousness which anticipates Freud's insights and compares with Shelley's concept of the imagination as the originator of metaphors leading to a universe of poetry.

Like Heidegger, Nietzsche cautioned us that we cannot get out of our own skin to see what we 'really are': 'the human intellect cannot avoid seeing itself in its own perspective forms; and only in those. We cannot look around our own corner' (*GS*, 336). Nor do we exist apart from that process of looking, by means of metaphor; it is not that we could see some transcendent truth if only our reason or vision were greater. 'Transcendent truth' is a contradictory concept. Truth is to be understood precisely as processes of figuration: of seeing things as 'like' other things, of assimilation and appropriation – of comparison and contrast – not of glimpsing some immutable thing-in-itself. For Nietzsche, the latter concept is a complete delusion; there are no things in themselves, no substances, no beings apart from the result of figuration.

We could describe and summarize Nietzsche's contributions to philosophy which are relevant to the present study as follows: (1) a mistrust of metaphysics and a questioning of the history of philosophy through rhetorical and philosophical gestures; (2) the questioning of traditional notions in philosophy, such as truth, meaning, and being; (3) Nietzsche's emphasis upon the concept of force, as in 'will to power', and differences of force; and, (4) Nietzsche's attention to creating a new language and style of philosophizing in order to demonstrate, not merely explain, his radicalization of concepts of evaluation, opposition, interpretation, and so on. Nietzsche freed philosophic language from its slavery to the signified (the world), freed it from meaning as referentiality, and liberated the sign from some notional dependence on the ideas of truth or *logos*, by showing, as Shelley had done, that the process of signification (of meaning) is figuration, not referentiality. Nothing is ever finally or completely comprehended; according to Nietzsche we only designate and distort – refigure – make metaphors. No conclusions are final, no origins are original. We need not 'resign' ourselves, however, as if this were an unhappy state of affairs. Nietzsche rejected what he saw as Schopenhauer's nihilism, pessimism, and resignation, for a joyous affirmation of uncertainty, of never-ending agility, and of endlessly inexhaustible figuration, interpretation, and play. He, like Shelley, embraced his knowledge of truth-as-metaphor (figuratively speaking, that is) as a liberation and a release from the lie of 'Truth'.

Nietzsche, like Shelley and Coleridge before him (not to mention the German romantics such as Friedrich Schlegel, Novalis, Tieck, and Jean Paul Richter), insisted, first, that a study of rhetoric should attend not pre-eminently to eloquence and persuasion, but to a theory about figuration and the making of tropes, upon which persuasion depends and from which it is derived: 'All that is generally called eloquence is figurative language.' More importantly, Nietzsche followed the English and German romantics in arguing that tropes, rhetoric, and figures of speech are not mere ornamentation of a pre-existing literal, scientific or philosophical language of truth. Figurative meanings are not somehow dependent upon or derivable from literal, non-metaphoric language. Nor do they lead away from truth towards passion, emotion or error, as eighteenth-century language theorists had insisted. As Shelley had showed in the 'Defence of poetry,' language is essentially metaphorical. What we perceive as literal language is, rather, 'dead metaphors'. Figuration is the character of language, not an optional elaboration which threatens knowledge with deceit, dissimulation, or error, as Paul de Man argued in his essays on Nietzsche. For Nietzsche:

> It is not difficult to demonstrate that what is called 'rhetorical', as the devices of a conscious art, is present as a device of unconscious art in language and its development. We can go so far as to say that rhetoric is an extension [Fortbildung] of the devices embedded in language at the clear light of reason. No such thing as an unrhetorical, 'natural' language exists that could be used as a point of reference: language is itself the result of purely rhetorical tricks and devices. . . . Language is rhetoric, for it only intends to convey a *doxa* (opinions), not an *episteme* (truth). . . . Tropes are not something that can be added or subtracted from language at will; they are its truest nature. There is no such thing as a proper meaning that can be communicated only in certain particular cases.[41]

Hence, Nietzsche's analysis of truth and its relation to art leads to the argument that language is meaningful not in so far as it is representational or is expressive of some literal, referential meaning; language is meaningful because it is rhetorical. Meaning involves appropriation, that process of 'making like', *Gleich machen*, of taking the new and relating it to old, familiar experience – so that we see the old, familiar experience in a new way, from a new point of view. Metaphor is the example par excellence of this vital relation of old to new, unlike allegory, for example, which simply compares old with old, or known with known. Consequently, Nietzsche viewed language as meaningful not because it mimetically represents some extralinguistic world or thing or thought. Language is preeminently expressive not of mimesis but of appropriation within the sphere of language – within Saussurean intralinguistic relations and functions of words to words, not in their supposed relation to some object outside of language. Nietzsche, like Wittgenstein, concluded that all our 'inner experience', our consciousness, is dependent upon finding a language which the individual grasps – which she or he understands because they can translate an unfamiliar, new experience into a familiar one: ' "to understand", naively put, merely means: to be able to express something old and familiar'. Nietzsche concluded that the external world of objects apparently existing independently – outside – inner conscious experience, as well as the mind itself, are figures of speech, or, to use Berkeley's phrase, they constitute a mere prejudice of 'outness'. Nietzsche thereby avoided hypostasizing either consciousness or the world into an ontological category. This is a central aspect of his critique of western metaphysics, and of its own tendency to hypostasize truth, reality, beauty, causality, the knowing subject, the known object, and so on, with all the irresolvable 'problems of traditional philosophy' which then arise and which cannot be solved, once the rhetorical and figurative (and essentially linguistic) nature of experience is 'forgotten'.

Much of *The Will to Power* reads like an early pragmatist treatise, and doubtless pragmatism, as expounded by C. S. Peirce, William James, and John Dewey, can look upon Nietzsche as its progenitor. Nietzsche's emphasis upon method as central to philosophy anticipates one of pragmatism's most central beliefs – though of course Socrates' own utterances repeatedly exhort his listeners to the critical role of method. In Nietzsche's Jamesean phrase: 'It is not the victory of science that distinguishes our nineteenth century, but the victory of scientific method over science' (*WP*, 261). And he argued paradoxically that 'the most valuable insights are arrived at last; but the most valuable insights are *methods*'. Nietzsche's incessant challenging of the traditional philosophical notion of truth and his rejection of it in favour of truth as interest, as to do with survival, is Deweyan, as is his emphasis upon the relation of physical bodily appropriation to linguistic figuration. Nietzsche's emphasis upon physical, bodily experience is closely akin to Dewey's naturalism. For example, the following quotation expresses Dewey's insistence upon the nature of intelligence and life as naturalistic when Nietzsche wrote:

The utility of preservation – not some abstract-theoretical need not to be deceived – stands as the motive behind the development of the organs of knowledge – they develop in such a way that their observations suffice for our preservation – a species grasps a certain amount of reality in order to become master of it, in order to press it into service.[42]

Like pragmatists from Peirce to Rorty and Goodman after him, Nietzsche insisted upon the need for plurality and relativity in the Socratic, sceptical sense: 'Profound aversion to reposing once and for all in any one total view of the world. Fascination of the opposing point of view: refusal to be deprived of the stimulus of the enigmatic' (*WP*, 262). Like Wittgenstein and Derrida – whose relations to pragmatism are not tenuous – Nietzsche rejected the naive notion of thinking as some kind of pre-existing, non-linguistic introspection (just as Plato had done when he argued, in the person of Socrates, that thinking is really a linguistic dialogue with oneself[43]): ' "Thinking", as epistemologists conceive it, simply does not occur: it is a quite arbitrary fiction' and 'nothing is so much deception as this inner world which we observe with the famous "inner sense" ' (*WP*, 264).

Like Wittgenstein, Dewey, and Derrida, Nietzsche believed that the so-called inner world of existence becomes conscious experience only after it has found a language which the individual can understand – while 'to understand' is only to translate from something older and more familiar into a newer language. This notion of understanding as translation leads directly to the idea of interpretation central to romanticism, pragmatism, and deconstruction: 'Against positivism, which halts at phenomena – "There are only *facts*" – I would say: No, fact is precisely what there is not, only interpretation' (*WP*, 267).[44] 'Knowledge' Nietzsche then defined as 'perspectivism', a metaphor taken up with enthusiasm by Richard Rorty,[45] and combined by the latter with the concept of irony as itself a definition of the perspectival nature of truth. In his criticisms of Cartesian metaphysics, Nietzsche arrived at Deweyan and Platonic notions, indeed, Blakean apocalyptic notions of 'coming into being', rather than essentialist notions of substantive being. Mind, language, and life emerge in interdependence with each other, and, with Socrates and Dewey, Nietzsche concluded that while 'we have to believe in time, space, and motion, [we do not have to feel] compelled to grant them absolute reality'.

Thus Nietzsche argued in words that could be taken from Dewey's *Experience and Nature* that 'it is improbable that our "knowledge" should extend further than is strictly necessary for the preservation of life.

Morphology shows us how the senses and the nerves, as well as the brain, develop in proportion to the difficulty of finding nourishment' (*WP*, 272). He concluded pragmatically that our apparatus for acquiring 'knowledge' is not designed for knowledge but for survival. Our intellect he described, as Dewey had done, as a consequence of our conditions of physical existence: 'we would not have it if we did not *need* to have it, and we would not have it *as it is* if we did not need to have it *as it is*, if we could live *otherwise*' (*WP*, 273).

Our entire intellectual apparatus is directed not, then, so much at knowledge acquisition, but at taking possession of things for the sake of survival. Nietzsche stated that we have senses only for a selection of perceptions which are useful, for those perceptions which concern our need to preserve ourselves in nature. Anticipating Dewey's naturalism yet again, Nietzsche wrote: '*Consciousness is present only to the extent that consciousness is useful*.' He then, like Dewey later, concluded that '*all sense perceptions are permeated with value judgments*' (*WP*, 275). The false dichotomy between the senses and the intellect, the aesthetic and the moral, is exposed as a typical dualism unsustainable in the face of experience. Nietzsche's repeated insistence upon the senses and the reason as physical apparatuses valuable for their usefulness in life, not for their truth-revealing function, places him firmly in a pragmatist tradition.

Like later philosophers such as Quine, Goodman, and Rorty, Nietzsche alleged that 'the most strongly believed *a priori* ' "truths" are for me – *provisional assumptions*' (*WP*, 273). Logic and reason grew out of the 'earthly kingdom of desires', of the desire specifically for stability and security – it did not spring from a will to truth, nor are its results or rules truths of nature. They are rather expressions of the human organism's struggle to find means to stabilize and control the environment, as Dewey might say. The categories of reason prevail only after much 'groping and fumbling, through their relative utility' (*WP*, 278). Nietzsche then scathingly ridiculed the raising of such utilities to *a priori* truths beyond experience and irrefutable. Categories are 'truths' only, he believed, in the sense that such logical or rational orderings are conditions of life for us, 'mere idiosyncrasy of a certain species of animal, and one among many -', a conclusion to which Kant himself came in his theory of morals.[46] And morals, like rules of logic, were for Nietzsche matters of conditions of interest, desire, survival, and expressions of our particular idiosyncratic human body – not some divine oracle. Neither the axioms of logic or of morality are adequate to some posited, independent reality, so much as the means by which the human organism creates reality – the concept 'reality' – for itself. Nietzsche concluded that the law of contradiction basic to traditional logic is itself a proof not of 'truth' but only of an incapacity, a physical inability, a subjective, empirical law, not the expression of some necessary truth about reality. Logic, then, is merely an imperative to posit and organize a world which is called true by us; it is no criterion of true being nor even an imperative to know the true: 'Logic is an attempt to comprehend the actual world by means of a scheme of being, posited by ourselves; more correctly, to make it formulatable and calculable for us' – (*WP*, 280) a conclusion which Blake embodied in his Urizen.[47]

Like Dewey, Nietzsche argued that we must 'start from the body and employ it as a guide' (*WP*, 289), proceeding to deny the absolute distinction between the physical and the psychological – two perspectives only. Nietzsche's analysis of the belief in a spirit, mind, self, and God also closely resembles Dewey's account in *Experience and Nature*, along with their conclusions that the notion of the soul led to a 'spectator theory of knowledge' which has dominated western philosophy and made it a dualistic dogma.[48] Nietzsche then generalized to attack the very notion at the heart of religion, namely 'Being – we have no idea of it apart from the idea of "living". How can anything dead "be"?' (*WP*, 313). Like Dewey, Nietzsche ridiculed the devaluation of the 'apparent' world as opposed to the 'real' world, and concluded satirically: 'I observe with astonishment that science has today resigned itself to the apparent world; a real world – whatever it may be like – we certainly have no organ for knowing it.' Apparently this real world is left to religious faith, until Nietzsche scathingly rejected this dichotomy as non-sensical: 'by means of what organ of knowledge can we posit even this antithesis?' Polemical to the end, Nietzsche concluded this passage nonchalantly:

There exists neither 'spirit', nor reason, nor thinking, nor consciousness, nor soul, nor will, nor truth: all are fictions that are of no use. There is no question of 'subject and object', but of a particular species of animal that can prosper only through a certain relative rightness; above all, regularity of its perceptions (so that it can accumulate experience). . . .

Knowledge works as a tool of power . . . the concept is to be regarded in a strict and narrow anthropocentric and biological sense.[49]

Or, in the words of a latter-day Nietzschean, 'Everything is only a metaphor; there is only poetry.'[50]

2

German Romantic Irony and Hegel: Creative Destruction

Speaking and writing is a crazy state of affairs really; true conversation is just a game with words. It is amazing the absurd error people make of imagining they are speaking for the sake of things; no one knows the essential thing about language, that it is concerned only with itself. That is why it is such a marvellous and fruitful mystery – for if someone merely speaks for the sake of speaking, he utters the most splendid, original truths. But if he wants to talk about something definite, the whims of language make him say the most ridiculous false stuff. Hence the hatred that so many serious people have for language. They notice its waywardness, but they do not notice that the babbling they scorn is the infinitely serious side of language . . . it is the same with language as it is with mathematical formulae – they constitute a world in itself – their play is self-sufficient, they express nothing but their own marvellous nature.[1]

The quotation above is from a short fragment-like essay of Friedrich von Hardenberg, called 'Monologue'. 'Monologue' is a concentrated and impressive example of romantic irony, in its fusing of content with method, subject matter with style, and in its use of what the German ironists called 'positive negation' and 'self-criticism', both at the heart of romantic irony. The related 'Dialogues' of 1798 continue the strong vein of playful irony explicit in their sister fragment, and are designed to illustrate again Novalis's self-referentiality principle that 'the genuine dialogue is sheer wordplay'.[2] In these and other carefully designed fragments, Novalis was exemplifying the romantic principle that the 'mystical fragment' was a formal symbol expressive of the method necessary for communicating with readers, since all communication was seen as only a beginning, a push given to the reader towards self-discovery and self-activity. Fragments were seeds that might become mature fruits if nourished by each individual reader with his or her own creative, imaginative response. The fragment as a form also symbolized the nature of language as suggestive of hidden, rhetorical dimensions, and of linguistic events as the impetus for intuitive acts.[3]

The German romantic ironists, such as Novalis, Friedrich Schlegel, Ludwig Tieck, Karl Solger, and Jean Paul Richter especially, developed their theorizing about literature, criticism, and philosophy in direct relation to inspiration from Shakespeare's works.[4] The tremendous impact of Shakespeare upon eighteenth-century German intellectual life was incalculable, especially as it was mediated by Lessing and Herder.[5] Literary theorists and creative artists alike were freed from crippling neo-classical constraints, and the results of this liberation suggest a direct line between the theorizing inspired by Shakespeare's works, which broke neo-classical inhibitions, and modern critical theory today. German romantic ironists found in Shakespeare the impetus for many of their most penetrating insights, and these insights constitute well-developed ideas coincident with some of the most exciting concepts of post-structuralist criticism in our own time. The concept of romantic irony is the locus for such anticipations developed further by Nietzsche, Dewey, Heidegger, Wittgenstein, and Derrida; 'irony', however, must be clearly distinguished from its tendency in Engish to be limited to sarcasm or satire.[6] For the Germans, it was a broad concept taken from Plato's Socrates and representing an entire way of life, as it later functioned in Kierkegaard's writings.[7] Moreover, it deeply influenced Coleridge, who was acquainted personally with Tieck, and who had read the writings of the Schlegel brothers, Solger, and Richter.[8]

The German romantic concept of irony, stemming from Plato's Socratic scepticism, constituted a challenge to both empirical and idealist (and absolutist) notions of truth, knowledge, and certainty. This challenge took the form of a sophisticated and dynamic relativism whose modern-day counterpart is the pragmatic approach to art, language, truth, and reality characteristic of Wittgenstein in his later works, and of Dewey, not to mention Nietzsche's and Derrida's rhetorical approaches, which form a basis for the first two philosophers. It would probably be mistaken to say that German Romanticism and the related English Romanticism of Coleridge, Blake, and Shelley was the origin of modern critical theory (since Romantic thought is based itself on Socratic Platonism, and was developed further in Kierkegaard and Nietzsche). German romantic irony, like modern criticism itself, was a stage in the reinterpretation of past theorizing which constituted a rewriting of it. It was based upon the belief that in such central figures as the Socratic Plato, Aristotle, and Shakespeare (for example) could be found the affirmation of the necessity for a continuous reanalysis of received opinion (which passes for fact and truth), and of the need for new and more adequate linguistic descriptions – not of reality or truth – but of previous descriptions, or, as Dewey and Samuel Johnson might have said, interpretations of other people's prior interpretations.

In the tradition of German aesthetics as well as in the Greek tradition, the concept 'irony' took on a more profound sense than the usual English usage of the word, even when irony is described as 'dramatic irony'.[9] The Socratic-German romantic tradition used the word to suggest a principle of art encompassing a Deweyan idea of 'art as experience'. This involved a dissolution of characteristic dualities and a rejection of aesthetic experience as a secondary activity – a passive beholding of another's creative product – in favour of a more Coleridgean-Barthean notion of aesthetic response as primary and imaginative.[10] Ideas of opposition and difference (which reject dualisms and hierarchies), self-consciousness and self-criticism (as central to intellectual activity), ideas of the mind as creative in basic perception (not just in artistic creation), reconceptualizations of language, truth, and reality – and other ideas familiar to modern theorists – have their roles to play in this German romantic theory of irony, and of art as inherently ironic, that is, as involving a level of self-criticism and including the reader-spectator within the work of art.

The concepts of irony developed by the German Romantics in their more overtly theoretical writings on metaphysics and aesthetics, and operative in their fictional works, have radical consequences for a theory of art and creativity and for perception and knowledge. The Germans made a clear distinction between 'common' and 'high' irony, in order to indicate that higher irony involved something philosophically more significant than mere satire. Frederich Schlegel had argued that romantic irony was the opposite of satire, since irony was self-criticism (*Selbst-polemik*), while Tieck had distinguished between the 'crude irony of Swift' and 'another far higher irony' found in Plato, which hovers over the whole and constitutes the best proof of true inspiration.[11] Some decades later, Kierkegaard saw irony as virtually synonymous with romanticism, revealing the roots of romanticism in Greek thought, by arguing that 'irony' had constant reference to Socrates. For the Germans, as for Socrates and Kierkegaard, self-criticism, self-consciousness, and self-knowledge were at the basis of the concept of irony.[12] Unlike English verbal or dramatic irony, German and Socratic conceptions of irony involved the collapsing of the duality between spectator and work of art, subject and object, mind and world, knower and known, or thought and thing, for example. Romantic irony broke through the conventional boundaries of the work of art (and of language) to include the spectator, the world, and the artist. Irony established a world as textual, a Shelleyan and Nietzschean universe of discourse where language is pre-eminently metaphorical, and the character of experience is rhetorical.

Romantic ironists set up a more encompassing Deweyan-Derridian context for investigation. The object of attention was the synthesis of subject and object, artist and product, spectator and work of art, and art as inherently self-critical, or self-consuming – containing within itself the means to deconstruct any investigation which seeks to fix or finalize meaning. Also postulated was a level of artistic experience which anticipated and mirrored the spectator's responses. Romantic irony demanded a flip of perspective on the part of the reader. The artist-spectator looks not only at the work of art as the object of attention. Attention is refocused by ironic devices onto the reader's own interaction with the work of art – on the experiencing of it, as Dewey would say. This enlarged context offers a new critical perspective, as the object of interest becomes a synthesis of the subject and the object.[13] Irony, understood as a principle of art, involves paradox, absurdity, and the notions of opposition, polarity, and difference. Schlegel described irony as a dialectic and tension of opposites, yet he insisted that the so-called dialectic leads not to any Hegelian reconciliation, but only to more uncompleted becoming and to perpetually renewing movement.[14]

Romantic ironists' concepts of annihilation and self-limitation relate interestingly to notions of deconstruction.[15] Nihilism and destruction are forcefully rejected as descriptions of the ironist's position, in favour of productive creation and play, humour and wit, the latter being Novalis's definition of irony.[16] These Germans appealed to Socrates' efforts to destroy prejudice by freeing the mind from habitual and unthinking attitudes, from unexamined traditions and conventional notions, which are taken for facts, knowledge, and objective traits. After this 'destruction', the mind was free to explore new possibilities, new ways of responding, conceiving, and perceiving than received opinion had previously allowed. Irony involved experience which encompassed both the rational and irrational, the conscious and unconscious, just as Socrates had done by seeing these two oppositions as only apparently conflicting sides of human nature. Reason was seen as intuitive and imaginative – *nous*, not *dianoia*, and as contingent, not absolute.

The concept of romantic irony arose in part from the efforts of Friedrich Schlegel and others to understand better the distinguishing characteristics of 'modern', as opposed to classical literature, in order thereby to arrive at principles of art which could encompass the widely divergent types of literature. 'Modern' literature was first described as ironic, but later romantic irony came to be seen as a principle of all art, uniting ancient and modern literature, leading Tieck to utter the polemical comment that all poetry is romantic, that there is nothing but romantic poetry. Schlegel was led to make claims for art as essentially a mixture of poetry, philosophy, and criticism, and he, like Coleridge, argued for a 'poetic prose', a movement away from distinct genres or hierarchies of value, all arguments based on his reading of Shakespeare.[17] Herder's aesthetic of philosophical and historical relativism had also pointed the way for the romantic transition which forms the basis of much modern theory today. Herder had emphasized the evolving, historical nature of concepts such as beauty, worth, truth, and perfection, much as Hegel was to do some decades later. Romantic critics sought to recognize a principle – or 'family resemblance' (to use Wittgenstein's term) – amongst aesthetic affects without postulating a metaphysical notion of shared essence and without losing sight of cultural and intellectual (historical)conventions which provide (limited) perspectives.

Some of the resulting characteristic emphases in German romantic irony involved: (1) a recognition of the element of autobiography in all writing; (2) a rejection of notions of purity of style, genre, unity, or originality, in favour of mixtures, shared authorship, 'plagiarism', fragments. The fantastic, marvellous, and grotesque were used as means for expressing the 'modern' tendency, while open-endedness and other challenges to conventional unity, beauty, form, and decorum were developed. Wit and play were mixed with seriousness and work, while the reader-spectator was written into texts, rhetoric was foregrounded, and language was used self-consciously. Criticism and philosophy were seen as crucial elements in art, while the two former disciplines were said to be genuine only if artistic. Friedrich Schlegel argued moreover that the difference between disparate literary forms and styles could not be one of fundamental aesthetic principle, but merely a matter of emphasis and artistic temperament. Not only was the absolute division of such genres and separate disciplines questioned. Assumptions about individual authorship and originality were challenged, especially by means of the publication of 'unauthorized' fragments. These collections of fragments of mixed and unidentified authorship were a further rejection of conventional notions about unity, structure, and development in art. The fragment form became a symbol for the notion that all literature, indeed all language and experience, is fragmentary and incomplete in part because of limited perspective and point of view involved in all gestures, as Shelley epitomized in 'Ozymandias'. Fragment collections of mixed and unidentified authorship expressed the romantic ironists' belief that all writing is borrowed from previous writings and essentially unoriginal, in part because deeply and unconsciously influenced by previous writers and the literary-philosophical tradition. Contrary to received opinion about romantic poets, authors were seen not as essentially discrete individuals originating new and individual works of art; individuality was looked upon as a function of communicating, whole works of art were seen as 'portions of one great poem' (to use Shelley's words). As the ironists saw it, they were, like Derrida, reminding their readers, for example, that influence and tradition permeate even the most apparently original texts, that the most 'objective' looking text is full of autobiography, and that unity is a matter of convention. Their efforts to emphasize the open-ended (organically evolving) nature of all genuine art and its irresolvable mystery of meaning led to the Hegelian inclusion of the irrational in the rational and to organic conceptions of unity which involved not static, fixed structures, but concepts of form as evolving, living, and vital.[18]

The fragment form expressed the nature of language and communication as indirect, imperfect, and rhetorical. Indeed, incomprehensibility became a way of parodying the literal language and immediate comprehension (demanded by some readers) as a delusion and as utterly unproductive of thought.[19] Like Socrates, ironists sought to stimulate readers to think for themselves, not to seek solutions from the author. Like such philosophers as Plato, Berkeley, Kierkegaard, and Coleridge, who used the method of art, that is, overtly indirect communication, the romantic ironists embraced carefully designed models of incomprehension as a way of stimulating readers, by means of fragmentary and oracular utterances, to grapple with thinking itself, and with words and language as both the substance and the 'vehicle of thought'. Such a style was designed, as was Hegel's, to frustrate passive acquiescence in linguistic formulations and mechanical acceptance or rejection of stereotyped conceptions. A too-readily accessible apparent surface sense would discourage actual reflection and fail to provoke active thinking, while appearing to offer determinate statements and solutions. Jean Paul Richter, for example, ironized (as did Coleridge) the reader who parrots and thus destroys words; he exhorted his reader to explore words further than the author has gone, arguing that the latter's works should be seen only as 'preparatives' – as prefaces for the readers' labours, and he wrote of his 'delaying techniques' and deferrals of meaning, much as Coleridge did, and as Derrida does today.

Jean Paul made extensive use of delays; his *School for Aesthetics* is an endless mass of interruptions, prefaces to prefaces, extra pages and notes to notes, which radically loosens narrative conventions and leads the reader to the recognition, as Coleridge put it, that the journey – the preparative – is itself the end or goal.[20] Thinking and writing became not only a means, but an end, as 'certain' truth was delayed, postponed, and dispensed with to give way to interpretation. As Karl Solger had repeatedly argued, situations of apparent, surface incomprehension were artistically designed to reveal the only goal to be reflection itself, arrived at through the very situation supposed to be only preparatory work.[21]

The fragment form expressed an aesthetic which rejected communication as direct and language as literal, insisting on irony and indirection, and on metaphor, symbol, and rhetoric generally as the character of language.[22] Moreover, for the romantics, nature was seen as a cultural hieroglyph in need of interpretation, or 'decipherment', as they termed it. Yet nature was understood as a hieroglyph to be deciphered not into a definable meaning or even a plurality of relative meanings. Rather, the never-finished activity of decipherment, either of nature or culture and art, was itself the only goal and solution, the antidote to literal-mindedness and lazy passivity. Friedrich Schlegel also argued that language, like art, has an indeterminate significance beyond the discursively expressible. Thus, he explained, a text must contain within itself the designed space and the stimulus for the reader to build and enliven the text with imaginative experience, the goal being a clear consciousness of 'eternal agility' and of an indefinite, 'teeming chaos'.[23] Schlegel and Solger both argued that the goal of the reader of literature is not ascertaining the meaning of a text, nor the author's values and beliefs. The Socratic goal is self-knowledge, self-criticism and self-cultivation, for art was said to show us the way to achieve greater moral, aesthetic, and intellectual development by exercising the imagination.[24]

Schlegel had used the notions of fragment and incomprehensibility as a parody and a paradox for expressing the non-absolute, incomplete nature of truth, the absurdity and incomprehensibility of notions of transcendent reality or being, and especially for expressing the extent to which human beings have not yet comprehended or cultivated themselves, anticipating Kierkegaard's 'projects of thought' and his existential insistence on self-development as the project of life.[25] Jean Paul spoke of the need for the reader to treat any work of art as if it were a sketch, an outline drawn by the artist for the reader to engage with in play – not as a repository of meanings, truths, or opinions for the reader to seek, determine, and adopt or reject. Karl Solger wrote of artifacts as symbolic designs whose meaning is unverifiable by the reason because undeterminate, because of the meaninglessness at the heart of meaning. He saw artists as offering readers the opportunity to sharpen by exercise their own faculties of wit and imagination.[26] Novalis also insisted that the truly imaginative reader must be an 'expanded author'; the context shows that he intended not to glorify the reader over the artist but to indicate the demands of art on the reader.[27] Many of Jean Paul's stylistic devices – his puns and descriptions, his extraordinary wit and imagery, along with surrealistic verbal acrobatics and outrageous mannerisms – are consciously-wrought aesthetic devices for shocking the reader out of compliance and complacency. Indeed Jean Paul's theory of indirect communication was based on a Coleridgean conception of mental faculties in which there is 'no such thing as [passive] perception' (to paraphrase Derrida). Coleridge argued that perception as mere receptivity of already constructed wholes was a myth: all perception involves production or creation, and imagination is active not merely at higher levels of artistic or aesthetic activity, but at the basic level of perception, synthesizing (relative) parts into (relative) wholes.

These romantic ironists developed, on the basis of the above described ideas, their own philosophy, which they named 'Symphilosophy'. Philosophy, they argued (with Schleiermacher), was not a matter of systems or dogmas or definite positions on traditional philosophical issues. Philosophy should be a matter not of such doctrines, rationalized discourses, words, or abstract thinking, so much as of living and experiencing, as Socrates exemplified, and as Kierkegaard later extolled. Solger's choice of the dialogue form was indicative of his Platonic commitment to the creative engagement of the reader – for the dialogue provided a model of response, as Berkeley had earlier realized.[28] Conversation, moreover, became the central character of philosophizing (as Richard Rorty, Dewey, and James argued), not the spinning of esoteric and abstract systems of thought according to chains of logical reasoning based on supposed first principles. Solger thereby sought to reunite philosophy with friendly enquiry in ordinary life situations – into a social game of interaction. Like Plato, he saw the dialogue form as a type of fragment form expressive of the character of genuine philosophy – understood as the art of evoking thinking and active response from the listener-reader as the only content to be taught, as opposed to some determined dogma or system. Like Schlegel, both Solger and Jean Paul believed philosophy and criticism to be kinds of art, because they shared with art the need for indirection and the goal of self-cultivation:

Where everything depends on knowledge being not merely spoken, heard, and stored up or preserved in the memory, but rather on becoming our own completely, and the material of our most inner experiences, then the dialogue form must be the best, for it lets our spirit, before our very eyes, come into being within us and develop in our daily lives.[29]

Philosophy (for Solger, Schlegel, Novalis, and Jean Paul), like art and criticism, is best understood as one of Wittgenstein's language games, and, as Rorty emphasized, not a search after ultimate truth, being, or metaphysical realities, but friendly conversation.[30]

In discussing the nature of communication, language, and art-philosophy-criticism as indirect, the romantic ironists made a sharp distinction between symbol and allegory, anticipating many of Coleridge's and Shelley's writings on symbol and metaphor respectively.[31] The value of the symbol (used similarly to Shelley's 'metaphor') over allegory was in its evocative power. Its content, incommensurate with its linguistic expression taken discursively and literally, is designed to stimulate the reader to active contemplation and energetic 'participation' (to use Plato's word) in the symbolic work. The symbol or metaphor cannot be translated, decoded, or determined in meaning, because it exceeds discursive discourse, eluding the very language which is its vehicle. There is always a residue of meaning beyond each interpretation. The romantics sought to make their fragments exemplary of this idea of residue, of excess, by using their symbolic mode, both through the genre itself, and in many cases through the contents of the fragments. Unlike allegories, which be can decoded hermeneutically, the symbolic fragment is an indeterminate rhetorical structure designed to proliferate a variety of responses from each reader, disseminating meaning by provoking inconsistent, paradoxical, and contradictory interpretations. This would explain in part why German romantics have been characterized so differently by different writers. Unlike some accounts of the biblical higher criticism of the time, however, the romantics veered not towards hermeneutical decodings to discover determinable, hidden meanings. The tendency was away from allegorizing determinacies and towards indeterminate, excessive dissemination. Novalis called his fragments literary seed-houses (in order to express a Nietzschean idea of wanton productivity), which could only germinate and disseminate through the reader's imaginative response. Unending striving – like free-play – characterized romantic descriptions of imaginative activity, and far from positing some transcendent, desirable infinity (as is often alleged about the romantic ironists and Shelley) they emphasized the infinite play of imaginative response for its own sake, not as a means towards some absolute truth or ultimate reality.

Such self-cultivation through creative play by the reader was said to be closely akin to the artist's work, and was the essential content of all works of art. Moreover, criticism, like creative reading, must, these ironists argued, become poetic if it was to fulfil its goal of helping readers to see how art and philosophy seek to engage them in self-development, by means of an awareness of the reader's present limitations through mirroring techniques, metaphors of reading, and ironic portrayals of passive reading. Criticism can begin the reader on her way to self-knowledge through self-criticism by helping her to delve into the depths of an artifact, to become conscious of its layers and stratifications of meaning, of its indeterminacy of form and content, of its rhetorical dimensions and multiple perspectives. It should, the ironist argued, show readers how, for example, unity and wholeness or integrity of form may be deliberately hidden and obscured by multifarity and apparent disorder. 'Symbolic individuality', the integrity and unity of a work of art, is not discernible to the reasoning faculty alone (understood as *Verstand* or *dianoia*), and as such must be sought in a creative intimacy with the text. 'Cultivated' randomness and surface miscellany mask innumerable deeper connections and multiple unities perceivable by the imagination alone, just as the symbol and metaphor must be grasped by an imaginative act.[32] Unity conceived of as a mechanical, surface, rationally perceived mode of organization is replaced by unity of imaginative perception and unity of intellectual perspective. The mind of a genius can provide the focus – or intellectual perspective – which may alone be enough to hold together apparent disunity and miscellaneous content, Schlegel argued, giving Goethe's *Meister* as an example. Genuine 'aesthetic unity' is not some objective, determinable, single formal quality inhering in a work of art, but suggests a variety of ways of focusing on a work of art and a variety of possible perspectives. The fragment genre was itself designed to break down conventional notions of surface unity in art, enticing readers to 'discover' (invent?) unities amongst the fragments through relating them in various and unique ways. Thus one fragment taken as a central focus would lead to one arrangement into a whole; another fragment would lead to another whole.

The importance of such a fluid, organic, and living conception of unity was illuminated by Novalis when in discussing deliberate randomness and disregard for conventional structural unity, he described Goethe as having 'no other intention than to find a poetic way of engaging the imagination in a mysterious kind of play'.[33] And in a comment startlingly similar to Coleridge's tireless distinction between genuine thinking as opposed to mere attention, Novalis remarked on the 'true disposition of mind toward reflection' as constituting the main means of progress of the spirit in cultivating itself, in contrast to the mere 'inclination to thinking this or that thought. . . . Many scholars do not have the true disposition':

> Where a true disposition of mind towards reflection prevails . . . there you will find Progredibility [or the potentiality to pro- gress] . . . [scholars] have learned how to draw inferences and conclusions in the same way as a showmaker . . . without ever coming upon the underlying design or troubling to discover the first principles behind the thought.[34]

Schlegel, Novalis, and Tieck developed this idea of genuine reflection – versus mere inclination 'to this or that' thought – with their emphasis upon the need for detachment and their distinction between the merely subjective, egotistical and the 'uniquely' human and personal. Self-conscious detachment raises both artist and spectator above naive and sentimental absorption either in the self or the work of art: 'The first step will be insight into ourselves – detached contemplation of ourselves.'[35] Tieck took up this Coleridgean version of self-consciousness to explain that irony helps the poet to have control over his material, protects her from losing herself in the work, thereby protecting from sentimentaliz- ing and empty idealizing.

Similarly to the artist's detachment, readers need to step back from the content of the artifact and reflect upon their responses to it. They thereby lift themselves out of an unconscious, sentimental reaction to the text in order to gain detachment and perspective upon their inter- action with it. For the German romantics, the Greek chorus and ironic prognostications had been designed to provide the means for such detachment, and they saw in Shakespeare numerous techniques such as plays within plays (audiences watching audiences, as in *Hamlet*), masks and disguises where characters play another character, self-referring prologues and epilogues, and the role of the fool as ironic observer. The ironists saw in Shakespeare techniques of imagery, metaphor, and simile in the style and languages designed to create mirroring devices, both implicating the reader's role and making life a theatre. They also knew of similar techniques in the fifth- and sixth-century Sanskrit plays of Kalidasa, Bhava and others, such as *Shakuntala* and *Rama's Later History* – in the latter the reality of life is seen by one of the characters in a series of paintings. Tieck, in his *Gestiefelter Kater*, Novalis in his *Heinrich von Ofterdingen* and *Blütenstaub*, and Schlegel in *Lucinde* (to give only a few examples) developed similar techniques of what today we might call disruption, *Verfremdung*, or defamiliarization, techniques which the modernists and such dramatists as Brecht and Beckett used freely. The goal was a self-consciousness about our own role in the experience of the work of art; the aim was to help us to see our own limited perspective in order to expand it. 'Agility', to use the ironists' word, meant the ability of the reader or artist to move from one perspective to another through imaginative detachment from egoistic preferences and prejudices. One transcended one's initial perspective or self, only, however, to have to transcend the next point of view, and the next; agility was needed since there was no question of art arriving at some unlimited, neutral perspective, some higher viewpoint transcending all others. For Jean Paul, one means of provoking readers out of stereotyped perspectives and conventional, unexamined points of view was through parody: 'the best reader of the best author would be one who could thoroughly enjoy a humorous lampoon on himself'.[36] Self-parody, self-criticism, self-knowledge, and self-consciousness – all interrelated in the ironists' analyses of reading – were ideas Schlegel remarked upon in relation to imaginative reading and the role of irony. Socratic irony, he wrote,

> will remain a riddle even after it is openly confessed. It is meant to deceive no one except those who consider it a deception and who either take pleasure in the delightful roguery of making fools of the whole world, or else become angry when they get an inkling they themselves might be included.[37]

Tieck emphasized the need, moreover, for the theatre to 'make fun of itself', and argued that the Greek tragedians were constantly ironizing themselves.[38] He and Jean Paul discussed the concept of 'Illusionsstörung' as one technique of romantic irony: authors appear on stage with audiences, actors become aware of themselves as fictions, narrators make a distinction between themselves and the author to the point of infinite regress. Fun, play, wit, and humour become almost analogous with the word 'irony', yet all the romantics argued that play was also the most earnest and serious work. The collapse of the divisions between work-play, comedy-tragedy, humour-earnestness, and art-life were shattered dualisms found in Shakespeare and other Renaissance writers, not to mention Chaucer. The destruction of illusion central to this shattering of dualities involved the recognition of the necessity for the artifact not only to 'criticize' itself, the author, or the reader-spectator, but also to destroy or 'annihilate' itself in a certain sense. Self-destruction or destructive creativity and Illusionsstörung led to the close involvement of tragedy with irony and humour. Rejecting any knowledge of an illusory reality, Goethe insisted that 'we know of no world but with relation to man; we desire no art but the art which is the imprint of this relation'.[39] The tendency for the mind to hypostasize such 'Dasein', as Heidegger would call it, into a super-human, transcendent reality explained the necessity for a restraining, ironic detachment, that self-watching, backward glance over the whole which deflates such transcendentalizing. This backward glance (exemplified in the final stanza of Coleridge's 'Kubla Khan') recognizes the interpenetration of all dualities in each other – of finite and infinite, of rational and irrational, of culture and nature. Reconciliation of opposites – rather than some notion of final resolution into a higher third – involved seeing each opposite element as a function of the other, as inextricably involved, but with no *tertium aliquid* as the ground.

One of the main dualisms the romantics overcame was that between art and criticism (and poetry and philosophy). Schlegel argued for excess and residue beyond univocal meaning in language and art, when he noted that 'all criticism must go beyond the visible work of art, because every great work, of whatever kind, knows more than it says, and aspires to more than it knows'.[40] Schlegel referred then to the best criticism as 'high poetry' on one occasion, and as 'poetic criticism' on another. Criticism, if it is to be valuable, must, he explained, become itself an art, because 'poetry can be criticized only by way of poetry'.[41] Modern literature, the romantics argued, has a level of self-criticism just as ancient literature did; correlatively, modern criticism must become poetical, at least in substance if not in verse-form. Criticism can become the 'reunderstanding of understanding' – but not in any final sense, for understanding is always from some empowering, as well as limiting, perspective. Every understanding for the German ironists was provisional, since *Symphilosophie* expressed the transcendence of subjectivity and solipsism only through *Gesellschaft*, that is, through a community of socially shared experience constituted by linguistic conventions and a naturalistic context.

Hegel: System and Desystematization

Hegel's pronouncements on the German romantic ironists were not generally enthusiastic, with the exception of his remarks on Karl Solger, whom he may have admired for certain specific contributions, such as the distinction between allegory and symbol central to the concept of irony.[42] It would be misleading, however, to deduce from his criticisms that his philosophy had little in common with theirs. More accurately, Hegel seemed to understand Solger's own more abstractly expressive temperament and Solger's more familiar mode of philosophizing while he was less in tune with other romantics' sensibility, and with their more artistic, less conventionally philosophic tendencies. Yet since Solger was in sympathy with the works of Tieck, Schlegel, and Novalis, his thoughts to some extent act as a bridge between Hegel and the ironists.[43] No account of Hegel's philosophy is attempted here, since discursive accounts tend to distort his texts beyond recognition, as is the case with many philosophers. Yet we can draw attention to some elements of Hegel's writings which share some common characteristics with romantic irony and with modern theory (in spite of the differences, too), such as that Hegel's texts are not so much discursive arguments and chains of reasoning as they are literary, philosophical works, just as are Plato's *Dialogues*, and Berkeley's, Nietzsche's, and Kierkegaard's writings.[44] To give an account of Hegel's philosophy would be like extracting discursive meaning from a piece of literature, or from an essay by Derrida. No account can state the truth or even the most important things about such texts, because the most important thing, for understanding at least, is, as Hegel alleged, the experience of the whole text as it functions in the reading experience. Like his contemporary, Coleridge, Hegel argued precisely for such experience, in the preface to the *Phenomenology of Mind*, which is the text we will be concerned with here. Accounts of philosophical or literary texts tend to oversimplify the elusiveness and complexity of such texts, seeking to establish determinations and definites for open-ended speculations. One can suggest ways of 'taking' Hegel's texts in lieu of offering accounts, however. The contexts of German romantic irony and modern theory – with their shared concerns for problems of reading and response – help to articulate possible ways of encountering Hegel's texts which do not ignore their artistry.

One indication of how to approach Hegel's philosophical writings is to say that Hegel 'intended' to baffle his readers. One has to be prepared to be baffled and puzzled to an extreme degree. Hegel was not conveying some opinions and dogma, some content, as if he had facts and information to tell the reader. For example, in *The Phenomenology of Mind*, Hegel was avowedly interested, like the German ironists, in the activity of thinking, in the phenomenology of consciousness, and tried, consequently, to get the reader actively to think. Moreover, his texts posed some basic questions, and they experimented with possible ways of posing those questions. Hence, Hegel was in the position, first, of confronting various conventional terms, notions, and prejudices in philosophy as well as in common sense. Things and words one had always taken for granted he questioned, and his texts help one to see the point of questioning terms, conventions, prejudices, and habitual thoughts by demonstrating clearly how self-contradictory, non-sensical, and baffling they are. More importantly, and this is central to Hegel's texts, he was using lauguage in the most highly self-conscious way imaginable. If the reader does not recognize this, if s/he reads as though the words Hegel used are to be taken in their usual vague, unconsidered, and ill-defined way, then readers will be lost and unnecessarily confused, not tactically confused. Hegel was drawing attention to a whole range of concepts, words, phrases and notions that arise in philosophy as in life. He was looking at them very hard, scrutinizing them, to try to find out what, if anything, they mean. In *The Phenomenology of Mind*, for example, he was examining, amongst others, the words or ideas of mind, spirit and consciousness. He was interested, like Coleridge, in looking at these words to see what they could possibly mean, how they could possibly be understood. He did this in several ways; he looked at how they have been used, how people have interpreted that use, and he looked at so-called immediate, that is, phenomenological experience. If one imagines, in reading Hegel, that he meant principally by spirit something like a Christian soul, we will be very far from having even a clue of what the text is about. Hegel was also investigating the concept 'reason';he experi-mented with it, as with 'Geist', to see what it could mean. As Merleau-Ponty wrote in 1946, 'it was [Hegel] who started the attempt to explore the irrational and integrate it into an expanded reason, which remains the task of our century'.[45] Merleau-Ponty was saying that Hegel changed our concept of reason, forced us to see that unreason, madness, or the irrational is in reason, and not outside it. Reason's other, its opposite, is part of itself. Hegel explored what on earth it could possibly mean, that unreason is within reason. Perhaps it is more correct to say that Hegel was trying to make a comment about language and how we use it, though of course this has consequences beyond that use (as Foucault and others have more recently demonstrated).[46] Rather, Hegel's main thrust was to get readers to rethink the word 'reason', and to see that whatever meaning it may have is utterly bound up with its opposite, unreason, madness, intuition, or whatever its 'opposite' is.[47]

This attention to discourse has its corollary, namely, consequences for the conceptual relation between reason and unreason, reason and madness, or reason and the irrational, consequences that appear to go beyond language-use, and to attack our notions and prejudices about things such as reasonableness and madness. Yet we will be better able to read Hegel if we realize that first and foremost he was writing, like Wittgenstein and Plato, about language, about how we use it, and about whether such usage is adequate to experience. That it almost never is, seems to be the conclusion, so that we are forced into a Socratic confrontation with words, concepts, and ideas that have been inadequately thought out. In Socrates' phrase, we have used words sloppily, passively, and unthinkingly; according to Berkeley, we pretend we know just what we mean by them, when a moment's reflection will show how vague and tenuous our grasp on nearly every word in philosophical discourse is, not to mention 'ordinary' language. As Plato's Socrates put it, this crude usage may be alright for the marketplace, but it is utterly useless in philosophical thinking. Yet even in the marketplace, he showed that it leads to gross hypostasizations and ridiculous literalizations of things that are often elusive and complex. A related pitfall in reading Hegel, even if one is aware that he was questioning language, is the tendency to read without genuinely thinking through what is being discussed. Consequently, one picks up words and parrots them; readers adopt Hegel's language and turn it into mere jargon, ungrounded in actual thinking experience; *in fine*, we misunderstand Hegel, just as we misunderstood Berkeley, even when we think we are saying exactly what he said, because we lack the self-consciousness that he had in saying it – that is, the awareness that the words are all, in Husserl's term, 'bracketed'. 'Bracketed' means on one level that the words are used by Hegel with question marks, because we don't really know what we are doing when we use them, since we don't know what they mean; yet they function rather centrally in some of our language games.

For example, suppose one quoted Hegel as saying that 'all that is real is rational'. Yet in so doing, we have misunderstood that sentence, unless we know that Hegel has 'bracketed' (questioned) the meaning of the word 'rational', so that unreason, madness and intuition are included in it. Or secondly, if we describe Hegel as an idealist, we are very likely somewhat out of touch with his enterprise, as we are with Berkeley's or Kant's, not only because the term 'idealist' is vague, but also because no such definition or simple category can encompass what Hegel had done. For example, if we define idealism in one usual way, as the theory that holds 'being' and 'being known' to be equivalent, with priority of reality given to the latter, then we have to ask what it means to talk of 'being' or 'being known' and of their relation as equivalent. For Hegel, as for Berkeley and Kant, these were interesting questions, but even more central was the questioning of language. If, for Hegel, being and being-known were said to be equivalent, then the point would still be more one about discourse than about ontology. That is, whatever we understand by the word 'being' is admittedly dependent upon 'being as known'. The word, being, Hegel explained (as did Coleridge), is not a word that denotes existence independent of knowledge; it denotes, rather, dependence on knowledge. To put it another way, the subject (being) and the object (being-known) are altogether tied up in each other – the meaning of the one word is interpenetrated by the meaning of its opposite. Their separateness is mere illusion, habit, prejudice.

Here we have, essentially, the infamous Hegelian dialectic, which has also, as one might guess, been often enough misconstrued. Jean Hyppolite has offered a rethinking of Hegel's philosophy, however, which gives more weight to the a-systematic, disruptive, and anti-metaphysical aspects of his thought, and which is more consistent than traditional readings of Hegel as a rationalist-idealist systematizer. As Hyppolite put it, the rational goes over into the irrational, the subject goes over into the object, mind goes over into nature, and back again.[48] When these words or concepts or thoughts have been thought in terms of their opposites, something happens to them; they no longer appear (falsely) as independent of each other. They take on a new meaning which is more complete for our understanding of them. They are 'Aufgehoben' – raised up to a higher level. This is not a metaphysical statement, as it is often interpreted to be. It is a statement about how better to use language, namely to come to the realization through 'Aufhebung' that words' meanings include their various opposites, and that when you realize this, words change. They become round and three-dimensional, we might say, instead of flat counters to be pushed around mechanically, like checkers on a board according to rules. They are themselves powers for the mind, to use Coleridge's phrase, if they are used actively and fully. Even then, however, even once 'dialectical thinking' is achieved (namely the thinking that is able to perceive the opposite in the word's meaning, the other in the same, the unreason in reason, the nature in spirit, subject in object and *vice versa*), even then, for Hegel, there is a measure of meaninglessness embedded in all meaning. This he called the 'absolute difference', – because for Hegel, as for Plato's Socrates, it was part of the very linguistic and intellectual structure of meaning that it is also meaningless. Language can only mean up to a point; it breaks off at that point where 'we grow dizzy to look down on the dark abyss of how little we know', to use Shelley's phrase.[49]

Hegel's language of dialectical method has another purpose, for it is designed to break down the barrier between disciplines. That is, a text such as *The Phenomenology of Mind* raises questions about the relations of philosophy, religion, and art to one another. More importantly, *The Phenomenology* challenges this categorization of human thinking and experience into separate disciplines. As a number of readers have noted, for Hegel, for example, there is no philosophic language peculiar to philosophy, surprising as this may seem to some of his readers. His use of German, like that of Heidegger, involved a play on words, an abuse of words, a misuse of words and syntax. This experimentation with language may give readers the sense that Hegel used a jargon, until one realizes what is at stake, namely, an effort to draw the reader's attention to the medium, language.

Hegel's style, that is to say, is, like Nietzsche's, more a part of the content, more an essential element of his message – of what he has to tell us – than is usual in discursive prose. Much of what Hegel has to tell us is, then, about language. As in a literary text, and as in many philosophical texts (Plato, Coleridge, Kierkegaard, Berkeley, Nietzsche, Heidegger, Wittgenstein, and others), the language is unusually fundamental to the meaning or content of the text. To use Hyppolite's words, there is no structure of method in Hegel anterior to the structure of the discourse itself. We could compare this with literary language and conclude that Hegel's philosophic style is self-consciously literary. And its level of self-criticism, as built into the style, hardly refutes this claim. For literary or poetical language can also be shown to contain inevitably a level of critical language and a philosophic awareness about itself. Any romantic poet contemporary with Hegel would be a good example, as would Wallace Stevens or Sylvia Plath in our own day. Such thinking is a metalinguistic meditation on itself, along with a level of awareness of the impossibility of any such meditation entirely detached from the language used to meditate.

Hegel's *Phenomenology* has been compared to the novel; indeed, some writers have insisted that it is a kind of novel.[50] That is, it is the story of the fluctuations and character of human thinking as experienced by one person. Yet, the author of the novel (Hegel) found it more and more difficult to narrate this story. For the story involved reflection on the very instrument used to tell the story. That is, the object of the narration, language and consciousness, is the instrument of the narration as well. To paraphrase Wittgenstein, thought and language, in order to analyse themselves, must use thought and language, as the 'tools' of analysis, while yet remaining the object of the study. Moreover, Hegel discovered, in the process of analysing thought, that ordinary, passive thinking usually relies upon a support, a firm subject, while a more critical, analytical thought sees the conventional nature of the support and opts to give it up. The subject – the firm, steady support – begins to evaporate. The support to which we are accustomed, in ordinary discourse, to attaching predicates, and thereby making sentences, disappears in Hegel's (as in Wittgenstein's) self-conscious thinking. For Hegel and his contemporary, Coleridge, the only subject is movement, becoming; it is phenomenological, not supportive or abstract. Subject and predicate cannot be kept separate; they pass into each other, and the dynamic movement becomes the focus and means of critical, dialectical thinking. Hegel also echoed Coleridge in warning his readers that his writing required of them an effort similar to that of a person walking on his head! In *The Phenomenology*, Hegel showed that thought and language are consubstantial – they are interdependent. The one cannot exist without the other. Language 'expresses' thought and thought can only express itself, indeed, exist, in language, as Dewey, James, and Wittgenstein maintained.

Hegel, Hyppolite explained, then employed various conventional philosophic language or idioms which relate to various ways of thinking. Each way of thinking has its own relatively distinct idiom, and Hegel examined these idioms. Using Plato's techniques or Berkeley's method in *The Three Dialogues*, he showed, by pushing them to their extremes, that they become inconsistent with themselves. Hence, that way of thinking about problems of philosophy is inconsistent or self-contradictory, as the pragmatist would say. Plato had done something similar when he developed his elenchic method of dialectics in some of the *Dialogues*. Hegel, like Derrida later, showed us, similarly, that the languages in question – the idioms used to express certain philosophic ways of thinking – have to use language that is self-contradictory, and which therefore, we have in a sense to give up. If we can't actually give the language up, however, since we can't step outside language, yet, being as it is self-contradictory, we will at least have to use it self-consciously – that is, with an awareness that we can't actually univocally mean what we say or say what we mean. We must put our words, phrases, syntax, our language, 'under erasure'. We must 'bracket' it, so that we don't take it literally, or forget that most of the words we use are saturated both with their opposites and with that 'absolute difference' which was referred to earlier. Words are saturated with a residue of meaninglessness which is part of the very nature of meaning and language. *The Phenomenology*, then, is both an analysis of 'ordinary language' and a record of what happens to ordinary language when subjected to analysis. What happens is that the subject and predicate become interdependent. The knower is involved in the thing known; or, being, as was said earlier, is equivalent to 'being-known'. Yet the priority of the latter is given up in dialectical thinking. For Hegel, as for Coleridge, there is then no means of understanding distinct from the thing-known, or, put another way, philosophic thought is thought in which knowledge is not an instrument exterior to the thing that is known. It is the thing-known which speaks and which expresses itself, to use Heidegger's idiom. This is dialectical thinking: the I, the subject, the support has forgotten itself.

In meditating in *The Phenomenology* on the nature of so-called ordinary experience and ordinary language, (as opposed to *The Logic*, which meditates on language as a relatively, humanly 'universal' phenomenon), Hegel wrote a novel of culture, or a novel of voyage and discovery. The philosopher seeks to *follow* ordinary consciousness (not lead it, ending in a self-analysis or ego-trip), but follow it in its theoretical and practical experiences, until the ordinary consciousness reaches the point of absolute knowledge, as it is called – the point where it says, 'but what you have just discovered, I knew it all along'. (Yet the notion of absolute knowledge, Hyppolite cautioned us, can only be understood in a bracketed, problematic sense. Otherwise, it is inconceivable in Hegel's dialectical, dynamic system).[51] Ordinary consciousness recognizes itself in philosophic consciousness – recognizes, for example, that there is no thought outside language. To experience and organize the world is to organize it with language, as Wittgenstein argued. To delineate a concept is to delineate with language. Moreover, for Hegel, philosophic consciousness reveals to ordinary consciousness that the I, the solid subject, the support, exists only in language, as Shelley later insisted. The linguistic environment is the humanly universal Being. It is the 'logos'. It is in language that the world takes on meaning and that thought exists, and can become both subject and object for itself. Language is that object which is reflected in itself. The mind (and subject) exists in language and in the use of language; for Coleridge, Shelley and the German ironists, language is the condition of knowledge, dialogue, and human intercourse.

It has often been said that one of Hegel's greatest contributions to philosophy was his emphasis upon the 'historical'. That is, Hegel took what we might term an apocalyptic view of mind, nature, language, the universe and self-consciousness, philosophy, and so on. For Hegel, unlike a number of earlier thinkers (though there are other notable exceptions, such as Plato and Berkeley, Blake, Coleridge, and Shelley), the world is not something fixed and static. The cosmos, the universe, is in a constant state of becoming. Humans are not confronted with an already achieved, fully-final product, the material world, which they receive passively on the surface of the senses, since the world is in a state of becoming. Yet, in addition, the mind of humankind is, first, a part of that world, not something metaphysical or super-empirical set over against it. And, secondly, the mind of humans is also not fixed; it hasn't reached some final, static state of development. Mind, like the world, is evolving. Mind, as a part of world, is developing and changing. For Hegel, in its expanded reconceptualization, mind, like nature, emerges (nature being the context for, not the opposite of, mind).[52]

Correlatively, 'reason' (bracketed), the character of mind for Hegel, emerges, and 'reason' is not conceived of as some super-empirical faculty, but as acts of (not merely analytic) reasoning by an active, evolving mind. Hegel's world, then, is a world of activity, of process, of goings-on, of events; therefore a historical world, an evolving world, including evolving mind and evolving reason. Mind, or (bracketed) 'reason' (and within it, unreason) – that elusive character of human mind – evolves through language. Language, logos, and 'reason' (bracketed) is the means by which mind becomes self-conscious, that is, aware of itself as existing in the world. Without language, humans would not be human, but only an animal with the historical possibility of self-consciousness or consciousness of being. Language for Hegel is reason, or reasoning, and language as expanded reason is the meaning of mind. Language, like mind, is also itself a historical phenomenon – it is constantly evolving and developing as the human mind comes to greater knowledge of itself, of reason (of unreason), of language – to greater self-knowledge we might say – though this is apt to mislead. For to Hegel, self-knowledge was a knowledge of the world, since subject and object are not independent or in opposition to each other, but are aspects or functions of the world as experienced. That is, the distinction of subject and object, within which human conscious experience exists, is held, as it is by Heidegger and Dewey, to be a distinction within a single unified experience. The form in which this 'unity in difference' reaches its highest known expression is self-consciousness. Whenever subject and object stand in the relation which constitutes experience, the 'unifying' principle is thought, (un-) reason, or language – the logos. Subject and object are inseparable in the life of experience. The subject, in the evolution or historical process of achieving self-consciousness, finds itself in its object, and thus comes to be 'at home' in the world. The subject is not, then, for Hegel, outside the world of nature – looking down on it from the heights of a superempirical soul-being. As for Heidegger, the subject dwells in the world essentially, not accidentally. (Yet 'essential' not in any transcendent sense – but linguistically speaking: to dwell in the world is part of the very meaning of the word 'subject'.) The Hegelian here and now (space and time) of existence are essential linguistically speaking, not accidental categories, in contrast to much philosophizing which insisted that only the eternal is essential or real. For Hegel, it is not some transcendent eternal which is the meaning of the word 'real', but the historical – the here and now – that is, time and space, that which is evolving and becoming – not that fiction which has 'pure being'.

Moreover, the so-called 'absolute knowledge' which Hegel depicted humans as striving toward, that more complete self-consciousness – that consciousness of the subject as in the object (dialectical thinking) – is not knowledge of an absolute conceived as beyond humans – as divine – as in a Platonic realm of transcendent reality. For Hegel, the absolute was historical, and the absolute is interpretable only in terms of mind, for mind is the individuality with which we have most acquaintance. It is futile, Hegel insisted along with Coleridge, to ask what the absolute may be over and above mind; for over and above mind there is nothing higher to which to appeal in any intelligible way. To be intelligible is to be mentally constituted, and intelligibility is the presupposition and the result of philosophy.

For Hegel, the 'being of mind is its *act*, and its act is to be aware of itself'. (This sentence could as easily be a quotation from Coleridge.) This act of self-consciousness, of reasonableness, is both analytic and synthetic, both reflective (discursive) and intuitive. Reason or mind, as redefined by Hegel, (not individual mentality, but *Dasein*) for Hegel, is self-complete, it is its own world and the law of its world. It does not, as Kant's reason tended to do, require a material external to itself in order to be synthetic and constructive and for the senses to 'receive'. Rather, reason, as reconceived by Hegel, contains both subject and object in an organic unity: difference in unity. The term 'experience' for Hegel, then, denotes the inseparable and continuous interrelation of subject and object. This is a redefinition of a familiar term in philosophy that had usually meant something subjective and private – something psychological. 'Experience', when used by Hegel, is neither subjective nor objective – or – you might say – it is both subjective and objective all at once – for experience is the integration in a being known of subject and object, mind and nature, if you will. This is what is meant by dialectical thinking. Mind is in nature and nature is the character of mind. Put another way, being, rightly understood, or pure being – *is* being known – is something intelligible. There is no such thing as being beyond the known – for that is to talk of unintelligible being – and such a being is unintelligible. To use Coleridge's terms, we could say that Hegel took Kant's metaphysics and banished the inconsistency of reason *versus* the notional manifold which, Coleridge argued, Kant himself had successfully achieved in his *Logic*.

Hegel was exploring language and experimenting with words and language, very much as Plato was doing especially in such a dialogue as the *Parmenides*, or as Heidegger, Nietzsche, and Derrida were doing. If one fails to attend to the fact that Hegel was questioning words, concepts, and language, and thereby questioning mind, and reason, thought and the world, then you will not know what to do when you read him as saying, for example, something similar to what Novalis was quoted as saying earlier:

> Those who put forward such assertions really themselves say, if we bear in mind what we remarked before, the direct opposite of what they mean: a fact which is perhaps best able to bring them to reflect on the nature of the certainty of sense-experience. They speak of the 'existence' of external objects, which can be more precisely characterized as actual, absolutely particular, wholly personal, individual things, each of them not like anything or anyone else; this is the existence which they say has absolute certainty and truth. They 'mean' this bit of paper I am writing on, or rather have written on: but they do not say what they 'mean'. If they really wanted to *say* this bit of paper which they 'mean', and they wanted to *say* so, that is impossible, because the This of sense, which is 'meant', cannot be reached by language, which belongs to consciousness, i.e. what is inherently universal. In the very attempt to say it, it would, therefore, crumble in their hands; those who have begun to describe it would not be able to finish doing so: they would have to hand it over to others, who would themselves in the last resort have to confess to speaking about a thing that has no being. They 'mean', then, doubtless this bit of paper here, which is quite different from that bit over there; but they speak of actual things, external or sensible objects, absolutely individual real, and so on; that is, they say about them what is simply universal. Consequently what is called unspeakable is nothing else than what is untrue, irrational, something barely and simply 'meant'.[53]

Likewise, you would be confused if in reading Plato's P*armenides*, you forgot that it was about words and language, and found yourself confronted with what we might anachronistically call a very Hegelian piece of language. For example:

> Let us, then, once more state what will follow, if a one is. Consider whether this supposition does not necessarily imply that the one is such as to have parts. That follows in this way. Since 'is' is asserted to belong to this one which is, and 'one' is asserted to belong to this being which is one, and since 'being' and 'one' are not the same thing, but both belong to the same thing, namely that 'one which is' that we are supposing, it follows that it is 'one being'

as a whole, and 'one' and 'being' will be its parts. So we must speak of each of these parts, not merely as a part, but as a part of a whole.

Therefore, any 'one that is' is a whole and also has parts.

Again, take each of these two parts of the one being – its unity and its being. Unity can never be lacking to the part 'being', nor being to the part 'unity'. Thus each of the two parts, in its turn, will possess both unity and being; any part proves to consist of at least two parts, and so on forever by the same reasoning. Whatever part we arrive at always possesses these two parts, for a 'one' always has being, and a 'being' always has unity. Hence any part always proves to be two and can never be one.

In this way, then, what is 'one being' must be unlimited in multitude. . . .

Therefore, if there is no one, the others neither are, nor can be imagined to be, one or many.

Nor yet, if there is no one, can the others be or appear like or unlike, or the same or different, or in contact or apart, and so on with all the other characters which we have just been saying they appear to have.

Thus, in sum, we may conclude, If there is no one, there is nothing at all.

To this we may add the conclusion. It seems that, whether there is or is not a one, both that one and the others alike are and are not, and appear and do not appear to be, all manner of things in all manner of ways, with respect to themselves and to one another.

Most true.[54]

In questioning words and language, Hegel, Plato, and others questioned the world. Yet if we read their texts as though they were questioning the world – reality – the way things are – and that language is merely instrumental to this thinking, then we will be utterly confused. Only by questioning language can we question 'ontologically'. For we dwell in language – language *is* our known world, and one main task in philosophy is to make us aware and conscious of this matter about our world – that first and foremost it is linguistic, not absolutely, of course, but relatively for human endeavours.

3

Johnson, Coleridge, and Method

English (as well as German) Romantic ideas about critical theory and aesthetics reveal connections with modern theory, deconstruction, and Derrida, connections which are in a general sense well known, as are the contrasts between them. An attempt is made here to elucidate these connections and contrasts in a more detailed way, in the implicit context of pragmatist philosophy and aesthetics. Recent pragmatist aesthetic theories, as expressed by Richard Rorty, for example, and based on John Dewey (especially his *Art as Experience*, and more briefly, chapters of *Experience and Nature*)[1] relate closely to Romantic aesthetic and critical principles. Hence, Dewey's ideas act along with Rorty's elaborations as a helpful bridge in spanning the time gap between, on the one hand, Coleridge's and Shelley's theories, and, on the other, modern post-structuralist views. Both the shared and the divergent aspects of these three periods can be said to stand out more clearly by relating them to each other. Given the strong connections between pragmatist and Derridean critiques of metaphysics (albeit wide differences in style and approach), a comparison of Dewey and Derrida on the critical-aesthetic level reveals much about Derrida's highly innovative strategies (and even more, about his advances beyond pragmatist practices). Before looking closely at Coleridge's critical ideas and practices, however, one can explore a (perhaps surprising) precursor, to establish earlier connections between eighteenth-century critical thought and modern theory, through one of the central ideas of Nietzsche, Dewey, and Derrida, namely, that interpretation is not so much of objects, but of other people's prior interpretations, the 'object' being understood as a kind of manifold of interpretations.

While English Romantic aesthetic and literary criticism was, in large part, a reaction against Samuel Johnson and his contemporaries, one of

Johnson's most penetrating, methodological procedures in criticism and in enquiry in general was taken up by the romantics wholeheartedly, as it was by Dewey nearly a century later. Like Coleridge, Johnson, probably a major influence on him, was often preoccupied with speculating about procedures and methods of criticism in a self-conscious way, though in his practice he, admittedly, often lost sight of his own discoveries. Johnson's methodological statements are scattered widely throughout the *Rambler*, the *Idler*, and other texts, a fact which has obscured a general recognition of the central role that sound method played in his critical procedures. John Wright has clarified this role of sound method in Johnson's thought, arguing that Johnson emphasized a literary-critical method which analyses and corrects received opinion about literature and texts, in contrast to literary critical endeavours to explain literature, or to explicate meaning in literary texts.[2] This preferred method, the analysis of either received or, for that matter, new opinion, acts, moreover, for Johnson, as a corrective to the second, less preferred criticism. For Johnson, the 'explanation of literature' or of phenomena in general, that is, the assigning of meanings and interpretations to texts, generates more opinion, which must then be tested for its value and cogency. This very Socratic (and even Cartesian, in certain respects) attitude of treating texts and objects as already interpreted entities is the view that informs Coleridge's and, later, Dewey's and Derrida's approaches to texts, artifacts, and to phenomena. Thus, its application to literature is a specification of a more general epistemological view of objects, whether artifacts or nature, whether physical or mental: objects are interpretive constructs in need of further interpretation, not pure, independent entities impinging on an independent, interpreting or, for that matter, a passive, receptive mind.

As John Wright explained, it could be said that Johnson learned, in part from Descartes, to treat experience and the information or judgments derived from observation as received opinion in need of analysis, and not as 'natural', 'pure' facts providing a substratum of objective reality for the mind to work upon. For Johnson, we can never record or observe objectively, since we are at all times applying prejudices and opinions in the very process of selection, attention, and conscious observation. There was for Johnson, as for Dewey, no objective observation: what we decide to analyse, which elements of an experience we attend to, all are dictated by values and interests of the observer. Johnson applied this insight to literary criticism and, combined with a Baconian, empiricist, experimental method of analysis derived from the methodological tradition of philosophy, he developed a sound method of literary-critical procedure analogous in many respects to general theories about sound scientific enquiry. As Dewey was to insist later, sound procedure is the common basis for all enquiry, whether in literature or the sciences. That our experience is received opinion (that is, already interpreted 'material', and not a neutral record or observation of reality, whether of texts or phenomena) is the basis, moreover, of the Socratic scepticism inherent in Samuel Johnson's outlook.

For Johnson, as for Coleridge, Shelley, Dewey, and Derrida, the human intellect is not properly described as apprehending 'reality', whether by reason, intuition, or imagination, since the concept is incomprehensible when taken as something monolithic, transcendent, or absolutely independent of experience. What we know as reality is received opinion or interpretation in need of constant reanalysis and reformulation. What we know analogously as texts is also received opinion (or prior interpretations of prior interpretations, as Dewey would say). Moreover, Johnson, Wright showed, denied the Cartesian view that we could obtain axioms which could be the basis of scientific certainty (as Plato had denied before him)[3] or the basis of certainty about the true meaning of a literary text. Thus Johnson's 'principles' were no basis for anything except enquiry: they were not axioms, but practical steps and procedures arrived at by trial and error, but not designed to serve the investigation of real things leading to certainty. They were to serve as tools to question received opinion and reveal its inconsistencies and inadequacies. Truth was never the object, nor did Johnson nourish illusions of fixing 'foundations' for knowledge.[4]

What Johnson tried to encourage us to pursue in our literary criticism, Wright suggested, was not true explanations of the text, but rather an analysis of the opinions and so-called 'true' meanings surrounding texts. Such analysis reveals whether the opinions and interpretations passed off as true meanings were based on sound experience, or merely on conjecture and prejudiced hypotheses. Johnson showed that in literary criticism we might better be interested, not in what is the true meaning or interpretation of a literary text. Rather, we should attend to what is *said* to be the meaning, and whether what is *said* is based on empirical observables of the text, arrived at by sound method of enquiry and testing of previously stated interpretations. Johnson recognized that there was no absolute point from which literary critical enquiry can begin, since in the first moment of reading a text we interpret, bringing to bear an entire background of literary tradition and personal literary experience upon it. We are forced to filter the experience that arises from such interpretive, 'first' readings by consciously analysing it and then making *it* an object of observation. Unlike some critics, who wrote and spoke as though literary criticism were a process of transcribing the feelings and responses of a critic, Johnson, like Dewey and Coleridge, saw criticism as the careful examination and testing of opinion about literary texts, opinion that may be the critic's own, or the traditional, received opinion surrounding the text. Johnson was a Socratic sceptic in his rejection of certainty about the essence or true meaning of texts as the goal of enquiry, in favour of certainty about the procedures of enquiry and analysis.

Thus he attacked, for example, the procedures of neo-classical critics who imposed by arbitrary edict the norms of tragic drama, making the three unities rules for texts that do not arise from the texts but are imposed externally upon them. Such importation is false procedure, and can be exposed by careful enquiry. For Johnson, one of the main roles of enquiry was to expose cases where such 'accidentals' as the three unities are raised by critics to the level of essentials and necessities. Johnson showed that a critic is never in a position to offer even a tentative or relative judgement on a text until s/he has established, from experience of the text, principles which can sustain opinion. (The three unities were never such a principle, he argued.) Moreover, such opinion and the principles they are derived from and which validate them (based as principles are in empirical experience of the text) must be constantly re-examined and reanalysed, in a process of self-correction. For, as Johnson admitted, with Socrates, we know only this: we are ignorant of the basic principles of things. We must be always sceptical of the principles we adopt, since experience and observation are themselves only a form of unexamined received opinion. There is no final foundation; a constant checking back and forth between experience and derived principles is necessary to make the alterations in the one that new development in the other requires. The result, John Wright explained, is a radical uncertainty in experience, as well as in aesthetic experience.

To search for knowledge of an ultimate, certain kind about reality was, to Johnson, futile, just as to search for univocal true meanings about texts was futile. It is not futile, though, to search for relative certainty or at least consistency in our method of enquiry. We can never settle the true, real, or even best meaning of a text, but we can establish that our critical steps of enquiry into the opinion about the text are sound. Some of Dewey's comments on enquiry in general (in *Logic: the theory of inquiry*), corroborate and extend Johnson's methodological insights enough to warrant brief discussion here, before we proceed with romantic criticism. Like Johnson, Dewey insisted that whatever the diversity of its subject matter, enquiry itself has a common structure and pattern; thus procedures of enquiry in science are precisely those we must use in enquiring into literary texts. And like Johnson, he insisted that enquiry, being a 'mode of conduct' is as much subject to objective study as is any other material, and that enquiry into clear procedures of analysis and into enquiry itself must interact with enquiry into other material. But, with Johnson, he made no pretence to any absolute science of enquiry, criticism, or 'philosophy' which could somehow offer certain principles or foundations for certain knowledge. On the contrary, Dewey jokingly compared the science of enquiry to that of farming! Like farming, he explained, enquiry (whether in art or science) is conducted in one way and not another because practice alone shows one way to be better for some purposes than other ways so far considered. New ways may be discovered that supersede the old, but the best enquiry is simply that method which experience has proven to be the best one available at a given time for certain purposes and results.

Much of Johnson's attention in the scattered comments on methodology and criticism concentrated, then, on establishing exactly what critics, as critics, should be trying to do: he distinguished the analysis of received opinion as their genuine object, not the establishing of determined meanings or truths about supposedly pure, independent, stable texts. Dewey likewise emphasized this point in *Art as Experience*, but in *Logic: the theory of enquiry*, he generalized it into a philosophical, methodological principle. For he noted that the first step of enquiry is to find out what the problem is which a situation represents, and that a problem well stated is already on its way to being solved. To mistake the problem, as, according to Johnson, most critics do, is to go badly astray. Moreover, Dewey reminded us that a problem only has meaning if there is reference to a possible solution; hence if the critic sets herself a solutionless problem (what is the true or best meaning of this text?; what is this text really telling us? etc.), then we could argue that those critical problems have no meaning in literature, in the absolute senses of those words, 'true', 'best', or 'really', because they deny context, and have no reference to a possible solution.

Dewey was more explicit than Johnson on certain issues, for aspects of Johnson's theory remain only implicit. For instance, it is an implication of Johnson's methodology that the facts that make up an observation, as well as empirical data, are themselves not fixed or absolute, but are as radically subject to change and reinterpretation as the opinions and deductions that arise from them. Dewey explicitly made clear this provisional nature of 'facts', and insisted that they are all 'trial' facts which must be treated symbolically, since if they lose their provisional character and are categorically asserted, they stop enquiry.[5] The facts, that is, may change, or come to have different meanings, as enquiry proceeds and the object/text is viewed from different perspectives or according to different interpretations. Like Johnson, Dewey insisted that the facts must be observed in the material under question, and that 'solutions', or suggestions, or ideas are arrived at by analysis of the facts, not by importations from outside, such as prejudices and authoritative dicta of how we ought to interpret the facts (as neo-classical rules were imported, or notions about pastoral poetry, as Johnson argued). These 'suggestions' or hypotheses for a solution must be carefully formulated and allowed to lead to more observed facts, or enquiry may lead to false conclusions, being thwarted by confused, untested ideas. Carefully formulated suggestions arising out of selected, provisional facts and tested by still more facts may be proved false or true, but the method, in either case, will be sound.

Dewey also elaborated the creativity involved in the practice of sound critical method, when he noted that 'suggestions' (which when carefully formulated and tested against more facts, become ideas) 'pop' mysteriously into our heads.[6] For they are not logical or deducible from the empirical matter under question, but are only suggested, and involve imaginative handling of the facts that are noted once the problem has been stated. Some suggestions are better than others in leading to resolving the subject of the enquiry in some way. Only by testing and careful formulation can we distinguish better from worse ones. Dewey concluded by suggesting romantic accounts of method when he defined enquiry as the controlled and directed transformation of less determinate situations into ones that are more determinate, that is, into ones where the constituents are more clearly determined and their possible relations clarified so as to reveal some unified wholes.[7] In contrast, the indeterminate situation is one in which the constituents do not relate, do not 'hang together', for they lack some unifying thread. For Dewey, as for the romantics (contrary to much general opinion) the constituent parts and their relations, not to mention the 'unified whole', are relative to the process of enquiry, and not absolute characters of the object or text. Other constituents, relations, and wholes will be perceived when the object/text is approached with other leading ideas, suggestions, or interests in view.

Like the 'facts' discussed above, all these elements are equally provisional. Every text, like every situation, is subject to numerous unities or 'solutions'. Nor must we forget that literally to ascribe these parts, relations, and wholes to the text-in-itself is to lose sight of Johnson's most penetrating critical principle, namely, that the object of criticism is not an objective text-in-itself, but is rather our own (or the received) opinion about the text. We distinguish the 'facts' from already interpreted, opined experience, not from some imaginary text-in-itself free from

human contact. Our constituent parts, relations, and wholes are those of
the received opinion, as analysed, and our conclusion tells us about that
opinion, that interpretation. It does not reveal to us unchanging, objective traits of an independent object, but only more opinion, then to
be subjected to enquiry. This is true whether the subject matter under
enquiry is literary texts or trees or black holes. What is said to be the case
about these objects is what is under enquiry, not what *is* the case. For
experimental scientific certainty about basic truth was for Johnson not
only impossible, it was unintelligible, since basic principles are unknown
to us, and since the concept of a founding principle outside of human
experience is nonsensical: we derive our principles from the very facts by
which we then seek to test them, and this circle allows for no external
anchor.[8]

Romanticism, pragmatism, and deconstruction share, in spite of their
differences, a common emphasis upon the need for a method and
theory of enquiry if literary criticism is ever to be something more than
unanalysed received opinion.[9] That is, there is a close relationship between the structure of enquiry and the task of criticism, and the difficulties rigorous enquiry and criticism face. John Wright has attributed to
Samuel Johnson the belief that 'criticism must confront the problem of
knowledge as a logical precondition of intelligent interpretive or
evaluative judgment'.[10] This remark applies equally well to Coleridge,
Shelley, James, Dewey, Derrida, de Man, and others associated with these
three major movements. Moreover, a strain of Platonic-Socratic scepticism pervades their thought, as they explore the intractable problems
involved in articulating a method of enquiry able to improve opinion
into knowledge.[11] The result of the sceptical view that experimental
scientific certainty about basic truth is impossible leads to a shift away
from the search for basic truth to an emphasis upon 'tracking opinion to
its sources'.[12] A method of enquiry that examines human opinion and
already existing systems of belief is sought, one that rectifies opinion
rather than establishing certain truths. Such scepticism common to all
these movements is a denial of the possibility that the human mind can
comprehend the real essence of nature or phenomena, a denial that
human reason can obtain axioms or principles of unquestionable truth.
Since it is argued that we cannot know ultimately what is the case, we
should attend to, analyse, and examine what is said to be the case: 'a
dialectical examination of opinion', whether about nature or literature,
to see whether received opinion is justifiable, appropriate, and based on
consistent principles. Our goal is procedural, relative certainty, not essential certainty. Rather, the goal of enquiry is to correct and improve
received opinion by analyzing its claims and principles and testing these

for their appropriateness, to ensure, for example, that received opinion is not based on unexamined elements: on fictions, prejudices, custom, unfounded authoritative pronouncements, unanalysed feelings, or elements not appropriate to the subject matter of the enquiry. We must test principles to ensure that those taken as relatively universal and necessary are not merely 'descriptive criteria or conventional principles' for specific literary procedures. Analysis into operative critical principles involves 'sifting opinions (actual or potential premises) about phenomena into those which the phenomena require and those somehow superadded'. What is often discovered in such analysis of received opinion into, for example, literary criticism, is that 'customary premises of critical judgment do not express principles of the phenomena' under question. Such customary premises turn out to be unjustifiable importations from without: or often, 'accidental characteristics of a genre' are made into a 'metaphysical or constitutive definition of its essential nature'.[13]

Coleridge is better known for his interest in methodological concerns than Johnson, but his investigations into the nature of enquiry and criticism follow directly from Johnson and are rarely at odds with that tradition of methodology. Like Johnson, he was concerned with establishing a sound method of enquiry, as his emphasis upon first principles in method, observation as evidence, and argumentation (rather than fiat) indicate. Coleridge, too, made his object of investigation received opinion, as his comments and his practice in the *Biographia* and *Shakespearean Criticism* show. He was constantly engaged in testing the validity of opinions (whether his own or received opinion) about Wordsworth, Shakespeare, and others, and this was usually the method of his criticism. He never confused what is said to be the case with what is the case, the latter being a spurious illusion of absolute knowledge that Coleridge took great pains to expose. In addition to saying much about criticism as a method of enquiry, however, Coleridge also discussed at length the nature of poetic language, a discussion that provides interesting comparisons and contrasts with an issue also central to deconstruction, with its emphasis on metaphor, rhetoric, and its exposure of divisions between ordinary and literary language.

Coleridge's exposition in the *Biographia* and *The Friend* of a methodology specifically related to literary criticism, but generalizable to other subject matters, exhibits the method of critical enquiry that both Johnson and, later, Dewey, advocated as the best method so far discovered, even though it is only capable itself of delivering opinion, albeit, 'right' opinion. Here 'right' means opinion tested by the inductive, deductive, and empirical observational elements that are all part of the described method. This opinion may not be knowledge, since it cannot be final or certain because its grounds are themselves suppositions. Yet it is an improvement over prejudice and untested opinion, in that it is at least consistent with itself and with the matter that is its object, namely a philosophical criticism of literature. Coleridge analysed the received opinion of the day about what critical enquiry into literary texts is, by looking at the practice of criticism in the various reviews and magazines that were the great purveyors of taste, judgement, and opinion in his day. Like Johnson and Dewey, he formulated his problem and then gathered evidence and facts from observation of the relevant material. His observation and analysis of the critical practices of the day suggested the idea to him that these critics had no method of criticism and no method of enquiry either into their literary objects, nor even any awareness that they should also be enquiring into their method of criticism! He concluded that not only was the prevailing 'criticism' unsound of method; it had no method. On this grounding assumption, that sound method is a prerequisite for reaching any sound opinion about things, Coleridge rejected such contemporary 'criticism' and sought, as his third stage of enquiry, to elucidate some principles of a method of enquiry (which he was already in practice demonstrating to the reader in his exposition of the reviews of the day). He drew his hypothetical principles from observations of his own and the critical practices of others. Finally, he tested those suggestive ideas about principles, by referring to more facts and opinions, in short, by analysing the received opinion about Wordsworth's poetry and by testing it against his own opinion. In the meantime, he had also established the necessity for defining terms concerning the objects of the enquiry and discussed at length the definitions of poetry, prose, a poem, and poetic language.[14]

The reader, then, sees Coleridge not only establishing a method of enquiry, but enacting and demonstrating it simultaneously with the exposition. Coleridge moved from observations, empiricals, and particulars, by means of analysis of received opinion, to more general, hypothetical ideas or suggestions for critical principles. Then he grounded his proposed principles, drawn from the observations and facts, in still more general, philosophical (not merely critical) propositions, involving, for example, defining terms, or noting the limits of knowledge and certainty, and finally he moved back into facts and observations, to test and validate his theoretic, hypothetical principles in a critical analysis of opinion about Wordsworth's poetry. Part of the richness and power of both the *Biographia* and *The Friend* is their impressive, simultaneous exposition of theory and the demonstration of practice. These texts collapse the concrete and abstract, the theory and the practice, into a single achievement. In the *Biographia* particularly, there is no break, for both theory and practice are fused in the text. The genius and uniqueness of this double-texture can be realized only when we try to identify any other text like it. The closest is perhaps Shelley's 'Defence of Poetry', or Kierkegaard's *Philosophical Fragments*, or Plato's *Meno*.

Before leaving this first stage, namely Coleridge's Johnsonian and Platonic concern about sound method as the generalized theory of criticism from which a specific theory of literary criticism emerges, we should note that, in the 'Essays on Method' in *The Friend*, he made his most systematic (indeed, only) statement of methodology (science of method, of enquiry, generalized theory of criticism). In the 'Essays' he not only searched for hypothetical principles on which to ground his investigation, including criticism, he also examined the nature of creative thought, since it is a necessary part of sound method (theories, hypothetical principles 'pop' into our heads, they are not logically deducible or mechanically derived from observations or facts). Already the distinction between method or general criticism and creative literary activity is challenged. Method and criticism are also creative, according to Coleridge, and not merely accidentally but essentially.

The need for principles and sound method was questioned by Coleridge. Why prefer method to prejudice or ungrounded opinion? Why not rely upon first reactions and the authority of established critics? Coleridge answered in a thoroughly pragmatic way: principles and sound method lead to power and consistency. Or, put another way, sound enquiry leads more often to understanding, clear apprehensions, and 'problem solving' than does mere prejudice or opinion.[15] We know this by practice, and we know that unquestioned opinion and prejudices are often inconsistent with themselves and even full of unintelligible elements, characteristics that prevent them from being the guides to greater understanding that they claim to be. Coleridge's first principle is to establish the need for sound method and principles over immethodical reactions to situations in general, and to literary texts, in particular (his answer to Leavis, amongst others). Hence he rejected the view that one could read intelligently by reading 'naturally', that is, unselfconsciously, and without an awareness of the principles and prejudices unconsciously guiding one's reading responses.[16] His insistence on sound method in criticism is an insistence upon the inevitability of theory saturating every concrete reading, and on the need to become conscious of that unconscious, selective, theoretical bias in order to read with greater intelligence. If, as readers, we do not know what the expectations and opinions are that guide our responses, we can never escape our own initial responses, we cannot ever escape our own prejudices and unexamined premises. For Johnson and Coleridge, to imagine that any reader can be free of prejudices and assumptions that restrict her response is naive. Moreover, an unconscious reader will forever remain ignorant, however impeccable her taste, of how the poetry she enjoys achieves its effects, a knowledge which itself increases the effects and the enjoyment of them. She will lack, Coleridge argued, 'power and consistency' of appreciation or apprehension.

Coleridge concluded that readers and critics need reasons and arguments for their opinions, not merely unanalysed reactions, and that the analysis of thought is the establishment of sound method. Method, he explained, is not mere arrangement; like thought itself (as opposed to mere attention), method involves 'progressive transition' or transition with continuity, and is 'unity with progression'.[17] 'Progression' is guided by a preconception or leading idea (Dewey's 'suggestion', 'idea'), an intuition or conjectural hypothesis arising not so much from empirical material, but arising from the creativity of the mind, which itself determines the limits of the preconception.[18] This intuitiveness, he insisted, like Dewey, is the 'initiative' of all method, and is never merely a product of observation; some 'hunch' is needed to make the choice amongst the innumerable particulars. Coleridge then noted that the notion, 'absolute knowledge', requires a ground for the conditioned, but the existence of such a ground outside human experience is an unintelligible notion. Hence, he argued ironically that such knowledge could never be attainable by men and would be divine, thereby adopting Johnson's Socratic scepticism. All our 'first principles', then, are relative and hypothetical, arising out of a culturally conditioned human mind itself, and so can never lead to knowledge independent of human, cultural experience. For Coleridge, principles are never absolute or ultimate, but are points of departure for reasoning.[19]

Coleridge's pursuit of a 'philosophical' criticism, as he called it, led him to a Deweyan enquiry into method or enquiry itself, and finally to an effort to establish principles 'in the component faculties of the human mind itself'.[20] This is less a positive claim than a negative, critical statement; that is, it is an admission that there exist no principles outside of human experience to provide any absolute ground. Or, as Coleridge said, he sought principles not of being, but of knowing, since beyond knowing it is impossible to enquire: 'The principle of our knowing is sought within the sphere of our knowing.'[21] He denied explicitly that he was engaged in any enquiry into ultimate grounds outside knowing. The rejection of absolute knowledge and of any independent ground places the Coleridge of the *Biographia* in the methodological tradition with its modest, Socratic scepticism, a scepticism based less on the notion of the limitation of the human intellect than on the view that ideas of grounds, absolute knowledge, and absolute reality are unintelligible and illusory, more matters of faith and religion than of reason, as William James would argue a century later.[22]

Coleridge's next move, to 'ground' human knowledge (or right opinion), involves establishing 'self-consciousness' as the only conceivable ground. But what does this ground of self-consciousness mean? Too often it has merely been interpreted as conventional idealism. Yet Coleridge's own elaboration makes it clear that 'self-consciousness' is the term he used to describe experience, and more particularly, human experience. It is not a transcendental entity or an idealist postulate, but a condition for human experience to be what it is. He then made a point precisely in keeping with the pragmatist and deconstructionist questioning of dualism, when he insisted that the experience of a dualism of subject-consciousness and object-world is a mere 'prejudice of outness' and not a character of 'primary' experience.[23] In 'primary' experience, or self-consciousness, as he termed it, subject and object are relative to each other, and can be reunited in an act of knowledge. Dualism is a description only of an intermediate stage of experience; it is a product of a stage of reflection, not a characteristic of reality.

Much of the problem of interpreting Coleridge lies in his apparently idealist terminology, which traps him in apparent dogmas, where critical scepticism is uppermost. Thus, his texts foster 'misreadings' that postulate the very idealist, transcendentalist positions against which he was often explicitly arguing. At points, the language leads not only his readers astray, but obfuscates and burdens his own best insights into his criticisms of dualism, empiricism, idealism, and so on. Similarly, Dewey struggled for years before divesting himself of Hegelian terms; only then was he able to free his thought for a less metaphysical way of philosophizing. No simple categorizing of Coleridge as an idealist, or Kantian, or transcendentalist, or pre-Hegelian will do justice to his tremendous efforts to grapple with and expose the assumptions of traditional metaphysics. However convenient a label may be, it only arrests thought about the issues he raised and sought more to explore than to answer. His critical stance towards the history of metaphysics is hindered and often deflected by a burdensome terminology, which prevented the more liberated stance that Nietzsche, Dewey, and later Derrida were able to adopt. Hence he can be easily misread if his specific use of terms is not respected.[24] The meaning of 'self-consciousness' as a methodological principle has greater operative force, however, when applied to his critical procedure, and we will return in chapter 7 to its practical, non-

metaphysical import. As we shall see in the discussion of Dewey's aesthetic and theory of criticism, Coleridge's enquiry likewise leads his
readers to a position not only compatible in the main with pragmatic
and deconstructionist theories and practices, but anticipatory of their
most central contributions. In all three cases, there is an emphasis upon
sound method and theory, rather than on determining meaning in texts.
Each emphasizes the nature of criticism as the analysis of received
opinion and interpretation, and not of some illusory pure text independent of experience. No expectation of arriving at a true or univocal
meaning or meanings of a text occurs at any point. Indeed, all three
approaches emphasize that the aim of criticism is not so much to restate
the text or to judge it, but to sharpen the reader's response and
awareness of the possible textual elements and their multiple interactions and unlimited effects. Coleridge is notable in his criticism for
almost never attending to interpreting poems or passages, that is, stating
their meaning. His practice of criticism, whether discussing Shakespeare, Wordsworth, Milton or others, is to look at the language, to
analyse the literary texture, to see how a text works, not wonder what it
means.[25] Moreover, all three approaches insist upon the active participation of the reader so that meaning adheres in the experience, in that
fusion of reader and text, not in the text or in the reader, separated as
objective versus subjective.

Coleridge's poetry and prose writings use techniques which demonstrate an awareness of the issues that post-structualists and pragmatists
raised regarding reading and interpretation. As will be discussed below,
texts such as 'Kubla Khan', 'The Ancient Mariner', 'Christabel', and
other poems and prose works such as *The Friend* and *Aids to Reflection*
indicate Coleridge's self-consciousness about his role as author, the
problematic nature of reading, the status of the text as self-critical and
self-referential, issues about language as constitutive of experience,
perception as actively imaginative, and experience as textual. In the
chapter below on Coleridge's rejection of dualism and idealism, his
Shelleyan concepts of imagination and of perception as radically metaphorical are discussed. It is argued there that his primary/secondary
imagination distinction conveys a continuity in experience from fundamental creative perceptual acts to the highest achievements of human
culture and the highest moral-emotional acts of love and empathy.
Correlatively, for Coleridge basic acts of reading involve, potentially,
creative responses (or stereotyped ones, if the reader is lazy) which
inform and are informed by meta-reading and critical acts of conscious
interpretation. As with Shelley and the German romantic ironists, perception and language are both vitally metaphorical (though Coleridge

used the word 'symbol' when Shelley used 'metaphor', drawing on the German tradition).

Coleridge's scattered remarks on organicism (which has been poorly understood as structuralist and static, rather than vital and evolving), on the nature of genius and passion, explicit discursive development of the Kierkegaardian notion of indirect communication in *The Friend* (and demonstrated fully in other texts) and its relation to irony, his exhortation to the reader to become a 'fellow labourer' in the appreciation and construction of aesthetic experience, all suggest anticipations of pragmatist and post-structuralist ideas. Questions about the relation of irony to metaphor, of criticism to art, and of the role of theory in practice, not to mention innumerable examples of personae in both the prose and poetry to emphasize multiple perspectives and raise questions about narrative point of view – these issues show Coleridge meditating about many of the themes that deconstruction has sought to explore and clarify.[26] Coleridge's texts challenge traditional genre notions, as he mixed philosophy, autobiography, criticism, and poetry. He strove to weave levels of critical awareness into his poems in order, as Dewey explained, that the artist should portray the audience's various viewpoints, as a central character of artistic works.[27] Coleridge's strategies, whether in prose or in poetry, act to deconstruct the traditionally authoritarian notion of author and text, while relations between spectator and work of art are radically altered by expanding the boundaries of the work of art to include the spectator (whether seen as author or as reader). His discursive statements and his texts lead to a unity of poetry and philososphy, as for example, when he argued that 'a great poet must be implicité, if not explicité, a profound metaphysician'.[28] For Coleridge it was clearly equally true that great philosophers are also, implicité at least, poets.

Related comments on the nature of genius, passion, and the poet are instructive of Coleridge's critical sophistication, as is his reconceptualization of the German concept of organic unity into a nonstructuralist, open-ended, evolutionary organicism which has more in common with radical interpretations of Hegel than with Friedrich Schelling or static conceptions. Coleridge's adaptation of the German idea of organic unity as the character of art expresses the vital, transformational character of living organisms in contrast to the mechanical and artificial. His emphasis was not on the closed structure of an individual organism, but upon its evolving, growing, and self-propelling qualities, not to mention the role of 'sports of nature' and of art in the genesis of new forms of life.[29] The related German romantic concept of irony further articulated the aspect of organicism which captured

Coleridge's imagination, as he realised that 'metaphor' was almost generically figured in organic unity and that irony, closely related to
metaphor, involved a self-criticism and detachment figured in the organic idea of self-propelling energy. The vitality and growth and change
characteristic of organic unity led to analogical distinctions between
living, vital knowledge and mere booklearning. The former involved the
reader as 'fellow-labourer', because the nature of communication is
indirect, Coleridge argued; hence, the need for irony as the tool of
indirectness and of metaphor. One of his favourite metaphors involved
the image of the serpent, whose movement he described in the following
three passages as emblematic both of the reader's activity and of the
faculty of imagination:

(a) Mackintosh intertrudes, not introduces his beauties. Nothing
grows out of his main argument but much is shoved between –
each digression occasions a move backward to find the road again
– like a sick man he recoils after every affection. The Serpent by
which the ancients emblem'd the Inventive faculty appears to me,
in its mode of motion most exactly to emblem a writer of Genius.
He varies his course yet still glides onwards – all lines of motion are
his – all beautiful, and all propulsive – . . . So varied he and of his
tortuous train / Curls many a wanton wreath; yet still he proceeds
& and is proceeding. –

(b) Even the most mobile of creatures, the serpent, makes a rest of
its own body, and drawing up its voluminous train from behind on
this fulcrum, propels itself onward. On the other hand, it is a
proverb in all languages, that (relatively to man at least) what
would stand still must retrograde.

(c) The reader should be carried forward, not merely or chiefly by
the mechanical impulse of curiosity, or by a restless desire to arrive
at the final solution; but by the pleasurable activity of mind excited
by the attractions of the journey itself. Like the motion of a
serpent, which the Egyptians made the emblem of intellectual
power, or like the path of sound through the air, at every step he
pauses and half recedes, and from the retrogressive movement
collects the force which again carries him onward.[30]

No substantive distinction is allowed here by Coleridge in describing the
making of art and the appreciation (or re-making) of it. In the above
three quotations, one might argue, we find a fascinating self-description

and a marvellous emblem of such writers as Derrida and Nietzsche, especially in the second notebook selection which re-evaluates the artistry of digression and 'wantonly curling wreaths', which still progress, in spite of digressing.

Coleridge devised a variety of strategies throughout his poetry and prose for deconstructing the traditionally authoritarian character of author and text, for raising the question of reading to philosophical dignity, and for revealing the saturation of experience by language. While his discursive accounts of criticism, method, art, and philosophy, burdened as they are by a Kantean vocabulary, may not seem as apocalyptic as those of Blake, Shelley, or Derrida, for example, there are nevertheless radical and innovative aspects of his thought which suggest a sophisticated anticipation of much modern thought. Even in such apparently conservative late works as *Aids to Reflection,* Coleridge can be seen to be investigating the language games dominating certain fields of knowledge, by examining the meaning and use of words and the effects of reorienting conceptual relations, rather than presenting us with a rather naive and moribund, dogmatic form of Christianity, as he is too often thought to be doing.[31] An alert reader will find more by the way of aids to thinking than s/he will find already accepted dogmas and unquestionable beliefs, if one takes to heart the first several chapters of aphorisms. These aphorisms exhort the reader to reflection, not to a passive beholding of someone else's thinking.[32] Like Berkeley's treatises and dialogues, Coleridge's prose is often mistaken as dogmatic idealism rather than the exercises in imaginative questioning and the 'projects of thought' that they were designed to be.

While Coleridge can hardly be said to have gone as far in challenging logocentric writing as Derrida – at least in his prose – the details of the hostile critical reception of *The Biographia*, and Ludwig Tieck's defence of it (see below page 70) are a warning not to discount the radical innovations *The Biographia* does represent, along with many sections of *The Friend*. In his poetry, it could be argued, Coleridge succeeded as much as Derrida or Nietzsche in putting logocentrism under erasure by means of imaginative, formal innovations and stylistic achievements. Coleridge's prose and poetry demonstrate carefully designed situations for enticing readers out of their logocentric stance of passivity into an imaginative, Barthesean participation, through their acknowledgment of the destructive role of the repression of desire as a recipe for sterotyped response. Moreover, Coleridge designed means of arousing readers to the imaginative awareness that their own modes of perceiving and reading are a central subject matter of the text, since without such self-knowledge, through these 'mirroring' techniques of parodying reading situations, the reader will fail to gain any new perspective on reading. Coleridge's texts demonstrate that passivity in reading or perception occurs only when these activities are allowed to degenerate from vital acts into stereotyped, lazy on-looker attitudes, into dead forms of dogma or received opinion through time, custom, and familiarity. Or, as Shelley put it, metaphors become dead metaphors, and language, Coleridge explained,degenerates: ' Truths . . . are too often considered as *so* true, that they lose all the life and efficiency of truth, and lie bed-ridden in the dormitory of the soul, side by side with the most despised and exploded errors.'[33]

Coleridge, like Shelley, was demonstrably more interested in speculating about experience as linguistic, about the debunking of eighteenth-century literalist interpretations of language, than he was in establishing some system of transcendental philosophy. While he immensely admired the sheer intellectual force of such systematizers as Kant,[34] he was more drawn to Plato's and Berkeley's ironic *Dialogues* than to discursive, academic philosophizing. His own style is conversational and undogmatic, anticipating James's and Rorty's descriptions of philosophy as, preferably, conversations rather than academic discourses. Nor was Coleridge prejudiced against innovative modes that rejected systematization, modes which the German romantics and, later, Nietzsche, developed. He recognized the hierarchical ordering of genres and forms as conventional and restrictive, never privileging artificial system over the stimulation well-conceived arguments could offer. In this speculative, open-minded mode, Coleridge designed texts which reveal to his readers the problematic nature of poetic language and its role in all kinds of thought, the nature of reading and the illusory notion that the text is independent of the reading of it. Like Samuel Johnson, he was sophisticated about the nature of reading as already interpretation, though he can be said to have gone further than Johnson in encouraging his readers to play with his texts to see what effects they could achieve. For reading, Coleridge argued, was a journey through uncharted territories, and the reader a traveller; while the author might be a helpful guide, she need not dictate what the reader sees or finds or experiences.[35] Nor, however, he cautioned, should the reader ascribe to the author her own experiences as a traveller, by ascribing intentions and purposes and beliefs to the text or its creator.

Many of Coleridge's poems are suggestive of his meditations on the constitutive nature of language regarding human experience, on the central role of metaphor in perception, and meditations on a Shelleyan universe of rhetoric. It is clear from Coleridge's philosophical musings that 'substance' is best understood as relationship and opposition (or differentiality), and this he also saw as the character of metaphor, just as Johnson had.[36] Through his rejection of the thought/thing duality, and through his repeated insistence upon the power of words as constitutive and on words as 'acts' of imaginative creation, he looked upon the notion of a non-linguistic reality as incomprehensible. Words, meaningful in a relational system, are involved in the very discrimination of both things, thoughts, and qualities.[37] Moreover, in his rejection of eighteenth-century language theories (postulating a literal, scientific, base language of truth, with metaphor as a deceptive supplement), Coleridge saw literal language as a dead metaphor, while scientific language conceived of as the language of truth was a misguided puritanism.[38] Coleridge's prose and poetry collapsed the genres and boundaries between philosophy, art, criticism, history, autobiography, and poetry, and he exposed the notion of a pure art or pure literature as a fantasy, embedding his poems with levels of critical interpretations, ironic commentators, and overtly naive personae, to show that literature and poetry are essentially criticism and philosophy, too.[39]

In one of his most sustained deconstructive acts, Coleridge embedded the history of seventeenth- and eighteenth-century literary and language disputes into his poem, 'Kubla Khan', so that this short, fifty-four-line ode becomes a richly-packed repository of the intellectual history of the period.[40] In a gesture of sophisticated detachment, Coleridge ironized the rage for oriental literature and imagery of the eighteenth century, emphasizing exotic lands and travel as literary conventions or metaphors for imaginative activity, reading, and aesthetic experience. His finely crafted contrast between art, the artificial, and nature challenged the orthodoxy of nature as prior to culture, reasserted the distinction between the fancy, the artificial, or the mechanical as opposed to creative acts of imaginative fusion, and stated the distinction between allegory and symbol. The poem's imagery of nature and garden and its further contrasting of genius with talent addressed the highly contentious issue of the nature of genius (as Coleridge had done in the *Shakespearean Criticism*), while Coleridge's abrupt change of narrative point of view in the final epode, to the poet as speaker, borrowed techniques from the *Arabian Nights* which shift attention to the storyteller as part of the story. Like 'Frost at Midnight', a central subject matter of 'Kubla Khan' turns out to be the process of 'figuration' and the making of metaphors, symbols, or tropes generally. Such self-conscious awareness about the nature of language was embedded, moreover, in the larger context of eighteenth-century disputes about theories of language which Coleridge compressed into the poem by means of imagery, symbol, form, and theme. Issues debated by Dryden, Pope, Locke, Burke, Johnson, Spratt, Watts, Baillie, and others are referred to by 'Kubla Khan', as it implicitly or explicitly addresses the distinction between the copy and the imitation, the mechanical and the organic, the nature of the sublime, the relative value of painting and poetry, and the distinction between fancy or allegory and the imagination or metaphor.

The enigmatic transition of 'Kubla Khan' from stanza ii to stanza iii and iv and the problematic nature of the relation of the final stanza to the rest of the poem involves a sophisticated shift in the function of imagery from pictorial to symbolic, and a crucial shift in narrative perspective which transforms the poem into a unified imaginative fusion of great integrity resulting from the extreme self-consciousness of its final paragraph. The 'after-song', incantatory character of stanza iv completes the poem's odic form, with strophe, anti-strophe and epode, while causing the narrative persona to cast a unifying glance back over the previous material of the first three stanzas and add a powerful metapoetical level of meditation about figuration itself. This final 'glance' is the glance of imagination whose purpose is: 'to convert a series into a *Whole*: to make those events, which in real or imagined History move on a straight line, assume to our Understanding a *circular* motion, the snake with its Tail in its Mouth'.[41]

'Kubla Khan' further illustrates Coleridge's rejection of dualisms such as that involving the senses and the reason. These are convenient distinctions only, not divisions of faculties of the human mind. In this poem, Coleridge portrayed imagination as the synthesizing faculty, the faculty which 'incorporates the reason in images of the senses' while the senses are 'imbued with Reason', [42] as they were for Dewey and James.[43]

Equally obvious deconstructive techniques are to be found in 'The Ancient Mariner', and 'Christabel', involving narrative personae flagrantly portrayed as naive and limited, while shifts of narrative create wider or different perspectives which confront the reader with an awareness of Henry Jamesian 'views'. Glosses, prefaces, notes, and prefatorial 'arguments' or prologues create a level of self-commentary and complex narrative strategy which raises questions about truth and interpretation. Stories within stories within stories lead to obfuscation of the distinction between fiction and reality, while the telling of the story becomes a central theme. Narrative authority is undermined and the distinction between fact and fiction is threatened, as in 'Christabel' the narrative persona is blatantly exposed as a superstitious interpreter. The bard Bracy's dream is interpreted in two inconsistent ways, while the heart of the poem – the encounter between Geraldine and Christabel – is completely under-determined: the reader has little notion of 'what really happened'. The characters in these poems become metaphors for typical readers, so that the poems are mirrors of stereotypic reading habits which jolt the reader when she realizes she is looking at herself.

In such poems as 'Frost at Midnight', 'This Lime-Tree Bower My Prison', the 'Eolian Harp' and 'Dejection: an Ode', the metapoetical, ironic devices used in the supernatural poems are more subtly deployed. 'Frost at Midnight' depicts the formation of figures of speech out of literal language and cliché with a breath-taking clarity. The power of language to bring things into being, the extent to which nature is a product of culture, the constructive role of figuration in intelligent experience, and the centrality of self-consciousness in poetry are all realized in this poem to a degree rarely surpassed in poetry. The poem encompasses as well an insightful analysis of the forces in nature, mind, or culture which impede and inhibit imaginative response. 'This Lime-Tree Bower My Prison' takes up the latter theme, but reverses the emphasis, and meditates on the power of imaginative figuration to liberate both poetry and the mind from conventions, stereotypes, and other constraints of time, place, and circumstance. No less than 'Frost at Midnight', however, 'Lime-Tree Bower' demonstrates the linguistic nature of experience and the absurdity of assuming nature to be prior to culture. It is also a Shelleyan testimony to the centrality of imagination in the moral sphere, as Coleridge took up Shelley's principle that love and empathic identification are the imagination in human intercourse. Art, for these poets, if it teaches anything, teaches the role of figuration in the moral sphere: by seeing the other as if s/he were ourselves, we overcome the chasm between self and other. We achieve the other's point of view, and cease to be trapped in the mundane shell of the ego. 'This Lime-Tree Bower' charts the way out of imprisonment in one's own ego, much as Blake's and Shelley's poetry is committed to doing, by means of imaginative acts which rely on metaphor and figuration in general. Nature itself becomes a figure of speech for imagination (as in Blake's poetry), while themes of growth and transformation define both.[44]

Coleridge's prose is saturated with strategies and devices which we have come to associate with deconstruction in spite of their prevalence throughout western literature.[45] Some of the narrative and stylistic practices of his prose are similar to the poetry. For example, he made use of extended metaphoric situations which illustrate the rhetoricity of language and which act as mirrors in which readers are confronted with unconscious prejudices and opinions. Coleridge made extensive use of the ancient rhetorical strategy called hypotyposis – the technique of metadiscursive commentary designed to draw attention to the text as opposed to its supposed theme or subject matter. In the vein of Sterne's *Tristram Shandy*, Coleridge allegedly eliminated from the *Biographia* his crucial chapter on imagination – the core content of the text – while supplementing the missing chapter with a letter from a 'friend' (himself) explaining the omission and describing 'what remains . . . as like the fragments of the winding steps of an old ruined tower'.[46] Earlier, the fictional letter-writer had explained that the Hegelian result of reading Coleridge's suppressed text was to feel as though he 'had been standing on his head'. The innovative genre of the *Biographia*, moreover, with its autobiographical frame, places it squarely in the tradition of 'deconstructive' texts, as Friedrich Schlegel, Tieck, and Solger realized. The *Biographia* has repeatedly been criticized for precisely those characteristics which Schlegel described as constituting the truly modern, romantic 'novel'.[47]

The contemporary reception of Coleridge's *Biographia Literaria* was not unlike the reaction to much of Derrida's work. Indeed, as recently as 1965 one critic described the *Biographia* as not only 'unread and largely unreadable', but totally lacking in any aesthetic unity: an 'immethodical miscellany', full of 'speculative obscurities' and 'dying under the weight of the theory supposed to elucidate his ideas'.[48] This sounds much like a description of complaints about Derrida's work. In his own time, Coleridge was accused of immorality and irreligion, 'corrupting the rising generation'. The *Biographia* showed a 'decrepitude of genius in its author', and, it was said, 'the work is most execrable . . . he has . . . little or no real feeling!'.[49] Almost the best that could be said of Coleridge was that as a poet of established genius, his was a 'wild, erratic genius' with 'wings but no hands'. His works were accused of lacking the very organic unity which he advocated; they were accused of inadequate attribution of sources and plagiarism; they were seen as vitiated by too much interest in that most monstrous absurdity of all, namely German philosophizing; they were hopelessly obscure and incomprehensible: 'a barren ridge of clouds piled on precipices and precipices piled on clouds';[50] the metaphysical bustards were said regrettably (by Coleridge himself!) to have ousted the poetic partridges. The *Biographia* was an unrecognizable genre of prose writing, a complete novelty, and Coleridge an unforgivable egotist, first for daring to write an autobiography, and second, for pretending to write about himself when really he was taking the chance to criticize Southey and Wordsworth.[51]

In Germany, the response was somewhat different, and can be summed up by a remark from Ludwig Tieck to Coleridge: 'Your *Biographia Literaria* utterly enchanted me, instructed me, and amused me; I should think, however, that for the greater number of English readers it is too weighty and profound.'[52] This remark is only a little less apt today than it was in 1825. To Coleridge's admirers in Germany, and to their friends Friedrich Schlegel, Jean Paul, and Novalis, Coleridge's *Biographia Literaria* must have seemed like the fulfilment of Friedrich Schlegel's description in 'Gespräch über Poesie', of that goal of the 'modern artist' namely, the truly modern novel. Friedrich Schlegel's theory of the 'modern novel' as the modern literary art form *par excellence* described no text of the period so exactly as it described the *Biographia*, that autobiographical synthesis of poetry and philosophy, that hybrid genre of creative criticism and art whose unity lies not on the surface but in its focusing intellectual point of view of irony and its detached, self-conscious criticism. Coleridge's playfulness, wit, irony, and Shandyesque rhetorical and narrative strategies were lost sight of in much of the criticism on his prose and poetry, so much so that his innovations were interpreted as flaws and uglinesses. One might characterize the gap between Coleridge and his readers to be an inability to comprehend the wit and play of Coleridge's 'weighty and profound' thought, as though the two were somehow inconsistent, when the most profound thought is usually allied with great wit.

The Friend is another prose text which illustrates Coleridge's deconstructive tactics; indeed, especially in the revised 1818 edition of *The Friend*, Coleridge's use of metadiscursive hypotyposis, reading analogies, framework techniques, irony, extended metaphor, and other narrative strategies is almost overwhelming. He began his several-hundred page *Friend* with an essay called 'The Fable of the Madning Rain', an extremely funny comedy-tragedy mirror of the reading situation and an indirect statement of his self-consciousness as author. Such comic devices have been dismissed by Urizenically minded readers as examples of 'special pleading', instead of the Sterne-like witticisms and Socratic ironies that a more genial attitude reveals. Essays on the communication of truth follow, which demonstrate the need for a Kierkegaardian indirection in language, and the reasons why indirect communication is more effective. Meanwhile, before *The Friend* culminates in its 'Essays on the Principles of Method', it goes through a miscellany ranging from serious topics to hilarious interruptive 'landing places' – both types of essays on every topic imaginable, yet clearly progressing according to the German romantic ironists' concept of unity as a focused intellectual perspective of a mind of genius. *The Friend*, no more miscellaneous than Goethe's *Wilhelm Meister*, that favourite text of Schlegel's, is also no less unified. In these prose texts, subject matter is reconceived as a process and a type of form, while our fundamental notions about the nature of reading, interpretation, description, and perception are re-examined and problematized, or put under erasure. Distinctions between attention and genuine thought, between understanding and reason, and between fancy and imagination operate throughout the texts not as static categorizations of mental faculties but as stimulants to imaginative activity, to thinking for oneself, and to a self-knowledge existentially conceived as construction of the self. Like Plato and Berkley before him, and like the great ironist Kierkegaard after, Coleridge sought to raise his reader into active thinking, and thereby into an existentialist self-creation through imaginative figuration.

Part II

Deconstructing Metaphysics

4

William James and Early Pragmatist Rejections of Metaphysics

The Method of Pragmatism

In an article in 1876, Charles Sanders Peirce remarked: 'Pragmatism shows that almost every proposition of ontological metaphysics is either meaningless or else absurd.'[1] Some decades later, John Dewey elaborated on Peirce's assessment, writing that 'a chief task of those who call themselves philosophers is to help get rid of the useless lumber that blocks our highways of thought, and strive to make straight and open the paths that lead to the future'.[2] Dewey attempted 'to forward the emancipation of philosophy from a too intimate and exclusive attachment to traditional problems', by raising the question of the genuineness of the problems. He further criticized the 'artificiality of much recent philosophizing', and pointed out that the subject-matter of past thought as formulated into received systems is not conducive to genuine reflection based upon immediate response.[3] Somewhat later than Peirce, but earlier than Dewey, William James was equally precise about the relation of pragmatism to traditional philosophy: 'It is astonishing to see how many philosophical disputes collapse into insignificance the moment you subject them to this simple test', that is, the pragmatic method.[4] Earlier, James had said that 'the pragmatic method is primarily a method of settling metaphysical disputes that otherwise might be interminable. Is the world one or many? – fated or free? – material or spiritual? – here are notions either of which may or may not hold good of the world; and disputes over such notions are unending'.[5]

James proceeded to demonstrate that many such disputes are also 'meaningless'. He used the word 'meaningless' in the same way as Peirce did (in the first quotation above), namely, to say that philosophical 'problems' or disputes can be tested for their 'genuineness'; in each disputed alternative answer, the practical consequences (the difference it would practically make to anyone), are traced, and if no practical difference whatever is found, 'then the alternatives mean practically the same thing, and all dispute is idle'.[6] Or as William James put it, 'there can *be* no difference anywhere that doesn't *make* a difference elsewhere'.[7]

James himself returned to Peirce to justify this definition of 'meaning-fulness', and, anticipating Wittgenstein, stated the principle of pragmatism to be that 'our beliefs are really rules for action':[8] to 'develop a thought's meaning, we need only determine what conduct it is fitted to produce: that conduct is for us its sole significance',[9] that is, its sole meaningfulness. This concept of meaningfulness as related to conduct is closely allied to the Jamesian notion of truth, as will be discussed further below. James modestly went on to insist, however, that 'there is absolutely nothing new in the pragmatic method'. He attributed it to numerous philosophers, beginning particularly with that thorough-going pragmatist philosopher, Socrates. He suggested that modern pragmatists were simply generalizing and making a method of the 'fragmentary' practice of many earlier thinkers. James reiterated that pragmatism does not offer dogmas, solutions, or a traditional content organized into a system: it stands for no special results, but is a method only. As James curtly remarked on another occasion, philosophic method is but a method of conducting discussions.[10] Pragmatism is essentially, moreover, the method of science; hence its empirical nature. Since it stands for no particular results, it has no dogmas, and no doctrines save its method: 'No particular results then, so far, but only an attitude or orientation.'[11] Later Dewey, along with James, also emphasized method rather than content, and further emphasized the scientific nature of the pragmatic method, when he summed up James's pragmatism as an epistemological statement of the implications of James's psychology.[12]

More recently, Richard Rorty has reminded us, however, that pragmatists, unlike positivists, never erected science as an idol to fill the place of God as rationalists did reason. Pragmatism views science as one more genre of 'literature', while literature and the arts are modes of enquiry like science.[13] With this scientific spirit of method in mind, James noted that:

> Pragmatism represents a perfectly familiar attitude in philosophy, the empiricist attitude, but it represents it, as it seems to me, both in a more radical and in a less objectionable form than it has ever yet assumed. A pragmatist turns his back resolutely and once for all upon a lot of inveterate habits dear to professional philosophers. He turns away from abstraction and insufficiency, from verbal

solutions, from bad *a priori* reasons, from fixed principles, closed systems, and pretended absolutes and origins. He turns towards concreteness and adequacy, towards facts, towards action, and towards power. That means the empiricist temper regnant, and the rationalist temper sincerely given up. It means the open air and possibilities of nature as against dogma, artificiality, and the pretence of finality in truth.[14]

Such a passage inevitably points up characteristics familiar to readers of Heidegger and Derrida, such as James's rejection of origins, finalities, and fixities. And this attitude James anticipated even more explicitly when he said:

Metaphysics has usually followed a very primitive kind of quest. You know how men have always hankered after unlawful magic, and you know what a great part, in magic, *words* have always played. If you have his name, or the formula of incantation that binds him, you can control the spirit, genie, afrite, or whatever the power may be. . . . So the universe has always appeared to the natural mind as a kind of enigma, of which the key must be sought in the shape of some illuminating or power-bringing word or name. That word names the universe's *principle*, and to possess it is, after a fashion, to possess the universe itself. 'God', 'Matter', 'Reason', 'the Absolute', 'Energy', are so many solving names. You can rest when you have them. You are at the end of your metaphysical quest. But if you follow the pragmatic method, you cannot look on any such word as closing your quest. You must bring out of each word its practical cash-value, set it at work within the stream of your experience. It appears less as a solution, then, than as a program for more work, and more particularly as an indication of the ways in which existing realities may be changed.[15]

Already, in 1890, William James was identifying the 'master-names' Derrida later ironized, and he was attacking 'logocentrism', as Derrida came to call it decades later. The Wittgensteinian concept of 'a programme for more work' which Rorty took over, and which James might be thought to have borrowed from Kierkegaard (his 'project for thought' in *Philosophical Fragments*), is also an aspect of Barthes' and Derrida's unravelling of systems. James concluded this passage by saying: '*Theories thus become instruments, not answers to enigmas, in which we can rest.* We don't lie back upon them, we move forward, and, on occasion, make nature over again by their aid. Pragmatism unstiffens all our theories, limbers them up and sets each one at work. Being nothing essentially new, it harmonizes with many ancient philosophic tendencies.'

Dewey summarized these ideas of James's on philosophy as method by describing James's great contribution to thought as the 'fundamental idea of an open universe in which uncertainty, choice, hypotheses, novelties and possibilities are *naturalized*' (my underlining).[16] That is, such things are not supernatural, but part of experience, as natural as the so-called 'stuff of experience' itself. Dewey, James, and Peirce, then, and most recently Richard Rorty, all emphasized, like Derrida, method and process over content, results, or solutions, though it can be said that method is the content for a genuinely critical philosophy. So-called solutions are viewed less as resting places than as programmes for more research, work, or play into the ways that existing realities may be reinterpreted and changed. To repeat, 'theories thus become instruments, not answers to enigmas in which we can rest'.[17]

So far then, pragmatism has two primary goals: first, as an anti-intellectualist tendency, it seeks to expose the absolutes, closed systems, fixities, and false origins of the rationalist attitude (which infects idealism and empiricism as well in varying degrees). Second, it seeks to transform any remaining content – for example, theories or results – into methods and instruments for further reflection and interpretation, for more work or play, much as Wittgenstein was later to change linguistic content into games, rules, and forms of human activity. There are several aspects to these two projects; they involve, first, a redefinition of truth, reality, and experience, an emphasis upon the social and conventional nature of our instruments and results, and a reminder that there is no final truth, but only 'interpretations and reinterpretations' of ways of describing experience, as Samuel Johnson would say. To take the latter point first, pragmatists reminded us that many scientists have gradually come to see that their laws are only approximations: no theory is a transcript of reality, though any one of them may from some point of view become useful. Their great use, according to James, is to summarize old facts and to lead to new facts. Theories are 'only a man-made language, a conceptual shorthand, in which we write our reports of nature; and languages, as is well known, tolerate much choice of expression and many dialects'.[18]

Rorty remarked that enquiry consists in large part in describing the world (and he is careful about his definition of 'world'), not in 'getting our representations into shape'.[19] Pragmatists all agreed that no interpretation or description is final, for new experiences may necessitate reinterpretation. Thus 'true' results are not to be conceived of as final truths, absolutes, fixities, unchanging ultimates. True results are simply the best descriptions and interpretation we have to date for our present purposes. As James put it, even the so-called theoretic truths upon which our most cherished, basic truths are based, are subject to revision in the light of new experiences and further evidence. Likewise, Dewey argued that 'it is not easy to break away from current and established classifications of the world . . . objects of knowledge are not given to us defined, classified, and labeled. . . . We bring to the simplest observation a complex apparatus of habits, of accepted meanings and techniques. Otherwise, observation is the blankest of stares, and the natural object is a tale told by an idiot, full only of sound and fury'.[20] And Rorty confirmed, likewise, that 'we never encounter reality except under a chosen description'.[21] Peirce had pointed out long before, Rorty explained, that the regress of interpretation can never be stopped once and for all. There may always be a new set of descriptions to throw everything into question once again.'[22] Dewey took Peirce and James's terms and described truth as 'interpretations of other people's interpretations', developing James's emphasis upon results as tools for further improvement of those statements that we presently accept or agree upon as true.

Rorty relatedly has suggested that truth and knowledge are better described as tools for coping with the world around us, not means of providing a foundation for reality or an ultimate definition of reality. For James, 'all our theories are instrumental, are mental modes of *adaptation* to reality, rather than revelations of gnostic answers to some divinely instituted world-enquirer'.[23] The pragmatist wants to show that purely objective truth, truth utterly independent of human experience, is nowhere to be found. There is no truth, to put it another way, without some 'interest'.[24] Because these points are often misunderstood, the pragmatist is accused of destroying all objective standards. Yet experience is surely a more objective standard than the rationalist-intellectualist hypotheses that claim absolute objectivity without verifying it by experience. Experience, said the pragmatist, has a way of 'boiling over' its own limits.[25] That is, it forces us to reconsider and correct what we once took for truths so that 'truth, really, is *made* just as health, wealth, and strength are *made*, in the course of experience'.[26] We must operate, then, with the regulative notion, as James put it, that potentially better truths will be established in the future on the basis of new and unforeseeable experiences, which lead us often to give up not only particular truths, but whole theories of organization if necessary:

> The absolutely true, meaning what no further experience will ever alter is that ideal vanishing-point towards which we imagine that all our temporary truths will some day converge. . . . Ptolemaic

astronomy, Euclidean space, Aristotelean logic, scholastic metaphysics, were expedient for centuries, but human experience has
boiled over those limits, and we now call these things only relatively true, or true within those borders of experience. 'Absolutely'
they are false; for we know that those limits were casual, and might
have been transcended by past theorists just as they are by present
thinkers.[27]

The True as *Bricolage*

To continue, we can look at that statement of James's which has been
most frequently quoted and most thoroughly misunderstood:

> *'The true', to put it very briefly, is only the expedient in the way of our
> thinking, just as 'the right' is only the expedient in the way of our behaving.*
> Expedient in almost any fashion; and expendient in the long run
> and on the whole *of course*; for what meets expediently all the
> experience in sight won't necessarily meet all farther experiences
> equally satisfactorily. Experience, as we know, has ways of boiling
> over, and making us correct our present formulas.[28]

Expedient 'in the long run and on the whole' is what all his critics fail to
attend to adequately, and is closely connected to his claim that truth so
conceived is good (see further below).

We need not, then, as the rationalist thinks, treat the name of a
concrete phenomenal reality as an independent prior entity, placing
such an entity behind that reality as its explanation. The pragmatic
account of truth is an account of 'truths in the plural, of processes of
leading, realized *in rebus*, and having only this quality in common, that
they *pay*'.[29] Therefore, no truth is so final and ultimate as not to be
challenged and altered by new experience. Moreover, James defined
truth as that which acts as a 'go-between', that which relates novel
experiences to our stock of old experience. Or, truth is a collective name
for verification processes.[30] An idea makes itself true by how well it works
to assimilate the new experience to the older – sometimes by mere
addition, sometimes by demanding rearrangements of the old; truth
dips back into experience to make connection with past concretes and
knowns.[31] Amongst rival theories or ideas, that idea is said to be the true,
or truest, which works best in this assimilation process. The notion that
there is some objective truth, some absolute correspondence of our
thoughts with an absolute reality, such that truth isn't a tool, isn't some-

thing practical, instrumental, and human, but august, remote, and non-utilitarian, is rejected outright. The pragmatist does not deny truth; he rejects this absolutist, subjective definition of truth which he claims has no ground in experience. For, people follow truth and call something true which 'works' in concrete life to solve problems and achieve needs, goals, and interests. This instrumentality is closely akin to Derrida's concept of 'bricolage', patch-work, do-it-yourself-work (or play), as will be discussed in a later chapter.

Truth is said, moreover, to be a 'species of good and not . . . a category distinct from good'.[32] For James, as for Socrates, we cannot keep what is better for us to believe and what is true for us to believe apart. James explained: 'the true is the name of whatever proves itself to be good in the way of belief and good, too, for definite, assignable reasons'.[33] Anticipating objections, James added the caveat that 'what is better for us to believe is true *unless the belief incidentally clashes with some other vital belief*'.[34] In confirmation of this claim, Plato reminded us that much of Socrates' life was spent in showing his fellow citizens that most of their beliefs clashed with each other. He then helped them to sort out the more true, because more useful and better for actual life, from the less true. James, like Socrates, concluded that, of course, the greatest enemy of any one of our truths may be the rest of our truths. Philosophy is the method of testing those conflicting truths, testing them against actual experiences and actual events. Dewey somewhat clarified this definition of the true by arguing for what he called 'warranted assertability', a concept designed to counteract stubborn misinterpretations of James's meaning.[35]

The True as a Copy of Reality?

Rorty emphasized another aspect of this bricoleur or 'instrumental' view of truth, in insisting that true sentences are not true because they correspond to reality, but because of social and cultural consensus. Truth for Rorty is not the name of a property shared by true statements.[36] It does not, he meant, have some mysterious essence needing investigation. The notion of truth as the simple duplication or copying by the mind of a ready-made reality, a 'given', is, says the pragmatist, a dream. There is no test for judging amongst the different rival claimants to such truth, as Samuel Johnson had earlier noted regarding rival literary interpretations which aspire to absolutism (see chapter 3). One of our most pressing needs is to get rid of this (supposedly) commonsense view of truth. We need to arrive at a view of truth more consistent with experience than the view that the true idea must copy reality or must agree with reality, with reality defined as ultimate, absolute, fixed, and remote from human experience. For James, truth is no copy of reality:

> The vulgar notion of correspondence is that the thoughts must *copy* the reality – cognito fit per *assimiliationem* cogniti et cognoscentis; and philosophy, without having ever fairly sat down to the question, seems to have instinctively accepted this idea: propositions are held true if they copy the eternal thought; terms are held true if they copy extra-mental realities. Implicitly, I think that the copy-theory has animated most of the criticisms that have been made on humanism. A priori, however, it is not self-evident that the sole business of our mind with realities should be to copy them. Let my reader suppose himself to constitute for a time all the reality there is in the universe, and then to receive the announcement that another being is to be created who shall know him truly. How will he represent the knowing in advance? What will he hope it to be? I doubt extremely whether it could ever occur to him to fancy it as a mere copying. Of what use to him would an imperfect second edition of himself in the new comer's interior be? It would seem pure waste of a propitious opportunity. The demand would more probably be for something absolutely new. The reader would conceive the knowing humanistically, 'the new comer', he would say, '*must take account of my presence by reacting on it in such a way that good would accrue to us both.* If copying be requisite to that end, let there be copying; otherwise not'. The essence in any case would not be the copying, but the enrichment of the previous world. . . . Why may not thought's mission be to increase and elevate, rather than simply to imitate and reduplicate, existence? The notion of a world complete in itself, to which thought comes as a passive mirror, adding nothing to fact . . . is irrational. Rather is thought itself a most momentous part of fact.[37]

For pragmatists, clearly, the function of thought is not to copy or image reality; it is rather to form ideas and guides for action (as it was for Nietzsche), so that we may satisfy our human needs and interests. Rorty took this idea up when writing that enquiry, whether in art or science, is not an effort to embody the True, the Good, or the Beautiful. It is rather an effort to solve problems, to modify our beliefs so that we are better able to shape a satisfying world and life for ourselves.[38]

We can apply these definitions of meaningfulness and truth to particular cases of truth, instead of just to truth in general, and conclude, with James, that 'the ultimate test for us of what a truth means is indeed the conduct it dictates or inspires. . . . The effective meaning of any philosophic proposition can always be brought down to some particular consequence in our future practical experience whether active or passive'.[39] Or as Peirce put it, 'the rational purport of a word or other expression, lies exclusively in its conceivable bearing upon the conduct of life'.[40] Meaningfulness only arises for Peirce and James, as for Nietzsche, in relation to purposes and conduct. Or, worded another way, the use of thinking is to help us change the world. Pragmatism rejected the rationalist notion that truth involves a relation or a world that is static and inert, final and unchanging. James and Dewey constantly emphasized that truth is not 'a stagnant property inherent in [an idea]' but something that actively happens to it. 'Man engenders truth upon reality', said James.[41] Our minds are not here simply to copy a reality that is already complete. Moreover, James insisted that in our cognitive as well as our active life we are creative. We add, both to the subjective and to the predicate part of reality.[42] Ideas become true by virtue of events that validate and verify them, that is, that lead to the possibility of assimilating new experiences into our fabric or field of present experience, whether by addition or transformation.

Such is James' formulation of Dewey's later idea that truth is 'warranted assertability' This is also the method of the natural sciences; the latter tend to identify the truth of particular cases with verification involving observation of particular facts. Thus, in seeking to define truth in this way, the pragmatist was applying his own pragmatic method to the effort to arrive at a definition of truth itself. The pragmatic method involves the view that, in philosophic conceptions, 'the affirmation of certain beliefs could be justified by means of the nature of their consequences, or by the difference which these beliefs make in existence'.[43] James then showed that, analogously, the meaning of truth in general is also determined by its consequences: 'True ideas are those that we can assimilate, validate, corroborate, and verify. False ideas are those that we cannot. That is the practical difference [consequence] it makes to us to have true ideas; that, therefore, is the meaning of truth, for it is all that truth is known as.'[44] Yet, since new experiences and observations may falsify previous ones, every true statement is, for James as for Derrida, ultimately hypothetical and provisional: 'But logical truth is an ideal which cannot be realized, unless all the facts and observations were "bagged".'[45] Thus, we have moved first from a definition of meaningfulness as the practical bearing or consequences in life of a concept, to the definition of truth as 'warranted assertability'[46], since this is the practical consequence of maintaining that some proposition is true, namely, whether experience verifies or warrants it.

Finally, having accepted Peirce's definition of meaningfulness as practical consequences and having anticipated Dewey's idea of truth as verifiability or warranted assertability, James proceeded, as Dewey did later, to apply these definitions to traditional philosophical problems in order to test their meaningfulness and the truth of their assertions. To come now full circle, James, along with Dewey and Peirce, concluded that most traditional problems had no authentic meaning and were purely trivial and verbal, since whatever solution to them was offered, no practical consequences ensued.[47] Other philosophical problems were authentic, and James demonstrated why, that is, what the practical consequences were in our lives for believing one solution or its rival.

Reality as *Bricolage*

The pragmatist definition of truth and the consequent rejection of many traditional problems of philosophy cannot be appreciated fully in relation to modern thought without looking at the pragmatist definitions of 'reality' and 'experience'. 'Reality' is a term that has been used in a myriad of different ways. For the pragmatist, it is a collective term for everything that happens, while truth and knowledge involve how all those things that happen 'hang together'. Things hang together in different ways depending upon different aims and purposes. 'Truth' is a name for activities that Derrida might be said to call bricolage; truth is a collective name for verification-phrases, just as health, wealth and strength, and so on, are names for other processes connected with life and also pursued because it 'pays' to pursue them. Just as the notion of the truth as the ultimate answer to some ultimate enigma is rejected, so the notion of 'a reality' as something ultimate, one, fixed, and eternal is rejected: There is no *general* stuff of which experience at large is made.

Just as our truths are man-made products arising from experience, aims, purposes, and needs – as does our language itself, the 'tool' of truth – so is reality best understood as 'in the making'. Truth and reality are the abstract names for the results of experience, and are subject to change in the light of future experiences. Quoting Ferdinand Schiller, James reminded us that the world is essentially:

> What we *make* of it. It is fruitless to define it by what it originally was or by what it is apart from us (ἡ ὕλη ἄγνωστος καθ' αὑτήν); it is

what is made of it. Hence . . . the world is plastic. We can learn the limits of the plasticity only by trying, and we ought to start as if it were wholly plastic, acting methodically on that assumption and stopping only when we are decisively rebuked.[48]

James balanced this idealist position by insisting that along with the plasticity of the world is the 'presence of resisting factors in every actual experience of truth-making'. He concluded, then, against idealism, that 'reality' is that with which truths concern themselves, and he called the *first* part of reality the flux of our sensations. Sensations, he argued, are pressed upon us; we do not know where they come from, and concerning their nature, order, and quantity, we have virtually no control. Sensations, explained James, cannot be said to be either true nor false; they simply are. What we say about them, and the names we give them, our theories of their origin and being and their interrelations, those things may be true or false, but not the sensations.

James further argued that the *second* part of reality is also something that our beliefs must take into account, namely, the relations occurring between our sensations or between their 'copies' in our minds. This second part of reality falls into two sub-parts. Firstly, we see relations that can be said to be mutable and accidental, such as those of time and space. Secondly, there are more fixed and essential relations because these relations are grounded in the inner natures of their *terms*. He gave as examples such relations as likeness and unlikeness. Both sorts of relation are, James insisted, matters of immediate perception, that is, both are 'facts'. Yet the latter kind of fact is the one which forms the more important aspect of reality for our theories of knowledge. Such relations are said to be relatively 'eternal', and they are perceived whenever their sensible terms are compared. It is of them that our thinking, both mathematical and logical thought, must constantly take account.

The *third* part of reality, James argued, which is additional to the other perceptions described above, while mainly based upon them, is the previous truths of which every new enquiry must take account. The third part of 'reality', is, James wrote, much less obdurately resisting, and often ends by giving way. James concluded that however fixed such elements of 'reality' are, one has nevertheless some freedom in dealing with them. We see for example that our sensations do happen, and are undoubtedly beyond our control. Yet James cautioned us that which sensations we attend to and select for emphasis in our conclusions depends on our own interests. Depending on where we lay the emphasis, quite different formulations of truth will result. Put another way, one can interpret or read the same facts differently: "Waterloo", with the same fixed details, spells a "victory" for an Englishman; for a Frenchman it spells a "defeat". So, for an optimist philosopher the universe spells victory, for a pessimist, defeat.'

For James, then, what we say about reality is dependent upon the point of view or context into which we throw it: 'The *that* of it is its own; but the *what* depends on the which; and the *which* depends on us. Both the sensational and the relational parts of reality are dumb: they say absolutely nothing about themselves. We it is who have to speak for them.[49] James cautioned his reader that he was not denying that sensations are pressed upon one. What he was arguing, rather, like Nietzsche, is that their meaningfulness is determined by human interests, ideals, needs, and purposes:

> When we talk of reality independent of human thinking, then, it seems a thing very hard to find. It reduces to the notion of what is just entering into experience, and yet to be named, or else to some imagined aboriginal presence in experience, before any belief about the presence had arisen, before any human conception had been applied. It is what is absolutely dumb and evanescent, the merely ideal limit of our minds. We may glimpse it, but we never grasp it; what we grasp is always some substitute for it which previous human thinking has peptonized and cooked.[50]

There may be a 'sensible flux', then, if we choose to talk that way (but what does it mean?), but what is true of such flux is a matter of our interests and needs. We may be said to 'encounter' a sensible element, but we do not 'possess' it. Nor do we (according to the pragmatist) structure it, as the idealist claims, according to absolute categories pre-existing before the origin of nature. Rather, relations and organizing principles gradually evolve in the course of human experience and give order to experience. Moreover, what we perceive as things, and the relations we 'find' between them, are selected by virtue of our own interests and aims. Had we other aims or needs, the reality we presently take for granted would be made up by us of other things; things would have been divided up differently and related differently. Reality does not start, then, ready-made and complete, such that the human mind looks on, seeking to copy it into true representations or descriptions. Reality, like truth, according to the pragmatist, is in an apocalyptic state, a state of being made:[51] interpretations and descriptions of it actually add to it in substantial and important ways. James explained, in distinguishing rationalism from pragmatism: 'for rationalism, reality is ready-made and complete from all eternity, while for pragmatism it is still in the making, and awaits part of its completion from the future. On the one side the universe is absolutely secure, on the other it is still pursuing its adventures'.[52]

Reality Evolves

Reality and truth are mutable, just as experience is. The rationalist, abstracting an idea (truth, reality) from the concretes of experience, then opposes and negates with it the very experience the idea was abstracted from. For the pragmatist, reality is a collective term for things that resist human endeavour, yet are also responsive to it. According to James the universe is growing and changing in response to human endeavour. 'Reality' is not necessarily a term to denote that which supports experiences, lies behind it, unifies it, or is the eternal and unalterable behind the changing. 'Reality' is simply the summarizing name for the whole spread-out and strung-along mass of phenomena.[53] There is no need to imagine that there *must* be a different entity that is prior to and unifying, holding together, this mass, this *bricolage*, in some concrete sense. There may be, but until we have some reason to believe this, the pragmatist can understand it only in a religious, not a philosophic sense. Yet even here, James explained, we are forced back on the pragmatic notion that truth is a matter of convention, a matter of 'workableness' for certain purposes. Thus, the idea of a world beyond our finite experience, an absolute, cannot be rejected wholesale. If such an idea, which works for many people, can be made to combine with all our other working truths, then it may be said to be true, in the pragmatist's sense of 'true' (which for her is the only sense that 'makes sense').[54]

What the pragmatist in part objects to is the rationalist tendency to oppose that immutable reality to the various realities that human experiences afford us. Rationalists ascribe to it certain qualities and structures, and say that it is *more* real, more perfect, than reality with a small 'r', 'reality' understood as a collective term for everything that experience (as *bricolage*) affords us. This privileging of reality we can reject as based on no experience, as pure prejudice. Some superhuman reality may exist, if such a concept is even intelligible; some 'absolute' may lie 'behind' experience but it is in no way more real than our experienced realities, James argued: 'But whether the other, the Universal *That*, has itself any definite inner structure, or whether, if it have any, the structure resembles any of our predicated "*whats*", – this is a question that pragmatism does not presume to answer.'[55] 'Reality' is just as well understood as an accumulation of tools for coping with the pressure of experience as it continually forces upon us novel events that must be assimilated with previous experience. Some of these 'tools' are, for example, categorizings of experience into thought, things, objects and subjects, time, space and so on.

The pragmatist does not, then, deny that reality is independent of thought, any more than Bishop Berkeley did. He does deny, however, that our experience of independence, of something in every experience that escapes our arbitrary control, is outside of experience itself:

> To say that our thought does not 'make' this reality means pragmatically that if our own particular thought were annihilated the reality would still be there in some shape, tho possibly it might be a shape that would lack something that our thought supplies. That reality is 'independent' means that there is something in every experience that escapes our arbitrary control. If it be a sensible experience it coerces our attention; if a sequence, we cannot invert it; if we compare two terms we can come to only one result. There is a push, an urgency, within our very experience, against which we are on the whole powerless, and which drives us in a direction that is the destiny of our belief. That this drift of experience itself is in the last result due to something independent of all possible experience may or may not be true. There may or may not be an extra-experiential 'ding an sich' that keeps the ball rolling, or an 'absolute' that lies eternally behind all the successive determinations which human thought has made. But within our experience *itself* at any rate, some determinations show themselves as being independent of others.[56]

The pragmatist cannot, then, be said idealistically to reject objectivity and independence in truth or reality.[57] Nature itself and subjective constructions are radically opposed.[58] Pragmatism appeals to the pressure of experience on all of us, to that which is verified in the long run. Yet, no point of view, no truth, can ever be the last word, in part because experience is a process of bringing new happenings and new perspectives to bear upon us. Experiences must validate each other, but this fact in no way pushes us to the view that experience *in general* must have an external, absolute support if objectivity is to be achieved. The actual meaning of objectivity, based on experience, is precisely that we must use experiences to validate and corroborate other experiences. There is no subjectivity in this, other than that a human element enters into all our experience, but not merely a personal, individual one.

The Meaning of 'Experience'

In conjunction with the word 'reality', then, we must examine the meaning of the word 'experience'. Like Peirce and Dewey after him, however (in relation to the meaning of truth, and, subsidiarily, of reality), James found it necessary to examine the way in which we understand 'experience' as a concept and then to examine our notions about what we mean by 'experience', in order to redefine it more intelligibly and more consistently with our experience. Dewey based his own repeated analyses of the concept of 'experience' on James's distinction between experience and knowing – the latter being only *one* type of experience – and on the relation of the knower to the known. To begin with, experience for the pragmatist is self-supporting:

> The generalized conclusion is that therefore the parts of experience hold together from next to next by relations that are themselves parts of experience. The directly apprehended universe needs, in short, no extraneous trans-empirical connective support, but possesses in its own right a concatenated or continuous structure. The great obstacle to radical empiricism in the contemporary mind is the rooted rationalist belief that experience as immediately given is all disjunction and no conjunction, and that to make one world out of this separateness, a higher unifying agency must be there. In the prevalent idealism this agency is represented as the absolute all-witness which 'relates' things together by throwing 'categories' over them like a net. The most peculiar and unique, perhaps of all these categories is supposed to be the truth-relation, which connects parts of reality in pairs, making of one of them a knower, and of the other a thing known, yet which is itself contentless experientially, neither describable, explicable, nor reduceable to lower terms, and denotable only by uttering the name 'truth'. The pragmatist view, on the contrary, of the truth-relation is that it has a definite content, and that everything in it is experienceable. Its whole nature can be told in positive terms. The 'workableness' which ideas must have, in order to be true, means particular workings, physical or intellectual, actual or possible, which they may set up from next to next inside of concrete experience. Were this pragmatic contention admitted, one great point in the victory of radical empiricism would also be scored, for the relation between an object and the idea that truly knows it, is held by rationalists to be nothing of this describable sort, but to stand outside of all possible temporal experience; and on the relation, so

interpreted, rationalism is wonted to make its last most obdurate rally.[59]

James then pointed out repeatedly what, as we shall see, Dewey also dealt with in detail, namely, that experience as immediately given is not atomistic, disjunctive, and without relations. On the contrary, experience itself is full of relations, connections, and organization: 'Our experience is all shot through with regularities.'[60] One of these relations is the truth relation: this truth relation has no content that is not experienceable; consequently truth does not stand outside of possible temporal experience.

To sum, a central principle of James's radical empiricism and his pragmatist theory of truth was the denial that sensations and ideas are discrete entities existing as atomic particles without inherent experiential relations or connections. He used the metaphor of the 'stream of consciousness' in order more adequately to describe the nature of sense experience as a continuous flow. Continuity, not discrete atoms or particles, is the fundamental character of sensation as experienced. Relations and connections, James insisted, were part of immediate experience, that is, an immediate part of the field of consciousness. Ideas, moreover, are not separate subjective entities that come and go through a consciousness conceived of as a receptacle for these unchanging, simple, Lockean entities. For James, the basic mental furniture of our minds – sensations, images, ideas – was not discrete parts, then, but a stream, a continuously connected flow. James thereby rejected the accounts of Locke and Hume regarding both the contents of consciousness and the nature of consciousness itself. Consciousness, for James, is a *function*, not an entity, as it was for the eighteenth- and nineteenth-century empiricists and idealists alike (this functional notion will be discussed in more detail below). James further rejected their account of complex ideas as being formed by means of mere associations. Complex ideas are formed, he insisted (along with Coleridge), by genuinely creative acts, as new experience forces a novel re-evaluation of previous experience. General ideas are not mere mechanical summaries or abstractions from concrete particulars. General ideas are 'instruments of thought' to be used for specific purposes, to use Coleridgean terminology. The atomism of Locke and Hume is, James believed, derived neither from observation nor from experiment. Atomism is a prejudice arrived at *via* a careless conception of experience imposed from without. It leads inevitably to the sceptical notion that all experienced objects – as opposed to mental constructs, connections, and relations – are mere 'appearances', and not 'realities'. Atomism irrevocably opposes thought (as reality) to experience (as mere appearance).

James, Dewey, and Peirce all saw that the atomistic fallacy of Locke and Hume had equally infected rationalism and idealism, for both accepted the atomism of the sensationalist doctrine. Each then felt the necessity of imposing or postulating a transempirical reason to organize, connect and relate the supposedly discrete and simple parts of sense and experience. For James, as for Dewey, however, this postulate led to absurdity and was unnecessary, since, as both insisted, experience itself is replete with connections; they are not foreign or superadded to it. In a sentence that gets at the heart of Berkeley's much misunderstood philosophy, James noted that relations are as much a fabric of experience as substance or so-called 'content' is. For James, there are no gaps between the felt, sensed 'substantive' states of consciousness that are not filled themselves by equally felt, sensed relations and connections that provide continuity and flow. Dewey indeed remarked: 'Long ago I learned from William James that there are immediate experiences of the connections linguistically expressed by conjunctives and prepositions.'[61] James, and later Dewey, spoke of the 'felt' nature of these relations and connections, these transitive elements that, along with 'substantive' ones (also made up of relations and connections) are woven into the web of experience like warp and woof. This view is in stark opposition to the traditional view of immediate experience as atomically substantive, or a 'presentation', a view that denies that felt, experienced relations occur at a primary level. James's position reveals the Coleridgean necessity to balance thought with feeling and to allow the felt side of experience its reality.

James openly admitted that this assertion of the felt nature of connections cannot be easily verified by introspection, because of the overwhelming number and variety of impressions. With Dewey, he insisted that we can nevertheless corroborate the felt nature of transitions, but only as given in our own experience. These feelings of the relations which exist between the objects or substances of our experience are as much qualities of experience as any other feeling or sensation, whether of colour, smell, touch, or whatever. In a sense, the feelings of relations are not even another order of quality, for all other qualities are themselves in a sense only relations, and as such are no more substantive than the qualities of conjunction, or disjunction, or sameness, or difference. For James, as for Berkeley before him, things are 'but special groups of sensible qualities'.[62]

For James then, experience of continuity is, relatively speaking, primary, and it is felt; it is not merely introduced as any kind of necessary or logical, mental connector, or product of thought. Thus, for James the unifying source of experience occurs as found within the stream or flow of experience itself, a fact which Coleridge expressed in his insistence on basic perception as itself highly imaginative and metaphorical (see below chapter 7). Continuity is not a supernatural or transempirical concept imposed from without, as intellectualist philosophers would have it, whereby experience and the world are unified by merely intellectual import. For James, as for Coleridge and Shelley, there is as much substance, vitality, and reality in the transitions and relations of immediate experience as in the 'things' connected and related, since these latter things are themselves only relations 'thingified' or concretized, as Berkeley and Coleridge would say – or process made into products according to human interest and selection. James clearly, then, determinedly rejected the atomistic or sensationalist psychology, whether in the English empiricist or rationalist – idealist version. He insisted that the introduction of transempirical constructs (such as reason) – in order to bridge the alleged divisions created in experience by denying the relations inherent in it – is an importation producing innumerable pseudo-problems of philosophy, which are trivial because based on a dualistic assumption having no ground in experience. Put another way, experience of duality occurs only upon reflection, and not in experience *per se.*

Consciousness is not an Entity

Clearly, a central issue for James's radical empiricism was to offer a more viable and coherent, non-dualistic account of the relation of subject-object, thought-thing, mind-matter, world-of-consciousness and world-of-objects than the numerous dualisms (whether empiricism, rationalism, or idealism) which pragmatists rejected, as not based on any experiential evidence. Idealism in any form, however disguised, was no solution for James, Peirce, or Dewey, as it was not for Coleridge or Shelley. Each of them spoke repeatedly of the uselessness of attributing too great a productive power to mind or thought in the face of the experienced obduracy and reality of the natural world. For the pragmatist, the fact of consciousness *assumes* the existence of a world of extramental reality; the stubborn irreducibility of facts was never questioned by pragmatists. The question, rather, is how the self penetrates and is penetrated by the world.[63]

James sought to avoid reducing experience either to the Cartesian ego (and the Kantian Reason) or to material substance, since all were counter-empirical conclusions. He did this by emphasizing, as Dewey also clearly elaborated later, the functional nature of experience and intelligibility. That is, intelligible experience is a function of the interplay between the world and the self, those two being figures of speech, as the romantics and Derrida (as well as Nietzsche) reminded us. Put another way, subject and object, thought and thing, mind and matter are but functional distinctions, and not absolute divisions in experience.[64] In *Essays in Radical Empiricism*, James graphically described his non-dualistic solution to the self–world relation, when in answer to the question 'Does consciousness exist?' James replied heuristically, and in true Derridean, paradoxical fashion, 'No!' (as Derrida denied later that perception exists).[65] James went on to explain: 'To deny plumply that consciousness exists seems so absurd on the face of it – for undeniably thoughts do exist – that I fear some readers will follow me no further. Let me then immediately explain that I mean only to deny that the word stands for any entity, but to insist most emphatically that it does stand for a function.'[66] Coleridge would have said that the word stands for an 'act'. Much later James further insisted upon the practical nature of the subject–object distinction in a very Coleridgean way: 'The attributes subject and object, represented and representative, thing and thought mean, then, a practical distinction which is of a functional order only, and not at all ontological as understood by classical dualism.'[67]

Consciousness is not, then, for James or Coleridge, as it is for dualists and idealists, an 'aboriginal stuff or quality of being'. It is not to be conceived as the nature of an ultimate reality; it is not a metaphysical entity. It is to be understood as an activity that arises in natural circumstances in the natural interaction of a sentient being with its environment. The interaction and distinction between subject and object occurs, then, within the whole field of experience, not, as traditionalists had it, with the object within and the subject without. Later, John Dewey gave a trenchant analysis of this unconscious dualistic assumption of consciousness as without (outside of) experience and objects as within, and insisted that, once assumed, there is no way of overcoming such a dualism (see below, chapter 5). The assumption itself is the error: it is a prejudice[68] that arises after reflection upon experience, a mistaking of distinctions for divisions (to use Coleridgean terms) and functions for entities. The subject – object distinction has no basis in experience except as a relative, functional distinction of aspects within the whole of experience, not one aspect within and one without. James and Dewey reexamined the concept 'experience' and, by removing the unconscious subjective connotation of previous philosophies, they established 'experience' as a neutral term for the field or context within which subjects *and* objects, consciousness *and* world, mind *and* matter, represented *and* representing, both occur as aspects or functions of a total experience.

What is Experience?

Yet what is this experience – this field or context of functional distinctions and human and material activities? James insisted that to ask what the nature of experience itself is, is a misleading question. For it assumes already that some pure, general, single nature of experience exists. For James, experience had no specific general nature. It is only virtual; it does not become any specific thing, he said (anticipating Dewey, Heidegger, and Derrida) until it occurs in *discourse*, until it is identified – and then categorized – by a mind. Experience, like consciousness, is no substance, no entity, no 'aboriginal stuff' or 'quality of being', nor is it a metaphysical reality. It is a heuristic device only, a 'metaphor', as Nietzsche would say, and not an *a priori* description or word for absolute reality or being: 'The question of Being is the darkest in all philosophy. All of us are beggars here'.[69]

'Experience' is not used by James or Dewey as a word denoting the substrate or foundation for subjects and objects. Nor is it a *tertium aliquid* uniting them both. For it is not a general stuff with two aspects, or a single unity – a one, out of which the many spring. It is rather a word, a metaphor, a figure of speech, like 'self' and 'world', used heuristically to name the field or context of activity of the functionally (not ontologically) distinguished elements of subject and object, etc. These categories of subject and object, thought/thing, and so on, are relational to each other. Experience for the pragmatist is not to be conceived of as the ontological totality within which this activity or dynamism of subject and object occurs. It is rather the acts, the activity itself, in constant flux, change, growth and yet also continuity. For James, as for Coleridge, experience is characterized by novelty and creativity: it is full of alternatives and possibilities. Reality is not fixed, it is still 'becoming'. Reality is not a unity or single totality; it is a plurality with new elements emerging and coming into being. The world, reality, or experience is a process in development, with many possible directions; it is not a mind or a matter with an already created or determined structure unrolling its true nature into existence through time.[70] It is not a primeval stuff developing itself according to its inner nature or true, already-fixed-from-eternity-structure. The world, reality, and experience are coming into being; they are relatively teleological, yet with no final end or totality involved. Experience is many, pluralistic, and is coming into being partly through human beings, and partly through other kinds of objects and processes. It is processive and pluralistic, not substantive and single in nature. 'Experience has no essence', no substrate. Nor is it the substrate of anything else. It is just the flux of life in all its variety and incompleteness, in its chancy and creatively incremental nature.

What, then is the essence of experience? For James, the notion of essence is teleological and instrumental; the conception and classification of essences are 'purely teleological weapons of the mind. The essence of a thing is that one of its properties which is so important for my interests that in comparison with it I may neglect the rest'.[71] Any description we give, then of the essence of experience, the world, reality, or being will be determined by our interests and, hence, restricted and relative to that extent, not absolute or metaphysical. This concept of interest as determinate for our conceptions is central to James's philosophy and to all pragmatists. According to James, as for Shelley, Coleridge, and Nietzsche, consciousness is natively selective; indeed, he asked, 'what are our very senses themselves but organs of selection?'.[72] Out of the flood of sensations, the 'undistinguishable, swarming, *continuum*, devoid of distinction and emphasis, – the senses made for us . . . a world of contrasts'.[73] Further, he insisted, 'Millions of items of the outward order are present to my senses which never properly enter into my experience. Why? Because they have no *interest* for me. *My experience is what I agree to attend to* . . . without selective interest, experience is an utter chaos.'[74] Consciousness is selective in the sense that it is interested more in some things than in others, more in the things that contribute to or threaten survival, comfort, or enjoyment, than in the things that do not impinge noticeably on such concerns.

More radically, James, like Coleridge and Berkeley before him, insisted that things themselves, external objects, do not pre-exist in any intelligible sense; the mind does not turn its attention and interest to certain sensations because they indicate external objects in the environment. Rather, things are but special groups of sensible qualities, which happen practically or aesthetically to interest us, to which we therefore give substantive names and which we exalt to this exclusive status of independence and dignity. Things are functional, not ontological; had our interests been different, the way we divide up the world as well as the objects we produce would be different. Perception itself is for James (as it was for Coleridge, Shelley, and Blake) constructive and creative, spontaneous and active. It is not a passive receptivity of already existing objects that are absolutely divided from an independent consciousness. James insisted upon the creative nature of human interaction with the environment, on the primacy of novelty and possibility, of chance and spontaneity. Yet he never exaggerated the role of thought and human creative perception into an idealism. He insisted upon the radical relativism of objects as known, yet never failed to emphasize the reality of a natural world distinct (but not absolutely divided) from an equally natural mind, thought, or consciousness.

World and mind are aspects of experience; neither has primacy over the other in any intelligible sense, however much we may want to give primacy to the world over consciousness, or vice versa, depending upon our temperaments. For James, the world as we know and perceive it (and what other world is there?) and consciousness are interdependent, not one dependent on the other, but both on each other as functions. Neither has any independent ontological status. For the 'world' is not something fixed, but something that keeps coming into being. While human consciousness has played a part in making the world what it is, this is not to say that something did not exist before human consciousness perceived and constructed things. Something patently did exist, for the human is clearly interdependent and continuous with nature. James insisted that the world and reality genuinely grow, and indeed 'in these very determinations which here and now are made.'[75] The attributes we give to nature, James concluded, must be said always to have been true of it; in one sense they are created, in another they are found. Nonetheless, these attributes are genuine additions made by our intellect to the world of fact, not additives of consciousness only, but additives of content: 'They copy nothing that pre-existed, yet they agree with what pre-existed, fit it, amplify it, relate and connect it with a "wain", a number-tally, or what not, and build it out . . . our judgment may actually be said to retroact and enrich the past.'[76]

The Role of Novelty in Experience

The world, reality, and experience grow and become other than what they were; humans contribute to novelty and change and make the world and 'reality' something other than what they once were. Thus there is a dependence. Yet reality – the world – also changes humans, and both frees and limits their activities, their creativity, and their effects. The only difficulty in grasping this acceptance of the interdependence of human being and world (along with the difficulty of understanding the admission that some world existed before humans) arises if we unconsciously assume the world to be fixed, that *this* world as we know it existed before humankind, and that our world is simply a copy of that preexisting world. James ridiculed this notion that our perceptions and thoughts are here to copy an independent, already fixed, nature. And, as is clear, he rejected the assumption of a world as fixed in its nature and pre-existing as a totality that reveals its inner structure to the human mind. James, like Dewey, Coleridge, and Shelley before him, emphasized that while the human creative role was not of the kind that idealism implied, humans are nevertheless genuinely creative in their activities in relation to their environment. If one major aspect of consciousness is continuity, by virtue of relations and connections (felt transitions) inhering in experience, this sensible continuity is in no way incompatible with novelty, which often means, in fact, re-evaluating the meaning and significance of past experiences in the light of a new, present context or point of view. For James, as for Dewey, the ability to handle novel experience is one of the surest signs of intelligence and mentality.

The concept of novelty involves, then, both the idea of new data impinging upon the mind and also the mind viewing old data in a new light, or recognizing that it overlooked data in a familiar situation by failing to appreciate its significance. This idea of the role of novelty is another aspect of radical empiricism, that is, that the world and the objects in the world are subject to change and growth. Not just the qualities of things, but our concepts of what constitutes things, change; indeed James insisted that 'there is no property *absolutely* essential to any one thing'.[77] Depending on our interests and the focus of our attention, the so-called essence of a thing may change, and the thing itself may cease to be a discrete entity or may break up into several previously undiscriminated parts, so that each part now demands to be seen as a unity. Our notion of what constitutes things, as well as what qualities belong to things, is relative and amenable to revision. Both the content, the substance, of experience (things) and the relations of experienced things (which constitute those 'things') is malleable. As was said earlier, things *are* but relations 'thingified' or exalted to substantive names out of the interest they have for us, whether practical, aesthetic, moral, or intellectual. Hence, metaphysically stated, process, not product, relation, not substance, is the more useful concept in analysing experience viewed empirically.

Empiricism, rationalism, and idealism all assumed that thought and experience were antithetical, that is, that inference, for example, goes beyond experience. But for James, Peirce, and Dewey alike, as for Coleridge and Shelley, there is no conscious experience without relations, and these relations include inference and reflection. Consequently, thought is intrinsic to experience, not an artificial by-product of it, not a transempirical import superadded to it, not a mere pigeon-holing or cumulative registration of particulars, as the traditional empiricists implied. Genuinely constructive and creative (or imaginative), thought – as Coleridge would say – is nevertheless constrained and limited by the pressures of non-thinking objects. (The idealist is criticized for magnifying the role of thought, to the point that it unintelligibly constitutes its object and even the universe.) Experience is understood to be shot through with inference and thought; it is not atomistic, discontinuous, unrelated and antithetical to thought. Moreover, thought and reflection are not activities primarily involving copying or reflecting – as in a mental mirror – an independent, pre-existing, static externality. Thinking and perception are there for the sake of behaviour, of solving problems, fulfilling desires, avoiding disasters: 'My thinking is first and last and always for the sake of my doing.'[78] That is, reflection, inference, perception, and thinking are all naturalistic forms of behaviour which help the organism adapt to its environment by intelligent response; they are not unnatural or supernatural additions to the practical fact of existence and physical activity. Inference and intelligence are natural, intrinsic elements of life and world activity, as Nietzsche would argue, not some mysterious, exalted, spiritual, or mental element directing a totally distinct physical entity.

However, just as inference, intelligence, thought, reflection, and perception are natural to and inherent in experience, the isolation of experience (as subjective) from nature is equally misguided. Nature and experience are continuous with each other. Note Dewey's Jamesian observation: 'Experience interpenetrates nature, it reaches into its depths and expands our understanding of it.'[79] Dewey further insisted that the contrast between the 'crudeness' of primary experience and the refinement of objects of reflection and culture is no reason for seeing experience as inherently dualistic, as physical *versus* mental, sensible *versus* intelligible, nature *versus* culture. On the contrary, primary experience is merely 'the result of a minimum of reflection, whereas the latter is the result of continual reflective enquiry and systematic thinking'.[80] Nature flows into and out of culture, and continuity is preserved between the world of natural and the world of human culture.

The 'evolutionism' inherent in pragmatism and radical empiricism is evident. For James, the universe is an unfinished one, an apocalyptic world truly in the making (as William Blake would have said), continuous, intelligible, meaningful, and purposive. It is purposive and directional relatively speaking, without any absolute certainty or unchanging truth.[81] It is historical without any sense of unfolding a pre-existing nature, or towards a pre-conceived end. The reality of James's universe is genuinely open-ended and pluralistic, as was Shelley's and Berkeley's before him.

5

John Dewey's Critique of Traditional Philosophizing

The 'Invasion of the Future'

Dewey's pragmatism and criticism of western philosophy owe much to Charles Sanders Peirce and William James, who freed him from the limits and constraints of Hegelian and idealist language, while still allowing him to profit from the historical emphasis of Hegel and the ensuing insights for philosophy of Darwinian evolutionary theories. Dewey, like James, found that much past and recent philosophy was artificial and trivially dialectical, because of a too-exclusive concern with and attachment to traditional issues and problems. He pithily remarked: 'Philosophy must cease to be a device for dealing with problems of philosophy, and become a method for dealing with problems of men.'[1] Dewey argued that when taught in received systems and preoccupied with past problems, such teaching was not conducive to what he called 'immediate response',[2] to, that is, genuine reflection and active participation in thought. Contrary to traditional views, philosophy for Dewey was not to be conceived of as concerned with ultimate reality. It is not a search for the real object or the truly real, whether fixed, as the absolutists would have it, or in flux, as some relativists insist. Dewey maintained that pragmatism has no theory of reality. Reality is a denotative term used to designate indifferently all that happens.[3] In criticizing traditional empiricists, Dewey denied that philosophy should be an analysis of a past 'given'; further, in criticizing idealists and rationalists, he alleged that 'philosophy is not a contemplative survey of existence . . . [it is] rather, an outlook on the future'.[4]

The emphasis upon the present and future as opposed to the past became a hallmark of pragmatism. From the pragmatist's point of view, our interest should be with what is actually going on in the world, the 'environment' (to use a familiar Deweyan term), not predominantly with what is already there in a finished form, contrary to the empiricists preoccupation with the past and the 'given'. Indeed, the latter can be of impact only as it affects present and future goings on, only, that is, because it is not really finished and done with at all, since it has future consequences that change its impact and character. Dewey nevertheless admitted, with the empiricist, that:

> the imaginative recovery of the bygone is indispensable to successful invasion of the future, but its status is that of an instrument . . . but to isolate the past, dwelling upon it for its own sake, and giving it the eulogistic name of knowledge, is to substitute the reminiscence of old age for effective intelligence.[5]

Previous philosophers are accused of failing to check their results against what Dewey metaphorically called primary experience. Instead of being genuinely empirical in this way, they have mistaken the nature of experience after reflection for a previous 'given' existing prior to reflection, explaining away or ignoring recalcitrant experiences, in contrast to scientists who are forced to adapt their theories, not the content of experience, if they are to assist at any adequate description or interpretation of experience.[6] The task of philosophy, Dewey argued in a Coleridgean statement, is the 'analytic dismemberment and synthetic reconstruction of experience'[7] according to the empirical methods of science. That is, philosophy, like science, must become an account of a method of enquiry to be followed, and will involve making predictions, as does science, on the basis of specific observations. Dewey repeatedly maintained that science, philosophy, and art share the same ends and methods, and that their subject matter alone differs.[8] Further, he believed that science as method is more basic than science as content or subject matter. Far from being a positivist, however, Dewey saw scientific enquiry as itself an art, based upon imaginative activity of the same quality as works of art.[9]

Dewey described one major task of pragmatism as the analysis and imaginative application of scientific method (and the conclusions of an experimental theory of knowledge) to human affairs, that is, a critique and 'reconstruction' of beliefs, values and institutions.[10] As an account of an empirical method, philosophy becomes 'a generalized theory of criticism'[11]; it provides a critique of the prejudices, beliefs, values, and institutions of our society by suggesting whether those beliefs and institutions will lead to or are consistent with other values, beliefs, and goals that a society espouses. Philosophy thereby involves value judgements;

this Socratic turn Dewey took further by insisting that philosophy should be a study of 'life experience', not exclusively of philosophy, or its past problems and concerns.[12] Philosophy as criticism, and as a theory of criticism, points to the crucial role of criticism as the means of the intelligent control of thought and experience in all its phases and aspects.

Naturalistic Metaphysics

Dewey's insistence upon life experience (values, beliefs, prejudices, social institutions, behaviour) as the material of philosophy (as opposed to philosophy's narcissistic preoccupation with itself) is reflected in his description of the meaning of metaphysics as well. Metaphysics, he explained, is the cognizance and description of generic traits of existence, not an endeavour to reconcile two separate realms of being, namely, appearance and reality.[13] For the so-called world of appearances, that world of incompleteness, change, precariousness, is just as real as the fixed, finished, and the permanent. The former should not be relegated to the status of incomplete or unreal being. Indeed, there is a genuine need for change, variety, uncertainty, and possibility in human action. Experience freed of preconceptions and prejudices shows us a world in continuous formation, a world in which there is still place for indeterminism, for novelty, for a genuinely new future full of unimagined possibilities.[14] Contrary to absolutists, idealists, and empiricists alike, the future, experience shows us, is open: the universe is still evolving, it is unfinished and 'in-the-making', to recall James's phrase. Experience, Dewey argued, does not show us that the universe is a totality whose truly real and forever fixed structure of reality needs to be revealed to us by reason. This notion is merely a hypostasizing from the fact that existence has generic traits to the notion that there exists one single, most real generic trait behind the multifarious and pluralistic world of experience. Rather, for Dewey and James, 'reality' is that denotative term for all that happens, while experience reveals a world in the process of becoming and still plastic.[15]

Given the Shelleyan and Blakean conception of a world in the making, mind has clearly a creative role to play in how this evolving world actually does evolve. Both James and Dewey had criticized empiricists for failing to appreciate the genuinely constructive and creative role of mind. Nevertheless, reason's function, the creative, is far more limited than the idealists had imagined: neo-Hegelian idealism had 'magnified the role of thought beyond all proportion' in asserting that thought constituted in the last analysis its object and the universe as a whole. Pragmatism, rather, sees a positive but limited function to thought. Thought does not merely know the past and present, as empiricists have it; it actually directs and creates to some extent the present and future; it can even recreate the past by interpreting it. Yet the extent of its participation is limited both by intelligent, imaginative use and control, and by the recalcitrance of the environment around it that resists total control. Therefore, things and events (as a world) are accepted 'for what they are independently of thought', yet 'thought gives birth to distinctive acts which modify future facts and events in such a way as to render them more reasonable, that is to say, more adequate to the ends which we proposed for ourselves'.[16]

There is, then, for Dewey, as for James, a real element and an ideal element, but this apparent dualism is temporary only. As Dewey's naturalistic metaphysics shows, these two elements are merely aspects or functions of experience: that is, thought and nature are inextricably bound up with each other. Briefly put, thought and nature, and experience and nature, are not two independent realms. The relations and connections that constitute thought are an immediate, natural, real part of the field of experience and nature. These relations are not superadded; they have rather the same reality and status as qualities, as James had already insisted. There is no absolute dualism because thought is intrinsic to experience and itself natural, and a part of the natural environment of which the thinking organism is a real, natural, influencing agent. (To conclude from this that the world or environment as we know it exists absolutely independently of thought in some form, is to fail to appreciate the functional emphasis of pragmatic analysis, and will be taken up in more detail below.)

Reconstructing Philosophy

In a very Jamesean comment, Dewey admitted that 'motives of instantive sympathy' and temperament 'play a greater role in our choice of philosophic system than do formal reasoning.'[17] Most philosophical problems (especially those regarding religious issues) are irresolvable except by temperamental preference, since decisive evidence is lacking. James and Dewey further undertook to prove, however, that many of these problems were based on false or contradictory or unempirical assumptions, and ceased to be problems when the prejudices that engendered them were exposed. Both James and Dewey were convinced, as is Derrida, that because of the artificiality of so many traditional problems in philosophy, philosophy was in need of moving in new directions, setting new problems, tasks and goals for itself. As Dewey presciently observed in 1930:

> if I read the cultural signs of the times right, the next synthetic movement in philosophy will emerge when the significance of the social sciences and arts has become an object of reflection in the same way that mathematical and physical sciences have been made the objects of thought in the past, and when their full impact is grasped.[18]

The last fifty years have certainly borne out this prediction; indeed, the concerns of recent theorizing lie squarely within the search for the 'significance of the social sciences and arts . . . [as] an object of reflection'.

Dewey spoke still more forcefully when he wrote:

> In any case, I think it shows a deplorable deadness of imagination to suppose that philosophy will indefinitely revolve within the scope of the problems and systems that two thousand years of European history have bequeathed to us. Seen in the long perspective of the future, the whole of Western European history is a provincial episode.[19]

Pragmatism for Dewey and James was empiricism pushed to its most radical, thoroughgoing conclusion, 'looking away from first things, principles, "categories", supposed necessities, and of looking towards last things, fruits, consequences, facts'.[20] The pragmatic method involves initially the Berkeleyan analysis of words (such as 'reality', 'truth', 'experience', 'mind', 'things', etc.) in order clearly to determine their meanings so that they are not used so loosely as to engender the merely verbal quarrels that Berkeley repeatedly bemoaned. Clarification of some of these terms has already been attempted in relation to James, but the discussion of some of these and of others will be expanded in this chapter. Similarly, Dewey's questioning of the genuineness of many traditional philosophical problems will clarify and carry forward James's project as the second major element in the pragmatic method. Third, the meaning of truth becomes a central project of the pragmatic method as an instrument for its determination, and lastly, pragmatism seeks to indicate that disputes (such as free will versus determinism) may not be resolvable by logical reasoning, since conclusive evidence is lacking. Nevertheless, certain beliefs lead to totally different consequences, and we can choose to act on beliefs because of a choice between consequences.

For Dewey, 'quarrels amongst conflicting types of philosophy are . . . family quarrels'.[21] That is, such quarrels make common assumptions: for example, the real is what is permanent and true or known, or, primary experience reveals independent subjects and objects, or, all experiences are knowledge experiences of varying clarity or obscurity; such assumptions often deny to the universe the character of contingency which it clearly reveals. Thus, they are fundamentally unempirical, for experience gives evidence of a world not complete, finished, and sure, but precarious, unstable, and evolving. Dewey criticized not only the absolutist view, however; he also believed that such philosophers as Lao Tze, Heraclitus, and later Bergson, had turned the principle of relativity into a finite and absolute description of reality. That is, change itself was deified and made universal, regular, and sure: something to be revered. Dewey insisted that reality has the character not of one or the other, but of both; that it is what is happening, and what is happening is in varying degrees permanent and impermanent, stable and in flux.

Aristotle is described by Dewey as having begun with a naturalistic metaphysics such as pragmatism encourages, that is, a metaphysics that insists upon the continuity between nature and experience or nature and thought. Yet, Aristotle became hypnotized by the fixed, certain, and finished, and thereupon created a hierarchy in which contingency and chance were made deficiencies of being or reality. Aristotle's philosophy 'was closer to empirical facts than most modern philosophies, in that it was neither monistic nor dualistic but openly pluralistic'.[22] His pluralism, however, was hierarchical of levels of being, so that, for example, Aristotle's conclusions led such philosophers as Kant to equate the realm of sense and sensation with chaos or low level or being (namely, mere appearance) while the regular, uniform, and ordered belonged to reason alone. Thus arose one of the most baffling (for the pragmatist, 'pseudo') problems of philosophy – how to reconcile the two realms.

Pluralism versus Particularism

For Dewey, pluralism is an established empirical fact, because the dynamic connections in experience are qualitative and diverse. But he further cautioned his reader:

> The attempt to establish monism from a consideration of the very nature of a relation is mere piece of dialectics. Equally dialectical is

the effort to establish by a consideration of the nature of relations an ontological Pluralism of Ultimates: simple and independent beings.[23]

Pluralism, for Dewey, implies contingency, novelty, liberty; accepting unity where it finds it, 'it does not attempt to force the vast diversity of events and things into a simple rational mould'.[24] Monism, on the other hand, suggests a world that is fixed and immutable, where inventions, free play, spontaneity, and unforeseen possibility have little place. Dewey had described James's philosophy as a revision of English empiricism wherein the value of fixed, past experience – the 'given' – is replaced by valuing the future, by what is yet mere possibility. Historical empiricism looks backward where pragmatism looks forward, and this change of emphasis, initiated by James, Dewey believed to be revolutionary. Experience, he claimed, is preoccupied not with the past but with the new; experience is a future complicated by a present. Adjustment or adaptation to the implied future is not a static, timeless state, but a continuing process of active, prospective human endeavour: 'we live forward' not backward, Dewey claimed.[25] For example, James was able to insist that general ideas do not merely report or register past experience: they are rather the foundation upon which future experiences are organized. In short, for historical empiricism, reason merely sums up the particular cases of the past; general ideas are just bunches of particulars.

For pragmatism, however, the inventiveness of reason cannot be reduced to mere summarizing and categorizing; reason has a truly constitutive function, a fact which led idealists to seek to correct historical empiricism by going to another extreme. James had shown that general ideas are modes of signifying particular things and not just an abstraction from particular cases or a super-empirical function such as the idealists assumed. Rather, general ideas were 'teleological instruments' or weapons for the intelligent control of the future. Clearly, then, the place of thought or intelligence in experience is one of the central and real issues common to empiricism and rationalism in their ancient controversy. The utterly mechanical, summarizing character of thought of the traditional empiricist, this 'cumulative registration' or pigeonholing, where thought is not constructive but a mere matter of bulk (and not qualitative), was rejected by idealism as wholly inadequate to the experience of creativity and novelty which is an empirical fact.

Use of the given as only relatively finished, to anticipate the consequences of processes going on is precisely what, for Dewey, is meant by 'ideas', by 'intelligence'. Present facts, then, are used as 'signs of things to come in evidence of absent things'.[26] We employ what has happened

as a means of inferring what may happen in the future, and this inference, this intelligence, is 'an intrinsic feature of experience' not an
accidental by-product as the empiricists would have it. Nor is this feature
best conceived of as a super-empirical, super-natural, already constituted
reason, as the idealist argued (as a corrective to empiricism): that al-
ready-made faculty of thought transcending experience.[27] In postulating
such a super-entity, rationalism and idealism rightly rejected the empiricists' mechanical account of thought, but accepted its 'stubborn
particularism', the basic, false assumption that the connections and
relations in experience (indeed, thought itself) are not intrinsic to
experience, but due to some super-empirical reason.

Dewey, like James, insisted that this shared doctrine of sensations and
ideas, of senses and intellect, as separate, disparate existences was totally
non-empirical. It is derived neither from observations nor experiment.
Indeed, Dewey further complained, 'Locke's account of discrete, simple
ideas or meanings, which are compounded and then distributed, does
palpable violence to the facts.'[28] For Dewey, experience reveals every
kind of connection within itself: the organism struggling in its environment is bound up with things by intimate bonds, connections, and
relations; its experience is 'of necessity a matter of ties and connections'.[29] This atomistic notion Dewey branded a mere logical deduction
from a prior unexamined notion of the nature of experience as a 'rigid
discontinuity' and as primarily inner and physical, or subjective. This
unwarranted, unempirical assumption led empiricists to the ridiculous
conclusion that the external, objective world of stable things and of real
connections and relations was a mere appearance, and that knowledge
was impossible (in the case of Hume at least). Idealism, rejecting such
scepticism, involved a transempirical reason to supply universal connections and relations which would restore objectivity and stability to this
'sensible manifold' of the sensationalists. Yet, Dewey pointed out, idealists could never solve the problem of how a reason extraneous to
experience could ever enter into constructive relation with it, for reason
and experience were by definition antithetical. As Dewey put it, the
concern of the idealists' reason was never 'expansion or guidance of
experience', but the creation of a 'realm of super-empirical entities'
chasmically separated from the sensational manifold it was supposed to
enter into.[30] For Dewey, the refutation of both historical empiricism and
rationalism is best achieved by rejecting their 'particularist' prejudices
and insisting on the empirical fact that experience is replete with connections intrinsic to it. There is no justification for postulating an empirical sensible 'manifold' of unconnected particulars, and there is
therefore no need to appeal to a superempirical Reason to connect

them, since the notion of a sensible manifold has no basis when experience is looked at with a less biased eye.[31]

Dualism: A Product of Reflection

The consequences of such traditional non-empirical 'methods' were, Dewey argued, first, the total separation of 'experience' from nature, and the real external world. That is, experience was seen as merely a veil cutting the subject off from the nature of true reality until such a subjectively conceived experience could be transcended by a super-empirical, non-natural reason.[32] Secondly, these non-empirical methods failed to lead back to any kind of actually occurring relatively 'primary' or 'genuine' experience, indeed, even denied it validity or reality, while secondary objects, that is, objects which were the products of systematic and refined reflection, became the only, or supremely real things. The 'original' materials of Dewey's actual 'primary experience' were called phenomenal, mere appearance, mere sensation, and a division in qualitative terms arose, one of true being versus non-being, or reality versus non-reality. Then the question of the very existence of experience and its objects at such initial primary levels arose. The mind had no access to real things, it was concluded, but only to copies, impressions, representations of them. These copies were neither things in themselves nor even 'real copies', but purely subjective inner mental states of an already constituted mind existing in a realm totally different from the realm of objectivity.

Put another way, Dewey maintained that the selection of the 'original' material for philosophical analysis is the difference between pragmatic, truly empirical and non-empirical methods and philosophies. The non-empirical methods of previous traditional philosophies began not with what is genuinely, empirically 'primary' experience (diversity and identity, interconnections and gaps, change and permanence, stability and instability, independent natural objects and organisms of all kinds, including the human organism). They began rather with 'a reflective product' and treated that as if it were primary, as if it were given. This reflective product was characterized by dualism: subject–object, mind–body, consciousness–matter, each absolutely separate from the other and wholly independent. This dualistic reflective product was assumed to be the essential character of primary experience. The age-old, resulting (pseudo-) problems of how mind–body, subject–object, and so on, ever interrelate, could be solved only by denying empirical aspects of experience. The idealist was forced to maintain that matter is really mentality disguised, while the materialist denied genuine reality to the mental. Moreover, in making these paired opposites absolutely, qualitatively distinct and independent of each other, the results of psychological experience were relegated to a separate mental world entirely sufficient unto itself and totally self-enclosed. According to this result, mental attributes became the given while, absurdly, objects of actual experience (trees, tables, etc.) were treated as mere questionable constructs of reason, or as complexes of sensations and ideas added together by a mechanical, pigeonholing understanding.

Dewey concluded that in such philosophies the very subject matter of experience is rendered dubious, though nevertheless assumed at every step of the way.[33] He pointed out that this traditional error arises in mistaking the act of observation for experience, and in often allowing a sense such as vision, for example, to tyrannize over all other experiences. He gave as an example the viewing, from various perspectives, of a chair, in one case, and the observation of a coin, in another, and pointed out that to assume that what we experience are discrete patches of colour in varying shapes without any 'real' connection (the connections being supplied by thought) is nonsense.[34] Experience properly understood really is of chairs, tables, stones, and trees, not of separate, atomic sensations and ideas. The latter are in fact products of reflection. It is not 'experience' which is experienced, but nature. Things interacting in certain ways are experienced.[35] That is, sensations, those patches of colours and shapes, are the traits connected with the *act of experiencing* – or seeing, in this case – when the act itself is made an *object of enquiry* as opposed to the chair or coin. Subjectivism arises, then, only when we mistake the act of seeing for the object seen. Reflection may discriminate a new factor in experience, namely the act of seeing, observation itself, or experience and enquiry; it can make an object of that and then enquire into that new object. But to mistake the act of experiencing for the original experience of a chair (or whatever object) is the gross blunder that leads to subjectivism. Thus, we observe things, not observations, though clearly the act of observation may itself *become* the object of enquiry, Dewey insisted.

Dewey, like Coleridge, did not deny the importance of making a distinction between physical and mental events; on the contrary, he emphasized that it is this distinction alone which allows humans to control and regulate their experienced world, unlike primitive people, who constantly attributed qualities to external objects that were more properly (from our cultural point of view, at least) traits of human modes of experiencing, feeling, and behaving.[36] The problem for pragmatism is not an insoluble one about how two absolutely independent realms of existence could ever interact (mind–body, mental–physical, consciousness–world). Rather, the problem is merely why experience, as a multifarious whole, *is* so distinguished, and the Nietzschean answer has already been given: to gain control over the physical we must distinguish it from the mental. The matter involves, however, a distinction only, not a division of experience into separate realms, as Coleridge would also have argued.

Furthermore, when we talk of primary versus secondary experience, no dualism is implied. For the distinction between the crude subject matter of so-called (metaphorically speaking) primary experience and the 'refined', 'derived' objects of reflection that make up 'secondary experience' is merely a distinction, Dewey explained, 'between what is experienced as the result of a minimum of incidental reflection and what is experienced in consequences of continued and regulated reflective enquiry . . . [that is] systematic thinking'.[37] These differing experiences do not belong to two realms, the one natural or absolutely, literally primary and physical in some originary sense, and the other super-natural, or mental. These two distinguished kinds of experience belong in a natural continuum; the distinction is relative and instrumental only. Systematic reflection leading to 'secondary' objects certainly makes it possible to understand the 'cruder' aspects of experience, so to speak, instead of merely having sense-contact with them.

Misconceptions of 'Experience'

To sum, Dewey argued that there are several major assumptions about experience in traditional philosophical systems that are unempirical and lead to the (pseudo) problems that have hypnotized western philosophy for two thousand years. Firstly, it has been assumed that experience is a knowledge affair, when actually, Dewey suggested, cognition is only one aspect of a whole complex process of experiencing better described as the 'intercourse of a living being with its environment'. Secondly, experience is said to be a physical matter, that is, tainted by subjectivity, mentality, whereas a thoroughgoing empirical view shows us that experience is rather of a genuinely objective world modified by the human's activities in it, and responses to it. Next, the emphasis on the bare present or past is too great – that alleged 'given', that 'sensible manifold', – whereas in actuality we find that our experience is full of projection, that it is future-oriented, towards control and change. Thus, the connection not with the past or even the present, but with the future, is the salient trait of experience. Fourthly, it has been assumed that experience is of discretes, particulars, simples, atoms, separates. No genuine connections, ties, bonds or relations exist in experience itself. These are supposed to be mere by-products. However, as James insisted, experience is replete with connections and relations; they are inherent in it, intrinsic and natural to it, if only we look at experience, and not at some alleged 'given' stripped of all the genuine traits of experience.[38] Connected with this denial of relations as inherent in experience and thus superadded to it is the mistaken notion that inference and reasoning, thought and intelligence somehow are separate from and beyond experience. For example, we have to make a great leap from experience of mere simple sensations to a stable world of things and other minds. With James, Dewey insisted on the naturalistic nature of inference, thought and reasoning. Experience is said to be full of inference. Indeed, Dewey maintained, 'there is, apparently, no conscious experience without inference' (or language, either; see chapter 8). As he put it, 'reflection is native and constant.'[39]

Traditional philosophical accounts of experience are described as mere deductions from unexamined premises of what, it is assumed, experience *must* be. Experience *must* be of separate simples, it *must* have no connections or relations. Inference *must* be extrinsic to it. Historical empiricism has been dominated by notions that it forced into experience instead of actual ideas gathered out of it.[40] Once it is understood that thought and relationship are inherent and genuine within experience, rationalism and empiricism are exposed, Dewey claimed, at one blow.[41] Both had assumed that experience collects around a centre or subject that is external to and set over against the natural course of events. This assumption probably arose, Dewey maintained, from religious preoccupations which rejected the human being as continuous with other forms of life. They viewed her as possessing a soul or belonging to a spiritual realm separate from and outside the world of natural existence. Experience was, then, centred in a non-natural subject, and thereby set over against the experienced world. The human being became a spectator of reality (reflecting copies of it, unreachable as reality was by any direct means) instead of a natural participant in the course of an evolving world.

Dewey insisted that the resulting problem of how the subject-consciousness can ever reach genuine knowledge of the real, external world is meaningless, since the assumption of the conscious subject as external to the world is contrary to fact.[42] When subjects are made centres of experience and made spectators outside the world, when objects are thereby isolated from the experiences in which they function, then experience is treated as it if were complete in itself, with no natural world actually needed. We are left with the nonsensical notion of experience experiencing only itself, instead of the things of nature.[43] A subjective, private consciousness is evoked which is set over against a nature that consists wholly of physical objects. Mental objects are not, however, isolated or self-sufficient, Dewey suggested. Mental events may be said to gather around a subject consciousness, but they do not inhere exclusively in it, nor do they place the 'real object' at some unreachable distance. Rather, 'experience' is a word better understood as denoting something wholly continuous with the natural, physical world. Experiencing, he wrote, is simply 'certain modes of interaction, of correlation, of natural objects amongst which the organism happens, so to say, to be one'.[44] Experiencing does not go on in a vacuum but in an environing medium while 'private consciousness is an accidental outcome of experience of a vital, objective sort; it is not its source'.[45]

Nature is not, then, to be conceived of as wholly mechanical and natural while experience is thought to belong to an ideal or spiritual realm of mentality. Dewey pointed out that, in science, nature and experience work together harmoniously; experience is 'a method of penetrating nature's secrets', while nature, thus disclosed, enriches experience. Experience is no veil or thin layer of nature. Reaching down into nature, it is capable of depth, expansion and penetration. Experience makes the past and the future accessible, as in cosmology, geology, and history.[46] Indeed, Dewey summarized that there would be no need for the word 'experience' if philosophy were to become genuinely empirical. For the word is actually merely a duplication *in general terms* of what is already covered in definite terms. Like the term 'reality', the word 'experience' refers to a plurality of events and modes of interaction, not to a simple generic substance behind the variety of forms of living and thriving.

In this way, the problem of the existence of the external world arose for orthodox empiricism, since it was assumed that experience was attached exclusively to a private consciousness. The world became external to experience instead of its subject matter. Dewey remarked that, nevertheless, 'if anything seems adequately grounded empirically it is the existence of a world which resists the . . . subject of experience'.[47] For traditional empiricism, with its concept of a spectator or knower outside the real world of nature, all that can be experienced is the transient mental state, 'purely' present, it alone being the object of any genuine knowledge. All else – the past, the future, stable objects, minds – are not included in this 'datum of experience'. As Dewey explained, traditional empiricism forces us to postulate all these external existents by an inference assumed to be beyond experience.[48] Idealism went a step further in recognizing the genuineness of the connections experienced, but it raised them to the supernatural level of rational (logical) connections, whereupon the real world became a synthesis of the 'sensible manifold of consciousness' through the agency of a supernatural reason supplying objectivity. The basic concept of experience in both philosophies is, however, Dewey showed, unempirical and fictional. Idealism at least recognized the role of thought, but, as Dewey put it, it presumed 'to reveal the world as already and eternally a self-luminous rational whole'.[49] It thus exalted thought, yet leaving it nothing to do! – since no growth or change or evolution was part of that eternal, unchanging realm called reality. Thought was there merely as a revelation of a pre-existing rational totality.

Experience is not merely Cognitive

Dewey emphatically denied the traditional assumption that 'experience' means primarily knowledge or cognitive conduct. He insisted that experience is a word denoting doings and sufferings of a whole variety of kinds.[50] He sharply accused the 'intellectualist philosophy' of falsely assuming that all experience is a mode of knowing, and that all nature and all subject matter of experience is to be defined in terms of refined products of scientific enquiry. He insisted that this reductive programme is utterly contrary to 'primary experience', that is, contrary to experience revealed for what it is when we actually reflect upon it, observe it empirically, as opposed to forcing it to fit our preconceived prejudices. In such empirically observed experience, things really are objects, not only to be known (in terms of electrons or mathematical calculations), but things to be enjoyed, used, and acted upon.[51] Dewey insisted that things of experience are *had* before they are cognized, and that cognitive experience must be seen to originate within experience of a non-cognitive sort since knowing and cognizing are merely factors in human enterprise and activity. Hence they are secondary and derived characteristics of 'primary, action-undergoing experience'.[52] It is a mistake and a source of much error in traditional philosophy to equate what things are with what they are known as, so that knowing and cognition are the sole or most real modes of experiencing.[53] Dewey claimed that when an experience becomes cognitive, a transformation has occurred – not of the kind usually suggested, namely, that an unreality has changed into a reality. Simply, the concrete, experienced reality has changed from being a 'had' experience to becoming a 'cognized' one. He gave the example of a noise that at first we experience as frightening, yet which upon investigation is discovered to be harmless: we can conclude that the noise as harmless is a more true account, but not more real than the noise as first experienced. The first experience is not cognitive (is not, 'I know I am frightened by the noise'), but non-cognitive ('Oh! frightful noise!'). One experiences fright, and only later does fright become the object observed ('I know I was frightened') and enquired into. Dewey reminded us that things are what they are experienced as, and that any one thing may be experienced in numerous ways, but that these alternatives are alternatives amongst several realms of experience, not alternatives between a reality and various approximations of it.[54]

Dewey concluded that the unempirical and *a priori* concept of the self, arising from early religious preoccupations, led to the notion that experience is primarily cognitive. Western philosophy has been hypnotized into looking upon all experiencing as a mode of knowing of various degrees of confusion and clarity.[55] Most experience is assumed to be a 'cognitive noting', whereas actually, knowledge – and the cognitive – are, rather, the use that is made of experiences and of experienced, natural happenings. While most experience is non-cognitive at the outset, it may become cognitive when its consequences and uses are realized by someone. Moreover, while a genuine transformation from non-cognitive to cognitive has occurred, the transition involves not a change from unreality to reality, or as the scepticist would have it, a change from objectivity to subjectivity. Rather, Dewey suggested, the original experience as 'felt' and 'had' has, when become 'known', acquired distinctively new features, namely a clarification of its uses and future consequences.[56] The object known, as opposed to had (or experienced non-cognitively), is no longer merely a physical occurrence; it has greater meaning and significance – given its enrichment by the anticipation of its consequences and uses – and it thereby becomes something with truth or falsity. Any experience may, then, become cognitive (an object of reflection), yet the cognitive aspect is never all-inclusive, Dewey reminded us, since the content of the non-cognitive experience is retained as the new, cognitive features are added. Both exist together, and knowledge can never wholly transcend its non-cognitive origins. Dewey pointed out that a stone subjected to scientific analysis may become chemical elements, atomic particles, and so on; yet it does not cease at the same time still to be a stone as had or felt in experience.

The error of equating all experience with cognitive experiences arises, as was said earlier, from a notion of the self as outside the course of natural objects and events, and set over against the world to be known, while knowing is said to be a 'presentative relation' between a knower and an object, a viewing of objects from outside the world they inhabit.[57]

Dewey described this as 'the spectator theory of knowledge', where knowing consists merely in the possession of 'a transcript, more or less accurate, but otiose, of real things'.[58] Genuine knowledge involves not, however, mere copying of some distant reality, or things-in-themselves; it is not a mere presentation. Knowledge involves inference, reasoning, testing, systematic observation, all vitally active, natural survival processes utterly distinct from the passive beholding by an already-constituted-mind of an already-constituted-reality. On the spectator theory of knowledge, the self or subject, the mind or knower, pre-existing before any activity, gazes down upon a distant reality 'feudally superior to the events of everyday occurrence'.[59] The knower is also not already consti-tuted or existing independent of activity and interaction with the world and natural events, as idealism and rationalism suggest. That is, the self *becomes* a knower when it anticipates future consequences and reads present things as signs of future things – that is, makes objects more meaningful and related. There is no absolute distinction between the knower (mind or consciousness) and the known (the world), as tradi-tional philosophy imagined. There are only distinctions between dif-ferent ways and modes of being involved in things, namely, 'brute physical ways and purposive, intelligent ways'.[60]

Experience is not merely Subjective

The notion that all experience is a knowledge experience of lesser or greater clarity and accuracy is at the root of the (pseudo) problem of subjectivity in experience. Dewey argued that this mistake arose because of mistaken conclusions drawn from examples of relativity in perception, as a bent stick in water, or the numerous shapes of a coin viewed from different angles. He pointed out that the different shapes of the bent stick and the coin are simply a natural result of certain specifiable, observable conditions. They are not cases of 'knowing', for these dif-ferent views of the coin are purely non-cognitive. That is, the shapes of the disk are, so to speak, 'primary' data of physical happenings that can be scientifically accounted for by the rules of optics, and the interaction of light and the human eye, and as such are not cognitive events. It is alleged, by traditional philosophy though, that, firstly, there is the real object of which the different views or shapes are mere modifications, secondly, that these modifications are cases of knowing and are intro-duced by a knower, and that thirdly, therefore,knowledge is subjective and tainted with relativity. But if these variations in the shape of the coin or stick are seen as the result of the dynamic interaction of two physical agents producing an effect, or several varying effects, and are understood as real effects of a 'had experience', knowledge or cognition enters in only afterwards. The experience of several varying shapes is certainly real, and only then can we even have any basis for going on to the experienced knowledge that the coin is viewed as round under certain other conditions, and that it feels or measures circular.[61] Truth and knowledge, then, Dewey succinctly reminded us, are no more real than error. That is, dreams, hallucinations, bent sticks in water, etc., are not distortions of real things; they are real natural events themselves that arise in certain natural settings. The experience of a bent stick in water is real, but is not at first cognitive, so it is not true or false of the stick. But it becomes a cognitive matter when we ask if the stick will feel bent or look bent out of the water as well. This pseudo-problem of subjectivity in perception, and the consequent alleged subjectivity or relativity of knowledge, rests on the old assumption that the self or knower is outside the world of things observed and known, and that, therefore, the organism ought not to make a difference when it interacts with other objects. Yet, human participation does not lead to subjectivity in the sense of altering the objective so that it becomes merely phenomenal, when once this 'spectator theory of knowledge' is relinquished, when once it is admitted that truth and error are both existential and real.[62] The word 'real' means simply 'existent'; Dewey denied it the eulogistic connotations that make the term 'reality' equivalent to true being; for all experiences – as real – stand on the same level of being.[63] As he put it elsewhere, 'illusions are illusions, but the occurrence of illusions is no illusion – that is a genuine reality'.[64] If, then, reality is arbitrarily equated, as in Rationalism, only with what is clear, distinct, and simple, as Descartes' interpreters would have it, and all other experience is relegated to secondary status, then knowledge as reality prevails. If we adopt an empirical method and actually look at experience, however, we discover that reality is also characterized by vagueness and obscurity. These things also really exist, as do ignorance and error.[65] These latter things may become distinct through enquiry and analysis, and then knowledge advances, but only, in fact, because reality is full of cases of real obscurity being really clarified.

Dewey concluded that what is 'in' experience or what is real extends much further than that which at any time is known. Moreover, if we reject the notion that only objects of knowledge are ultimately real (so that all other objects of had and felt experience are not real), then we need not, for example, assume that emotions and sensations are merely confused thoughts which may reach cognitive status by becoming clear and distinct.[66] On the contrary, not only intellectual experience, but emotive, aesthetic, and moral experiences reveal the character of real things, too. Hence the traits of objects discovered and postulated by science (elements, atoms, electrons, etc.) are no more real than that reached by poetry, art and myth. Or, as Dewey put it, 'Poetry may have a metaphysical import just as science does, in not just a mystical or esoteric sense.'[67] The traits which the subject matter of experience possesses, whether aesthetic, moral, emotive, or truly physical, are just as real as the characteristics reached by physics or biology.[68]

Dewey analysed the traditional notions of reality psychologically when he curtly remarked that 'reality is made into what we wish existence to be':[69] namely, stable and eternal, so that we degrade the so-called defects of existence, such as change, instability, and impermanence, to a lower order of being. We are then trapped in the (pseudo) problem of how these two realms of being or reality could possibly interact, whereas a more genuine problem for metaphysics would be to discover and describe the 'generic traits of existence'. That is, for Dewey, both change and permanence are real, and change is not merely negative, but could be seen as a challenge to action and endeavour.[70] In a world of confusion, complexity and precariousness – where change is feared – certainty, simplicity and permanence are assumed to constitute true being. All else is a passive beholding of this already determined, finished totality, where nothing is to be accomplished except the passive reverencing of it.[71] A truly empirical method rejects this *a priori* account and refers to the dynamic nature of the interaction of natural agents, some possessing mentality, others not, as the material which cognitive experience arises from and enriches.

Mind and Matter: Characteristics of Natural Events

There is no basis, then, for assuming that consciousness or the subject-knower is outside the real world and different in kind from the objects known, so as to infect them with subjectivity. Mind and consciousness need not be viewed as supernatural. The problem of the relation of subject and object dissolves, said Dewey, when this totally unempirical account of mind, originating from religious conceptions of a world beyond this temporal world – is replaced by an empirical, naturalistic view arising from biological and evolutionary facts.[72] Both mind and matter can be viewed as simply different characters of natural events, 'in which matter expresses their sequential order and mind the order of their meanings in their logical connections and dependencies'.[73] Dewey cautioned us against concluding, however, that mind and matter are two aspects of some *tertium aliquid*; this view, he argued, is literally unthinkable. The alternative to such a view is to recognize mind and matter as belonging simply to 'the complex of events that constitute nature, not to some *tertium aliquid*, mysterious and incapable of designation of which mind and matter are static structures instead of functional characters'.[74] Like James, Dewey emphasized the functional character of both the concepts of mind and matter. He defined matter as:

> that character of natural events which is so tied up with changes that are sufficiently rapid to be perceptible as to give the latter a characteristic rhythmic order, the caused sequence. [Matter] is no cause or source of events or processes; no absolute monarch; no principle of explanation; no substance behind or underlying changes . . . the name designates a character in operation, not an entity.[75]

If mind and matter are taken as entities, as static structures, rather than functions, then the mysterious, unthinkable *tertium aliquid* needed to unite them both arises; when taken as functions belonging to the complex and varied world of natural events, no such mystery is evolved, nor any unsolvable dualism.

For Dewey, the term experience does not mean some 'aboriginal stuff out of which things are evolved',[76] nor is it suggestive of an endless flux or an indefinite totality.[77] Experience means rather what humans do and how they do it, and as such, it recognizes no absolute dualism between subject and object, act and material, thing and thought – since each of the pairs refers to a product discriminated by reflecting on life experience. The word experience denotes both an organism and an environment, both being contained in an unanalysed plurality. Only upon reflection does life break up into (external) environment and (internal) organic structure. The inclusive integrity of experience so conceived dissolves questions of the relations of mind and matter and the question of the possibility of knowledge into moot points, questions arising only when the integrated, functional conception of experience as a starting point for analysis is replaced by a dualistic account – which is always a product of systematic reflection, and not prior to it. Dewey is not, however, to be understood as postulating a 'pure', primary, originary experience freed of all reflection contrasting with 'reflected' experience. Dewey's is rather a relative and functional distinction between had or felt experiences (which are nevertheless full of the traits of thoughts and reflection – relations, connections, inference, but in which reflection is at a minimum), and experience as a product either of systematic, highly intensified or imaginative reflection. Dewey's distinction implies a continuum between these two types of relatively distinguishable experience. Non-empirical philosophy mistakes that experience, which is a high-level cultural product of systematic reflection, for an aboriginal primary material freed of all traits of reflection. Dewey's point is a polemical one; it is not an effort to establish a dualism between some notion of 'primary experience' as absolutely different from reflective, secondary experience, but an effort to expose the traditional mistaking of a product of systematic reflection for a primary, original material. 'Primary experience' as Dewey uses the term, is no more a reference to some generic stuff or *a priori* of which experience at large is made than is James's notion of pure experience. To argue so would be wilfully to misinterpret all else that they wrote. By 'experience' is meant the complex plurality of natural events in all their diversity of character, not some 'indefinite, total, comprehensive experience which somehow engenders an endless flux'.[78] Experience means, for Dewey and James, a plurality of interacting aspects and functions; it offers no absolute stability, but does offer concreteness and an emphasis upon processes as well as products, entities, stability.

Like James, Dewey rejected the notion that words such as mind, matter, subject, object, etc., denote absolutely stable entities, entities already constituted before interaction. He offered the Coleridgean idea of organism in place of the loaded concept of something purely mental as implied by 'soul', 'consciousness', or 'subject', meaning by 'organism' a biological, natural being continuous with nature, with mentality as a natural product and process in nature.[79] Mentality is defined as the activity of seeing future possibilities and consequences in present things. As James wrote: 'the pursuance of future ends and the choice of means for their attainment are thus the mark and criterion of the presence of mentality in a phenomenon'.[80]

Mind, for Dewey, as for Heidegger, is 'a genuine character of natural events at their most complex'.[81] Moreover, nature is said to interact not with something purely mental (subject-consciousness), but rather with human beings that are biological-cultural, natural organisms.[82] There is no gap between mind and nature since environmental energies constitute those very organic functions that are human beings. Neither mind nor reason are entities pre-existing or independent of their environment. They come into existence through action; mind is engendered, said Dewey, and reason comes into being with rational activity. Dewey went further, in fact, and insisted, as did Wittgenstein and Derrida later, that 'mind is a function of social interaction', that it arises in the process of human communication and participation, and that consciousness is inconceivable without the social interaction called language (see below p. 177).

Reflection, then, and thought or mentality, originate in the biological behaviour of an organism struggling to adapt to environmental influences.[83] Reflection guides the choices, efforts and actions of human beings, and, as such, is native and intrinsic to experience, a natural activity, not a supernatural entity. Indeed, reflection, reason, or thought is not an entity, but is rather acts involving the control of the future through intelligent grasp of the meaning of the present. The function of thought is not one of copying already constituted objects of the environment, but of relating more effectively to them.[84] As Dewey succinctly put it, 'intelligence is not a distorting eye registering in a remote and alien medium the spectacle of nature and of life'.[85] Reflection, he insisted, is a natural event that occurs because of the trials and struggles that nature affords; it is a natural function that philosophers have converted into a causal, antecedent reality.[86] For Dewey, thinking is one in kind with other natural materials and energies, such as fire or tools: it refines, reorders, and reshapes other materials of nature. It is not a specific power, but a process of reorganization continuous with the world of objects experienced. Thought contributes to the origin and development of things as experienced: yet those things are not its exclusive product. Dewey cautioned us against the excesses of idealism when he wrote:

> the constructive or organizing activity of 'thought' does not inhere in thought as a transcendental function, a form or mode of some supra-empirical ego, mind, or consciousness but in thought as itself a vital activity . . . we have passed to the idea of thought as reflectively reconstructive and directive, and away from the notion of thought as imminently constitutional and organizational. To make this passage and yet to ignore its import is essential to objective idealism.[87]

Continuity between Mind and Nature

Given this account common to Dewey and James (and to Nietzsche) of mind, knowing, thought, and consciousness as not entities but constructive functions, an account modified by their rejection of idealism, the question of how we are to understand 'things' inevitably arises. Dewey had repeatedly insisted that we experience things – rocks, stones, nature, cultural objects – not experience itself – not mere sensations or ideas isolated and discrete, not patches of colours – but things. Yet he insisted upon the constructive role of intelligence and rejected the notion that things, or objects, or experience – as we experience them – exist absolutely independently of the human organism's activities. He rejected the basic dualism of both idealism and historical empiricism, by insisting upon the continuity of the human organism with the objects of the natural world, so that the living being is *in* the world experienced, not outside it looking on passively, either reflecting an already created world or creating by means of thought the world it experiences. In addition to this Heideggerian insistence on continuity and context is the insistence that objects as we experience them are as much a function of experience as mind or consciousness is. Objects, like mind or reason, are engendered, come into being, and are always in the making, just as the world is unfinished and in the making. If reason is a function rather than an entity, it itself is in a state of growth and development through reasonable activity and intelligent conduct. Likewise, objects change, grow and evolve; for example, some of them become more reasonable, more meaningful, due to the effects of human interaction. Reason 'makes the world really more reasonable; it gives to it an intrinsic value'.[88]

Objects then, are no more those static, fixed, final entities existing in their true nature as absolutely independent of humans than is Dewey's evolving, changing world fixed and permanent. As we come to experience objects more rationally or aesthetically or practically, they change, and evolve into something different; our most basic characterizations of objects may change through scientific investigation or aesthetic representation. Thus, Dewey emphasized objects as processes constantly in the making, in evolution and in development, not as products fixed, determined, and final in their true nature. He utterly rejected the notion of perception as a passive receptivity of already existing, permanent object-structures, as does Derrida. Like Coleridge, Shelley, and Blake, he insisted that perception is a vitally active affair, which while practical in character, carries at its heart cognitive and aesthetic qualities.[89] Perception is not a merely passive reflex act or instinctive response. Perception at its most basic levels involves not only imaginative grasping of relations amongst objects for the sake of overcoming obstacles and adapting to changes, as Coleridge and Shelley tirelessly emphasized. It is also fundamentally aesthetic.[90] Perception is itself saturated with intellectual and aesthetic material, and as such cannot be viewed as antithetical to thought, since 'thoughtful' selection of stimuli and choice of courses of behaviour are basic to it.

We do not, then, divide perception and thought into two distinct aspects or phases of experience, but recognize in experience varying degrees of thoughtfulness and imaginative response. Thus Dewey contrasted, for example, the 'crude subject matter in primary experience and the refined, derived objects of reflection'.[91] No dualism is suggested here, not is any aboriginal stuff of general experience even implicit. To repeat: 'The distinction is one between what is experienced as the result of a minimum of incidental reflection and what is experienced in consequence of continued and regulated reflective enquiry.'[92] Reflection and intelligence are involved at all levels in the discrimination of objects. Moreover, the so-called secondary objects, when referred back to primary, cruder objects, explain and enrich the more primary levels of experience. They are thereby actually altered and enriched. Objects are then grasped with greater understanding, or imbued with more meaning, instead of merely being had *via* sense contact, containing a minimum of awareness or appreciation. So-called secondary and primary objects and experience are continuous with each other and with nature. Things, objects, acquire new properties as a result of systematic reflection and imaginative enquiry, and then actually become new objects. There are no basic, stable, 'crude' objects that are then refined or ornamented by language or thought, as James had already pointed out (see pp. 85–90). The most basic, crude 'objects' are subject to change and evolution, because they are the result of selection of stimuli according to the needs, concerns, and interests of the organism. These objects are better understood as processes, temporarily concretized into stable, apparently fixed objects for certain aims and purposes. That is, what is going on or happening, the processes and course of natural events, could have been broken up into different objects had our needs and aims been other than they are.

Nor for Dewey is there any sense in talking of a basic content of sense qualities which provides us with some stable, crude material. Not only are sense qualities sifted and selected by the organism, noticed or not noticed; they have the same status as relations and connections, which are equally an immediate part of the field of experience.[93] They do not form the solid content of mind, but rather the social character of meaning forms the solid content of mind.

For Dewey, experience is characterized by a variety of generic traits, none of them reducible to the same one, ultimate, crude content or substance out of which all else evolves. The world is irreducibly plural. Any attempt to force overall unity when there are only limited examples of unity will involve the denial of some basic trait or traits of experience and existence. There is no more any truly real, fixed, irreducible, solid matter or 'somewhat' of crude sense experience than there are 'states of mind known in their very presence' (a comment Derrida might have made, so close is the terminology).[94] To ask, 'What is the stuff that impinges on the mind, that it selects and relates and organizes, that limits the constructive function of thought in contrast to idealism', is a question that arises only because a dualistic assumption has already been made unconsciously, namely that mind is an entity already constituted and outside of the world it experiences. If mind comes into being as the world it experiences comes into being, if the two are functions, not stable, exclusive entities, then no such question arises. Once it does arise, it is unanswerable without doing violence to the nature of experience, if experience is viewed in a genuinely empirical, unbiased way. There is no pre-existing mind in need of some stuff to act upon. Mind evolves as a result of organized biological activities; indeed, it *is* those activities at a highly systematic and complex level.

The Rejection of Idealism

Yet, we ask, did the world, the environment in which the human organism acts, exist before it or did it not? This question, reasonable as it seems, also has a hidden dualistic assumption, namely that the environment, the world, is something fixed and static set over against humans, who eventually appear in this already established scheme of things. If we recognize that experience shows us a world in the making, partly making, and being made by, humans, then we need not be trapped in such blind alleys and puzzles. Everywhere we have evidence of past events, but those events exist as events with meanings that arise only in the course of human interaction. There are no original basic events preceding the human organism. As Dewey argued, 'a bare event is no event. *Something* happens. What it is is only found out by study'.[95] When we say the world really exists apart from thought or human organisms, we mean that thought and humans and mentality are only some of the traits of natural events, which also include non-organic traits and objects without mentality. These traits limit and circumscribe the extent to which thinking organisms influence natural events. Moreover, when we say the world existed prior to humankind, we mean that we have evidence everywhere that had organisms like humans been present, they would have found a world somewhat like the world we see evolving further today. To say that natural events occur and that a world exists independent of human involvement is to say no more than that. If we go on to conclude from that the metaphysical assumption that matter is more fundamental than mind, or that the mind encounters an essentially already ordered world, then we err. For we forget that all our concepts of world, order, natural events, existence, and matter, are human ways of thinking that we have no business projecting into past eternity.[96] That is, all the attributes with which we imbue the world, including world and existence, may be seen as always having been true, *once you come to think of it.* The world – not mind – dictates what attributes are true, once the mind considers them at all; the stars are such and such, the laws of gravity are so and so, and not due to thought exactly. Yet they are also genuine ways of making meaning of things, and as such, are physical, intellectual, aesthetic, or moral additions to a world that before now was only implicitly or virtually these things. Neither science nor mathematics can be said to have 'been forced upon the mind *ab extra*';[97] our own aims, interests, needs, and concerns have much to do with the construction of both.[98] Dewey remarked, in a Nietzschean vein, 'there is assuredly something *a priori* – that is to say native, unlearned, original – in human experience, that something is not knowledge, but is activities made possible by established connections of neurones'.[99] Dewey went on to discuss even the most fundamental qualities of experience – paraphrasing William James before him and rejecting the notion of necessary truths or universal categories:

> many of our most important modes of perception and conception of the world or sensible objects are not the cumulative products of particular experience, but rather original biological sports, spontaneous variations, which are maintained because of their applicability to concrete experiences after once having been created. Number, space, time, resemblance and other important 'categories' could have been brought into existence . . . , [James] says, as a consequence of some cerebral instability, but they could by no means have been registered on the mind by outside influence. Many significant and useless concepts also arise in the same manner. But the fundamental categories have been cumulatively extended and reinforced because of their value when applied to concrete instances and things of experience.[100]

If an obnoxious and disturbing relativity seems to be the conclusion of such a criticism of metaphysics and a pragmatic reappraisal of experience, Dewey argued that relativity does not mean something regrettable:

> That red, or far and near, or hard and soft, or big and little involves a relation between organism and environment, is no more an argument for idealism than is the fact that water involves a relation

between hydrogen and oxygen. It is, however, an argument for the ultimately practical value of these distinctions – that they are *differences* made in what things would have been without organic behaviour – differences made not by 'consciousness' or 'mind', but by the organism as the acting centre of a system of activities. Moreover, the whole agnostic sting of the doctrine of relativity lies in the assumption that the ideal or aim of knowledge is to repeat or copy a prior existence – in which case, of course, the making of contemporaneous differences by the organism in the very fact of awareness would get in the way and forever hinder the knowledge function from the fulfilment of its proper end. Knowledge awareness, in this case, suffers from an impediment which no surgery can better. But if the aim of knowing be precisely to carry on to *favourable* issue, by the readjustment of the organism, certain changes going on indifferently in the environment, then the fact that the changes of the organism enter pervasively into the subject matter of awareness is no restriction or perversion of knowledge, but part of the fulfilment of its office.[101]

Dewey warned us that from the postulates about experience of such a pragmatic empiricism as described in this chapter (for example, things are what they are experienced to be, and every experience is something) nothing can be deduced. The value of such empiricism lies rather in the recommended method of philosophical analysis, namely, to go to experience to see what things are experienced as and to find out what words like subjective, objective, mind, and matter mean. The empirical method suggested here gives no solutions, Dewey wrote, to God, freedom, immortality, ultimate reality, or the true nature of mind or matter. Yet it might supply us with a way of telling what these things mean, if anything. And, as Berkeley noted, this is the first step (and often the last) in clearing up otherwise interminable philosophical quibbles.

6

Jacques Derrida: Deconstructing Metaphysics

Derrida's deconstructive project can be approached from several different directions, many of which impinge upon and clarify romanticism, as well as pragmatists' concerns. One can begin by focusing upon Derrida's comments about language as the condition of human consciousness, an issue which Dewey had explored in *Experience and Nature* (see below chapter 8). Familiar themes, such as speech versus writing, rhetoric versus logic, the analysis of Saussure's and structuralists' views of language, and Wittgenstein's philosophy of language, articulate issues which Derrida's precursors engaged with in their own individual styles. This focus will lead directly into, firstly, Derrida's critique of dualism and metaphysics (that is, his deconstruction of such notions that language 'represents' a non-linguistic ground); secondly, his critique regarding the positing of origins, presences, signifieds, Being, and other transcendent unifiers; and, finally, his discussions about the concepts of truth, trace, differance, pure perception, and others. This initial analysis of traditional philosophical projects will relate Derrida closely to previous critiques of metaphysics, and leads to an application to practical problems of a literary critical nature, namely, the reading and interpretation of texts. What Derrida meant by intertextuality, free play, interpretations, and decoding will be examined, implying close relations with some pragmatic and romantic concepts. Derrida's anti-formalist, anti-hermeneutic, anti-structuralist activities will also be examined, along with his questioning of the dichotomy between ordinary language and figurative language, his analysis of meaning in texts as non-referential, his 'absurd' claim that everything is a text ('there is nothing outside the text'), and his relation to other theorists such as Barbara Johnson, Hillis Miller, and Hartman. Some suggestions of how to read Derrida's texts, how to avoid the pitfalls of taking him literally, how to avoid reading his polemics as dogma, how to come to terms with his style, and what some of the 'rules' of the new games are that he is proposing will be discussed in relation to romanticism and pragmatism.

In his essay 'Differance' (in *Speech and Phenomena*, and other collections), Derrida attributed to Saussure the notion that language is not a function of the speaking subject, but that, paradoxically, self-consciousness, 'subjectness', or the subject, is rather a function of language: 'the subject . . . is inscribed in the language'. Moreover, not just the speaking subject (the signifying subject) is inscribed in language, but the subject in the full sense. It is not even possible to conceive of a presence and a self-presence of the subject qua subject before speech or its signs, 'a subject's self-presence in a silent and intuitive consciousness'.[1] Derrida deconstructed the notion that something such as consciousness is possible, some pure self-presence, prior to language or speech, outside of signs. Like Dewey and Wittgenstein, he rejected the definition of consciousness as such self-presence, and insisted that subject, self-consciousness, and presence are only the other side, the difference, of object and not something substantial in themselves: these words express already a relation, a function to 'the other' – whose likeness is only a relation, a difference.

Derrida denied, however, that he destroyed the subject. He insisted that it is absolutely indispensable; rather, he explained, he 'situates it'.[2] Like Dewey, he emphasized that the subject is a function, not an independent being; its reality is as a function, as a relation – not as a substance or an independent centre or origin of perception or consciousness. Consciousness arises out of language use, as does the consciousness of being a subject, and even the 'reality' of the subject, as Shelley had argued before. We do not become conscious, even through language, of an already constituted subject, origin, or self-presence. The subject, the centre, are gradually, historically constituted and evolved by language use, as Dewey had explained.[3] Language, then, is, in Heidegger's terms, the house of being, not a tool for expressing being.[4] It is the context of being, the place, so to speak, where being dwells. In Shelley's and Nietzsche's words, the self is a figure or effect of language, and (as Wittgenstein had maintained) all awareness is a linguistic affair. Dewey had similarly emphasized that human experience is irreducibly linguistic; as Derrida suggested, experience becomes experience only when it is uttered:

> experience is inseparable from the field of the mark, which is to say, from the network of effacement and of difference, of units of iterability . . . the very iterability which constituted their identity

does not permit them ever to be a unity that is identical to itself, there is no experience consisting of pure presence but only of chains of differential marks.[5]

This pure presence, this Cartesian cogito, this Husserlian pure intentionality is put by Derrida 'under erasure' (its meaning and reality as a useful concept is questioned, not denied). The cogito is instead said to be not a substance, or soul independent of objects, of the world, or of language, but rather a relation in a system of functions, relations, or differences.[6]

In Derrida's objection to the secondary status given to writing against speech, this denial of the intelligibility of the notion of pure presence is reiterated. Writing is not merely a supplement to a speech which is to be understood as more closely situated to the original subject, the pure presence of thought, than writing itself can ever be. Writing is not encumbered with a distance from perception that speech avoids. Rather, Derrida's insistence that writing is 'always already' there, his replacement of semiology with grammatology, his reversal of the priority of speech and writing is a polemical device. He insisted thereby that speech is infected by the same secondarity, the same supplementary character as writing, because there is no pure thought, perception, or pure self-presence to which speech has better access than writing. The secondarity ascribed only to writing affects all signifieds, including speech.[7] Speech has no privileged access, over writing, to some private language or interior realm, to some more real monologue of thoughts, because there is no such pure interiority. There is no 'full presence', no pure self that speech has direct access to, for the self is itself a 'text', a result of language, a 'figure of speech'. Derrida agreed with Wittgenstein that there is no private language and no something in our minds to which speech refers, or which makes speech have sense. (His critique of Plato's texts on the speech/writing relation may be an example of polemical 'misreading'.)[8]

The rejection of the anteriority of speech over writing is another way of expressing Derrida's desire to deconstruct the notion that language is meaningful by reference to some non-linguistic reality, to external objects, or to some transcendental signified. He took up Wittgenstein's project of constant concern with what it means to mean something, what the conditions of a statement's having sense are. Wittgenstein had latterly denied that sense depends on words being correlated either with the objects they 'stand for', or with something in our minds such as thoughts or ideas or mental representations or intentionalities of some kind. On the contrary, he rejected the notion that sense depends on reference; indeed, he rejected, as did Derrida later, the idea that sense and reference are two absolutely distinct modes. First, Wittgenstein showed that a proposition's having sense depends upon other propositions being accepted as 'true' by a community of speakers, and this truth involves not reference to or representation of (correspondence to) some ground that is non-linguistic, some external substance or reality. This truth involves human agreement about what we do, which is what makes language possible. That is, meaning depends upon use, upon the human context, upon convention, as Dewey had argued. This agreement involves not an agreement about our opinions as to the so-called content of language, so much as about our activities in playing what Wittgenstein referred to as 'language games'. Moreover, there is a plurality, a multiplicity of ways in which language makes sense, has meaning; a plurality, that is, of ways in which we use language. There are numerous language games, not just one. All language, then, does not have sense in the same way. Reference of word to object is never, Wittgenstein maintained, the deciding factor, since our language games can only be played if agreement takes place, agreement in 'forms of life' in his technical terms. The phrase 'forms of life' suggests conventions of behaviour, that is, activities of human communities.[9]

As C. S. Peirce had suggested decades earlier, there is no ground of non-signification that can be conceived as a foundation for signs and language. Nor is language a tool for the communication of already existing, independent, determinate meanings. Such meanings only come into existence through language.[10] Derrida insisted that the great dream and delusion of metaphysics is that meaning is a matter of reference to some transcendental signified, to some intuitively grasped and immediately present extralinguistic reality.[11] Meaning is not present outside words and language and inside objects, thoughts, minds, ideas, or mental images; rather it is a function of the system of signs, of the language itself. Derrida challenged the intelligibility and usefulness of the notion that the meaningfulness of language resides in the attempt at representation of something else. It is a conceptual confusion to view language as representing something non-linguistic. Richard Rorty described Derrida's project as an attack upon the Kantian notion that language is a tool for representation, instead of the context for our consciousness and existence as such. Rorty denied that there is a word on the one hand and a thing denuded of words on the other, which the word is supposed to represent. But he criticized Derrida for suggesting that because the structuralist term 'sign' suggests some thing outside language (a signified), that 'trace' can substitute for it. 'Trace' also suggests something that has left a trace – a presence, an original something before the trace. Put another way, 'trace' can be hypostasized just as can be the word 'sign'. Rorty preferred Derrida's concept of 'differance', which resists such reification or subjection to a logocentric interpretation (logocentric meaning here the elevation of some principle, or 'logos', to a transcendental status, or the suggestion of a cosmic order – how things really are – accessible to reason or intuition).[12]

Derrida's concept, differance, arose in part out of his analysis of Saussure's language theory, and its insistence upon the arbitrariness and differential character of signs.[13] That is, a sign is constituted by its difference from another sign, not by reference to any substantiality, some pure, independent being, not by fullness nor by identity to some signified. Signs have meanings through a network of oppositions that relate signs to each other. There is no substance or substrate in language, or some external world to which language refers for meaningfulness. Signs are meaningful neither because they have content, substance, nor because they refer to something else that does. There are no substances in language, only oppositions – or relations. All language, whether written or spoken, is characterized by this differentiality, this fact of relationship as the only 'substance'. Language is better described as a system of functions of differences, than as a representation of some Absolute, Origin, Centre, some thing which has presence or meaning or existence outside language. Language is the play of differential sign systems. Derrida quoted Saussure, saying, 'Let us only cite Saussure where it interests us':

> The conceptual side of value is made up solely of relations and differences with respect to the other terms of language, and the same can be said of its material side. . . . Everything that has been said up to this point boils down to this: in language there are only differences. Even more important: a difference generally implies positive terms between which the difference is set up; but in language there are only differences *without positive terms*. Whether we take the signified or the signifier, language has neither ideas nor sounds that existed before the linguistic system, but only conceptual and phonic differences that have issued from the system. The idea or phonic substance that a sign contains is of less importance than the other signs that surround it.[14]

Roman Jacobson also defined meaning in language as a differential rather than a substantial system. Jakobson's binary analysis of phonemes into distinctive features showed that the phonic substance heard by the listener is no substance at all, but only a relation of opposition.[15] What is heard is arbirary, variable, relational to other sounds, not some identical sound or phonemic substance. Thus, speech is no more substantial or primary than the written word; like the written word's system of signs, the phonemes in speech are not atoms of substance that constitute and ground the speech, but only relations of difference and opposition. Thus, what is important for the meaningfulness of any sign is not some substantial phonic substance, but rather the other signs that surround and relate to it, that situate it. Language is meaningful and signifies something, not because its signs refer to some outside object signified, nor because the signs themselves carry a fixed, atomic, substantive meaning. Language signifies by virtue of differential relations and patterns established by convention; language is a 'fabric of difference'. Derrida illustrated the temptation to substantialize even this functionality, applying Nietzschean ideas:

> Differences are thus 'produced' – differed – by differance. But what differs, or who differs? In other words, what is differance? With this question we attain another stage and another source of the problem.
>
> What differs? Who differs? What is differance?
>
> If we answered these questions even before examining them as questions, even before going back over them and questioning their form (even what seems to be most natural and necessary about them), we would fall below the level we have now reached. For if we accepted the form of the question in its own sense and syntax . . . we would have to admit that differance is derived, super-venient, controlled, and ordered from the starting point of a being-present, one capable of being some thing, a force, a state, or power in the world, to which we could give all kinds of names: a what, or being-present as a subject, a who. In the latter case, notably, we would implicitly admit that the being-present (for example, as a self-present being or consciousness) would eventually result in differing: in delaying or in diverting the fulfillment of a 'need' or 'desire', or in differing from itself. But in none of these cases would such a being-present be 'constituted' by this differance.[16]

If, conventionally (by agreement of human communities), language is a system of differences which signifies by means of differential relations, and not by reference to or representation of an 'other', then interpretation of meaning and significance involves not the 'disclosure of truth as a presentation of the thing itself in its presence'. It involves, rather, a process of incessant deciphering of the endless play of interpretation, by suggesting or proposing new possible ways of agreeing about other

people's interpretations. The 'thing-in-itself', for example, and the signifying subject (the self, self-consciousness) are 'always already' interpretations or decipherings, as Dewey had said, while all experience is
interpretation. There is no collection of objective facts already existing
and to be objectively described by the tool, language. All description is
interpretation, but interpretation is not to be understood as a pre-
existent subject analysing an independent object via language. It is the
free play of a subject and object which are interrelated, which are
functions, are effects, of each other in the text of language. Subject and
object are already figures of speech, interpretations (not things-in-
themselves), which then evolve more figures of speech in an experience
that itself is interpretation and free play. Experience is not an immediate
presentation of pure object presence to a pure subject mind.

Thus, when Derrida said 'there is no such thing as perception',[17] he
was rejecting, as had Coleridge, Shelley, and the German romantics, the
conventional concept of perception as the passive, immediate receptivity
of already constituted objects. Such objects were supposed to be independent of and pre-existent to language, and received by a consciousness that itself is privileged as a being present prior to language – a
self-presence, as if 'consciousness can gather itself up in its own presence'. Consciousness is, in a sense, an effect, a determination within a
system of differences. Perception conceived of as an interpretation of
difference deconstructs the traditional, passive notion: no privilege is to
be given to some notion of immediate, innocent perception, perception
as full presence, free from the taint of interpretation, or perception as
the immediate intuition of 'the other', that object of the self, both
viewed as prior to signs and difference, and as substantive. There is no
such thing as pure perception. All perception involves interpretation, as
Samuel Johnson had implied. Perception is not representational, but
interpretive; we cannot be aware of pure immediacy, for awareness
involves differentiation, terms, relations, and therefore cannot be immediate. All perception is the recognition of patterns and relationships, not
the recognition or reception of substance or pure simples, atoms, or
sensations. Consequently, everything is, for Derrida, relationship and
differance.

Free play of interpretation, or one non-ultimate, intermediate interpretation replacing another, substitutes for the notion that one is engaged in a search for truth or the ultimate logic of things – their 'deep
structures'. Truths, Derrida said, in accord with Nietzsche, are merely
'solidified figures of speech'; truth is not to be understood as the correct
relationship between representations (signs) and the things represented. Truth, as Rorty put it in pragmatist terms, is the reinterpretation

of our predecessors' reinterpretations of their predecessors' reinterpretations. Consequently, there is no teleology here, no ontotheology – free play and reinterpretation are not directed towards the goal ultimately of finding some final, best interpretation, that structure of all interpretation. We are not in search of the right interpretation, of some absolute knowledge. Interpretation doesn't lead to these things; it leads to more interpretation, sometimes to contradictory interpretations. Writing leads to more writing, history to more history.[18]

Derrida criticized the structuralists, hermeneuticists, and formalists for seeing interpretation as ultimately teleological, instead of an endless free play. Saussure, Jakobson, Levi-Strauss, Ricoeur, and others failed, he seemed to suggest, to carry through their insights into the differential, relational character of sign-systems and the nature of interpretation.[19] Ultimately, they gave in, Derrida suggested, to the nostalgia of a presence, an origin, a substance, a ground that is already significant before language and signs. 'Differance' is Derrida's expression of the determination to avoid the search for how language looks into reality – that search for the structure of all interpretation as representations of non-represented things. With the concepts of endless free play and differance, Derrida was not, however, making the claim that meaning is totally arbitrary. Nor was he claiming that any interpretation is as correct as any other. Rather, he was suggesting that there is no final, last word about a text or about anything else, because the concept of a final commentary, a last word, is unintelligible. For any useful interpretation (any truth, pragmatically speaking) is only the opportunity for stimulating us to more interpretation, more commentary, more writing. Meanings resolve endlessly into other meanings, and we are therefore related to a changing, non-teleological historical experience, not to some ultimate, unchanging cosmic order, fixed and determined, ahistorical and outside language and experience, which we should seek to know, represent, interpret, or intuit.

Derrida rejected the temptation to settle upon a master name, a *tertium aliquid,* a unique name for what it is that differs; indeed he rejected the terms of such a statement. Nothing differs; differance is not a name: 'There is neither Being nor truth to the play of writing, insofar as it involves differance.'[20] Difference is not a new name (nor is 'trace') for some ultimate, for some essence, for an origin, centre, being, or presence – nor for any underlying substance or transcendental signified. Difference is the putting-under-erasure of these concepts, and is the first rule in a new language game that no longer asks the old questions or tries to solve the pseudo-problems of traditional philosophy, as Richard Rorty would put it. In other words:

In marking out differance, everything is a matter of strategy and risk. It is a question of strategy because no transcendent truth present outside the sphere of writing can theologically command the totality of this field. It is hazardous because this strategy is not simply one in the sense that we say that strategy orients the tactics according to a final aim, a telos or the theme of a domination, a mastery or an ultimate reappropriation of movement and fields. In the end, it is a strategy without finality. We might call it blind tactics or empirical errance, if the value of empiricism did not itself derive all its meaning from its opposition to philosophical responsibility. If there is a certain errance in the tracing-out of differance, it no longer follows the line of logico-philosophical speech or that of its integral and symmetrical opposite, logico-empirical speech. The concept of play [*jeu*] remains beyond this opposition. . . . Let us introduce ourselves to the thought of differance by way of the theme of strategy or strategem . . . the efficacy of this thematics of differance very well may, and even one day must, be sublated, i.e., lend itself, if not to its own replacement, at least to its involvement in a series of events which in fact it never commanded.[21]

According to the strategy of differance, meaning and signifying activities are the condition, not the results, of concepts and experiences of self, object, presence, being. Meaning does not supervene from without; it results, as was earlier insisted, from the linguistic rules or conventions of the 'game'. It is a result of convention and practice for Wittgenstein, and as C. S. Peirce explained, 'Use determines meaning.' There is no meaning that hovers above the play of differences, informing it and to which it refers. Meaning is, therefore, contextual, as Dewey argued tirelessly, anticipating Heidegger. It is never independent of its historical, social, human, and linguistic context, its system of reference. In Heidegger's terms, we dwell within language, not it within us.[22] Derrida argued, then against any notion of a first cause, an absolute, non-empirical, non-contextual being, meaningful in itself as a necessary element for the possibility of meaningful language.[23]

Derrida's emphasis upon interpretation and free play as the basis of meaning and significance can then be interpreted as a rejection of the traditional emphasis upon pre-existent conceptions independent of language, which devolve significance and meaning upon words and signs. If meanings are to be understood within the human context of interpretations, then the emphasis is upon usage, as Wittgenstein insisted, upon operations, human activities. Thus C. S. Peirce, Dewey, and Wittgenstein anticipated Derrida's emphasis upon the contextual nature of meaningfulness, the view of the later Wittgenstein, that language and meaning are 'always already' embedded in human activities and do not exist outside the human context. Meaning, for all these writers, arises in the role that it plays in human affairs, not in some external non-linguistic thought, intention, signified, or existent.[24] Derrida expressed this emphasis upon usage, human activity, and human context as the condition of meaning in his privileging of rhetoric over logic, contrary to western metaphysics, which had always made logic the ground and rhetoric the supplement of language meaning. Logic, he insisted with Nietzsche and Shelley, is derivative of rhetoric. By reversing this priority, Derrida reiterated the inherent metaphoricity of language and its differential character, a claim consistent with Shelley's emphasis upon metaphor. To privilege logic over rhetoric is to posit a signified whose nature or essence is independent of the nature of the sign; something pure and simple which is the ground for the meaning of signs. It is to deny the historicity of the human context and to posit an ahistorical presence which involves direct, unmediated awareness of logical structures and atoms forming the content and structure of language. Meanings are, however, significant by convention (results of rules of social games governing relations and differences and how they can be patterned) and subject to change, to historical development. They are not pre-linguistic, fixed, logical intentions, atoms, essences, or deep structures which language expresses. Hence, neither meanings nor things can be conceived apart from the signs representing them, and signs themselves are not pure simples or atomic substances, but functions and relations within a system.

These strategies of Derrida can be understood as challenges to the history of metaphysics, which he read as the continous replacement of one unique or master name, one version of presence, with another, by thinkers who had failed to note that their corrections to their predecessors' names always involved them in logocentrism, or the elevation of some principle to a transcendental status, whether consciously or unconsciously. Each thinker centred his discourse in some new way, but never managed to attend to the activity of centring itself which prohibits free play. Derrida accounted for this repetitive pattern party by suggesting that metaphysical implications (implied presences, centres, origins, transcendents, absolutes) are 'sedimented' into our language, and his task is, to use Foucault's metaphor,[25] one of desedimentation – of exposing to the light of day the concealed (unconscious) metaphysical assumptions that prevent free play. Hence, not destruction, but a deconstruction, was his programme: revealing to conscious thought the unconscious assumptions which tyrannize over our intellect, which centre our systems and posit origins that deny the differential, relational character of experience in favour of a substantialist view. Derrida proposed that we should put under erasure (not deny the existence of, but consciously question the intelligibility of) notions such as the centre or origin. We can criticize whatever displays any metaphysical presupposition incompatible with the theme of differance. Derrida sought to deconstruct, to subject to conscious questioning the assumptions of the metaphysics of presence, which have dominated the history of western thought.

Moreover, like Dewey, Derrida refused to engage with traditional philosophical (usually dualistic) problems (mind/body, sensible/intelligible, how we can know versus scepticism, the nature of reality and how language and thought represent it, and so on). Richard Rorty described Derrida's project as one of 'debunking' Kantianism and of showing us how we could look at things if the Kantian vocabulary were not embedded into the very fabric of our intellectual life.[26] Kantianism involved the search for truth about the relation between the word and the world, he argued. Derrida rejected the search as unintelligible, since word and world are interdependent; they are functions and relations meaningful within the context of language, not one within and one without. Thus, he rejected the tradition of philosophizing which questioned the relation between words and things or words and world, with the view to reaching some truth about ultimate reality, where truth means the 'correct relationship between representations and things represented'. Derrida was interested, rather, in how our signs, words, and representations interrelate, not in how they refer to some alterity, some other. Philosophers have tried in the past to represent accurately how things really are; philosophy was supposed to make clear to the human gaze something fixed, unchanging, and atemporally, eternally true. Derrida proposed that philosophy is yet another version of literature, a literary text to be interpreted, and not a science searching for truth. Indeed, science is literary, too, in that it offers new models and metaphors for interpreting the book of nature (as Berkeley had demonstrated centuries earlier with his essays on vision). The promise in science of an ultimate, true description or interpretation of nature or reality is as delusory as it is in philosophy or in literature, if we imagine that any text could have a single, true meaning or interpretation. Like Samuel Johnson, Derrida and Dewey insisted that our object of investigation is not a thing-in-itself, but is the received opinion that constitutes objects of experience, and then the reinterpretations of that received opinion.

Rorty, however, cautioned us against imagining that Derrida makes positive claims. He does not, Rorty insisted, claim that language is *not* a system of representations; he does not claim that philosophy is not an effort to understand how representation and knowledge are possible. Rather, Derrida implied that such questions and problems are unintelligible, uninteresting, and contain contradictory assumptions. He queried such pseudo-problems as the claim that objects exist prior to words, that consciousness exists prior to language, that signifieds are absolutely independent of signs, and so on. Languages can, for certain limited purposes, be viewed as representational. Yet we risk metaphysical errors when we imagine that we can arrive at some eternal, absolutely true answer. Rorty argued that for Derrida one can only talk about the usefulness and intelligibility of specific ways of looking at language, not about whether language is really, ultimately a system of representations, a view of reality, or whatever. Derrida analysed the motives behind our past obsessions with representation, epistemology, and ontotheology (the positing of a transcendental, teleological being).[27]

In 'Structure, sign, and play', Derrida exposed the unintelligibility of the metaphysics of presence in terms of the centre. 'Centre' refers again to a transcendental being meaningful prior to any language-system or sign-system. Derrida insisted that to deconstruct such implicit metaphysics, we must play with the notion of a structure without a centre, which, he said, represents the unthinkable itself. Yet centre is itself also a contradictory, unintelligible notion, for in all centred structures of western metaphysics, the centre itself escapes structurality and is seen as unique. Contradictorily, it is both within and without the structure. It is at the centre, yet not a part of the structure: 'center is not center'. That is, the concept of centre, origin, presence, or absolute is unintelligible. The history of metaphysics is the history of the metaphors and metonomies that were the different forms or names of centres substituted for previous centres. Metaphysics itself cannot escape the centred structure. Derrida proposed a 'rupture', a breach, with this repetitive game of substitution of one kerygmatic name for another. He proposed a new game, a new project, namely to cease offering new metaphors for centre, and to reflect instead upon the 'law that governs the desire for the center that was never itself, always already transported outside itself in its surrogate'.[28] Presence is never present to us: it is always absent, because unreachable, transcendental, yet it is allegedly present in some realm beyond experience, yet it is present to us in vitiated, incomplete non-plenitude.

Derrida asked us to rethink the concept of such a centre, to reject its meaning as being-present, since it is contradictory and unintelligible when subjected to reflection. He asked us to think of centre as a relative function, a relation, which has no fixed locus, as Shelley had urged; it is always on the move within the structure or system. Yet, if we do this, if we give up the notion of a central signified that is transcendent and originary, present before reflection or language, then everything becomes discourse. The centre always was conceived as prior to language, as the transcendental signified with one or another kerygmatic names. If this centre, this signified-prior-to-the-sign notion is relinquished, language becomes the context for experience as decentred structure, as Dewey argued (see chapter 8). Once we reject the centre, the sign-independent signified, we are left only with signs. By decentring the structure, by freeing ourselves of the notion of a non-representative ground of our signs (representations), Derrida argued that the opportunity for free play of interpretation is opened up, as he demonstrated so vividly in *Glas*, 'Living On: BORDERLINES', and in other of his most playful writings. As long as the absolute signified retained authority, signs were restricted to accurate representations of it. Only by erasing this centre can genuinely free interpretation occur, by which we mean that all propositions and signs are conventionally meaningful as relations, differences, and functions of other propositions and signs. Moreover, the rules of the games of language and interpretation are not limited by the structure of an absolute reality, but rather are determined by conventional agreement and are subject to free play, to change, and development. Illusions of stability and certainty are given up for the notion of the freedom and responsibility to interpret, and the infinite regress of interpretation, never leading to some stable, certain, final interpretaion. All conclusions, then, are provisional and inconclusive, all origins are relative origins subject to shiftings. Moreover, signs always lead to other signs: the play of signs refers to nothing other, but only to other signs. Signs are not means to meanings as ends. Or, as Derrida explained regarding Nietzsche, a thematic of active interpretation substitutes an incessant deciphering in place of the disclosure of truth as a presentation of the thing itself.

This challenge to metaphysics, along with the concepts of differance and trace, expose, moreover, the fallacy of the dualism that underlay all western philosophy, as Dewey, James, and Coleridge had shown. When we put a concept under erasure, we deny its independent existence, we insist that it is meaningful only as an opposition, only, that is, in relation to its opposite. Differance posits terms as in binary opposition, with each as an accomplice of the other. Thus, all distinctions and oppositions are provisional and relative, and not primary. Every concept's meaning involves its opposite; thus there is identity in difference. Presence, Derrida suggested, is merely the deferral of absence; it is nothing in itself, not independent or pure. Its substance or meaning is only differential and relational. What Derrida meant by the 'economy of difference' was that one concept is involved essentially in its opposite, both deferred and differing from the other. The sign, for example, is the signified deferred. Sign and signified are interchangeable: neither has any priority or primacy over the other. The ablility to turn signifieds (socalled facts, events, things) into signs of other events, facts, or things, is a measure of intelligence, as Dewey would argue. Intelligence is a deconstructed hermeneutics, a taking relative presences for signs of present absence, but without assigning absolute priority to any presence or absence, without trying to fix any one signified over all others. For all signifieds become signs when used intelligently.

One can connect these primarily philosophic, linguistic concerns to literary theory and practice by noting Derria'a polemical argument that all language is figurative 'from the beginning': all words are metaphorical. Rhetoric precedes logic, not vice versa. Figures of speech are not derived from a literal, objective, scientific language base. They are not mere ornaments and decorations on a fundamentally literal language. As Stanley Fish suggested, there is no plain, ordinary language, no logical language at the base of figurative speech.[29] On the contrary, logic is only a type of rhetoric and metaphoricity (and it, too, is a figure of speech). Indeed, the notions of literal language and plain speech are themselves both figures of speech, or 'dead metaphors', as Shelley was fond of calling them. The notion that logic precedes rhetoric, that there is a literal, logical, base language, to which can be added figures of speech as ornaments, is rejected. For it is based upon the unintelligible and contradictory notion that signs refer to ideas that are timeless and have semantic (meaningful) content independent of the signs: there are ideas to which signs refer which have meaning without reference to contexts of communication, without reference to the 'stream of life' or to 'forms of life'. Ideas are assumed to stand in a logical relation to each other prior to language or human contexts or usage, which the sign seeks to represent. These signs and ideas are radically disparate entities, and, on the view of logic as prior to rhetoric, the delusion that language is meaningful referentially to non-lingustic entities arises again.

It is assumed that meaning is independent of use; sense and reference are absolutely distinct aspects of a sign. In *Speech and Phenomena*, Derrida, like Wittgenstein, Dewey, and Peirce before him insisted that meaning and use – sense and reference – are inextricably intertwined. This position is another restatement of Quine's rejection of *a priori* statements and of the analytic/synthetic distinction, the latter type of proposition involving context-dependent signs and statements, the former involving alleged context-free statements and signs, such as are imagined to be logical, timeless, and transcendent to human use and concerns. Quine explained that such analytic statements are better understood as synthetic statements which a community is hesitant to give up because to do so would involve a vast and radical reordering of a large portion of its less central, synthetic, agreed truths. Analytic, like logical terms and propositions, are only a type of synthetic (rhetorical) proposition – namely, the type that, by agreement and convention, plays a central role in our human usage and activities at the present time.[30]

Deconstruction involves putting under erasure the apparent referentiality of language and of texts, in order to focus upon their figurative, metaphorical, rhetorical nature. If language is 'always already' figurative and rhetorical, then the notion that it refers in order to mean is unintelligible. For reference involves the logical, the literal, while figuration involves the play of relations of one sign or word to another. That is, 'rhetorical' signifies the role words play in human activities, in human use; human context is the condition for meaning. Figures of speech result from human usages and activities of relating signs to signs; logic is better understood as figures of speech solidified by means of implicit communal agreement. Thus, logic, like even the most hallowed scientific and mathematical propositions, is subject to revision; it too is a product of history and prone to development. Moreover, for Derrida, since all writing is figurative to some extent, all writing can also be said to be fiction. There is no qualitative distinction between fact and fiction, for fact is merely a species of fiction, as logic is a species of rhetoric. Facts, like Nietzsche's truths, are solidified figures of speech, dead metaphors. Fact and fiction, like literature and science or history, are not absolutely distinct categories. History and science are alleged to be genres of literature, of fiction. They use models and metaphors freely, though they repress and deny this, and are interpretations, not objective, neutral description. For they, like interpretations of literary texts, are subject to revision, change, and replacement. Language understood as fictional, as figurative, is not merely a tool for the communication of determinate meanings, as the positivists would have it, for there are no determinate meanings to put into words. Thus literature and literary criticism are no longer absolutely distinct genres; both are fictional, both are figurative, as the German romantics insisted two hundred years ago. Criticism is itself, Derrida showed, subject to interpretation, and is characterized by the richness and inexhaustibility of meaning, *aporiae*, and figurations natural to 'literature' and to language generally. The difference between criticism and literature is one of relationship, of function, not one of substance,[31] as each is embedded in the other, like the conscious in the unconscious, the rational in the irrational.

Derrida set up the opposition between the text (writing, interpretation, play) and the book in order to illustrate the unintelligibility of language conceived as, first, a logic which is then overlaid by rhetoric. The book is conceived as something fixed, final, a unity or totality essentially independent of anything else. It is an object with an organic unity, in the sense of a fixed structure and a centre of meaning, not organic in the Coleridgean and Jamesian sense of growth. Its fixed, centred meaning can be searched out by careful reading, and it is the project of the critic to do precisely that, to find the meaning of the book. The book is conceived as a thing-in-itself, not essentially dependent on its relation to other books or to readers for its meaning. It is a totality, fixed, unchanging, ahistorical. There can be a last word about the book, a final commentary or best interpretation of it, because its meaning involves representation of some reality to which it refers. The book is a kind of writing that seeks truth.

The text, on the other hand, is profoundly determined by other texts. It is not some totality with a fixed, determinable meaning; it has no core content, no presence to which it refers for truth or meaning; indeed, it has neither a single meaning nor a specifiable plurality of meanings. Such a text, as Derrida conceived it, is not a thing-in-itself, the way the book is. The text is not organically unified into one best unity or structure behind its textured surface, one univocal form, as the structuralists, formalists, and hermeneuticists would have it. A text, as opposed to a book, is meaningful, like signs, in relation to other texts, not as it refers to something outside the text, such as life, or history (for these are shot through with textuality too, and not prior to it). Signs are understood as meaningful in their differences and relations to other signs, and not in themselves, as substances. Likewise, texts are meaningful in their relations and differences to other texts. As Bloom explained, all texts are readings or interpretations of previous texts under the anxiety of influence.[32] Likewise, criticism is the reading and interpretation of previous criticism (received opinion), also under the anxiety of influence. The object of criticism is not the objective text-in-itself, as Samuel Johnson had already noted. It is the received opinion (previous interpretation and criticism) about it that passes for the text. Poems, critical texts, novels, all are saturated by interpretations and critical layers of opinion, and are not accessible to the reader in some pure form freed from the accretion of opinion, nor even freed from the opinion and interpretation that arises on a fresh reading of a new text. The boundary between literature and criticism, description and interpretation, is 'under erasure'. Criticism is understood as a genre of literature, and literature itself is not a pure art, because saturated with criticism and interpretation.

There is no pure work of art floating above interpretation to be experienced purely and aesthetically, just as there is no pure perception or self-presence. Perception, whether of objects or of works of art, is not pure, immediate or unspoiled; perception of all kinds involves interpretation.

As Richard Rorty argued in relation to Derrida, writing is about texts and about the interpretation of texts. It is not about extralinguistic reality. Only books are about extralinguistic things; yet the concept of book is unintelligible. Texts comment on other texts, texts are always changing, growing, developing in meaning, they have a history, and have no end or origin. There is no last word, no true explanation or meaning of the text. There are only provisional interpretations and temporary resting places. When Derrida wrote, 'there is nothing outside the text', he was speaking polemically, denying that texts are meaningful insofar as they accurately represent something else: 'active interpretation . . . substitutes an incessant deciphering for the disclosure of truth as presentation of the thing in its presence. . . . What results is a cipher without truth, or at least a system of ciphers that is not dominated by truth value, which only then becomes a function that is understood, inscribed and circumscribed'.[33]

In *Of Grammatology*, Derrida went on to propose that 'reading . . . cannot legitimately transgress the text toward something other than it, toward the referent (a reality that is metaphysical, historical, psychological) or toward a signifier outside the text, whose content could take place, could have taken place, outside of language'.[34] Like the sign, the text refers to other texts; its meaning resides in its rhetorical character, its irreducible textuality, not in referentiality to non-textual things. We mistake these quotations, and Derrida's pithy summation, that there is nothing outside the text, if we take 'text' in a narrow, conventional sense. Texts – such as poems, novels, and essays – do refer to self, experience, world, objects, but only as the latter are conceived as themselves saturated by textuality, as existing within the context of language, textuality, and literature, as themselves figures of speech. Conceived as substantive and independent of language, texts do not refer to them, because they are unintelligible notions. Referentiality is a word that need not be taken as reference only to extra-linguistic presence, to non-textual centres, to logical structures existing prior to textuality. Referentiality is understood by Derrida not as referring to some absolute alterity, but as intertextual: as signs refer only to other signs, so texts refer only to other texts, but the word sign includes the signified, as text includes the world. For the latter term is understood as itself textual, not pre-linguistic, as residing within the context of human language activity.

In explanation of Derrida's concept of intertextuality, Schneidau quoted Wofflein in saying that 'all paintings owe more to other paintings than to nature. The art of painting is in its rendering, precisely in its representation, not in what it takes for a subject'.[35] In discussing the concepts of intertextuality and interpretation as free play, Derrida suggested the creative role of the reader as a kind of author, as had Barthes and Coleridge. The reader is not merely a passive perceiver and recipient of the author's or the text's autonomous meaning. Her primary aim is not to cleanse her subjective spectacles so she can get to the text-in-itself. To this delusory, unintelligible objectivity one need not imagine our only alternative to be a solipsistic subjectivism, however. Even if one decries as unintelligible the notion of a final, true, or best reading, subjectivism is hardly the result. These points will be taken up more explicitly in the discussion of Dewey's theory of criticism, but one can argue that if objectivity in criticism be an intelligible concept, it cannot mean accurate representation of a non-linguistic signified. Objectivity involves, rather, a community of agreement about relations and differences in a language game, an agreement that is subject to repeated change.

If one is to avoid the frequent errors that critics of deconstruction fall into (some criticism is clearly based on genuine misunderstanding), one needs to read Derrida's statements not as dogmatic or literal truths, but as stylistically innovative and polemical, heuristic devices to draw our attention to words and concepts that we have failed adequately to reflect upon. Hence, we have been blinded to their inconsistencies and unintelligibility. If we take Derrida literally, we may become enmeshed in idealist, metaphysical claims, but if we emphasize the heuristic, polemical nature of his writings, we can get much more insight from them. We need to keep questioning all the answers and interpretations we come up with regarding Derrida. For he sought to expose every final reading as just more interpretation:

> If Derrida is on the right track in his post-Grammatology treatment of philosophical texts, . . . the Kantian versus non-Kantian contrast now appears as that between the man who wants to take (and see) things as they are, and thus make sure that the right pieces go in the right holes, and the man who wants to change the vocabulary presently used of isolating pieces and holes. . . . Unspeakable possibilities, unmentionable acts are those which are spoken and mentioned in the new, revolutionary, Hegelian, abnormal vocabulary. . . . To think [of philosophy as a kind of writing] is to stop trying to have a philosophy of language which is 'first

philosophy,' a view of all possible views . . . the attempt to divinize oneself by seeing in advance the terms in which all possible problems are to be set. . . . Derrida's point is that no one can make sense of the notion of a last commentary, a last discussion note, a good piece of writing which is more than the occasion for a better piece.[36]

Derrida challenged humanist notions that art is the great purveyor of human experience; he challenged formalist notions of a single order, unity, or univocal meaning at some level of the text, notions of the autonomous literary text and the notion of an essence to literariness, all notions that traditional criticism had failed to scrutinize adequately. He challenged the hermeneutic nostalgia for some ultimate origin or truth that it might decipher, so that hermeneutics 'lives like an exile the necessity of interpretation'.[37] He described deconstruction as the other, which

is no longer turned toward the origin, affirms freeplay and tries to pass beyond man and humanism, the name man being the name of that being who, throughout the history of metaphysics or of ontotheology – in other words, through the history of all of his history – has dreamed of full presence, the reassuring foundation, the origin and the end of the game.[38]

These two alternatives are not unlike the alternatives between the weak textualist and the strong textualist that Rorty described; he concluded that deconstruction taken to its logical, radical conclusions, is a thoroughgoing pragmatism. (But this is to underestimate the vital importance of Derrida's revolution in vocabulary, genre, and style.) Rorty read Derrida heuristically, and polemically, emphasizing Derrida's efforts to deconstruct Kantianism as well as so-called serious, logical, literal discourse, supposedly essentially free from figurative elements, that writing which seeks truth, is non-literary, which eschews metaphor, wit, and pun. According to Rorty, Derrida challenged the notion that writing gets in the way of pure presence, of a vision of reality, and replaced the notion that writing should seek truth with the idea that writing should stimulate further writing:

Consider Derrida as trying . . . to create a new thing for writing to be about – not the world, but texts. Books tell the truth about things. Texts comment on other texts, and we should stop trying to test texts for accuracy of representation. . . . He doesn't want to

write a book about the nature of language; he wants to play with
the texts which other poeple have thought they were writing about
language.[39]

Deconstruction is not even a rhetorical science of truth, for it destroys its
own basic axiom, namely, that rhetoric is the 'essence' of language.[40] For
Derrida and other deconstructors, texts contain both the traditional
materials of metaphysics and the subversion of these materials. Consequently, deconstruction is not to be understood as a destruction of the
tradition, nor as a destructuring of the structure of a text; it is rather 'a
demonstration that the text has already dismantled itself'.[41] As Hillis
Miller explained, deconstruction reaches its own *aporia*, or impasse,
since it can never offer interpretations that do not need to be
deconstructed in their turn.[42] This is hardly an impasse; it is, on the
contrary, the invitation to keep on passing beyond to new activities, new
games, new free play. It is true that we are caught within *bricolage*, 'the
necessity of borrowing one's concepts from the text of a heritage which
is more or less coherent or ruined'.[43] (Quine used a similar metaphor in
Two Dogmas of Empiricism, when he invoked the image of rebuilding a
ship in mid-ocean.) Metaphysical assumptions may be cemented into
our language, but we can expose those sediments to light, and become
conscious of them, instead of being unconsciously mastered and vic-
timized by them. Derrida further cautioned us:

> What I want to emphasize is simply that the passage beyond
> philosophy does not consist in turning the page of philosophy
> (which usually comes down to philosophizing badly), but in
> continuing to read philosophers *in a certain way*.[44]

Reading Derrida confronts us with still another fascinating event,
namely, how are we to interpret the history of western philosophy? Are
we always to interpret it as naively logocentric, or can we deconstruct that
interpretation too, and read philosophical texts in that 'certain way'
which suggests sophisticated critiques of logocentrism? That is, we can
change the story of the history of philosophy, and suggest that we read
it not as one endless series of substitutions for the old logocentrisms, but
as deconstructive of prior texts as is Derrida. Or, as Dewey put it, he, like
Shelley, read Plato's *Dialogues* not as the dogmatic, idealist system, but as
the restless, searching, open-ended speculation that was not conven-
iently fitted into university syllabuses. Coleridge read Berkeley similarly,
and Yeats was equally scathing of reduction of philosophical texts to
closed systems. Kojève rewrote the interpretation of Hegel's texts, as

handed down by systematizing readers, too. In any case, Derrida's own story about western philosophy is a fiction designed not to be taken literally, nor the last word on Plato, Hegel, or Kant. As Plato said, the true philosopher plants in the soul of his listener 'words, which instead of remaining barren, contain a seed whence new words grow up in new characters.'[45] So much for the newness of 'dissemination'.

7

Coleridge's Attack on Dualism

In this chapter we examine how Coleridge, like Dewey, James, and Derrida, deconstructed the accepted metaphysics of western thought by attacking the dualisms at the centre.[1] These thinkers were also concerned to reveal the consequences of such a deconstruction for our beliefs about language and art.[2] Theories about art and literature, and their appreciation, are shown to relate closely to some philosophical position, whether conscious or unconscious, while a theory of criticism must engage with the question of methodology (or method of enquiry) if it is to be intelligible. In the context of the background of chapters one, two, and three, the following exposition, suggestive of the various interrelations – the similarities and differences, especially in vocabulary – between Coleridge and these other three groups of thinkers will, it is hoped, clarify their thinking on issues of interest today, as we continue to struggle with the insoluble problem of improving opinion into knowledge via sound enquiry on the one hand, and via imaginative creation on the other, the two being interdependent for Coleridge, Dewey, and Derrida.[3]

Coleridge's questioning of the metaphysical and epistemological tradition occurs in specifically philosophical contexts, while Shelley, Blake, Keats, and most of the German romantics (except Solger) wrote more from an aesthetically emphasized orientation. The latter do reveal a thoroughgoing jettisoning of the dualisms underpinning traditional western thought, however, in their sophisticated attitudes to language, art, and experience generally. Blake, with the 'Marriage of Heaven and Hell', for example, Shelley, with his theories of metaphor, and his apocalyptic vision of experience and the universe as one great poem, and Keats, with his fusion of thought and feeling and his concepts of negative capability, and of 'vision' as the source of truth (rather than 'consecutive reasoning'), all suggest a rejection of the tyranny of 'Urizen' over the senses or the imagination, and connect these romantic poets with Dewey, James, and Derrida. Dewey, moreover, was steeped in romanticism, to the extent that his aesthetic treatise, *Art as Experience*, is as nearly a systematization of romantic insights into art and æsthetics as we have available, albeit wonderfully enriched and informed by Dewey's own original perspective, his innovative vocabulary, an historical sense learned from Hegel, and his naturalistic orientation.[4] Nearly four out of five names mentioned in *Art as Experience* are romantics, and even when he does not expressly name one of these precursors, their own central concepts and even explicit modes of expression are shaping Dewey's thoughts.

First, one may examine Coleridge's deconstruction of western metaphysics (having discussed in chapter 3 the central methodological issues that informed romantic theory) and relate it to pragmatist and deconstructionist ideas, confusing and often misleading as the differences in terminology may be. Through these early years, Coleridge was fascinated by the western philosophical tradition, fascinated by the contradictions which he found in it and sought to untangle for himself. Exposed early to the alternative tradition of Plotinus and other neo-Platonists, of Jacob Boehme and Giordano Bruno, of the 'mystics' who also influenced Blake, Coleridge was deeply impressed by the world, life, and experience 'in all its uncertainty, mystery, doubt, and half-knowledge'.[5] This profound respect for the ineffability of things protected Coleridge from the superficialities of much western philosophizing, which reduced experience to knowledge experience, and mind to reason alone, as Dewey was to complain a century later. Like Keats, Coleridge seems to have been struck early by the realization that nothing 'can be known for truth by consecutive reasoning': no reasoning which excludes imagination, sense, or intuition can ever reach truth, that wisdom by which humankind lives.[6] As a consequence, Coleridge was never satisfied with the traditional rationalisms, idealisms, or empiricisms, which tended to deify reason in one way or another, to dismiss imagination, to reduce experience to mere knowledge experience or cognition, and to assume dualisms whose possibility of (evident) interaction was tortuously and endlessly debated. To anticipate, we may argue that Coleridge's (and for that matter, Shelley's) challenge to traditional philosophy takes the form of a dynamic synthesis of Platonic/Socratic philosophy with empiricism, as did Berkeley's (who taught Coleridge much), expressing itself through the ancient conceptualization of the reconciliation of opposites. This challenge specifically attacked the dualisms of thought and feeling, subject and object, poetry and philosophy, and so on, which underpin traditional interpretations of western thought.

Early influences from Kant set Coleridge to pondering the specific faults of most traditional philosophizing, namely of unconsciously assuming barren dualisms which leave interaction impossible and deny growth, change and evolution.[7] In *The Philosophical Lectures* (1949), Coleridge remarked that philosophy had its origins in the distinction between subject and object, but, like Dewey and James, he saw that this distinction had become an abstracted, absolute division, an unconsciously assumed dualism, and hence, 'the whole of progress from that time to this present moment is nothing more than an attempt to reconcile the same'.[8] For reconciled they must be, given that experience is a testimony to the constant interaction of subjects and objects, mind and nature, and so on. The problem arose from the assumed division, however, Coleridge saw, since no two existences essentially dissimilar could interact or be made sensible of each other in any way. For interaction involves things similar in essence, according to the law of homogeneity of experience. The 'outness prejudice' was at the root of this barren dualism infecting philosophy 'from that time to this' a prejudice which Berkeley had sought to overcome by redefining the word 'idea' (though he failed to get this redefinition accepted by his readership, who read him, and continue to read him, as a subjective idealist, in spite of the evidence to the contrary). From Berkeley, Coleridge saw that the outness prejudice must be thoroughly analysed and understood if it is to be overcome:

> We have been accustomed by all our affections, by all our wants, to seek after outward images; and by the love of association, therefore, to whole truth we attach that particular condition of truth which belongs to sensible bodies or to bodies which can be touched.[9]

The sense of outness must be, Coleridge argued, a habit, a prejudice unconsciously involved in the immediate sense of a subject, since it is otherwise inconceivable how objects absolutely separate from ourselves could ever become part of our consciousness.[10] Subjective idealism Coleridge scathingly described as rejecting 'all that was objective and real, and affirmed that the whole existed only in the mind and for the mind ... that in mind itself was to be found the sole reality of things'.[11] The rejection of materialism, on the other hand, as wholly inadequate to experience, takes numerous (often equally scathing) forms, but the most central was the insistence that mind and consciousness could not be reduced to a barren conception of lifeless matter without doing palpable violence to the most central facts of experience.[12] The rejection of materialism involves, then, two central arguments: first, that matter itself is misconceived by materialists in a way contrary to experience; and second, that 'it is admitted by all now not prejudiced, not biased by sceptical prepossession, that mind is distinct from matter. The mind of man, however, is involved in inscrutable darkness . . . and is to be estimated (if at all) alone by an inductive process; that is by its effect'.[13] Mind, for Coleridge, is distinct, but not absolutely divided from matter, however, for matter itself, if defined as utterly lifeless, cold, and dead, was for him a mere fiction of the abstracting mind, and hardly a description of anything experienced empirically. This assumed, fictional, material substrate – that thing-in-itself, the noumenon, the substantive cold reality behind appearance – Coleridge viewed as nonsense, having no empirical basis. He accused Descartes of being the first philosopher to make nature 'utterly lifeless and godless . . . who introduced the absolute and essential heterogeneity of the soul as intelligence, and the body as matter'.[14] Coleridge's later definition of matter as 'the pause by interpenetration of opposite energies',[15] suggested his own efforts to conceive it in a more Jamesian, dynamic, vital way, a way which anticipates, moreover, modern physics.

Two other statements alert the reader to the completeness of Coleridge's rejection of the traditional dualism which infected much of western philosophy. Greatly though he admired Spinoza, Coleridge accused him of the same error which many of his predecessors had fallen into:

> The πρῶτον ψεῦδος of Spinoza is . . . one in which all his Antagonists were as deeply immersed as himself . . . [it] consists in the assumed idea of a pure independent Object – in assuming a Substance beyond the I; of which therefore the I *could* only be a modification.[16]

Contrastingly, the related though apparently opposite error of his predecessors, whether rationalists, empiricists, or idealists alike, was described by Coleridge when he complained:

> Our Senses [allegedly] in no way acquaint us with Things, as they are in and of themselves . . . the properties, which we attribute to Things without us, yea . . . this very Outness, are not strictly properties of the things themselves, but either constituents or modifications of our own minds.[17]

Unlike in the *Logic,* where Kant himself had avoided these two errors by retaining experience whole and continuous from perceiver to perceived (no assumption of a separate noumenon), Coleridge argued that in Kant's metaphysics he had abandoned this continuity and unity, assumed a noumenon outside reason to provide objectivity for knowledge, and had thereby arrived at a subjective reason: 'The Subjectivity of Reason is the great error of the Kantean system.'[18] Kant's partial resolution of dualism occurred in his astute insistence on the nature of reason, in the *Logic,* as not merely analytic but also synthetic – productive and generative, that is, and hence both objective and subjective, thanks in part to 'unity of apperception', as established by the categories being limited in themselves in the *Logic,* and not by an external noumenon, as was supposed by Kant in his metaphysics.

Coleridge's solution was to challenge the accounts of experience as fundamentally and primarily dualistic, by arguing, as did James and Dewey later, that dualism is not a primary quality of experience, but a product of reflection, and therefore only relative. The 'prejudice of outness' alone prevents us from easily arriving at this realization that the primary quality of experience is its continuousness from subject to object, that 'unity of experience', to which Coleridge's 'One Life' theme, later in his *Theory of Life,* addresses itself on a grand scale.[19] So-called inorganic nature itself is part of life, Coleridge, like Blake before him, had argued. Self-consciousness, or reason, must be reconceived as found:

> therefore neither in object nor subject taken separately . . . it must
> be found in that which is neither subject nor object exclusively, but
> which is the identity of both. . . . This principle . . . manifests itself
> in the SUM or I AM; which I shall hereafter . . . express by the
> words spirit, self, and self-consciousness.[20]

The main purpose of this passage for Coleridge was, like Berkeley before him (with the word 'idea') and Dewey after him (with 'experience'), to reconceptualize the words spirit, self, and self-consciousness, so as to create a word to represent non-duality and continuousness in experience between the old hypostasized pairs of mind/body, nature/culture and so on. As with Heidegger's *Dasein,* and as with 'idea' and 'experience', readers were unable to grasp the import of the revitalization of such words, and ended up reading them as idealisms.[21]

The notebooks, letters, marginalia, and published writings of Coleridge contain dozens of passages relevant to his rejection of the dualism he found inherent in the western tradition, and his efforts to resolve this barren dualism by insisting, essentially, on a Deweyan continuity between subject/object, mind/nature, thoughts/things, thought/feeling, poetry/philosophy, and so on. This continuity he had seen Berkeley trying to establish with his innovative redefinition of 'idea'.[22] Coleridge had also learned from Plato, Plotinus, Cudworth, and others (such as Boehme and the mystical tradition) first, not to hypostasize a lifeless material substrate 'behind' appearance (thereby preserving nature as part of the 'One Life'), and second, not to imagine that 'consecutive reasoning' could lead to truth. Induction and intuition are indispensable in a world where, as Blake put it, the greatest mystery of all is perception itself. Kant in part had already confirmed Coleridge's efforts to keep experience unified, when in the *Logic* he made the reason both analytic and synthetic, hence neither subjective nor objective, and in no need of a noumenon outside itself. But when, according to Coleridge, Kant 'retrograded' to postulating the thing-in-itself, thereby separating objective from subjective reason,[23] Coleridge returned to the Platonic, neo-Platonic, and mystic traditions of thought. These strengthened the insight needed to ward off dualism and the outness prejudice infecting much of philosophy, so as to retain experience one and entire, as Hegel also sought to do.

Impressed by the continuity in experience, as were Dewey and James, Coleridge turned specifically to the ancient philosophy of the reconciliation of opposites (which took a more mundane, witty form in his delightful collection of aphorisms on 'Extremes Meet'). This philosophy of opposition has, arguably, much in common with Derrida's idea of 'differance' and with Dewey's and Heidegger's emphasis on the importance of continuity, context, and *Dasein*. Coleridge attributed it at times to Heraclitus and Giordano Bruno, alerted perhaps to its possibilities as a solution to the barren, dualist 'psilosophy' of Friedrich Schelling. Schelling's (flawed, according to Coleridge) articulation of it Coleridge had encountered sometime after 1810. As Owen Barfield has explained in his thorough examination of the 'Law of Polarity', the 'essence of polarity is a *dynamic* conflict between coinciding opposites'.[24] Barfield cited numerous philosophers (Lull, Cusa, Bruno, and Boehme) as having developed a Heraclitean *coincidentia oppositorum*, while Coleridge related polarity to Plato's *Parmenides* and to his truly Pythagorean logic, as he called it, as opposed to the Aristotelian, dichotomous logic of the mere understanding.[25] Coleridge also related the coincidence of opposites to Scotus, Bruno, Boehme, and to some extent, parts of Spinoza's thought.

In articulating the importance of the philosophy of the coincidence or reconciliation of opposites, Coleridge sought both to clarify the dynamic nature of the opposition and to relate this ancient conundrum to the philosophy of polarity:

> Every Power in Nature and in Spirit must evolve an opposite as the sole means and condition of its manifestation; *and all opposition is a tendency to reunion.* This is the universal Law of Polarity or essential dualism, first promulgated by Heraclitus.[26]

The concept of dynamic opposition contained within itself the notion of 'a tendency to reunion', that is, what Coleridge called an essential dualism, as opposed to the barren dualism which failed to distinguish contraries (defined as independent dualities with little relation to each other) and opposites (which are only relative dualities dependent on each other for existence). Anticipating Blake's argument that there is no such thing as contraries, but only opposites, Coleridge remarked, 'He alone deserves the name of philosopher, who has attained to see and learnt to supply the difference between Contraries that preclude, and opposites that reciprocally suppose and require each other.'[27]

The essential difference between opposites and contraries, he said, in *The Constitution of the Church and State,* is that 'opposite powers are always of the same kind, and tend to union, either by equipoise or by common product'. Coleridge then stated what constitutes more an attack on Friedrich Schelling's absolute dualism than any dogmatic claim, namely that 'in the Deity is an absolute synthesis of opposites'. Within experience and self-consciousness as a unified organic system, the dialectic of oppositions occurs which makes experience and knowledge possible. Coleridge also cautioned his readers (as Owen Barfield has argued) about the need to ensure that the opposition is understood as dynamic and not static, when he pointed out the danger of misunderstanding his Kantian critique on several fronts, one concerning the meaning of synthesis: 'It is the object of mechanical atomistic Philosophy to confound Synthesis with Synartesis, or *rather,* with mere juxtaposition of corpuscles separated by invisible interspaces.' The proper understanding of 'Synthesis' is clarified by further statements on the nature of essential dualism, as opposed to Kant's barren dualism.[28]

Coleridge's 'philosophy of difference' is scattered throughout his marginal notes, letters, and notebooks. In those writings, Coleridge traced all Kant's defects to the 'barren dualism of the Reflective system'. Dualism is the consequence of the assumption of the noumenon, whether in relation to reason or to imagination: 'The assumption of two Powers only, was the occasion of all the errors and imperfections of this theory.'[29] Essential dualism, reconciliation of opposites, and polar philosophy were indications that Coleridge, like Hegel, saw the necessity for an opposition or 'negative quantity' to occur within reason itself if there was to be an intelligible account of a world of experience, representation, and knowledge.[30] The negative for Hegel and the somewhat analogous concept of opposition for Coleridge became the solution to Kant's positing of a noumenon outside reason, experience, and self-consciousness. Coleridge then explained that matter is best understood as the product, or 'coagulum spiritus, the pause, by interpenetration of opposite energies'. Coleridge further stated that he held no matter as real otherwise than as the copula of these energies.[31] The notions of copula, pause, interpenetration, identity, and relation all became elements in a more complete understanding of the meaning of synthesis as occurring within experience and reason itself, in order to account for matter, that 'coagulum spiritus', as well as all other objects, including individual perceiving organisms. In formal terminology, Coleridge explained that the 'Identity of thesis and Anti-thesis is the substance of all *Being*'; opposition, on the other hand, is the condition of all existence, or 'Being manifested'.[32] This distinction between existence and being is the cornerstone of Coleridge's rejection of Schelling's misconceived account of static polarity.

While there is then, no proper opposition except within a single sphere, Schelling erred in actually 'establishing Polarity in the Absolute', making dualism absolute, a consequence, Coleridge alleged, of his making nature itself absolute.[33] Coleridge explained further:

> Schelling who . . . had seen the inadequacy of Kant's two Powers as constituting Matter, and had supplied a third as the copula and realization of the two, has yet succeeded no better in fact: though by stealing-in the Law of Polarity he has counterfeited a more successful appearance.[34]

To Coleridge's mind, Schelling had both made nature absolute and the absolute absolutely dual. Yet Coleridge himself, contrary to Schelling, placed the so-called absolute in the Act, in the Reason (conceived not as consecutive reasoning but as imaginative will), and kept unity and identity (or rather, continuity), not duality, as the nature of all knowable being:

> The reality of all alike is the A and W, or rather that Ineffable which is neither Alpha separately, Omega separately, nor Alpha and Omega by composition, but the Identity of both, which can become an object of Consciousness or Thought, even as all powers

of the material world can become objects of Perception, only as two
poles or Counterpoints of the same line.[35]

This idea of a non-dynamic juxtaposition of opposites (as opposed to
coincidence or tendency to reunion, or polarity) is at the basis of the
dualism characteristic of Schelling, of Kant, and of many other philosophers. Coleridge formulated this distinction further when he insisted upon the difference between true synthesis and mechanical
synarthesis, or 'mere juxtapositions . . . [of elements] separated by invisible interspaces'.[36] Believing that Schelling had merely paid a formal
obeisance to polarity and dynamic opposition, Coleridge sought to pro-
tect his own formulation from this counterfeit by ensuring that, first,
neither one pole (or opposition) nor the other would be privileged, and,
second, that the dualism be essential rather than barren – that is, only a
relative, or differential, or functional, not an absolute dualism. Such a
relative dualism is, paradoxically, not ultimately a dualism at all,
Coleridge argued, but a philosophy which expresses 'unity in multeity',
'identity in difference', or irrationality in rationality. It expresses also the
one life theme which Coleridge came to articulate more fully later, when
he sought thoroughly to explore the continuity between mind and
nature, and experience and nature. There, he emphasized a conception
of nature as itself vital and generative, rather than the dead, lifeless,
souless matter he accused Descartes and even Kant of inventing.[37] Before
Coleridge developed his one life theme of natural continuity between
specifically mental and other, more physical aspects of experience, he
had already asserted an organic conception of art and the world more
consistent with Shelleyan views and with Dewey's and Heidegger's concepts of naturally evolved living organisms than the philosophies of most
of his empiricist, rationalist, or idealist precursors.

Through the phrase, 'humanizing nature' (applied to Shakespeare's
genius in the *Shakespearean Criticism*),[38] Coleridge expressed the unity of
experience of mental and physical, mind and matter, also characteristic
of pragmatism. He too came at the problem of the unity of experience,
in spite of apparent duality, by exposing duality as a product of reflection
and not a fundamental or absolute character of experience, as James,
Dewey, and Heidegger later argued. Thus, Coleridge was able to insist
on the Pythagorean view, as he called it, that those very powers, which in
humans reflect and contemplate, are basically the same as those powers
which in nature produce the objects contemplated.[39]

As stated above, Coleridge adapted the terms self-consciousness, and
spirit to express this Deweyan continuity, terms often misconstrued as
idealist or transcendentalist by his readers. Before we assume that these

terms brand Coleridge a useless, transcendentalizing metaphysician from whom we can learn little, we might look first at how he tried to redefine and revitalize these terms and, second, at how to interpret their meaning in the context of his specific metaphors and images, and in the context of his philosophy and aesthetics as a whole. Coleridge certainly used the two terms in part to express the continuity and unity of experience, what Dewey sought to express by redefining the word experience itself. Likewise, Berkeley had sought to redefine the word idea to express continuity and reject dualism and idealism. Yet he was misunderstood by his readership, and still is often today, as is Dewey. Dewey acknowledged that his readers had interpreted 'experience' in precisely the way he had hoped and worked to avoid. Namely, they took it as implying a subjectivity or mentality, when Dewey sought to revitalize a familiar word to express the unity of subject and object met with in empirical acounts of experience. Berkeley's readers took his word idea in the same mistaken way, while Coleridge's readers have subjectivized his words self-conscious and spirit. All three writers were motivated by historical considerations about the use and etymology of these words, as well as the need to avoid the pitfalls of both materialism and idealism.

Like Derrida, with the words trace and differance, these writers were looking for a new way to express the relationship between mind and matter, subject and object, nature and culture as one of functional relation, not in need of any bridging *tertium aliquid*. For all these elements were seen only as distinctions within the sphere of experience, not palpable divisions in need of reunification. If their choice of words seems to be a choice of a 'master name', and, moreover, a name which privileges one element of duality over its opposite, then they are certainly toying with metaphysics, embedded in a vocabulary which even Derrida cannot escape, as 'trace', 'sign', and 'differance' gradually take on metaphysical dimensions they were explicitly invoked to eschew. Nearly every thinker has been accused of sliding into metaphysics, however vociferously his texts seek to deconstruct it. Vocabulary saturated with prior metaphysics cannot be rescued it seems, even when each of these philosophers puts crucial words under erasure, brackets them, and tries to redefine them. Yet, clearly, each one of these philosopher's texts also has a deconstructive, anti-patriarchal tale to tell, as opposed to the metaphysics they are said to propound. Yet the two alternative tales are oppositions, not contraries, and inhabit each other.

There are a number of reasons for respecting Coleridge's choice of 'self-consciousness' or 'spirit' as expressive of this Dewey-Derrida continuity of differences and oppositions which characterizes experience. The choice of words was, arguably, an effort to offer not a transcendentalist or idealist account, as this would be entirely inconsistent with the context of Coleridge's philosophizing. Coleridge could be seen as offering a way of acknowledging the interrelatedness of consciousness, nature, and experience, along with the limited role of reason, while seeking to preserve the mystery and ineffability in the fact of any existence whatever. Materialist accounts stripped life and existence of all its mystery, uncertainty, and doubt, resolving them, Coleridge complained, into a ludicrously self-contradictory notion of matter, substance, or noumenon. Non-materialist accounts, on the other hand, adopted, of course, non-materialist language, and thereby found themselves burdened with the idealist-subjectivist-transcendentalist vocabulary of the language.

The reader is often unresponsive to revitalization and reconceptualizations, to putting words under erasure, Coleridge's constant concern in *Aids to Reflection*. Coleridge's and Berkeley's 'theological' speculations led, it seems, automatically to accusations that they were constructing metaphysics. When carefully read in context, both these writers, and others such as Plato and Kierkegaard, seem to be writing a deconstruction of traditional dualistic metaphysics and transcendentalist-dualist religions. Coleridge himself had attacked much enlightenment thinking for its superficial and misleading 'clarification' of the insoluble mysteries of existence and consciousness into matter and reason, turning philosophy into 'psilosophy'. Coleridge argued that such 'psilosophers' imagine they can know the reality of things, can have absolute knowledge, instead of only right opinion, to use Socrates' distinction.

Hence Coleridge's emphasis on traditional methodology: the goal of the science of knowledge is sound method of enquiry, not truth about reality. This is the knowledge we can obtain, and even this is reliant not just on reasoning, but upon inductive, intuitional thinking, and especially on a revitalized language which puts central words 'under erasure'. When we start seeking to know or comprehend with our reasoning faculties the 'ground' of existence, we begin metaphysics and end inevitably in hypostasization, dualism, and error. For we immediately posit a metaphysical entity which is to be known somehow, but which, paradoxically, is beyond the reach of knowing. This entity is not knowable, because it is a fiction of an abstracting mind, an unintelligible notion, and not because our faculties are too limited to grasp its reality.

Coleridge, along with Plato, Berkeley, Kierkegaard, and others, is read metaphysically and as an idealist partly because he, like Keats, Blake, Shelley, and many other artists, sought to emphasize the folly of believing that materiality is the real, and that anything can be known for truth by mere deductive reasoning. Coleridge's, (like Kierkegaard's and Berkeley's) theological speculations are an examination of the traditions of Christianity from a critical and imaginative perspective which denies the notion that 'consecutive reasoning' is independent of imagination and induction. The concept of imagination, itself impenetrable to the reason, is a way of articulating this commitment. To read such aesthetic and theological writings as merely another version of metaphysics or transcendentalism is to miss valuable opportunities to grasp critically the movements of western thought and the history of human efforts to come to terms with death, life, good, evil, and so on. Each of these writers argued passionately against the notion that reason, understood as the faculty of analysis and logic, could lead to truth. Each of them attacked the eighteenth-century notions (still strongly held today) that science is somehow more true or real than art or history or literature. Science, the rationalist argument goes, is not subject to relativities, to mere right opinion, to mere interpretations. By means of reason, science, through univocal propositions, can lead to non-relative truths, it is alleged. The hegemony of science throughout the world today is alleged to be a proof of this superior reality and truth. This worship of the God, reason, and its human manifestation, science, ignores the reliance of science on metaphor, the constant necessity for scientists to revise dramatically their theories, and the effects of new, recalcitrant experiences which force complete reappraisals of previously 'true' theories.[40] Science is the human way of describing phenomena principally in relation to each other, as Dewey reminded us. Yet as observers, we affect the observed, and select, according to our own needs and interests, what to investigate, often for reasons of survival. More sinister is the unconscious assumption that reason-science, the new religion, leads in the main to good, to progress, and necessarily to a better way of life. The reality around us tells a more embiguous tale, namely that reason and science are one small aspect of human life desperately needing control by imagination and by informed moral and aesthetic discussion, if we are to use our scientific discoveries wisely. Without constant re-evaluation and revision, without constant renewal of dead metaphors and outmoded theories, science – like unrevitalized poetry – ceases to enrich culture. Science is no less and no more true or relative, for Dewey, Coleridge, or Derrida, than art and moral life. Art and moral life are as widely spread over the globe as science, share many common features, and contribute as much if not more to enhanced experience. It could indeed be argued that science and reason are the master names of the twentieth century, the new metaphysical dogma of our times.

Coleridge, like his predecessors, had searched for an appropriate word to express the continuity of experience and to analyse dualisms as differential relations. A closer examination of Coleridge's use of such terms as spirit and self-consciousness establishes better the position these terms take in his deconstruction of dualistic and atomistic philosophies, a critique which resists materialist or rationalist reductions of 'mystery, doubt, and uncertainty' into 'jam datum', as he scathingly described such simplifications. In a notebook entry Coleridge wrote:

> The I = Self Spirit is definable as a Subject whose only possible Predicate is itself – Ergo, a Subject which is its own Object, i.e., a Subject-Object. . . . The Spirit . . . cannot be an Object {'object' means necessarily dead, inert}, . . . it becomes an Object through its own act. . . . The Spirit is Power self-bounded by retroition on itself, and is only for itself . . . in it subsists the primary Union of Finity and Infinity . . . absolute Co-presence of the Infinite and Finite. . . . However, we yet do distinguish our Self from the Object, though not in the primary Intuition – now that is impossible without an act of abstraction – we abstract from our own product – the Spirit snatches itself loose from its own self-immersion. . . . But this is absolutely impossible otherwise than by a free Act.[41]

Taken out of the context of Coleridge's writings, such a passage seems the basis for a conventional idealism until one remember, first, Coleridge's efforts to reconceptualize 'self' to mean continuity between inner and outer, second, his constant criticism of idealist philosophies, and, third, the relation of the 'word' to 'act', which is discussed below. In the following passage the emphasis upon 'Act' is reiterated, which forms the most consistent character of Coleridge's Jamesian, dynamic philosophy: not idealism, not transcendentalism, so much as an evolving, natural supernaturalism:

> As an absolute Principle it can be neither Subject nor Object . . . but the identity of both. . . . And yet to be known, this Identity must be dissolved – and yet it cannot be dissolved. For its Essence consists in this Identity. This Contradiction can be solved no otherwise, than by an Act . . . the Principle makes itself its own Object, [and] in and thus becomes a Subject. The Self affirmative is therefore a Will; and Freedom is a primary intuition, and can never be deduced. . . . All Truths therefore are but deductions from, or rather parts of the History of Self-Consciousness.[42]

This emphasis on 'Act' will be elaborated below. But one of Coleridge's favourite ways of overcoming dualism and the outness prejudice, which

Berkeley had taught him to suspect, was to argue, first, that thoughts and things are not absolutely heterogeneous, not one prior to the other, but that they are continous one with the other, as Shelley had argued. Relatedly, Coleridge explained that the spirit (as he reconceived the word), in its observation of the so-called external world of nature, views only itself,[43] or rather, the very powers which in humans reflect and contemplate are in their essence the very same as those in nature which produce the objects contemplated. Blake's expression of this 'Pythagorean view' was to say that 'to the Eyes of the Man of Imagination, Nature is Imagination itself'.[44]

Coleridge's tireless insistence on the thought/thing relation was a central mode of rejecting the idealism he is often mistakenly believed to have espoused. The resolution of this distinction is another gesture of differential, non-dualistic thinking, but overcoming this dualistic prejudice was no easy matter to teach. In a passage instructive of Coleridge's anticipation of Heidegger's central principle of the power of words to bring things into being, Coleridge argued for the imaginative nature of perception at all levels of mentality: 'To think (*Ding, denken; res, reor*) is to thingify.'[45] In the following statement, Coleridge affirmed not just the continuous, unbroken, Shelleyan, Berkeleyan progression in experience from things to thoughts that he had argued for elsewhere, but an analogy between the relation of thoughts to the mind and things to the mind. Not only thoughts, but things as well, are 'portions of the act of producing', thus anticipating Shelley's radically Berkeleyan reappraisal of experience as dynamic, evolving, and apocalyptic:

> Even so as thoughts, from Images even up to ideas, are distinct but not divided Existences of the Mind, [quasi proles semper in utero] so are the Products of Nature, which we call things or Fixes (res fixae, intellectiones coagulatae) are never really producta jam et vere fixa; but themselves portions of the act of producing.[46]

This quotation relates closely to numerous accounts in Shelley's prefaces and his 'Defence of Poetry'. The importance of the word, act, for Coleridge's analysis of dualism and metaphysics, will become more evident below. The point made here, that products are not merely or strictly products, but processes viewed from a specific perspective which makes them look static, should suggest that the above quotation is not expressing an idealist position, so much as arguing for a distinction only, not a division between process and product. This very Deweyan relation of process to product, verb to noun, and the privileging of energy over matter – thus rejecting a conception of products as lifeless, soulless, and independent of the acts of producing – led eventually to Coleridge's characterization of experience, life, nature, matter, and reason itself as vital, growing, and essentially active, rather than fixed, static and unchanging.[47] Hints of the importance of transformation and evolution and, finally, a strong historical sense, suggest anticipations of Hegel. In the following passage the word reason, like spirit, is reconceptualized by Coleridge to mean the 'full' reason, not only subjective, but objective reason. Reason is both analytic and synthetic, nous and dianoia; it is both deductive and inductive, understanding and imagination, sense and intellect, and finally, reason and unreason. Coleridge reconceived 'reason' not as some discrete faculty pre-existing in a distinct thing called mind, but as dynamic, as productive, as Shelley was to do. Thus Coleridge anticipated Shelley's composition theory of experience, characterized by growth, evolution, and transformation, all of which relate to Derrida's concept of 'system as writing', as endless productivity and free play.

Coleridge's organicism emphasizes an organic system of reason and self-consciousness whose 'essence' is processes and acts, growth and productivity, not products, completion, and stasis. He distinguished the products 'of the mechanic Understanding . . . from the ποιησεις of the imaginative Reason. . . . Products in antithesis to Produce – or Growths'. He also remarked that the 'higher life of Reason is naturally symbolized in the process of growth in nature'.[48] Reason is best understood in terms of production, activity, and process, not as a predetermined, innate faculty already formed and waiting to be put to work. Furthermore, the essence of knowledge was, for Coleridge, activity,[49] while intelligence and imaginativeness are conceived as self-development, not 'qualities supervening'. Like Dewey, then, Coleridge denied any role to a Kantian noumenon or substance external to reason. Imagination, and consequently perception, is essentially vital, as James would have said, for 'all objects (as objects) are essentially fixed and dead'.[50] Coleridge explained further:

> 'Eclectic Philosophy', 'Syncretism' . . . is the Death of all Philosophy. Truth is one and entire because it is vital. Whatever lives is contradistinguished from all juxtaposition – and mechanism . . . by its oneness, its impartibility; – and mechanism itself could not have had existence, except as a counterfeit of a living whole.[51]

For Coleridge, products and mechanisms are 'dead metaphors'. Like truth and imagination, reason must be understood to be one and entire; it is vital. That it is 'one', a 'unity', does not mean it is a dead, finished, totally determined, closed structure. On the contrary, Coleridge, like Dewey, saw the reason as emerging into life with active, free productivity, through language. Coleridge argued that 'in Kant's system there can be of course no intelligible Genesis, or real Production – in Heraclitus it is all in perpetual Genesis'.[52] The barren dualism of Kant's philosophy, which allegedly introduced an element foreign to reason to explain synthesis, allows of no 'intelligible Genesis'. Any account which suggests that perception receives its materials from without, reduced, for Coleridge, to a static dualism. Structural 'organicism' is itself a contradiction in terms, a dead metaphor, and a 'disguised dualism'. It mistakes structures and products, those familiar forms of processes, as different in kind from the processes, activities, and growth that are the essence of all products and objects. Or it mistakes the powers of growth and production for *ab extra*, instead of *ab intra*, principles, and thus degenerates unwittingly into a structural dualism as barren as that of Kant. The difference between growth and generation and the mechanism of fabrication is that, in the first case, form is evolved *ab intra*, the other *ab extra* – impressed, that is, from without. The latter is representative always of something not itself, 'but the former . . . of its own cause within itself, i.e., its causative self'.[53]

Through his organic conceptions – of intelligence as self-development, of perception and imagination as acts, of nature's products as processes, and of reason's educts as growths, – Coleridge cleansed from his system the last trace of passivity and stasis, and rejected any trace of a substance external to experience. He defined mind in a Nietzschean way, 'as a pure active and proper Perceptivity', rejecting the passive account of the object as an affect of the perceiving subject. Coleridge sought to redefine the word object itself, to reveal its more essential connection with life as conceivable only in terms of growth: 'But/Observe! that in my system the Object is not, as in the Fichtean Idealism the dead, the substanceless, the mere Idol, but the absolutely free Productivity in the always perfected Product.'[54] Here he echoed familiar words from the German romantics, Friedrich Schlegel and Novalis. Coleridge's statement reveals that our conception of object and product are a natural consequence of a 'degeneration' of imaginative Blakean, twofold vision, which if activated would reveal all objects and products (for example, artifacts) to be themselves essentially living growths and processes, which, through time, degenerate into dead metaphors or products. With this emphasis upon growth, productivity, and acts, Coleridge concluded, in a Berkeleyan statement: 'God is . . . one eternal Act, in which all other Acts are comprehended. All else arises out of the Relations in which Finites exist to Finites.'[55] Later we shall see 'Act' become the definition of reason, while the above statement says more about dynamic life than a transcendent God of metaphysics.

In his tirelessly repeated insistence on distinction versus division, Coleridge expressed in another way the 'differentiality' of experience, and the relative nature of inner and outer worlds. He explained to his reader that:

> the office of philosophical disquisition consists in just distinction; while it is the privilege of the philosopher to preserve himself constantly aware, that distinction is not division. In order to obtain adequate notions of any truth, we must intellectually separate its distinguishable parts [analysis]; and this is the technical process of philosophy. But having so done, we must then restore them in our conceptions to the unity, in which they actually co-exist [synthesis]; and this is the result of philosophy.[56]

Elsewhere Coleridge had remarked that 'it is a dull and obtuse mind, that must divide in order to distinguish: but it is a still worse mind, that distinguishes in order to divide'.[57] Coleridge's 'distinction versus division' is a central pivot of his attack on dualism and metaphysics, and anticipates the concepts that guided Dewey's challenge to dualism as well as Derrida's concept of differance. It also relates closely to Shelley's distinction in 'A Defence of Poetry', between synthesis and analysis, the former being the province of imagination, intuition, and induction, while the latter is the province of reason (understood as '*dianoia*', not as '*nous*', as Coleridge was later to redefine 'Reason'). Likewise, the distinguish/divide opposition is another related way of expressing the difference between 'contraries that preclude, and opposites that presuppose each other' – the cornerstone of the *coincidentia oppositum* philosophy and the law of polarity. For both polarity and dynamic opposition involve distinctions between two forces which are not divided, but merely two poles of one power. The distinction/division duality also suggests a central principle of Coleridge's aesthetics and philosophy, namely the concept of unity in multeity, which is later articulated into the part–whole aesthetics of organic unity. The thrust of the distinction between division and distinction is that all oppositions are relative, interdependent, functional, and differential, not positing absolutely distinct entities. Indeed, Coleridge seems to have adopted Blake's more flamboyant attack on the notion of contraries, the existence of which he polemically flatly denied, implying that contraries (divided dualities) are dead metaphors.

Blake's marriage of opposites throughout his poetry is another aspect of the romantic philosophy which anticipates 'differance', while other aspects of Blake's writings show startling similarities with Derrida's 'writing'. The central role of delight in Blake's poetry corresponds to notions of *plaisir* and free play. The habitation of unreason in reason is evident everywhere, as is Blake's commitment to challenge decorum, propriety, repression (whether sexual, emotional, or intellectual), patriarchy, and stereotype. This Blakean critique creates a congruence between thematics and stylistics in Blake, not seen again until Nietzsche's and Derrida's remarkable innovations. Blake challenged the boundaries between painting as well as poetry, criticism, and philosophy, as Derrida has done. He created a new, composite art, transforming both poetry and etching techniques in the process. He embedded a level of ironic self-parody and parody of reading and interpretation which even Derrida has hardly equalled.

Coleridge's Blakean redefinition, revitalization, and reconceptualization of the word Reason is instructive and needs to be distinguished further from traditional, dogmatic interpretations of a static Kantian kind (it is more similar to Hegel's 'reason', understood in Kojève's sense). Unlike Shelley, who in 'A Defence of Poetry' equated the term reason with understanding or *dianoia*, Coleridge distinguished between understanding and reason according to the Greek and German terminological distinctions between *dianoia* and *nous*, or *Verstand* and *Vernunft*. Moreover, Coleridge criticized Kant for his separation of 'the Reason from the Reason in the Will or the theoric from the practical Man'. He then queried 'whether the Division of Reason into Speculative and Practical, amounting to the Assumption of two Reasons, different in function and extent of jurisdiction, was not arbitrary, and an hypostasizing of mere logical entities'. Then, the barren dualism affecting Kant's account of reason Coleridge criticized still more fully in the same marginal note:

> even Kant makes the fundamental error of ... the derivation of ideas from the Speculative Reason entirely, for the behoof of the practical Reason and the Active Principle, but not by Means thereof, or in conjunction therewith; which latter is nevertheless the true and Platonic theory of Ideas ... according to which the Reason and Will are the Parents ... and the Idea itself the transcendent Analogon of the Image or die Spirituelle Anschauung.[58]

Coleridge sought through this distinction to attack both mechanistic, materialist philosophies and passive-mind theories, which attributed to the mind only an associative power of the lowest, most superficial kind, and which, therefore, assumed perception to be essentially passive and receptive. He went further to characterize more fully the concept of reason. From this, it becomes evident that the emphasis in Coleridge's constructive philosophy was far from metaphysical. For it is based in the entirely natural and empirically experienced process of growth and evolution, as is Derrida's central idea of 'system as writing': 'the higher life of Reason is naturally symbolized in the process of growth in nature'.[59] At times, the reason is almost synonymous with imagination. Indeed, Coleridge's 'reason' is very close to Shelley's concept of imagination, though Coleridge elaborated it further in his later writings, so that reason comes to synthesize the Greek *nous* with the Christian 'will'.[60] Coleridge's use of the word reason is repeatedly distinguished from the enlightenment 'Reason', that mere 'organ of science' or logic, as Blake, Shelley, Coleridge, and Keats branded it.

Like Dewey, Coleridge's constitutive philosophy states that reason is in the process of elucidating itself in and through both the individual mind (not externally to it), and through culture. Moreover, mind (and reason) gradually evolves ideas of itself which actually change it. Reason grows and alters in the process of knowing itself, for it is 'one and vital'. Reason, as Hegel and Coleridge conceived it, is not a fixed, determined, static, fully formed faculty, gradually revealing itself to itself through time, either from the point of view of the individual or from that of history. Rather, as for Dewey, reason is actually in the process of making itself for itself. Knowledge is both its product and a process influencing its development. Thus, the constitutive philosophy, that Pythagorean view, does not suggest that relatively subjective ideas can be raised to objective forms or an absolute validity, in the sense of giving us a glimpse of the structures of nature or an already whole, totalized Reason, Reality, or God, revealing itself to us as it will in time. These ideas of reason are themselves gradually evolving in significance and meaning for the individual thinker and for the social consciousness. They are not static and fixed ideas. The verbal formulations of such ideas from the reason are continuously being altered and rearticulated in new ways, as *Aids to Reflection*, for example, testifies. There, Coleridge sought to re-examine, like Berkeley before him and Kierkegaard after him, ideas of reason central to Christianity, and to insist on revolutionizing worn-out, dead metaphors.

In *The Statesman's Manual*, Coleridge sought to make clearer his clarification and redefinition of 'reason':

> The Reason (not the abstract reason, not the reason as the mere
> organ of science, or as the faculty of scientific principles and

schemes a priori, but reason) . . . reason substantiated and vital, 'one only, yet manifold, overseeing all, going through all understanding' . . . the Reason, without being either the sense, the Understanding, or the Imagination contains all three within itself, even as the mind contains the thoughts, and is present in and through them all. Each individual must bear witness of it to his own mind, even as he describes life and light . . . and it dwells in us only so far as we dwell in it. It cannot in strict language be called a faculty, much less a personal property of any human mind![61]

Later, in *Aids to Reflection*, Coleridge simply stated, 'there is no such thing as a particular Reason'. This dynamic distinction between 'reason' and 'Reason' is, we must remember, not a division: 'There is no such thing as a particular reason.' Reason cannot properly be called a faculty, much less a personal property, Coleridge insisted. 'Reason', as reconceptualized, designates a dwelling, to use Heidegger's language as well; it means an active Platonic 'participation' in reasoning by an individual mind. Coleridge concluded, 'the whole human Species . . . may be considered as One Individual Mind'.[62] Later Shelley was to make an almost identical comment in 'A defence of poetry'. Coleridge described his '12 Lectures on the History of Philosophy as the gradual Evolution of the Mind of the world, contemplated as a single Mind in the different successive states of its development'.[63] Elsewhere, he designated 'Reason' as 'Supreme Reason'; he insisted that its 'knowledge is creative, and antecedent to the things known'.[64] But one of the things known is reason – that is, reason realized in so far as an individual dwells in it. Knowledge is not only a product of reason, but creative of it, as Dewey had insisted, and as had Hegel: 'the more we dwell in Reason, the more it dwells in us'. Reason reasons, and in reasoning it realizes itself. In realizing itself, it develops itself and creates itself further in new and quite unpredictable ways, evolving into greater and greater power. Coleridge explained, in an apocalyptic passage:

> All Knowledge, I say, that enlightens and liberalizes, is a form and a means of self-knowledge . . . the whole of Euclid's Elements is but a History and graphic Exposition of the powers and processes of the Intuitive Faculty. . . . We learn to construe our own perceptive power, while we educe into distinct consciousness its inexhaustible constructive energies.[65]

It would, arguably, be regrettable to deduce (from taking the metaphors in these passages too literally) that Coleridge and Shelley had postulated some transcendental Mind or Reason as the reality behind appearance.

The purpose of such metaphors is to establish, as Heidegger tried to do later, that logos and reason are the conditions for experience and consciousness, not the results of it; that language and words saturate and structure our experience, and that to see them as outcomes of an independent noumenon, whether conceived as material or spiritual, is to hypostasize unintelligible entities. For as Coleridge insisted repeatedly, being is a function of knowing; we cannot know of being as prior to knowing; nor is knowing prior to being, he argued, in his anti-idealist strain. They are inhabited by each other, functions of each other, differences of each other, as are reason and Reason.

Coleridge argued then, that 'Truth and Being are correlative'[66] in the *Biographia*, and he explained further:

> The term, Philosophy, defines itself as an affectionate seeking after Truth; but Truth is the correlative of Being. This again is in no way conceivable, but by assuming as a postulate, that both are *sub initio*, identical and coinherent; that intelligence and being are reciprocally each other's substrate.[67]

Put in modern terminology, we could say that intelligence and being inhabit each other, are differential functions. Instead of 'intelligence', we could say that 'reason is a self-development, not a quality supervening',[68] a remark Dewey was to reiterate a hundred years later in *Experience and Nature*. In Nietzschean language, Coleridge pithily noted that 'God is . . . one eternal Act'. For Coleridge, as for Nietzsche, Dewey, and Derrida, knowledge too is 'essentially a verb active'. Thus, intelligence, truth, and knowledge, not to mention reason, are not qualities supervening to the fixed, predetermined, fully formed entity or substrate, Being. Their reality resides in act, in active self-development, that is. For Coleridge, in this existentialist strain, this meant that intelligence, knowledge, truth and reason cannot be properly understood apart from the 'coinherence' of the activating principle, the will:

> We (that is, the human race), live by faith. Whatever we do or know, that in kind is different from the brute Creation has its origin in a determination of the Reason to have faith and trust in itself. This, its first act of faith, is scarcely less than identical with its own being.[69]

Shelley had argued in the same terms, when he spoke of the mind's acts as deriving their integrity only from within themselves; no outside authority or God or Being could authorize the mind's productions. It itself must choose, according to its own laws, which ideas and metaphors have integrity, and which must be discarded as inadequate. Both Shelley and Coleridge show a pragmatic, Socratic admission that we can only act as if we had knowledge (thus reiterating Socratic, relative scepticism), at least as long as we insist upon defining knowledge as independent and objective in some absolute, non-relative sense.

Coleridge had also described reason as the spirit of the regenerated man, and spoke of it religiously as an essence or vital act, or activity, the Will in its supreme form. 'Reason' in Coleridge's philosophizing is to be understood as having little to do with the enlightenment notion, then, or with 'consecutive reasoning', as Keats described the faculty of Blakean analysis, Urizen. Coleridge's 'Reason' is rather a mode of expressing the continuity of and differential relation of nature and mind as two forces of one power, whose being is better understood as activity, growth, and vitality. Nature and reason are, as for Blake, analogies of the generative powers and energies which Dewey had also described, but in his more naturalistic terminology. Coleridge, like Hegel, took over and sought to revitalize a cumbersome terminology which often may seem to hinder his thought from breaking more cleanly with western idealist thinking. But if read carefully, Coleridge's attack on dualism and idealism is still surprisingly effective, while his excursions into metaphysical and Christian theology are also instructive as he, like Kierkegaard, struggled mightily to avoid dogmatism. Coleridge can be said to liberate the careful reader into the opportunity to appreciate the balancing act required if Coleridge is to sustain the Shakespearean/Keatsian respect for the mystery and uncertainty of experience and existence, yet not give in to any dogmatic metaphysics or mystical and superstitious religion. *Aids to Reflection* is a fine example of the non-doctrinaire, questioning thrust of his readerly communications, following in the tradition of a Socratic Plato and a radically re-read Berkeley.

Coleridge's concept of reason, then, and his 'self-consciousness' can be compared to Dewey's concept of experience, and like the latter, was probably not a felicitous choice of words, since it carries with it not only the alleged privileging of subjective over objective, but also the whole tradition of enlightenment reason as consecutive reasoning, that 'mere organ of science', and the privileging of the narrowly conceived concept of the rational over the irrational. Yet Coleridge's efforts to challenge traditional meanings show his awareness of the need to put these words under erasure, and also show his realization that there is no way of escaping from logocentric language, since metaphysics seems embedded into the very elements of our discourse, and creeps back in however much we seek to exclude it.

Like Socrates, and like Hegel, for that matter, Coleridge never under-estimated the importance of the so-called irrational (the non-analytical, non-deductive) in human experience. His concepts of reason, imagi-nation, and symbol, amongst others, were designed to emphasize this depth and complexity of human experience. His choice of language at this level, however, suggests to some readers a shift towards an idealist metaphysics, a fascination for ultimate causes and notions of reality as intelligence, which Dewey and Derrida eschewed as master names. Nevertheless, a careful and sensitive study of Coleridge's widely scattered philosophical, theological, and other writings reveals a similarly radical, existentialist strain as, for example, in Kierkegaard's attack on Christi-anity or in Nietzsche's and Shelley's idea of a universe of poetry, to which it is difficult to append a metaphysical and idealist reading without distorting the texts. What comes across is radically innovative and chal-lenging, open-ended speculations about such issues. These issues are illuminated when kept closely in relation to the use of words such as being, intelligence, and concepts of growth, activity, and the 'Logos as communicative intelligence', a phrase anticipatory of Dewey's strong emphasis on communication in his theories about language (see chapter 8).Coleridge's constant emphasis upon revitalizing dead metaphors and central philosophical terms by redefining such concepts as reason into act, growth, and evolution, suggests the possibility of interpreting his writing as reaching towards a more naturalistic, Deweyan conception of mind as expressive of natural, continuous processes of experience. Given the Coleridgean organic emphasis upon activity (understood as transformation and evolution), and given his existentialist emphasis on self-development, it would seem perverse to interpret Coleridge's 'Rea-son' or 'self-consciousness' as some metaphysical, fixed, static Being or reality (as it is with Hegel perverse to do so), since everywhere in his philosophy Coleridge emphasized vitality, activity, and productivity, as William James was to do a half century later. Reason and its sister, imagination, are for Coleridge creative in the fullest sense of the word. That is, they are creative subjectively as well as objectively, their activity leads both to further self-development and to more sophisticated per-ceptions of nature, culture, and society.

In his well-known definition of the imagination, Coleridge had an-ticipated Shelley's constructive theory of experience:

The imagination then, I consider either as primary, or secondary. The Primary Imagination I hold to be the living Power and prime Agent of all human Perception, and as a repetition in the finite mind of the eternal act of creation in the infinite I AM.[70]

This early use of the term imagination later took on almost entirely the character of the later term, reason. The imagination is 'that synthetic and magical power'.[71] Or, 'Imagination is the laboratory in which the thought elaborates essence into existence', it 'dissolves, diffuses, dissipates, in order to recreate'.[72] Imagination is a sort of 'fusion to force many into one'. Elsewhere Coleridge spoke of the 'philosophic imagination, the sacred power of self-intuition',[73] and of the 'imaginative Reason'; and, as the above quotations suggest, 'it is wonderful how closely Reason and Imagination are connected'. The eventual, latterly developed distinction between Coleridge's use of 'reason' and his use of 'imagination' seems to consist in his applying and confining the latter term to the aesthetic and perceptual activities of the finite, human mind; reason, on the other hand, is also present in the finite, individual mind as a power, too. But it seems to seek to refer more explicitly to the shared, natural character of individuality in persons and in nature generally. It also seems to refer to a more general 'Act of causative generation' evident everywhere in nature, rather than to specific acts of aesthetic or perceptive powers. The term imagination is used as the 'repetition in the finite mind of the eternal act of creation in the infinite I AM'.[74] We can further understand Coleridge's eventual distinction between reason and imagination by noting that the former is, strictly speaking, the source of all ideas, while the latter, he explained is:

> that reconciling and mediatory power, which incorporating the Reason in Images of the Sense, and organizing (as it were) the flux of the Senses by the permanence and self-circling energies of the reason, gives birth to a system of symbols, harmonious in themselves, and consubstantial with the truths, of which they are the conductors.[75]

Imagination is the activity of embodying the ideas or truths of the reason into symbols. Symbols are characterized by the 'translucence of the Eternal through and in the Temporal'. A symbol 'always partakes of the Reality which it renders intelligible; and while it enunciates the whole, abides itself as a living part of the Unity, of which it is the representative'. We could conclude that the imagination is itself a symbol of reason, and, consequently, that it, while it 'enunciates the whole, abides as a living part of the Unity, of which it is the representative'.[76] As such, it is reason embodied, manifested, and made finitely perceivable. Imagination is the reason individualized into a finite act of a perceiving mind. If we relate the finite acts of perceiving minds to the perceived world and remember that, for Coleridge, the character of the perceiving individual mind is imaginative activity (while nature too is all 'Imagination itself'), then these two 'opposing finite objects or forces (of mind and nature) are related to reason as symbols of it. They partake of its 'intelligibly rendered Reality'. Nature and imagination, that is, as reason individualized into relative object and relative subject, both inhere within experience, not one within and one without, and inhabit each other.

Coleridge's theory of the imagination as primary and secondary in distinction from the fancy leads to the concept of experience as self-sufficient and in no need of an external ground for synthetic-imaginative acts, whether primary (perceptual) or secondary (artistic). Perception, for Coleridge, at its most basic levels, is not passive and receptive, but imaginative, connecting and relating and figuring experience *ab initio*. As with Shelley, Coleridge saw perception as operating as a process of figuration; through metaphors and other figures of speech, experience is structured and ordered from its most basic, initial levels up to the higher orderings of culture. Like Shelley, Coleridge's primary and secondary imagination distinction (so poorly understood by many critics) indicates his full commitment to a rejection of the notion of perception as passive receptivity of already constituted objects. As Derrida said, such perception does not exist. For Blake, as for Coleridge, perception was the great mystery of human experience, not some passive copying or mirroring of an already existent nature. In this dynamic conception of perception lies Coleridge's greatest criticism of dualistic thinking and metaphysics generally, as he held that metaphor and symbol are the primary constituents of knowledge experience, and that figuration and artistic activity are the pre-eminent character, not merely of the production of cultural artifacts, such as poems or paintings. They are the character of basic perception itself, and, given this analogy between perception and artistic creation, perception becomes almost synonymous with imagination, while passivity is simply an example of dead metaphor, of the degeneration of imaginative energy into familiars, fixities, and determinates. 'Things', then, are metaphors, made from other metaphors and figures of speech, eventually mistaken as objects in themselves and somehow independent of the figuration processes of perception itself which produced them.

Coleridge adopted the essentially Hegelian and Shelleyan solution that reason and experience are not subjective and therefore in no need of an object, an externality. Reason is synthetic by virtue of making itself an object of itself, through an original act. There are scattered hints and indications in Coleridge, however, of a further elaboration of his conception of a Shelleyan composition theory of experience, which also suggest anticipations of Heidegger's emphasis upon language and being. Indeed, they suggest that reason, when properly understood, is language, and that the emphasis upon language in modern theory is an elaboration of earlier insights in a new terminology.

Indeed, one could deduce from Coleridge's many definitions of reason that he was moving towards a concept of reason not as a master name, but as a word with the multifold functions of: (1) denoting the continuity between relative, dynamic dualities; (2) taking in the whole of experience, so that both the rational and the irrational, for example, and nature and culture, or mind and world, are bound up together, as Hegel sought to do; (3) having connotations which not only reject materialist and empiricist accounts, but which affirm the centrality of language as the 'house of being,' while eschewing as far as possible idealist, metaphysical implications. To interpret Coleridge as an idealist because of his use of the words reason, or spirit, or self-consciousness would be to ignore his repeated efforts to redefine such words. It would be to ignore their function as emphasizing the linguistic (not the logical) character of experience, and would require readers to ignore his theory of imagination as primary perception, as well as to discount hundreds of other scattered anti-metaphysical, anti-idealist statements. Coleridge's choice of words may be as regrettable as Berkeley's 'idea' or Dewey's 'experience', or even eventually Derrida's 'trace' (trace of a something?). But this is more an observation about the nature of logocentrism embedded into our language and about the difficulty of prising readers out of entrenched, metaphysical, logocentric attitudes, with the related resistance to efforts to revitalizing language, as Shelley described the poet's task. Or perhaps it is simply a fact indicating the way in which language and texts inevitably degenerate with time, from innovative, powerful forces of change to familiar conventions, which finish by shoring up the prejudices and stereotyped metaphysics they had sought to bracket.

Coleridge's remarkable insights into language are scattered widely throughout his published works, as well as in letters, notebooks, and marginalia. Here we must conclude by mentioning only a few of his comments on the relation of language to reason. In an early notebook entry, Coleridge mused on the power of words to affect reason: 'Not only as far as relates to speaking but the knowledge of words, as distinct component parts, which we learn by learning to read – What an immense effect it must have on our reasoning faculties?'[77] Earlier it was suggested that reason develops and further creates itself by reasoning and imagining; but words, said Coleridge, are the tools and powers of thought. He repeatedly insisted that it was a mistake to think that words have significance because they refer to, represent, or correspond to things or thoughts.[78] Words, he explained, are 'learnt by us in clusters, even those that most expressly refer to Images and other Impressions are not all learnt by us determinately'. He then concluded:

> Words therefore become a sort of Nature to us, and Nature is a sort of Words. Both Words and Ideas derive their whole significancy from their coherence. The simple Idea Red dissevered from all, with which it had ever been conjoined would be as unintelligible as the word Red; the one would be a sight, the other a Sound, meaning only themselves, that is in common language, meaning nothing. But this [disseverance] is perhaps not in our power with regard to Ideas, but much more easily to Words. Hence the greater Stability of the Language of Ideas.[79]

(Note that Coleridge is not suggesting that ideas exist before language; he speaks of the language of ideas.)

The 'immense effect . . . upon our reasoning faculties' of words led Coleridge to enthuse on this immense effect: 'Reason, Proportion, communicable Intelligibility intelligent and communicant, the WORD which last expression strikes me as the profoundest and most comprehensive energy of the human Mind.'[80] 'Word', then, is seen here to have been raised to an even higher power, a move that is naturally consequent upon the previous reflections. In *The Philosophical Lectures*, Coleridge took a step further towards the goal he sought of avoiding dogmatic metaphysics, when he equated 'Reason' with 'Logos', 'word', and '*nous*'. Correlatively, he had insisted that, in early Christian times, 'logos' was used to mean 'personal being'.[81] And in a passage in *The Statesman's Manual*, he had changed a quotation from John 1:4 to read 'in the Word [instead of 'in him'] was life; and the life was the light of man'. Here 'word' seems to be equated with 'God' for Coleridge, which suggests interesting interpretations of his own unconventional religion, very biblical perhaps, but far from the orthodoxy of Christian Church versions. In a late letter, he further equated not 'word', but 'reason' with 'God': 'in the Reason is God'.[82] In Greek ὁ λόγος means both the word as expressive of thinking, and the thought, and reason itself. Coleridge seems to have led to the very brink of this double meaning of ὁ λόγος as reason and language. It is not unlikely that Heidegger's meditations on λόγος and λέγω would have been a familiar kind of speculation to Coleridge, as would Heidegger's conclusion that we dwell in language and not it in us.

Coleridge's sophisticated lucubrations on such words as truth, God, Being, and other 'master words', especially in *Aids to Reflection*, his radical

challenge to religious orthodoxy, reveal his connections with later pragmatist and deconstructionist philosophies, however much we wish to
acknowledge his individuality and difference from them. Closely related
to his theory of perception as essentially imaginative and creative (by
means of the imagination construed as both primary and secondary) is
Shelley's composition theory of experience and his belief in language as
essentially metaphorical. The related insistence by both men that poetic
(and all artistic) activity is not a special kind of mental activity, but the
paradigmatic form of human mental activity, from basic perceptual acts
to the highest intellectual exercises, relates them to Nietzsche's universe
of figuration, Dewey's idea of art as itself experience, and Derrida's
differance, free play, and dissemination.

Part III

Art as Experience

8

John Dewey: Language Reconceptualized

Heidegger and Wittgenstein relocated the forms of twentieth-century philosophical thought by reflecting upon language in a way that rejected positivistic emphases on meaning and reference and the distinction between sense and reference.[1] The course of Wittgenstein's (and to some extent Heidegger's) philosophical development illustrates this shift towards viewing language as the context for consciousness, and not merely as an instrument of an already constructed consciousness vis à vis an already constructed world external to it. Later, Derrida applied this shift to literature and literary criticism, showing how radically such a shift affects our notions of the subject, the text, interpretative activity, relations of text to subject and world, the concept of the unity of the text, notions about meaning and truth in texts, and so on. Recent Anglo-American philosophy and criticism had at first some difficulty in assimilating these continental developments, partly due to terminological difficulties and simple linguistic hindrances, such as the problems of translating Heidegger, Derrida, and Wittgenstein, particularly, into an English that could attempt to do justice to the German and French. In Heidegger's case, much is lost because of his poetic style – that is, his efforts actually to embody or 'reduplicate' (to use Kierkegaard's word), in the language, his conceptual insights. In this sense, his prose is almost as dense and compressed as poetry, and as difficult to translate.[2] Even with Wittgenstein, much in the way of fascinating illustration in German is lost. Derrida's writing poses a similar problem of translation, though for different reasons in some cases, one of the most important being the playfulness of his style. The allusiveness of his work – a demonstration of his concept of intertextuality (that interdependence of texts upon other textualities) – along with the rejection of traditional notions of boundaries and discrete, unified texts, further increases problems of comprehension.[3] With Derrida the situation is exacerbated because his style is central, even more than is usually the case, to his project. Another difficulty in reading these writers on language is their rootedness in Husserl's work, and in phenomenology in general, which has been (until the last decade or two), not very well understood in much Anglo-American thinking.[4]

These several difficulties – of terminology, translation, and tradition – are far from insuperable, as many English-speaking literary theorists and philosophers have admirably demonstrated. It seems important that a still wider audience of theorists, critics, and readers should gain access to these liberating insights, readers who do not, for example, know German or French fluently, and who are not very conversant with the phenomenological, terminological traditions that make access easier. This is not to suggest that Heidegger, Derrida, or Wittgenstein's texts are reducible to easy formulae. There is no substitute for reading and con-templating Heidegger in German, no substitute for grappling with Derrida's trapeze-like intertextual stylistic fireworks in its original French, and with Wittgenstein's tantalizing Germanic constructions. It may be possible, however, to clarify some of the central thematic issues with which these writers were grappling by means of John Dewey's earlier, more pedestrian-looking efforts, which, upon analysis, become surprisingly prescient and exciting.

One effective way of gaining access to the significance of the shift from viewing language as a medium (or tool) between two already constructed independent beings – subject and world – to viewing it as the context for world and consciousness, is to look at John Dewey's lucid and systematic treatment of language in *Experience and Nature* (pub-lished first in 1925, having been given as the Carus lectures in 1922). In these lectures, Dewey drew out with great clarity the implications of pragmatism for a reconceptualization of language, anticipating Heidegger, Wittgenstein, and Derrida in quite explicit ways. Since some of Dewey's work (from very early) was translated into French, it is not unlikely that pragmatist influences were exerted on French philosophiz-ing leading up to Derrida, however unconsciously. Richard Rorty has already briefly pointed out the interesting connections between Heidegger and Dewey, in *Consequences of Pragmatism*. Wittgenstein's 'pragmatism' has long been noted, but not to the extent, it seems, of tracing it back in thorough and systematic ways to early twentieth-cen-tury pragmatic texts of Peirce, James, and Dewey.[5] Such interconnec-tions could throw some helpful light on the nature of the insights about language that these three continental philosophers and the pragmatists came to, and corroborated, in each other's work, whatever their obvious differences.

Dewey's most systematic treatment of language came in the fifth chapter of *Experience and Nature*, the text in which he expounded his own most explicit critique of western metaphysics, anticipating Heidegger's and Derrida's great contributions, preparing readers for their penetrating exposures of the assumptions underlying this tradition. This critique of the metaphysics which infects language, as well, is implicit in all Dewey's philosophical writings, as it is in James and C. S. Peirce. Indeed, pragmatism began, and could be defined, as a critique of the dualistic and other (for example, absolutist) assumptions underlying rationalism, empiricism, and idealism alike (as was described in chapters 4 and 5 above). Dewey included in his critique of previous philosophy an account of language, long before either Heidegger or Derrida had made modern readers acutely aware of the importance of an analysis of conventional notions about language and discourse. We need to make ourselves conscious of the unconscious assumptions that have slipped into our speech and writing, forming the foundations for our (unconscious?) epistemology and metaphysics. Hence, Dewey set out in *Experience and Nature* to emphasize the contextual and constructive nature of language, in terms which are often startlingly Heideggerian, and which anticipate some of Derrida's most central ideas. An examination of Dewey's exposition does much to promote an understanding of pragmatism's relation to Derrida, and to deconstruction. As with Coleridge, Dewey's lucid and readable style may tend to lull his reader into a sense that nothing very profound is being said. On the contrary, the profundity is in close relation to the lucidity, as with Plato. Moreover, one can easily misread and misinterpret Dewey, if one takes his remarks out of the context that his pragmatism provides.

Dewey began in *Experience and Nature* by remarking on the fact that while philosophers 'have discussed so fluently about many topics, they have discussed little about discourse itself', and we must take seriously his comment that 'of all affairs, communication is the most wonderful',[6] an evaluation that he went on to justify in detail. Characteristically, Dewey gave a brief exposition of traditional philosophical views of language, sketchy as they are, and pointed out their errors as well as their insights. For example, he noted emphatically that transcendental, rationalist, and idealist philosophers had been more aware of the identification between logos or language and mind than traditional empiricists. Language is the 'condition for mind and consciousness'; mind 'emerges' as language develops. Transcendentalists, Dewey maintained, nevertheless conceived of both mind and language, or logos, as supernatural, instead of arriving at a naturalistic conception of the origin and status of language of the kind which Dewey offered. ('Naturalistic' is a key conception in any discussion of Dewey's ideas on language and philosophy.) He also pointed out the strengths of the traditional views of language as well as their weaknesses, which in this, as in most philosophical cases, involved some kind of dualistic assumption, whether conscious or unconscious. In this case, the dualism involved the unconscious assumption that mind is absolutely independent of physical existence. From a critically penetrating and insightful realization of the nature of the relation between language or logos and mind, transcendental philosophers erroneously moved to a division of the physical and the rational, the real and the ideal, and thus lost the most important implications of the original insight. For they unconsciously assumed an absolute dualism between the physical and mental, and by identifying the logos with mind, the rational became separated from the physical as well, in a conscious way. Language and mind were no longer conceived as natural, but as supernatural.[7]

Dewey contrasted this with the equally faulty empiricist account, which correctly rejected the errors of the transcendentalists, but supplied errors of its own. That is, language was conceived by the empiricists as a mere 'mechanical go-between', a 'practical convenience and not of fundamental intellectual significance'. The historical empiricist's view was of a language that 'expresses thought as a pipe conducts water, and with even less transforming function that is exhibited when a wine-press "expressed" the juice of the grapes'.[8] Such an unimaginative view of language, which Coleridge had bitterly derided, resulted first from the assumption of a world of observations and ideas (a world of existence) absolutely independent of language. Then, social interaction was treated as the product of a 'ready-made specific physical or mental endowment of a self-sufficing individual'. Dewey insisted, on the contrary, as did Derrida (see above, chapter 7), that observations, things, and ideas, as we know them, are to a large extent dependent upon language and social interaction. Nevertheless, Dewey denied the idealist view that some specific mental endowment exists; mentality, he believed, comes into being only with use, with social interaction. Relatedly, Dewey maintained that no concept of the individual is self-sufficing, but exists only in relation to a concept of community.[9]

Empiricists had furthermore failed adequately to note the creative role of language and signs, just as they had traditionally been criticized for failing adequately to acknowledge the creative role of mind while, Dewey argued, like Coleridge, idealists had exaggerated this role and postulated pure mentality. Signs, Dewey emphasized, actually have a centrally creative role in reflection, foresight, and memory; they are not to be conceived as 'mere words, sounds, that happen to be associated with perceptions, sentiments and thoughts which are completely prior to language'.[10] That is, referentiality is not the primary way in which language is meaningful, and Dewey anticipated Wittgenstein in his next step forward. Dewey was arguing a point that Derrida had also tirelessly emphasized, namely that neither objects, whether physical or mental, nor subjects, as we understand or consciously experience them, exist in any intelligible sense of the word prior to language. Indeed, the dichotomy between subjects and objects, and between world and language, is a result of language, Dewey concluded, with Coleridge and Shelley.

Communication through some form of language (some form of artificial signs) is, Dewey explained, in Heideggerean phraseology, a 'condition of consciousness'.[11] Or, put another way, Dewey explained that 'mind emerges'; it does not exist ready-made and prior to language. Language and mind emerge together, and with them the world as known and meaningful emerges, too. Heidegger spoke of this point clearly when he described language as 'the house of being', as the context and condition of conscious existence.[12] Psychic events which are anything more than the unconscious reflex reactions of a creature susceptible to pain and comfort have, we are assured, language as a condition of their existence as such. 'Events' become perceptible, meaningful, or identifiable objects or happenings only through their 'concretion in discourse'; or, as Coleridge put it, by thinking, we 'thingify'.[13] We objectify and make perceptible and meaningful (bring into conscious existence) things, thoughts, or objects, whether physical or mental. In a very Heideggerean statement, Dewey wrote:

> That things should be able to pass from the plane of external pushing and pulling to that of revealing themselves to man, and thereby to themselves; and that the fruit of communication should be participation, sharing, is a wonder by the side of which transubstantiation pales. . . . Events turn into objects, things with a meaning.[14]

Dewey elaborated this revelatory, Wallace Stevens-like quality of language further when he continued:

> to reorganize the thing is to grasp its definition. Thus we become capable of perceiving things instead of merely feeling and having them. To perceive is to acknowledge unattained possibilities; it is to refer the present to consequences . . . and thereby to behave in deference to the connections of events . . . perception or aware-

ness is predictive by expectancy, wariness. The meaningful event –
the event marked by potential consequences, becomes an object of
contemplation; as meaning, future consequences already belong
to the thing.[15]

Dewey explained that the belief that sensory affections discriminate and
identify themselves apart from discourse into colours and sounds, thus
ipso facto constituting certain elementary modes of knowledge (even if it
be only knowledge of their own existence) is inherently absurd. Indeed,
no one would ever have entertained such a notion were it not for
familiar preconceptions and prejudices about mind and knowledge.
Dewey insisted that sentiency in itself is anoetic. Yet while it exists as any
immediate quality exists, it nevertheless is an indispensable means of any
noetic function:

> The qualities of situations in which organisms and surrounding
> conditions interact, when discriminated, make sense. Sense is
> distinct from feeling, for it has a recognized reference; it is the
> qualitative characteristic of something, not just a submerged
> unidentified quality of tone. Sense is also different from sig-
> nification. The latter involves use of a quality as a sign or index of
> something else, as when the red of a light signifies danger, and the
> need of bringing a moving locomotive to a stop. The sense of a
> thing, on the other hand, is an immediate and immanent meaning;
> it is meaning which is itself felt or directly had. When we are baffled
> by perplexing conditions, and finally hit upon a clew, and every-
> thing falls into place, the whole thing suddenly, as we say, 'makes
> sense.' In such a situation, the clew has signification in virtue of
> being an indication, a guide to interpretation. But the meaning of
> the whole situation as apprehended is sense.[16]

Dewey went on to note that this apparently idiomatic use of the word
sense is actually nearer the empirical facts than is our usual restriction of
the word to a single, simple quality, like red or bitter. These, he says,
simply apply as cases of minimum sense, limited for the purposes of
philosophical definition. He concluded, however, that when any situation has both the double function of meaning, namely, signification and
sense, then we can conclude that mind or intellect is present. He then
rejected categorically any division between physical, psycho-physical,
and mental events: all are natural, they do not represent separate kinds
of Being.
Dewey concluded that the heart of language, far from being either

referentiality or a copying of reality, far from being moreover the expression of something antecedent (and certainly not of antecedent thought), is, rather, communication, and, as such, enables us to live in a world of things that have meaning through language, while we are also engaged in a social sharing that enhances their meanings still further. The importance of this insight has rarely been grasped, partly because it seems so obvious. Yet its consequences for a view of language and literature are incalculable, as it establishes the overcoming of the individual/society dualism, the private/public dichotomy, and as it establishes a profound connection with Derrida's ideas of writing as inscribed in nature/culture. For communication also relates to Wittgenstein's deeply pragmatic commitment to social life as the context for individuality and his rejection of notions of private language and intentionality. Dewey's use of the word communication, taken in context, is almost a synonym for Derrida's 'writing'.

Dewey gave another example of the way language 'brings objects into being', in the following case:

A stick, even though once used as a lever, would revert to the status of being just a stick, unless the relationship between it and its consequences were distinguished and retained. Only language, or some form of artifical signs, serves to register the relationship and make it fruitful in other contexts.[17]

He concluded that to made another person aware of the possibility of a use, or of an objective relationship , as he called 'instrumentality', is to perpetuate as an 'agency' what otherwise would be a mere incident or bare happening, without meaning; communication, he repeatedly emphasized, is a condition of consciousness. Language and communication bring objects into meaningful existence, as Heidegger tirelessly argued, a point more often made by poets than philosophers. As for Derrida, then, for Dewey too there are no objects *per se*, existing prior to language and revealed or copied by it. Nor, however, are there pre-existing subjects, as idealists imply. The occurrence of language, Dewey noted, changed dumb creatures – as we call them so significantly – into thinking and knowing animals, and created the realm of meanings. Perceiving, knowing subjects come into being through language.

The nature of the distinction Dewey described between animal and human experience is enlightening. He explained that animals, complex and active as they are, have, therefore, feelings which vary enormously in quality, corresponding to activities bound up in distinctive connections with environmental affairs. Animals do have feelings, but they do not know that they have them. Activity, Dewey explained, is psycho-physical, for animals, but not specifically 'mental'. To act is not necessarily to be aware of meanings. Mind, on the other hand, is an added 'property' achieved by a natural organism, by a creature that engages in activity, when it reaches that natural but highly organized interaction with other living creatures called language or communication. Then only do the qualities of feelings become significant as specifying objective differences in external things and as identifying episodes as past, or present, or to come. When qualitatively different feelings or activities are not just 'had', but are significant of objective differences, then can we speak of mind. Feelings, Dewey concluded, are no longer just felt or had, they have and they make sense; they record past meanings and prophesy future ones.

There was for Dewey, as for Coleridge and Nietzsche, no doctrine more absurd than the empiricist notion that general ideas or meanings could arise by comparison of a number of particulars, eventuating in the recognition of something common to them all.[18] Comparison, Dewey maintained, is used only to check a suggested wider application of a rule. Rather, mind spontaneously carries generalization as far as it can be pushed:

> Meanings are self-moving to new cases. To call [generalization] *a priori* is to express a fact; but to impute the *a priori* character of the generalizing force to reason is to invent the facts. Rationality is acquired when the tendency becomes circumspect, based upon observation and tested by deliberate experiment.[19]

Dewey carefully and systematically examined the 'meaning of meaning', and, more particularly the nature of communication. He argued that while the Greeks had a more adequate conception of discourse than modern philosophers, they seemed to mistake 'the structure of discourse for the structure of things, instead of for the forms which things assume under the pressure and opportunity of social cooperation and exchange'.[20] This error was mentioned earlier when it was said that transcendentalists identified logos and mind and made them into supernatural entities. The Greeks, Dewey believed, like many philosophers after them, elevated meanings into ultimate, independent forms of things, forms which then dictated the evolution of the world of becoming. As he succinctly described this error, the Greeks, as did their followers, 'took a work of social art to be nature independent'. This mistaking of social products for independent nature is at the core of all forms of dualism and absolutism. It might be said then that the world of nature as we know it, a world including both subjects (minds) and objects (whether mental or physical), is a work of 'social art' which is mistaken as nature independent. Hence Derrida's famous reversal of nature and culture.[21] This position is also not to be mistaken as idealism, however; Dewey, like Coleridge and Derrida, criticized the idealist for making mind absurdly creative and, indeed, supernatural. Mind, for Dewey, did not create the world or exist prior to it and above the physical. Rather, the world and mind are both works of social art, or figures of speech, if you will. They are the objective results of social cooperation, of sharing and experience, of participation and exchange. And this social cooperation is effected through language. Put more forcibly, Dewey described communication as the 'queen of social arts'. As the product of social art, of shared experience, the resulting evolving world (including humans as they see themselves through the consciousness that language makes possible) is neither subjective nor objective in itself, but can be subjected to those perspectives depending on one's particular interest at a given time.[22]

Dewey more specifically anticipated Derrida when he pointed out that the theory of substances and essences, which resulted from elevating the structure of discourse to the structure of things, 'controlled the whole scheme of physics and metaphysics, which formed the philosophic tradition of Europe'.[23] Or, as Derrida might put it, certainly things, words, and meanings correspond; but the correspondences of things and meanings was falsely conceived to be prior to discourse and to social intercourse. Dewey can hardly be said to have exaggerated when he stated that the discovery of the relation between things and meanings was the 'greatest single discovery of man', but he noted that this discovery was perverted by the assumption that some sort of correspondence existed prior to language. The result of that false assumption was a belief in ideal essences, with philosophy, science, and morals turning into a stale dialectic of their relationships, of definitions, classifications, and so on. The universe was viewed as 'an incarnate grammatical order constructed after the model of discourse',[24] a view which Dewey rejected as yet another absurd form of idealism. He also rejected the corresponding solipsism of much modern thought, which he insisted was based upon a failure to recognize that the world of inner, private experience is also equally dependent upon an extension of language; inner experience is also a social product and a communal operation. Thus, he complained, modern philosophers, in contrast to the ancients, composed nature not after a grammatical mode, but after the model of 'personal soliloquizing'. Introspecion, then, Dewey argued, is not a matter of looking into a realm of wholly private events of mental stuff, utterly disparate from the world of social and physical events. Introspection may well be soliloquy, but soliloquy is merely the result of converse with others, and entirely dependent upon it. Dewey concluded that, contrary to much philosophy, it is not social communication which is an effect of soliloquy, of some notion of private thought prior to language, but the other way round. Or rather, like Wittgenstein and Derrida, he reversed the priorities and then insisted on the interdependence of the two.[25]

Dewey concluded that language is a *natural* function of human association. Its results have consequences for other events, whether physical or specifically human: language gives events meaning and significance. This is not to say that human association in any meaningful sense existed prior to language, or the other way around. Both these concepts are interdependent for meaning: any notion of priority is simply unintelligible. Through the use of language, then, 'bare' events, metaphorically speaking, are enriched and accrue greater meaning, thereby enriching language. As Dewey explained, events come to possess 'character.' When events come to have communicable meaning through social intercourse, they have marks, notations, and are capable of connotation and denotation. Events become more than mere occurrences, Dewey insisted. Events come to have implications, and thereby more inference and reasoning are possible.

In words that Heidegger might have used, indeed, vrtually did use, Dewey wrote that inference and reasoning are 'reading the message of things, which things utter because they are involved in human associations'.[26] The world, for Dewey, is a kind of textual entity, in interdependence with human experience understood as saturated by language. Dewey concluded that the Aristotelian distinction between the sensible and the rational is better understood as a distinction between things that operate in a local, restricted context or universe of discourse, and things which are easily extended to larger, more extensive universes of discourse. (Dewey did not read Plato as advocating an intellectualist distinction, either.) The distinction is not an absolute division amongst things, as Coleridge, for example, would also argue, but a simple variation of emphasis in the extent of human association. Moreover, just as there is an absurdity in contemplating the priority of language over human association or vice versa, there is an equal absurdity in posing the question of the priority of individuals over social intercourse and association, or asking how individuals become social. For the two concepts, individuality and sociability, are interdependent, not one prior to another, as Derrida and Shelley had also urged. For Dewey, immediacy (individuality) is not 'the whole of existence. . . . Everything that exists, in as far as it is known and knowable, is in interaction with other things. It is associated, as well as solitary, single'.[27] Human association is in itself then, nothing new; and individuality is relative to association and interaction. What is new is the element and extent of participation at the heart of communication. One thinks immediately of Plato, for whom things 'participate' in reality. With human participation in association, individuality emerged in the context of social intercourse; but social intercourse is dependent on individuality. There is no privileging, or hierarchy, of originary forms.

In order to explain this concept of participation as a central character of language (rather than, for example, referentiality), Dewey insisted that gestures and cries are not the origin of language. They are not primarily expressive or communicative, but mere organic modes of behaviour such as locomotion, chewing, and others. Language arises from the use made of sounds and gestures. These latter become language only when used in a context of participation, that is, of mutual sharing and directed activity. Such a context alone brings about the transformation of mere sounds or cries into names, signs, and significations. The crucial transformation from sounds to names occurs, Dewey explained, when sounds are treated as signs of an ulterior event, or rather, when sounds and events are treated as of interest, not in themselves, but as 'preparatory to a desired consummation'. Thus, response is not to some 'bare event' or bare sound, but to its meaning. Moreover, the essential peculiarity of language as distinct from mere gestures, cries, sounds, or events, is that the latter are egocentric, that is, of interest only as they function in the experience of the originator of them, while genuine signs or linguistic events are 'participatory': another human being is involved. Something, then, is made common in at least two different centres of behaviour. Moreover, sounds and gestures are responded to not in themselves, but as an index of something else. Dewey gave a lucid account of this difference between sounds and signs in discussing the way one interprets the act of pointing, relating to a similar discussion in Wittgenstein. Dewey succinctly reminded us that, 'In pointing, you have to learn to interpret the straight arm and finger as pointing. You have to learn, that is, that the straight arm and finger are meaning something at all.'[28]

Speech, therefore, is markedly different from the signalling acts or reflexes of animals, though the latter might be construed as manipulable material, so to speak, for language. These acts, however, are not signs, as pointing is, or as words are, but direct stimuli to which other animals respond by a performed mechanism such as habit or conditioned reflex.

Such acts are responded to in themselves, and not as indices of something else, not as part of a system of participation and human association.

Meaning is a property of behaviour, but of a very distinctive behaviour that is cooperative, systemic, and inferential. Meaning is not, Dewey insisted, a psychic existence or an occult quality supervening.[29] The co-operative behaviour that characterizes meaningfulness is described by Dewey as the responsiveness to acts by another person, which responsiveness itself involves yet again response to a thing as it enters into the other's behaviour. Indeed, Dewey saw this cooperative engagement as the very sign of intelligence itself. Further, in analysing meaning, a relatively primary and a relatively secondary characteristic are noted. First, meaning is said to be intent. Yet intent is not to be understood as a personal or private affair exclusively, as some phenomenologists would seem to suggest. For meaning originates in communicative, cooperative contexts. Second, meaning is the 'acquisition of significance by things in their status in making possible and fulfilling shared cooperation'. Or, in other words, things gain meaning when they cease to be just what they are brutely at the moment, and are responded to as means to ends, for example, or as 'indices of further potentialities', as 'effects of later consequences'.[30] Elsewhere, Dewey defined the ability to discern conse-quences as intelligence: to see the absent in the present, to see events as signs of future happenings. Intelligence creates or enriches things as meaningful, while meanings contribute to the emergence, development, and growth of mind and intelligence.

Dewey defined 'essence' as merely a pronounced instance of mean-ing. The meaningfulness of an event involves most integrally its potential consequences, Dewey argued, which, when repeated and when impor-tant to the observer or participant, can be said to be the essence of a thing. Thus, essences are not independent of human experience, not pure logicality or intellectuality, not any kind of metaphysical entity. They are merely meanings that are said to designate extensive and recurrent consequences. Yet since things have more than one meaning, more than one set of consequences, to assign one meaning as essence is to be partial to a set of consequences for a particular goal. At another time, another set of consequences may be seen as more significant. Thus, supposedly 'immutable essences' are subject to change, and are only, anyway, a result of a history of repeated, preferred contexts or consequences in meanings: 'essence emerges from the various meanings which vary with varying conditions and transitory intents'.[31] Essences are hypostasized by phiolosophers, however, into primary and constitutive forms of existence when they are treated as final and ultimate in nature itself, instead of as the 'distilled import', as Dewey described it, of meanings that result from social activities and human cooperation.

Nevertheless, essence and meaning are not arbitrary or solipsistically relative. Words, Dewey explained, are modes of social interaction which function to realize the goals of human association. They are not, Dewey reminded his reader, the expression of 'a ready-made, exclusively individual mental state'. For example, sounds do not become words by expressing a mental existence (a sensation, image, feeling, or idea) in the mind of a particular individual. Rather, sounds become words when they accrue meaning, that is, when the use of a sound establishes a genuine community of action. Meanings are rules and a community devises rules for using and interpreting things. Interpretation, moreover, involves the imputation or ascription by someone of the existence of a potentiality for some consequences.

Meanings are not, then, either univocal or private, not a property of ghostly psychic existences, as Wittgenstein had also emphatically insisted. They are, he too argued, communally developed in the process of human activities, human 'games', rules, and 'forms of life'. They are not essentially subjective (though they of course have personal associations), precisely because they are not absolute, transcendent, or eternal forms of things. It is precisely their origin in communal acts that assures their relative objectivity, though they are, of course, subject to change, as human activities or forms of association ('forms of life', as Wittgenstein called these) and human interests and values change.[32] Meanings are objective, then, precisely because they are modes of natural interaction and relative rules of social action. Meaning and essence are best understood as the 'persisting rules of social and natural interaction', not as expressions of eternal relations pre-existing amongst objects independent of human intercourse. (It is doubtful whether even Berkeley could be interpreted, with his 'language of nature', as saying anything more 'metaphysical' than Dewey, given his empirical commitment, and the context in which his metaphor occurred. One could argue that Berkeley was expressing the 'textuality' of nature, and rejecting the priority of nature over culture.)

For Dewey, every meaning, then, is generic or universal. A meaning is, he said, a method of action, a way of using things as a means to a shared consummation. Dewey also noted that while method may be general, the things to which it is applied are themselves concrete and particular. To sum, for Dewey as for Wittgenstein, meanings were relative rules for using and interpreting things. Yet interpretation itself was always understood as an 'imputation of potentiality for some consequence'.[33]

Hence, the classical philosophers rightly asserted the objectivity of meanings, essences, and ideas: 'Meaning is objective as well as universal . . . it indicates a possible interaction, not a thing in separate stillness.' In seeming to attribute, however, to essence and meaning, in *rerum natura*, the consequences they possessed only within the transmitted culture of the group, the classical philosophers erred. Dewey explained:

> Some meanings are meanings communally developed in the process of communal festivity and control, and do not represent the politics, and ways and means of nature apart from social arts. Scientific meanings were superadded to aesthetical and affectional meanings when objects, instead of being defined in terms of their consequences in social interactions and discussion, were defined in terms of their consequences with respect to one another.[34]

Meanings are not private, psychic existences, as much philosophy would have us believe. They have, as Dewey's vocabulary and arguments show, a naturalistic origin in communal interaction and social intercourse. Nevertheless, scientific and mathematical meanings are no more objective than other meanings, Dewey believed.[35] They are, rather, a result of objects being related and defined by humans in terms of human interests and in terms of the interactions and consequences of the objects with respect to each other, instead of being defined directly in terms of their specific effects in social interaction or human relation, as are aesthetic and moral meanings. Hence, scientific meanings are additional meanings of things. They are not qualitatively more true or more real, nor are they essential aspects of those things. For the purposes of science, we may choose to ignore the ulterior meanings that things have in relation to humankind, directing our attention relatively exclusively to the meanings determined in terms of what we call causal relationships of things amongst themselves and apart from direct human interaction. However, to repeat, these are no more real, or objective, than the aesthetic, moral, affective, or religious meanings things have in terms of human association.

Ancient philosophy, and its survival in later modern idealism, assumed that the ulterior human meanings, or meanings of direct association in discourse, as Dewey put it, are forms of nature isolated and independent from their place in human discourse. Modern thought marks a sharp disjunction between meanings determined in terms of the causal relationships of things and meanings in terms of human associations. The latter, Dewey complained, are treated as negligible or purely private, not the meanings of natural events at all, so that 'abstract relations become an idol'. A distinction valid for purposes of science controlling natural events becomes invalidated when philosophers abstract it into a value judgement about hierarchies of reality. In science, then, symbols are used to define things in their consequences with respect to each other alone. But, as Dewey insisted, 'water still has the meanings of the water of everyday experience when it becomes the essence H_2O, or else H_2O would be totally meaningless, a mere sound, not an intelligible name'.[36] Thus, Dewey concluded, the natural bridge between existence and essence, when abstracted, opens up a gulf that is 'fictitious, gratuitous, and unbridgeable'.

Language for Dewey is an experienced event, and, like meaning, language involves relationships. It is not a thing; it is a function, not an entity. Moreover, meanings are also, like language, relational, differential, functional, instrumental, as Saussure was later to argue, and not substantive or essential and unchanging. Meanings indicate possible interactions; they are not 'things in separate singleness', immutable and eternal. Language is always a form of action, an expression of interest and survival. (For this vital, dynamic view of language Dewey was deeply influenced by William James, and by Nietzsche.) Moreover, as a specific mode of interaction of two or more people, language presupposes 'an organized group to which these creatures belong, and from whom they have acquired, their habits of speech'. This community of partaking (which is meaning, for Dewey) involves not only a speaker and an audience: 'The meaning of signs moreover always includes something common as between persons and an object, . . . Persons and things must alike serve as means in a common, shared consequence.'[37] Meanings, to be objective, need not be elevated to a realm separate from and superior to the realm of existence, nor treated as an order of entity independent of human invention and use, as if they were not themselves significant terms of discourse. Dewey concluded:

> Meanings are evolved in human experience, not prior to it or independently of it. But they are objective and compelling with respect to present particular physical and psychical processes; they are general methods of reaching consequences; they are interactions of previously existing physical existences.[38]

With this lucid example in mind, one can see that the same observations apply to meanings and essences, though they are conceived neither as physical nor as psychical existences; they are, rather, 'continuous ways of organized action.' While, like machines, meanings are demonstrably dependent on human interaction, they are functions which act, Dewey

insisted, to expand that very interaction in order to make it more significant and rich. Meanings and essences, then, build upon each other; they
can be so 'dialectically fruitful' that complex cultural structures emerge.
Yet such cultural structures and constructs are, nevertheless, continuous
with their naturalistic and linguistic 'origins'.

Clearly, for Dewey, then, as for Heidegger and Derrida, nature and
culture emerge together, not the one prior to the other. As was concluded in the chapter on metaphysics, Dewey argued that mind emerges
with language and reasoning. No faculty of reason, no entity called
mind, exists prior to acts of reasoning. Coleridge had argued similarly
throughout his writings, culminating in *Aids to Reflection,* that the development of a faculty of 'imaginative reason' (not the calculating faculty,
but Reason) was in direct proportion to the intelligent use of words and
language as exercises in acts of imaginative thinking. Shelley had viewed
the imagination and its vehicle, metaphor, in the same way, following
English terminology with his use of 'imagination', insisting that nature is
part of human culture just as culture is part of 'nature', and that only by
exercising the imaginative faculty, as one does in art, can the human
mind and human culture develop further and, with them, a complex
nature emerge.

9

Dewey's 'Romantic' Aesthetic

Coleridge and Johnson founded their theories of criticism on the belief first, that all criticism is an analysis of received opinion and not a search for the true meaning of a text. Nor were they under the illusion that the object of critical enquiry is a text-in-itself. Second, both Johnson and Coleridge were anxious to stress the importance of striving for certainty in critical methods of procedure, and not in striving for clarity about the work of art in itself. Hence their emphasis upon the importance of establishing and clearly stating principles, along with a careful elaboration of the Platonic method of analysis and synthesis in the formation of critical opinion and judgment. Both repeatedly assured their readers that one major role of criticism was to help readers to improve their critical practice, their reading, and to develop powers of discrimination, analysis, and acts of synthetic unification, rather than that criticism should tell readers what to read or think, and save them the trouble of articulating and sophisticating their own responses. Coleridge, perhaps more than Johnson, emphasized the importance of what he called geniality,[1] that is, of establishing some sympathetic rapport with authors by at first seeking to dwell upon their strengths. This would create in the reader a more perceptive frame of mind, so that new, original forms and techniques might be at least temporarily tolerated until a better understanding could judge their adequacy to the intent. Otherwise, the reader-critic might be inclined to reject the new out of hand, before allowing time and familiarity to reveal the appropriateness of new forms of expression to new experiences. This idea of geniality is, at ground, simply the well-attested truth that unless two people agree about something, there is no basis for argument. It asks further for a suspension of distrust for a time; or, as Coleridge put it, 'until I understand a writer's ignorance, I will presume myself ignorant of his understanding'.[2]

Coleridge and Johnson also insisted that the reader-critic must be highly trained, like any expert in any field of enquiry. That is, she must have developed a sense of beauty through education and experience, and must have a rich and well-informed knowledge of the artist and the tradition, as well as a knowledge of other traditions, in order that taste should not be provincially limited. It might be thought that Coleridge's insistence upon the idea that taste is relatively universal, that every human mind has within it a 'regulative principle' or sense of beauty, postulates a non-empirical, transcendent faculty at odds with pragmatism and deconstruction. This is in fact not the case. Rather, standards of beauty are understood by Coleridge to be human conventions, not absolute, objective, and independent rules from without the human mind and human culture.[3] Also apparently at odds with deconstructionism is Coleridge's insistence on organic unity as a character of art and genius. As was discussed briefly in chapter 2, however, his concept of organicism has little to do with static structure, emphasizing instead evolution, transformation, and growth.[4] Coleridge, like pragmatists and deconstructors, moreover, insisted that there can be no rigid distinction between art and criticism. The latter at its best is art. The *Biographia Literaria* was a testimony to this new genre, and a more successful effort than any contemporary piece of writing, only equalled by Shelley's 'Defence of poetry'.

Implicit in Johnson's theory and explicit in Coleridge's was the pragmatist-deconstructionist insistence on the active-creative role of the reader. Related to this active-creative reader role, a role that in kind (if not in degree) is one with that of the artist-maker, is the consequence that any given interpretation is only one of many possible ones. For John Dewey, this plurality of possible meanings did not mean that all interpretations are as useful as all others; this feared relativity and total subjectivity or solipsism is hardly the outcome of such theories of criticism, any more than it is the outcome of science. The method of critical procedure is, according to Dewey, that of science, and the same result accrues: namely, hypotheses that arise via imaginative reflection from a selection of observed material can be tested for their adequacy against the demands and constraints of the material. Like scientific hypotheses, Dewey argued, some interpretations are better than others for a stated purpose, because they account more or less elegantly for the given material. But hypotheses that, once tested, are regarded as established theories, like interpretations of poems that have been tested, are nevertheless subject to revision in the light of new evidence, or, in the case of works of art, in the light of new ways of perceiving or viewing the object. Thus no interpretation is absolute or final; it does not preclude further investigation, but it is nevertheless objective in the only meaningful sense of that word, namely publicly testable against the materials of the work of art which are available to every reader. Not surprisingly, Dewey's account of critical method in some chapters of *Experience and Nature*, and more fully developed later in *Art as Experience*, acts as an intermediary between Johnson and Coleridge (and romantic theory generally), and the deconstructionist emphasis on the apparently incongruous principles of criticism as play and criticism as rigorous method of procedure (without the positivist encumbrance of logical certainty, however). Indeed, Dewey's elaboration of his own critical principles not only establishes a link between Johnson, Coleridge, and the deconstructors; the development of his argument parallels that of Coleridge's in the *Biographia* in some important respects, though it remains more discursive in style than either Coleridge, Shelley, or Derrida, more akin to the most exemplary theorists amongst the American deconstructors.

Judgement, for Dewey and for Coleridge, formed an essential and central role in the act of criticism of an aesthetic object. Yet both these terms, criticism and judgement, are frequently used in ways that suggest a misunderstanding of the nature of critical activities in regard to art and literature. Modern critical theory has forced us to a careful re-evaluation and reanalysis of such terms as judgement and criticism in our critical tool-chest,[5] in order to bring about a greater awareness of the most profitable ways in which we, as readers and critics, can approach literature, more consciously aware of what we are doing to it (whether as readers or as critics). According to Dewey, one might expect that judgement, which both ideally and etymologically, *is* criticism, is an act of intelligence performed upon an object of direct perception with the view towards a more adequate, improved perception. Unfortunately, Dewey noted, judgement has another import, namely, that of passing verdicts on texts or making authoritative statements of preferences about texts. Criticism, rather than being seen as explicative of the content of an object with regard to its substance and form (to use Dewey's phraseology), is seen as a process of condemnation or acquittal. Criticism has been erected into something 'judicial' and desire for authoritative standing leads many critics to speak like attorneys for established principles of unquestioned authority. Or, as one critic has described the process of settling the claim of rival hypotheses, the latter look like 'little people battling beneath a throne over whose appearance is most consonant with court standards'.[6] Perception is thereby obstructed by the remembering of an influential rule or by the substitution of precedent and prestige in place of direct experience.

Hence, as Coleridge complained, many critics assume their role as literary explicators to be one that involves judgements about a text which are final and which settle the matter.[7] For Dewey, as for Coleridge, judgement and criticism should be an 'act of controlled enquiry', a 'development in thought of a deeply realized perception'. As one notes from much of the secondary criticism of our own century, and from complaints made by writers such as Coleridge in earlier times, critics prefer to 'tell' their readers what they should believe, and, as Johnson and Coleridge complained, their audience itself prefers to be told. To teach readers to 'discriminate and unify', to teach them to school themselves in thoughtful enquiry, is a much more difficult, though rewarding task which, Dewey believed, was one major aim of criticism. According to Johnson, Dewey, and Coleridge, such judicial decision, which passes itself off as objective criticism, assumes that antecedent authoritative standards exist by means of which one judges and pronounces verdicts on texts, as, for example, in the neo-classicism of the eighteenth century, and as in the unconscious, unreflective criticism of traditional, 'anti-theory' critics unwilling to analyse their own methods – if methods they can be called which substitute existing prejudice for thoughtful enquiry. Dewey complained that notions such as Arnold's of an 'infallible test' – provided by the ancients – limit direct response and introduce extraneous factors that are harmful to the individual's development of appreciation. Great artists, Johnson, Coleridge, and Dewey insisted, follow neither rules nor ancient models, but subdue both of these to serve the enlargement of their own personal experience and the expression of that experience.[8]

Such judicial criticism as Coleridge and Dewey rejected sees itself as the guardian of tradition; it constantly refers to the so-called true art of previous artists, set up against new and unacceptable inventions. The main failure of the best of judicial criticism arises, Dewey explained, precisely from its inability to cope with the emergence of new art forms and new modes of experience that demand new modes of expression. New artists almost always master the techniques of the artists that preceded them. Yet as artists grow, they see experience and the world in new ways, and this new subject-matter demands new forms. Technique being relative to form, artists are forced to try to develop new technical procedures to render these new forms of expression. Coleridge argued that new movements in art, such as the poetry of the *Lyrical Ballads*, express something new in human experience to which judicial criticism, which relies on standards from the past, is inevitably blind and insensitive.

The opposite form of criticism from the judicial type discussed so far, is, as one would expect, equally ineffectual. 'Impressionist criticism', as

Dewey liked to label it, or subjective criticism, as Coleridge called it, is a denial that criticism in the sense of judgement is even possible. Judgement, according to impressionist criticism, should be replaced by a simple statement of the responses of feeling and imagining which the art object evokes. Such criticism is clearly a reaction against the 'standardized pseudo-objectivity' of the ready-made rules and precedents of judicial criticism, and a reaction in favour of the chaos of a subjectivity that is lacking in any objective control. Impressionist criticism asserts that criticism can do no more than utter and catalogue the impressions made on the reader or spectator by a work of art. Dewey complained that a mere 'it seems to me' is all such criticism can honestly offer. Hence, Dewey and Coleridge objected, the insight of a cultivated mind and the gush of the immature enthusiastic stand on the same level. Or, as Friedrich Schlegel complained, the most we can say is WOW![9] Because judicial criticism set up false notions of objective values – or indeed unconscious notions that cater to tradition – the impressionist critic has reacted by denying that there *are* any objective values at all. No criteria of any sort are allowed, since the criteria used by judicial criticism involve standards of an external and extraneous nature.

Both Coleridge and Dewey realized, however, that judgement of the value of an idea or the value of a work of art involves a conception of 'standard' that is quite different from the usual notion of standard as quantitative (and which can be applied equally well by a child as by an experienced, mature expert). There is, Dewey suggested, no external and public thinking defined by law that can be applied to works of art, whose traits are also qualitative, not merely quantitative experiences. Dewey, like Coleridge, however, insisted that it does not follow from the acknowledgement of an absence of a uniform and publicly determined external object that objective criticism is impossible. What does follow is precisely that criticism *is* judgement – and that like all judgement, it involves a 'hypothetical element'. Criticism is not the mere authoritative pronouncement of a valuation of works of art. It is concerned with the objective properties of the object under consideration, Dewey explained; it is a search for the properties of the object that may justify or invalidate the direct reactions had to it. The astute critic, argued Dewey, will lay far more emphasis upon the objective traits of the object than upon pronouncements of good or bad. Authoritative statements about worth tend to limit personal experience rather than enrich it, while the astute critics' survey of 'objective traits' may be of assistance in heightening the perception of other readers about the texts under question.[10]

While, then, no standards *per se* exist for works of art or for criticism (at least in the sense of standards of measurement, since these apply to quantitative, not qualitative traits), there are, nevertheless criteria in judgement, so that criticism does not fall into the field of mere impressionism. Yet such criteria are not rules or prescriptions applied from without, as Coleridge would put it; they are the result, as Dewey would say, of efforts to find out what a work of art is as an experience, that is, what the kind of experience is that constitutes it. This question of what a work of art is as an experience, or what the kinds of experiences are that constitute the work of art, is another way, paradoxically, of speaking of the objective traits of an object which provide part of that objective control missing from impressionist criticism (the other part of objective control being provided for by the critics' commitment to a procedure for justifying his comments, by grounding them in the objective traits of the object so that any reader can check his or her conclusions against those traits). That the experience of a work of art, to use Dewey's expression, should be a way of talking about objective traits, seems paradoxical, since 'experience' usually is taken to refer to something subjective. Yet for both Coleridge and Dewey, as for Kant, the word experience necessarily involves the unification of subject and object. Hence, experience can be neither wholly subjective not wholly objective. Our task, as critics, is, in part, to render our experience of texts as public and accessible to other readers as possible by discriminating objective traits in the work of art that are perceivable to other readers. Yet, objective traits, like the word experience, does not mean absolutely objective – but objective in the sense of testable within the context of experience; for 'traits' exist only as discriminated in experience; they do not exist outside experience and in the object. Criticism based on such criteria as are arrived at by looking at the experience arising from a text becomes, as Coleridge, Johnson, Dewey and others have asserted, a public document which can be tested by others against their own direct perceptual experience of the work of art. The objective traits of the object as object supply part of the objectivity of such criticism. These traits do not exist in the object in the sense of being outside the experience of it. They exist within the experience of the object as objective, as public, for they are grounded on experienced perceptions available to other spectators.

Criticism as judgement has, according to Coleridge and Dewey, two main functions to perform, namely analysis and synthesis, or, in Dewey's terms, discrimination and unification. First, with regard to discrimination, it is for the reader's judgement to evoke a clear consciousness of constituent parts in the work of art (not the constituent parts, but simply some constituent parts), and then to discover how the parts relate to form a whole (not *the* whole, but *a* whole). This Coleridgean part-whole concept is at the basis of an organic concept of art. But this concept has been poorly understood, especially in modern theory, as denoting something static and fixed, structural and final. On the contrary, the organic theory of art as expressed by Coleridge and Dewey denotes anything but fixity and finality: it constantly evokes concepts of growth and development, of change, life, movement, and relativity. In organic criticism, all forms are open-ended and in the process of change, growth, and development. Forms and unities are never static and fixed as in structuralism. New forms, shapes, parts, wholes, and unities are constantly growing out of the old ones. Hence, a work of art does not have fixed parts and a static whole or unity. It has the character of living things, things that are in growth, change, development: evolution without any final aim. Organic unity suggests discriminable parts related in perceivable ways to discriminable wholes. Yet the main characteristic of works of art conceived organically is that they are rich with innumerable perspectives and evolving possibilities as parts relating to some whole. There is, however, no single unity or form for each work of art, and no single set of fixed parts. According to Dewey, there is a variety of ways of seeing a work of art as a unity, a variety of sets of parts, or, a variety of experiences: hence, a variety of possible objective traits.[11]

This variety of parts and wholes and unities and forms, like the variety of meanings a work of art offers, constitutes the experiences a work of art can inspire. The astute reader and critic can articulate some of these experiences, meanings, forms, unities, parts, or whatever you will call these objective traits of the artifact. Readers of such criticism can see some of the ways in which the critic arrived at his or her responses, and test them against their own experience, with a view not merely to verifying their initial experience of the text, but to enlarging, transforming, or modifying it. Attention is, in such criticism, drawn to traits in the object, whether parts or wholes, unnoticed before by most readers; or attention can be drawn to the fact that traits previously ascribed by readers to the text are not demonstrably there, but imposed from without due to traditions and expectations. These traits (of part/whole, for example), objective as they are, are the result of acts of discrimination, which itself is an experience – but not subjective. For experience is neither subjective nor objective in itself; it becomes so when it is either grounded in intelligent enquiry or not grounded, but made obscure and subjective by prejudice, habit, and custom.

For Dewey, the moment of discrimination, or analytic judgement – as he and Coleridge liked to call it, after Kant – is the moment when that hypothetical element spoken of earlier enters into criticism. Analysis, or the discrimination of parts (as contrasted with synthesis, or the perception of a whole) cannot be separated absolutely from synthesis, since parts involve wholes and wholes involve parts. In Coleridge's terms, analysis and synthesis, parts and wholes, can be distinguished but not divided from each other absolutely. This composite mental operation involved in criticism, understood as a process of analysis and synthesis, is the opposite of dissection, or the arbitrary picking to pieces of an artifact. A hypothetical element enters since no rules can be laid down for the performance of analysis-synthesis, or the determination of significant parts and their respective place and weight within a unifying whole. Dewey remarked that the delicacy of mind required for analysis-synthesis as opposed to arbitrary picking apart of an artifact probably explains why 'scholarly dissertations upon literature are so often merely scholastic enumerations of pedantic details, minutiae, and so-called criticisms of paintings are of the order of analyses of handwriting by experts'.[12]

Both Coleridge and Johnson had argued that analysis-synthesis is a real test of the mind of the critic, and that here the richness of a critic's intelligence and experience come into play, contrary to judicial criticism, which implies, in spite of itself, that standards can be applied irrespective of the expertise of the one applying them, and contrary to impressionist criticism, which implies that the outpourings of an inexperienced audience are as useful for improving aesthetic experience as the critical judgements of the expert. Both Coleridge and Dewey noted, however, that an informed, experienced critic can be a cold, ungenial critic, and that even experience and wide-learning without being combined with a consuming, passionate interest in art leads to academic pedantry. Such a critic always remains outside the work of art and can never penetrate to the heart of the matter. On the other hand, Dewey warned explicitly that a passionate interest not modified by wide learning and rich experience leads to gushy sentimentalism. Here one can see the judicial/impressionist dichotomy returning again. As Coleridge might say, intelligence (or expertise) uninformed by affection leads to authoritative pronouncements that do not encourage individual readers to an original, enlarged appreciation. Such pronouncements force upon a reader the views and experiences of an expert whose conclusions are not made for the purpose of improving the reading experience, but made for the purpose of legislating opinion about a text. On the other hand, affection and passionate interest without wide experience leads to ungrounded, misguided enthusiasm that may equally well tyrannize over a central aim of criticism, namely, encouraging the enlargement of each individual's experience and response to an artifact. Enlargement as a central goal of criticism suggests not only Barthes' and Derrida's concepts of interminable play and enactment of desire by the reader. It also suggests Shelleyan and Coleridgean beliefs that initial response needs to be developed, modified, and even often abandoned for more experienced perceptions which may arise out of both genial, playful response and out of reflection, those sustained periods of analysis-synthesis – or informed appreciation, we may call it, upon works of art. Appreciation when subjected to sophistication is something that grows and develops out of, and often away from, initial experience and response to a text. Aesthetic appreciation involves, for Dewey, enlargement of perception, experience, and response.[13]

According to both Coleridge and Dewey, the critic must also be acquainted with the tradition of a particular art. Such acquaintance involves not merely a knowledge of the objects in that tradition but a personal intimacy with them. Moreover, Dewey argued that the acknowledged 'masterpieces' in a tradition may provide a 'touchstone' (as Arnold put it), but they should never be dictators of appraisals. Moreover, every field of art has more than one tradition, and a critic unaware of the variety of traditions in the field will be limited and one-sided. Indeed, for Dewey much of the controversy of critics arises from a lack of a sense for the variety of traditions in any given field of art. The unstable swing of fashions marking the attitude of different periods towards works of art was an unfortunate testimony to such a lack. A critic appreciative of the variety of traditions is also aware, Dewey believed, of the variety of materials, techniques, and forms usable in art, and such a critic will hesitate to condemn new experiments in form, technique, or matter when she comes across them. An adequate knowledge of the variety of traditions already existing protects both from over-praise of works only technically skilful, and from underpraise or condemnation of works accused of lack of technique or accused of extreme personal traits when new techniques and new experiences are being discovered and invented. The danger for all critics, Dewey explained, is that if guided only by personal predilection or partisan conventionalism, the critic will take some one procedure, form, technique, or matter as the criterion of judgement, and condemn all deviation from it as departures from true art or good art itself. One major point of much art is then missed, namely, a unity of form and matter, because of a lack of sympathy for the variety of interactions of form and matter possible, a lack arising from both natural and acquired one-sidedness. Criticism for Dewey can be said, then, to be an effort to enlarge experience in yet another sense. It can show us how to break out of both the natural and acquired one-sidedness that characterizes our responses until reflection attends to the individuality of background, temperament, personality, and experience which can work to stimulate – or to hinder – fresh response.

Coleridge and Dewey both insisted that a large degree of a hypothetical element is introduced into criticism even in analysis – or the discrimination of parts. For intelligent analysis depends upon both the penetration and sophistication of the critic's mind. A still larger degree of this hypothetical element enters into synthesis: the unifying phase, the phase of discrimination of the integrity of some whole or some unity, requires even more of a creative response. This response, this insight, is itself an art; criticism itself becomes art, Dewey argued, anticipating Barthes and Derrida, since no rules can be laid down for the performance of insight, whether in art, science, or criticism. Criticism, however, is no more a matter of mere subjective opinion than is science or art itself. Differences of opinion and controversy arise in criticism, as in art and science, because, Dewey believed, individual, personal predilection or partisan conventionalism takes some one procedure or form or technique to be *the* criterion of judgement, and excludes all variations and deviations from this preferred mode as illegitimate or bad art.

Such criticism as Dewey and Coleridge exhort us to, criticism as art, is contrasted first with criticism as a mere mechanism worked by precept according to a ready-made blue-print. Criticism as art moves from analysis or discrimination of parts to unification, or to the discrimination of some integral experience. For without some one or another unifying point of view based on the objective form of the work of art, criticism, for Dewey, as for the English and German romantics, becomes mere enumeration of details. This is not to say, however, that discrimination of a unity is discrimination of *the* unity of an artifact. *Some* unity, rather, is discovered, some unifying thread or pattern that runs throughout the details. A work of art rich in experience inevitably leads to the discrimination of many possible unifications. No one conception of unity is the only way in which the elements of a single work of art can be brought into focus. Dewey maintained that there is never just one unifying idea or form in a work of art. There are many, in proportion to the richness of the artifact. Criticism, then, is a focusing activity for the variety and welter of details in any artifact, and moreover, a focusing activity that respects what the relatively objective traits of the artifact are (those traits communicable to others). It is not an activity that introduces traits from outside, in order to preserve convention or traditions. Dewey alleged that the test for whether any discriminated mode of unification is more or less legitimate than any other involves meeting two conditions: first, the alleged unity (whether in terms of form, theme, structure, design, subject matter, or whatever) must actually be present in the work of art, that is, perceivable by others and not a merely fanciful importation. Second, this alleged unity must be shown to be consistently maintained throughout the parts of the work.

For Dewey, the two main fallacies operative in criticism across all fields of art, are first, reduction, and second, confusion of categories. The fallacy in criticism of reduction occurs when some one constituent of a work of art is isolated and then the whole reduced to the terms of this single isolated example. He offered psychoanalytical criticism as one type which tends to practise the fallacy of reduction. It too often explains the aesthetic content of the work of art by means of such factors as are relevant primarily to a biography. Biographical factors are taken as substitutes for the appreciation of the work of art as aesthetic. Sociological criticism is also, Dewey wrote, guilty of the reductive fallacy, for Dewey insisted that while economic, historical, social, and cultural information throw light on the causes of the production of art, each artifact is still 'just what it is' aesthetically and artistically, and its aesthetic merits and demerits are inherent in the work. Knowledge of the social conditions of production is really of genuine value, Dewey acknowledged, but it is no substitute for understanding the object in terms of its own qualities and relations.

The second great fallacy in criticism (closely related to reductionism), namely, the confusion of categories, Dewey described by pointing out that there are categories or controlling conceptions of enquiry appropriate to history, psychology, economics, biography, sociology, and political science, to name a few, but only confusion results when they are used to control enquiry into art, ignoring the artistic conceptions. Critics are tempted to try to translate the 'distinctively aesthetic strain in experience' over into terms of some other kind of experience. Dewey gave as an example the fact that while religious values have exercised an incomparable influence upon art, seen aesthetically, each concrete painting or text has its own distinctive qualities apart from the religious ideas, beliefs, or values expressed. Moreover, *artistic* substance is not identical with theme. Theme is best understood as the 'vehicle' or 'intellectual carrier' through which an artist receives his subject matter and transmits it, and this theme is quite distinct from both the form and matter of the work, aesthetically speaking. Dewey also criticized the confusion of aesthetic and philosophic values, using as his example T. S. Eliot's notion that 'the truest philosophy is the best material for the greatest poet'. What Eliot allegedly did was to make philosophic content more viable by adding poetical qualities of the sensuous and the emotional sort. Dewey pointed out, however, not only that what the truest philosophy is, is a matter of no small dispute. He also stated that great poets have had fundamentally different philosophies, and that acceptance of their poetry as great does not by any means entail acceptance of their philosophy. Otherwise, he warned, we must condemn Milton if we approve Dante or Goethe.

Both Coleridge and Dewey agreed that much poor criticism proceeds from the same source, namely, the neglect of the intrinsic significance of the medium. The source of every art, whether science, philosophy, mathematics, or art *per se,* lies, Dewey believed, in the use of a particular medium having its own characteristics. All fields of human cultural activity, whether science, religion, history, art, or philosophy have the same *material,* namely experience: 'the interaction of a living organism' with its surroundings. Fields of activity differ in the medium by which they convey and express this material, Dewey explained, not in the material itself. The medium of science, for example, is adapted to the purposes of control and prediction, yet science is an art in the widest sense of the word. Indeed, under very specific conditions its material can even become art in the aesthetic sense. The purpose of 'aesthetic art', on the other hand (that is literature, painting, etc.), is the 'enhancement of direct perception and experience itself', and for this purpose, Dewey argued, art adopts specific media to accomplish enlargement of perception and experience.

Artists may of course have philosophical, religious, or moral values or psychological experiences which influence their artistic work. In Dewey's view, the question for the critic, however, is the adequacy of form to matter, and not that of the presence or absence of any particular form, idea, or value. Moreover, critics tend to be less sensitive to signs of change and innovation than to the recurrent and enduring, and therefore, he explained, they use the criterion of past tradition, without remembering that 'every past was once a future', and that the models and patterns of the past were once the inventions and divergencies from the conventions and traditions of the previous era. Coleridge and Dewey both remind us, however, that every critic, like every artist, has a bias and a predilection bound up with our very individuality as human beings. It is a central task of the critic to convert this predilection, this individuality, into an 'organ of perception and insight' guided, Dewey believed, by the instinctive preferences from which are derived our very sincerity and direction as critics. But, he cautioned, when natural and personal predilections 'harden into fixed moulds', and when selective modes of response become preferred modes, the critic's judgement is crippled. The critic, like the artist, must seek to direct the perceptions of others not towards his or her own personal predilections and preferences (whether in philosophy, religion, morality, or art), but towards the ability to cultivate a fuller appreciation of the objective content and the aesthetic content of works of art. For Coleridge, as for Dewey, one major function of criticism is the re-education of our perceptions of works of art, or – put more generally – of the process of learning to see and hear intelligently. The notion that the primary business of criticism is to judge, in a legal or moral sense, precisely inhibits the perception of those influenced by such criticism. Individuals can be encouraged, Dewey alleged, to make for themselves their own appraisals, out of an enlarged and sophisticated response. Echoing a central tenet of Coleridge's writings, Dewey said that readers must go through the same vital processes as the artist, and criticism can assist them, not try to do it for them. The function of criticism, like the function of art, is to perfect the power to perceive, to remove from the eyes the scales of prejudice that prevent insight.[14]

In *Experience and Nature*, Dewey had sought to expose the dualistic assumptions of much traditional philosophizing, arguing that these assumptions are prejudices and importations which lead to pseudo-problems. In the last two chapters of that 'deconstruction of metaphysics', he continued his exposé of dualism in the domain of art and criticism. He criticized Greek thought for its depreciation of practice (including the fine arts) in favour of theory (philosophy, mathematics, science). Modern thought, on the other hand, viewed experience as merely 'subjective', unlike the Greeks, who had equated it with art, craft, making, thus using the term in a more honorific sense. Modern thought, Dewey complained, tends to view art as a mere arbitrary addition to a preconceived nature. The latter is understood to be the more genuine objective reality,the authentic expression of which is not art, but science and rational knowledge. Even when art is esteemed equally with science, as a social good, knowledge is still regarded as a direct grasp of ultimate reality, instead of as a practice. That is, knowledge is contemplation rather than a productive practice or art involving natural energies, so that practice will always appear inferior to contemplation. Even within art, a dualistic hierarchy arises involving a notionally creative, artistic production of artifacts, and a merely passive, secondary aesthetic appreciation of already constituted artifacts-in-themselves, which turns the hierarchy on its head, esteeming practice over contemplation, unlike Greek thought, which was at least consistent.

Dewey argued against the distinction between practice and theory, as yet another dualism imported into experience because of prejudices, insisting that the only distinction worth drawing is between 'the modes of practices that are not intelligent, not inherently and immediately enjoyable, and those which are full of enjoyed meaning'. Art, as the mode of activity charged with meanings most capable of enjoyed possession, is said, then, to be not distinct from nature, not some arbitrary addition to nature, but the culmination of nature. Art is a continuation, by means of intelligent selection and fusion, of natural energies and events, not some peculiar addition to nature, with an esoteric character and an occult source. On the latter view, art and the aesthetic become isolated from ordinary experience, whether art is demoted to the expression of emotion or to objects with so-called 'significant form', secluded from ordinary life activities and experiences. But, Dewey argued, both emotion and significant form are intrinsic aspects of ordinary, natural events and activities, if the words have any meaning; far from making art exclusive and esoteric, they reveal it to have the very continuity with nature that proponents of emotive and formalist theories of art deny.

Dewey maintained that art trains our organs of perception to perceive in new, non-stereotyped ways, much as Blake had done, by giving us new objects to be enjoyed: 'The "magic" of poetry – and pregnant experience has poetical quality – is precisely the revelation of meaning in the old effected by its presentation through the new. It radiates the light that never was on land and sea but that is henceforth an abiding illumination of objects'. Put another way, art is both instrumental and consummatory: 'meanings that are signs and clews and meanings that are immediately possessed, suffered, and enjoyed, come together' in art.[15] Moreover, Dewey believed, echoing Shelley, that art is a practice or a process of making the world a different place, involving disruption and protest, which becomes apparently arbitrary and eccentric when frustration in communication of meanings occurs. Attempts by the artist to find new modes of expression, language, or technique often involve violent departures from received canons and method, as Derrida's writings show. But for Dewey, such departures and experiments are precisely the condition of growth of new forms, and, he argued, they are 'a condition of salvation from that mortal arrest and decay called academic art', a comment with distinct relevance to critics of Derrida's innovations.

In describing aesthetic experience, Dewey used the terms 'appropriate enjoyment' and 'appreciative possession', metaphors which explicitly acknowledge the active, participatory nature of response. He also argued that the difference between the aesthetic or appreciative and the artistic or productive was one of degree; later, he seemed to minimize even this degree of difference in acknowledging that criticism and philosophy are themselves arts. The more sustainable distinction is not that between the aesthetic or critical and the creative, but between perceptions that are diffuse and inchoate and those which are connected and focused so as to bring forth further perceptions. Dewey concluded that thinking is itself pre-eminently an art, 'a light radiating to other things',[16] and thinking is always inductive: 'there is only one mode of thinking, the inductive, when thinking denotes anything that actually happens'. Knowledge is itself a product of art, a result of modes of interaction and natural practices and processes, not a perversion or distortion of the real by adding traits that do not belong to it. Knowledge is the conferral upon previously non-cognitive material of meanings which transform it into cognitive material. Knowledge is the art of achieving meanings of events, and as such science itself is an art, and, Dewey concluded, 'the separation of science from art, and the diversion of arts into those concerned with mere means and those concerned with ends in themselves, is a mask for lack of conjunction between power and the goods of life'.[17] Nature, Dewey concluded, is at its most free and active in art, while consciousness itself is not a separate realm of being but a natural quality of existence. Art trains the mind in new modes of perception, and brings into being new objects, thus enlarging the world of human experience.

Dewey's *Art as Experience* is a profoundly 'romantic' exposition, invoking many of Coleridge's and Shelley's explicit and implicit theories. While Dewey rejected the privileging of historical, social, or intellectual context over the artifact (understood as an aesthetic object), like Coleridge, Shelley, and the German romantics he never succumbed to the formalist fallacy of treating the artifact as in isolation from its context. As anyone familiar with pragmatism knows, context is a crucial element in the deconstruction of dualistic metaphysics. Dewey's emphasis upon congruence in works of art between form and material (distinguishable elements only, not 'real' divisions in experience) was one mode of rejecting formalist extremes, while at the same time condemning the excesses of thematic criticism which treats works of art as if they were repositories of ideas to be restated in discursive language. Dewey's most profound connection with later writers such as Derrida and Barthes involves his most central aesthetic belief, that art *is* experience, and that criticism and judgement are best understood as modes of improving aesthetic perception and enriching appreciation by active involvement of the reader or critic. 'Art as experience' is another way of stating the rejection of dualistic and essentialist notions; indeed, it is another aspect of Dewey's and Coleridge's theory of organicism – of art as vital, living, evolving, experiencing. The concept of art as experience links Dewey with Barthes's and Derrida's notions of dissemination and play, and to American deconstructors' related ideas of generating effects from works of art. Dewey, like Coleridge and Derrida, explicitly rejected the notion that the aim of criticism was to extract meanings and reduce aesthetic forms to discursive accounts. Enrichment of perception and improved appreciation meant, for Dewey, the enlarged experience of an artifact by intimate, intelligent acquaintance with its qualities and their irreducibly rich significances. This emphasis on rich experience is Dewey's way of describing Barthes' and Derrida's playfulness with texts.

Dewey's insistence that the aim of criticism is not to assign meanings but to help others to experience art more fully sets him squarely within the romantic and deconstructionist tradition, of the reader as active participant and fellow labourer in aesthetic experience. His rejection of the essentialist notion that art is a special quality supervening to objects independent of the experience of them involves equally a rejection of the notion that literary language is a special language distinct from ordinary language. The use of the simile 'art as experience' (reverberating with references to Plato's 'knowledge as recollection') expressed Dewey's awareness of the centrality of rhetoric in language, as did his repeated reliance on figures of speech such as the idea of 'congruence', 'enrichment', 'part–whole' relations, 'radiation' and 'illumination', his emphasis upon 'discrimination *and* unification' as two aspects of one imaginative process, and his constant reference to the metaphor, 'hypothetical element'.

In *Democracy and Education,* Dewey had based his philosophy of education upon the idea that playful, imaginative participation in activities was the way in which children could best be stimulated to learn. In his experimental schools, he insisted upon the learning process as involving the child in play, activity, and designed situations which would provoke interest and involvement, rejecting passivity, memorization, or acquiescence as unacceptable. He took William Blake's adage of 'instruction as delight', and sought to develop the idea that education takes place only when active participation and development of imaginative individuality are fostered within a community. Otherwise, mere indoctrination and socialization occur. Education, like criticism, became for Dewey an art of developing individual potential through the sharpening of perception and the exercise of imaginative response. Play and artistic activities were essential to an educative process that was truly democratic, that is, which sought not to impose a system of beliefs upon children, but to develop their capacities for thinking and feeling. He took this democratic principle into all areas of his thought, interpreting philosophy, for example, as the human endeavour not to communicate a thinker's beliefs, so much as to design intelligent situations in which the reader is stimulated to think through issues herself. Art (in the narrow sense of the word) Dewey saw as another arena in which the imagination is exercised and enriched. 'Art' in the broadest, sense meant deeply realised and intelligently structured experience. Any experience can take on aesthetic qualities when intelligent discrimination and unification of elements in an experience occur through imaginative participation. In the next chapter, Derrida will be shown exploring this Deweyan idea of imaginative participation, making criticism an art, and making art experience.

10

Derrida, Textuality, and Criticism

Deconstructive criticism sought to bring about a transformation in traditional thinking and critical approaches to literature. For Derrida, deconstruction initially involved the thorough analysis and exposure of critical dogmatics and the self-contradictory notions upon which such thinking rests. Deconstruction was conceived not so much as a simple critical operation; criticism itself was its object. It was not merely a criticism of criticism, however, since it sought to subvert the kind of activities traditionally thought of as criticism. It was not a rigorous method or a science of interpretation, so much as a playing with tactics and manoeuvres that were designed to challenge the hegemony of traditional methods and practices. As such, it emphasized not a hermeneutical search for decoding meaning of any kind, but an unloosening of the concept of meaning; it privileged the idea of 'misreading' over reading, play over decorum and rational, academic seriousness, fragmentation over unity, and dissemination over definite meaning or discursive truth or knowledge.

In order to privilege these alternative, new concepts, Derrida proceeded by reversing the usual hierarchy within a dualism, a theory, or a set of terms. By inverting traditional oppositions, he revealed the 'difference within', to use Barbara Johnson's terms, that is, he marked the 'disorganizing play of hitherto invisible concepts that reside unnamed in the gap between opposing terms'.[1] There is no question of a reconciliation or transcendence of opposing concepts or terms, no *Aufhebung*, no diffusing or reforming. Disorganization, not organization, was the aim, disorganization with no end, no aim to resolve or reorganize into a new, rational account or whole view. Vincent Leitch thus identified the two stages in the deconstructive activity of Derrida, but these stages are also evident in the criticism of the Yale deconstructors. He noted that

Derrida's texts reveal and identify, by means of traditional practices, the stable truths which seem to inhere in a text. Derrida's texts then proceeded to undermine those truths and practices by an active production of 'undecidables', an exposure of the indeterminacy within the very fabric of those truths that appeared determinate, definite, and well-defined until closely scrutinized. Derrida began by using the resources of traditional criticism to initiate its breakdown, 'dramatizing its closure'.[2] He further emphasized the necessity of questioning and examining received notions about meaning, text, author, self, truth, presence, and so on, in order that these notions should not be allowed to serve unexamined as a supporting structure for the traditional modes of analysis, whether thematic, formal, psychological, historical, sociological, or biographical. Leitch described these two now well-known stages of deconstructive criticism as 'repeat and undermine'. The first stage is the conventional, while the second is the deconstructive advance. Barbara Johnson described the process similarly, when she noted in relation to her account of Mallarmé that she was taking the traditional view of his poetry, and then showing that the poems do not simply express these views, they repeat them in order to analyse, question, and expose them to scrutiny, and finally to expose them to disorganization.[3] As she stated elsewhere, deconstruction is the 'strategic, rigorous decentering of the structure described by someone, not by abandoning the structure, but by multiplying the forces at work in the field of which that structure is a part'.[4] 'Multiplying forces' suggests a revealing of the undecidables, indeterminacies, and indefinites that reside in the difference within identities as opposed to adhering to dualistic, 'difference between'-type thinking.

Llewelyn described Derrida's method as the working through of a text in order to let it speak for itself, while, as critic, avoiding positions, theses, or theories for the sake of focusing on what is in question (*il s'agit*) rather than supplying answers. He, like Leitch, identified two stages in Derrida's activity, noting the reversal of priority or hierarchy in binary oppositions as the first stage. He cautioned too that the language of the old order must be used in the second stage of deconstruction, the latter being not a synthesis positing a common ground at a higher level, but a move away from such meaning, truth, logic – all examples of organization – towards being devoid of truth and falsity. As Llewelyn described it, in the first stage priority has been reversed (mind/body, nature/culture, intelligible/sensible, and so on). In the second deconstructive stage, Derrida intervened between the terms to expose them as 'not-terms', and to expose the stroke between them as 'not-a-boundary'. Difference between is shown as difference within, and the identity of separate/opposite entities is subverted as they are shown to be inextricably involved the one in the other. The stroke, being 'stroked out', becomes a 'chiasmus marking the parasitism of one pole on the other and vice versa'.[5] Nature is not prior to culture, culture is not a supplement to nature; the concept of nature is dependent upon and involved in that of culture. Speech is not prior to writing and writing is not supplementary to speech, to take an analogy. Speech is marked by a kind of writing. Oppositions are not made to vanish or to be transcended, but in order to show the necessity that one of the terms appears as the difference of the other, as marked by the other, as 'the other differed within the economy of the same'.[6] The intelligible is not distinct from and opposed to the sensible; it is the 'sensible differed.' Derrida's target is no less than the deconstruction of the notions of absolute distinction, or what Coleridge called division and 'barren dualism'. Deconstruction functioned not to resolve ambiguities or to clarify differences. It, like pragmatism, 'makes clear only the limits of clarification'. By exposing the ambivalence in the superficially opposed relations between terms, Derrida brought out the deeper structural contradiction inherent in all dualisms, where difference inhabits the self-identity of every entity or concept; every concept is inhabited by its opposite and cannot exist without it. The limits between them are thereby de-limited, revealed as non-absolute, arbitrary, and provisional, much as Coleridge had argued.

Deconstruction destabilized dualisms as well as other interpretive structures and practices, denaturalizing the conventions that perpetuate authority and traditions.[7] In opposing philosophies of representation and construction, it resisted any positive truth built into critical systems and, like pragmatism, became an anti-methodical method. It worked as a 'system of differences with no positive terms; the elements of the "system" are multivocal, undecidable, indeterminate, differential', and such a system replaced the tradition of the metaphysics of identity with a new 'tradition' of differences.[8]

This differential system, as opposed to the traditional systems of identity (consisting of self-identical entities opposed to and distinct from the 'other', as in much traditional philosophizing), arose from the Saussurean view of language as system in which the relation of sign to signified is problematic in the extreme; words do not mean exactly what they say, and signifiers are not related simply to signifieds as inviolate givens. The 'substance' of any sign is not a signified, an identity, but merely its difference from other signs. Moreover, signs only exist within a system; they do not pre-exist outside it as discrete elements. There is no before or outside language – everything is, polemically speaking, a text.

We construct the world, self, and consciousness in and by language, in rhetorical, figurative language, so that self and world are tropes or figures of speech, understood, that is, as results of language. Derrida deconstructed Saussure's notion of the sign as signifier by dissociating it from the signified. The signifier allegedly transports truth, for Saussure, but the sign is merely a 'trace', not a sign for anything outside itself. De Man compared such a differential conception of the system of language with music. The signs in music exist in a system of relations having no dependence on any substantive presence, either sensible or intelligible. Music, like language, is a play of relationships whose signs are grounded in no substance, have no assurance of existence outside music, and are never self-identical, but only exist in difference from other signs.[9] Hillis Miller futher assured us that we must choose between the tradition of presence and that of difference.[10] Though what he surely meant is that we may choose to remain fixed at the first stage of deconstructive analysis, avoiding the second, since Derrida insisted that there is no choice, no opposition, no either/or, between deconstructive criticism and traditional approaches. (For further discussion of this non-choice and refusal of oppositions see above, chapter 7.) Yet what does this concept of differance, and the differential nature of relation as contrasted with opposition, mean? 'Differance' is neither a word nor a concept, Derrida provocatively assured us. It can never be affirmed as an ultimate value 'because it is that which subverts the very foundation of any affirmation of value'.[11] There is nothing kerygmatic about it; it does not spring from a prior moment of unity; it is not an event. Rather it is the begetting of substitutions and displacements. With regard to language, differance affirms that there is neither substance nor presence in the sign, but only the play of differences. The sign operates as a 'trace', not as a self-present sign.

John Llewelyn contrasted Derrida's 'differance' with Hegel on difference, and conceded that Kojève and Hyppolite's readings of Hegel bring Hegel's concept closer to Derrida's than traditional readings. Yet, he argued, Hegel's concept cannot do Derrida's job. For Derrida, for example, contradiction is a conflict of forces and energies, not of concepts or propositions, a view that loosens the grip of concepts, such as 'dialectical difference' and 'metaphysics of meaning', on the project Derrida undertook with 'differance'. As Llewelyn put it, 'differance', unlike Hegel's word, acts as a 'metalinguistic excluder' of the meaningful and the meaningless, not just as the opposite of meaningful.[12] The notion of a conflict of forces, unlike the conflict of concepts, is not really either meaningful or meaningless. Meaning is delayed, reserved, postponed, deferred. Hegel's thinking does not achieve the deferral that Derrida's activity does, Llewelyn argued. For the latter puts in brackets or under erasure the concept of meaning, neither affirming nor rejecting, but suspending it, suspending logic, reason, truth, to leave space for other activities, as yet perhaps virtually inconceivable. (Whether Llewelyn's evaluation of Hegel is convincing is another matter.) Yet Llewelyn cautioned us that differance, while it aids in helping us to delimit our metaphysical epoch, is also a form of mastery to which we can only pretend, since we cannot so easily escape the assumptions and languages that bind us within metaphysical, dualistic, identity–thinking. He contrasted differance, however, with metaphysics, in saying that differance is not already built, but is 'endlessly a-building'; it is a house with no name or fixed address, and no construction engineer, but a product of *bricolage*, of improvisation (borrowing from Levi-Strauss).

Derrida's differance as displacement and deferral allows us to come up behind or between oppositions and 'trace the logic of their complicity', unlike Hegel's, or for that matter Bachelard's or Kuhn's, notions of breaks in the scale of continuity.[13] Derrida showed that in traditional philosophical opposites, each term is the differance of the other, the other differed in the economy, or field, of the same. And in classical logic, difference is opposed to identity, whereas differance is not opposed; it is 'a mongrel neographism' that subverts difference or opposition and identity. Llewelyn cautioned us, however, that Derrida's neographisms become so familiar that we think we come gradually to comprehend their sense. He argued that we must resist this deadening familiarity: 'There is no sense to be understood.'[14] (In time, of course, Derrida's new words will become 'master names', and he may be read as Hegel or Plato is, today.) Such neographisms are the disorganization, rupture, and dissemination of sense, not so much into nonsense as into a questioning of our notion of sense, reason, and understanding – a suspending of an assumption that we know what these things are. This is in contrast to Hegel, Llewelyn believed, who was, allegedly, opposed to 'undecidability', even though he went further than Schelling, for example, in recognizing that not merely identity but difference inheres in opposition. Yet 'diaphorism' is needed he said, not Hegelian negative dialectics. For there is no third value in differance, no static or even active reconciliation, a no coincidence of opposites. (It is arguable whether Hegel's philosophy posits a positive third value; see above, chapter 2). There is only an 'undecidable', a 'middle voice' which is neither active nor passive, but which exceeds or subverts the contrast – not a mean, but a spacing.

Llewelyn concluded that deconstruction should not be seen as an attack on – or weapon against – philosophical structures, but a 'tool for teasing out the illogicality of texts', and for showing us that the notion of theory as direct seeing or *eidos* – immediate presence to mental vision – and logos as substantive hearing or speech, is self-contradictory.[15] Derrida aimed at a 'hermeneutics of indeterminacy' (an apparently self-contractory phrase), at a revaluation of criticism and of values, while renouncing the ambition to master, control, or demystify the text, the author's psyche, or the act of reading and making sense, in favour of the joy of interpretation, constant movement, no final rest. Signs may be said to mean, Geoffrey Hartman explained, but only in the sense of being indefinite of meaning, where meaning involves not the presencing, but the deferral of absolute knowledge.[16] Indeed, such activity leads to the sacrifice of conventional readability (as much Modernist writing had done), and such readability is viewed as a rejection of play, activity, and sexuality. It is the closure into authorized meaning and limited notions of reason. According to Howard Felperin, criticism becomes deconstructive when it 'realizes the inadequacy of its own law-making, the obsolescence of it'.[17] He saw deconstruction as language-scepticism in the mode of play, an exacting mode, but still play. He objected strongly to the notion that deconstruction annihilates the text, maintaining rather that it defamiliarizes it, in order to refresh perception. It redirects our attention to the problematics of signification that were overlooked in traditional criticism, which always took meaning for granted as simple, univocal, and referential, and which grounded itself on extralinguistic meaning. Felperin noted that deconstructive practice denied that critics need justify or guarantee critical practice on some convincing rationale, on some human good.[18]

That is, criticism leads to no truths, no revelations of meaning; it is grounded in no such illusions: it merely leads to more writing. Derrida placed writing under scrutiny, and reversed the traditional priority of speech as antecedent to writing, as closer to self-present truth. In a second movement or stage he also gave up the priority of writing over speech, once he had shown the absurdity of the former priority. He gave up 'grammatology', that is, as equally logocentric – redefining and extending the function of the word writing, so that it is no longer conventionally, unconsciously logocentrically used. For mere reversal, mere privileging of the supplementary element in the dualism of speech/writing cannot escape logocentrism. He adumbrated the 'non-science of "writing"', (newly defined) as graphematics, as opposed to grammatology. 'Writing' is not opposed to speech, but is that which enables conventionally conceived-of writing and speech to occur. 'Writing', as 'arche-writing', does not, however (Llewlyn warned us) denote an arche or telos: 'It is not a term but a monstrosity.' It is the 'formation of a form.'[19] Derrida, he explained, used words like writing and sign to graft on to them new forces, as writing comes to mean not something supplementary to speech, but a marking, a tracing, a spacing that inhabits speech and writing and puts their referentiality into suspension. Thus, 'sign' no longer is used to imply signified; signs merely indicate relations with other signs. And 'writing' refers to any practice of spacing, articulation, or differentiation, practices that produce language, instead of being the supplement of speech and, as such, devoid or distanced from pure presence, eidos, or viewing of truth. Writing, not speech, gives the logical model for all language, with its deferral, dispersion, and dissemination of present meaning beyond the author's power to control or even know.[20] 'Writing', newly conceived, undoes the illusion of self-presence fostered by speech and by the voice. Hartman, moreover, noted that writing cannot be an antidote to anything other than itself, as it questions its own referential and representational claims.[21] Like writing, the sign, no longer used to imply any signified, but only signs of other signs, is replaced by the 'trace' as the force and formation in writing. Sign is displaced by trace, understood as a writing, a spacing, rather than a representation.

Put another way, the signified is itself originally merely a writing, a sign, a trace, always partaking of a signifier; it never existed before or outside a linguistic system of writing. The trace is a decentring concept, for the pure trace does not exist, according to Derrida, since to exist is to be an entity, a being-present, while the trace is only a spacing, a writing. 'Spacing' designates the divisive, traditionally obscured gaps between things, such as the writing within speech which makes writing not a supplement to speech, but the possibility of it as articulation, marking the creating of the borders that Derrida constantly then exposed and subjected to questioning. Derrida constantly breached the borders of words and texts, showing the spacing as within supposed entities, and not just (or even) between them. When he deconstructed the notions of sign and writing as supplements to speech and signifieds, he also played with the concept of supplement, and made it into an undecidable, like trace, mark, differance, *écriture*, dissemination, border, and so on. He showed that the entity to which something is a supplement is in fact constituted by its supplement, as speech is constituted by writing. The 'after' is actually a 'before' – as, for example, culture is before nature. Yet the concept of supplement does not merely reverse the priority of binary opposites, as was said earlier. Rather, it seeks to disorganize or disrupt the binary opposition while rejecting inclusion of a third term, or, as Barbara Johnson paradoxically noted, these undecidables of Derrida's reveal the rhetorical indetermination of all our theoretical discourse, the impossibility of any ultimate, analytical metalanguage: 'undecidability can never be the last word. What is undecidable is whether a thing is decidable or not'.[22]

Hence, the avoidance by Derrida of theories held straightforwardly, of posited theses; hence, Derrida's stylistic manoeuvres and his 'disinclination for ratiocinative argumentation [which] is not just a matter of taste'.[23] A change of style is needed, Leitch admonished, from the decorous, scholarly, or serious, self-important works of writing, to something new. For the old assumptions embedded in language imprison us in logocentrisms. Leitch cited *Glas* as an example of this something new, of 'split writing' as he called it, whose 'excesses court unreadability' with its stolen citations, puns, and its verbal play foregrounding the materiality or physicality of language at the expense of sense, erasing itself at the moment it instantiated itself.[24]

This emphasis upon style is at the heart of Derrida's project, of course, and it distinguishes him from the Yale, and other, American deconstructionist practitioners. For example, only the most cursory glance at *Deconstruction and Criticism*, a collection of essays by Derrida, Bloom, de Man, Miller, and Hartman, will alert the reader to the gulf that separated Derrida's practice from the conventional critical practice of the other four. Indeed, Derrida's essay acts quite openly as a ribald parody of such critical writings which implicitly claim to have advanced beyond conventional, traditional criticism, yet actually remain rather firmly within its limited idioms. A borrowing of Derrida's 'ideas', or his methods and approaches, which merely applies and reiterates them within the limits of ordinary critical discourse and practice, is an example of the inevitable process of 'taming' Derrida's rather wild originality – that Derridean deconstruction – a taming which, admittedly, many critics have deplored. Leitch decried the way some American deconstructors mechanized Derrida's approach into a virtually mechanical method of critical procedures, and described the three simple steps, namely, thesis, antithesis, and *aporia*,[25] so that deconstruction has become hypostasized into a fixed theory and a slide-rule practice. Felperin too noted that American deconstruction had often become a practice and a theory 'totally amenable to routinization at the hands of the institution to whose authority it once seemed to pose such a challenge of incompatibility'.[26] Indeed, he bemoaned the fact that it virtually had become the institution, and set himself the project of writing from within theory against the institutionalization of theory, since deconstruction ceases to be deconstruction once it is institutionalized (the fate of Hegel, Plato, and so many other philosophies, as Dewey argued). American deconstruction, unlike Derrida's texts, often became a set of mechanical procedures for identifying throughout literature *aporias*, *mise-en-abîmes*, and so on. Felperin's advice 'not to tame this cat' is another reminder of the gulf that separates Derrida from those practising in his name.[27] Leitch also insisted upon the sharp and no-nonsense distinction between French and Yale deconstruction, and his emphasis, too, is upon Derrida's style. Derrida, as well as Barthes to a large extent, engaged in a mode of writing that was structurally, stylistically, generically, thematically, and academically a genuine rupture with tradition, while the texts of many American deconstructors are decorous, well-made, and remain quite within the bounds of academic propriety, good taste, scholarly procedure, all the while that they proclaim the free play of textuality. Derrida actually enacted the 'free play of textuality', he did not merely subscribe to it as a theory, or talk about it in acceptable, conventionally, logically rational, argumentative discourse.[28]

By his 'unreadable', innovative style, Derrida challenged the hierarchical, dualistic opposition between creative writing and so-called criticism as rational discourse, just as Friedrich Schlegel and other German romantic ironists had done before him. He dared to import into the rational discourse of criticism and philosophy (thus breaching the proper borders of texts) most of the techniques of 'creative' writing, as well as some new ones of his own. He challenged the authority of rational discourse because it simply repeats *ad infinitum* the logocentric errors, unconscious assumptions, and notions of dualism, self-presence, and so on, which Derrida sought to bring to light. Hence 'readable' texts, texts that, allegedly, communicate univocal meaning, are shoring up the old logocentric tradition. This is why Derrida sacrificed readability and communication of the comfortable, familiar type: it reiterates the same old logocentric story in infinite numbers of disguises. What he sought was a text which could rupture the old story, dissipate it, and reveal its meaninglessness, since it is based on 'phony' principles. This meant, however, that we need to learn new ways of reading and of approaching texts, to unsettle our expectations about what a text should do, and most importantly of all, accept that our requirement to make sense in the usual way is merely a law of logocentric, rationalist discourse, which is challengeable, which indeed has always been at odds with poetry and fiction, anyway.

Thus the basic tools of poets and artists become his means for disrupting the conventions of style, structure, genre, theme, decorum, diction, and so on, that bind us within the academic proprieties of the logocentric tradition. His 'unreadability' is a concerted challenge to forms of rational discourse which have rarely been questioned before to the extent that Derrida questioned them, at least in practice, except by such writers as Blake, Nietzsche, and a few German romantics. The illusion of rational discourse – that it can communicate and mean univocally and exactly what it says – is shattered by Derrida's parody of it and by his practical innovations. He achieved with dexterity and erudition a change of style and a rejection of the ratiocinative argumentation that is the hallmark of logocentrism. He showed that the solid path of discourse is, upon analysis, saturated and potted with the indeterminacies, ambiguities, and figurative/rhetorical dimensions that undermine its claim to univocal meaning, and which it seeks to repress for the sake of the illusion of clarity, solidity, and meaning. His own style is technically a dramatization of the essential indeterminacy and figurative nature of ordinary discourse.

The pretence that rational discourse is the expression of already constituted, fully present, univocal meanings was a major target of Derrida's stylistic devices, as he played with words to reveal their role as multifaceted differences in relation to other differing words, rather than as signs standing for self-identical, substantial concepts. The notion that some determinate, signified concept springs to mind at the sound of a word is shown to be a myth: words are toyed with etymologically and in terms of connotations, sound assonances and dissonances, puns, oppositions, and so on. With Wittgenstein, Derrida argued against the requirement that sense should be determinate. There is no single, or determinate, or even primary meaning adhering to any utterance, for an utterance makes sense at the very moment that it opens up the possibility for innumerable senses or meanings. Meaning is no longer imagined to derive from an originary speaker's intention, but is seen to exceed – by its very nature of repeatability – the intention of the speaker in indeterminate ways. Our responses to each others' utterances often repress and ignore the penumbra of alternative, ambiguous, and equivocal meanings which surround the sense we selectively decide to acknowledge.

Derrida's texts are unreadable partly because of their hybrid nature – he mixed philosophy, sociology, psychology, anthropology, literature, classics, linguistics, and so on, a mixing which made it possible for him to avoid being bogged down in any specific conceptual structure peculiar to the terms, vocabulary, and practices of these various disciplines. As a consequence, his varied vocabulary is beyond the grasp of the average reader, but makes it possible for Derrida to be 'everywhere at once', ungrounded in the limitation of any specific discourse. He thus 'decentres' his texts from any particular tradition or discipline, subverting the crucial terms of other traditions. Derrida also took key terms within a given discipline and exposed the dualism and contradictory assumptions within them, as he had done with Saussure, Rousseau, Levi-Strauss, Plato, Hegel, and others. He showed that, our discourses being so saturated with hierarchical dualisms, the only way to begin even to expose the extent of the dualisms is from within discourse. Hence, he invented new 'words', or rather monstrous, offensive neologisms, based on the old words, but different enough to rupture the usual associations. These monstrosities, these neologisms, are non-concepts rather than new concepts, that is, they are 'words' which indicate the context or implicate the possibility of conceptuality itself, rather than being yet another concept subsumable under the umbrella of logocentric thinking. Hence Derrida's coinages, his traces, marks, differance, supplements, arche-writings, spacings, dissemination, alterity, iterability, and so on.

Derrida's hybrid texts, his mixtures of philosophy, literature, linguistics, sociology, and autobiography, not altogether different from Coleridgean and German ironists' devices, are also a way of breaking down the borders between genres, to show how arbitrary and logocentric these categorizations are. He especially challenged the border between creative writing and rational, discursive discourse. The imaginative, creative, irrational element already inherent in so-called rational discourse is brought out into the open by Derrida from the repression that it has always suffered, for the sake of univocity, definiteness, and clarity. Rational discourse is shown, as in Hegel, to be marred at every point by its irrational, repressed opposite. His indecorous parodies of literary critical exercises, of biography or logical argumentation, expose the repressed elements of these types of rationalism and leave them ragged and in ruins. He ridiculed the 'phony' distinction between text and commentary, between quotation and paraphrase, by refusing to discriminate between them in his own texts, in order to demonstrate that the boundaries are arbitrary and illusory, or merely another aspect of the false dichotomy between creative/discursive writing. As Hartman put it, Derrida multiplied citation and texts, framed them in unexpected ways, and produced elegant opacity rather than the illusion of translucence of rational discourse.[29] He mocked and parodied such literary commentaries as totally at war with the very style and nature of the texts they were supposedly explicating, in their efforts to define meanings and truths left undefinable in the texts. He encouraged a Barthean 'manhandling' of the texts he discussed, since, he maintained, criticism has always manhandled texts while pretending to respect their integrity. He made no pretence to such prevalent hypocrisy, and openly manhandled the text in order to see what unexpected surprises might burst out of it, to disrupt our preconceptions. In *Spurs*, for example, his essay, 'I have forgotten my umbrella', is a sophisticated, detailed, and ruthless parody of biographical, often pedantic, literary criticism – while the whole of *Glas* ('not since *Finnegan's Wake* has there been such a work as *Glas*')[30] is a parodic attack not only upon literary, critical, and philosophical discourse and conventions, but upon the type of institutional mentality that encourages the hypocrisies and illusions of definites and clarity common to each.

Derrida's unreadability is not an absolute unreadability, however, any more than Blake's or Nietzsche's was. It is the highly sophisticated style of a writer who has worked through and then turned a critical backward glance upon everything he had learned. This glance showed that the content/form/style distinction was preventing any genuinely critical perspective, because criticism was confined to 'content', by and large, while the form-language-style dimension, where the roots of the content were buried, remained intact, even to some extent in formalist criticism itself. The question of Derrida's style is crucial, and not merely a question of embroidering craft. Derrida, through his stylistic advances, can be said to be offering readers a different way of reading, thinking, and approaching texts, whether philosophy, history, literature, or whatever. Even scientific texts are implicated, once their rhetorical dimensions are admitted. As long as we insist upon approaching Derrida for univocal meanings and definitive, communicated truths, for information, or for opinions, or for theories, he will remain unreadable. We are habituated to this kind of content-oriented reading, which Derrida was, like Blake, trying to frustrate. For example, Derrida's texts expose the repression and selection of material involved in a statement's making sense, as well as the metaphysical assumptions behind it, by proliferating the material that is usually repressed in ordinary discourse (those connotations, alternative meanings, ambiguities, puns, etymological nuances, and contradictions), for the sake of univocal meaning. This 'irrational' element in all rational discourse is elevated to an intensely active role in his writings, as it is, for example, in poetry, in order to expose rational discourse and determinate meaning for the restricted and limited aspects of experience that they are when their archaeological layers are ignored. As with the romantics, the claims of reason are returned to their proper place, having a limited sphere within an experience that reaches out far beyond the circumference of reason, decorum, and logic. Reason is not rejected, but restored to its habitation within, as Hegel might say, unreason, within the irrational; it is shown to be the irrational tamed by familiarity and convention, and another dualism collapses.

The dichotomy or absolute duality between reason – or rational discourse – and unreason – or non-rational discourse – is exposed as another illusion and hypocrisy of the metaphysics of presence. The point is not that unreason should be unleashed upon the world in some terrifying way, but that unreason already flourishes destructively (because repressed) behind the phony mask of a phony reason that parades as the only permitted way of thinking, acting, feeling, writing, or reading. Derrida's texts reveal the unreasonableness of conventional reason, the irrationality and authoritarianism of rational discourse, showing that more imaginative ways of thinking, reading, feeling, and experiencing are open to us, if we can only confront the limitations of a mode that passes itself off as the only acceptable or best way amongst educated people. That way has its uses, no doubt great uses, as Dewey and James argued. Yet its tyrannical entrenchment has reduced these uses to a shoring up of entrenched ways of thinking and writing, which hinder, rather than foster, innovation and fresh response. Derrida's style, then, enacts the refusal of repression into an entrenched, acceptable, rational, discursive language for the sake of tradition, decorum, and propriety. His puns, jokes, alliterations, abusive or obscene etymological experiments, his witty rechartings of word associations, his gimmicks with phonetic and typographical elements, his use of forbidden, debased, or obscene words, his barbarous, unnatural word creations, neologisms, archaisms, foreign and technical terms, his equivocations, catachreses, erudite allusions – these techniques are not only frivolous play, though they are that. They are also the heart of a writing that seeks to criticize the logocentric tradition. For as long as we use the language of that tradition with its dualistic, hierarchical assumptions hidden or embedded within it, we cannot even begin to revitalize our thinking. Derrida's stylistic innovations directly relate to his mixing of genres and subject matters, to his confusion of commentary and quotation and rampant allusiveness, for they indicate the parasitism of all our speech and language on other speech, other texts. Nearly everything we say, he revealed, is borrowed and second-hand: our speech is ridden with clichés, and our writing is saturated with the thoughts of others, as Blake had demonstrated.

Such innovations, which lead to texts and textuality instead of 'books' and meaning ('textuality' also being a play on texture, or the importance of medium, of style), demand a new approach to reading (as the opening remarks above indicated), as well as a new approach to criticism. One of the most taxing demands on our habits of reading is made when Derrida presents us with fragments instead of unities, or rather, with a spiraling concatenation of associations, endless word plays, chains of connotations, interminable deviations and side-trackings, instead of the linear, stately, deductive, reasoning style of argumentation with a central, developed theme that we have come to define as readability (in sharp contradiction to what we expect from creative writing, especially poetry). If one could 'suspend' one's expectations about prose writing, and approach Derrida's disorderly conduct more in the way one expects to read, say, modern poetry or Blake, or even at times Shakespeare, one might feel less defensive and irritated at the frustration that he 'doesn't make obvious sense', that Derrida leaves no themes or metaphysics in place. One might quit insisting that he should write to make himself better understood. To be better understood is to be drawn back into the logocentric circle and placed into neat categories within that circle. Derrida has no apparent wish to make sense or be understood within the traditional terms of western thinking; he did, however, suggest ways of resisting the forces that confine us within the limited logic and narrow channels of experience of the logocentric tradition, or Blake's Urizen. Derrida also suggested that his techniques were not imported from without, but actually inherent and essential within ordering, rational discourse. He is, allegedly, dramatizing and intensifying characteristics inherent in all language, in order to make them more visible. For a tendency to deny and repress these qualities for the sake of clarity and secure, determinate meanings blinds us to their dwelling place in logocentric discourse itself. Thus, all language and all books are 'texts', riddled with the sorts of traces of Derrida's own tactics and practices, but in repressed and obscured forms.

Derrida's narrative techniques question linear, discursive argumentation as an illusion perpetuated by the repression of the disruptive elements within such writing itself. Readers find this challenge one of the hardest to tolerate, as the mind resists change and craves to absorb some information, some concept, some definite meaning or argument, evading the opportunity to set off into new directions of thinking for oneself. Dissemination, however, the 'goal' of Derrida's texts, is not the production of meaning or many meanings so much as the diffusion or bracketing of meaning itself, the dissemination of the concept of meaning and the search for it. Derrida's words slip the leash of meaning without exactly escaping meaning. Dissemination is deconceptualization out of the imprisoning categories of western thought and out of its binding modes of writing. The deformation of familiar modes of writing and thinking brings to the fore the language that usually conceals itself behind subject matter. Language itself and nothing else, or the 'no-thing that is language', is the motivating residue, argued Hartman.[31] Language is said to be a palimpsest, a layering or archaeology of legitimate, decorous, words and phrases repressing layers of obscene, forbidden, tabooed words and phrases – a layer of standard, acceptable thought and feelings concealing a layer of deviant, threatening, alternative thoughts and feelings. Derrida, like Nietzsche and Carlyle, ripped off the facade of propriety with 'violent' tactics and strategies, in order to show the far more violent strategies of hypocrisy and repression inherent in our decorous linguistic activities, and to liberate these pre-packaged, manacled, and repressed energies of language. Writing, as Hartman put it, becomes a disaffiliation, a revealing of the absence of a unique meaning, a logos, a 'father'.[32] Derrida's style, his 'poetic prose joke words' are not, to repeat, merely frivolous play, as Johnson, Felperin, and Llewelyn also argued: yet this comment is marked by erasure, as we realize that frivolity and play had a central role in Derridean activities. Deconstructive reading was said to be a work, a labour, but a work that is play, indeed, that plays beyond the control of any subject, a *bricolage*, nor a logic or science.

Derrida's critique of the language of the logocentric tradition analyses the desire to escape the so-called prison-house of language (as the concept, language, has logocentrically functioned), to stand outside of it in order to analyse it, understand, or perhaps even cure it. Can we assume that the epoch of logocentrism is coming to an end, as Derrida's followers sometimes seemed to narrate? At other times, Derrida clearly indicated that deconstruction cannot free itself from the metaphysics that it contests, since it is compelled to use concepts and metaphors from that tradition. There is no 'outside' beyond the metaphysics of presence. Logocentrism is said to hold within itself the resources, however, for deconstruction. There is no question of a denial of the logocentrism inherent in language, of an escape either simple or complex. A critique of the closure imposed in language and thought by the logocentric tradition and its dualistic assumptions is not in itself something occurring outside the tradition. The critique of logocentric language by other languages is not a cure, or a therapy. For such languages of critique are themselves saturated with the assumptions of logocentrism, and their new metaphors, moreover, will degenerate in time into familiar conceptualizations. The desire for presence, meaning, definiteness, or self-identity is exposed as inhabiting all discourse, but the exposure is not a cure. We can at least recognize, however, the illusions of duality and hierarchy that constitute the desire for presence, even if we cannot escape them, but only alter our perspectives to see things in (temporarily, at least) new ways. Deconstruction involves the destruction only of the ignorance of those desires, those illusions, not of texts. This cannot be accomplished by a simple rejection, for, in the first place, a simple negative is a surrender to logocentrism's logic of non-contradiction, to its dualistic oppositions. And all attempts to displace opposition are dependent upon the logocentric philosophy of oppositional, dualistic thinking.

In his analysis of Hegel, Husserl, Heidegger, and others, Derrida concluded that some adherence to the logocentric tradition is inevitable, due to the assumptions embedded in language. He insisted, however, that adherence should be tactical and strategic, not doctrinal and naive, and that all three of these philosophers' texts exceed the inevitable adherence that arises from the language used by the deconstructor. Yet he refused to deny Hegel, Husserl, or Heidegger's philosophies, for he insisted that the texts deconstruct themselves, that is, that they defeat the theories they are purported by their readers to establish. Deconstruction is not denial, but the drawing out of inconsistencies and warring contradictions – of differences – within the text. The drawing out is, admittedly, locked within the language of presence. This emphasis upon differences within the text itself leads to the concept of differance discussed above, and as Llewelyn put it, differance is the aid to help us to delimit our metaphysical epoch, but it is also a form of mastery to which we can only pretend: 'The thinking of this presence does nothing but metaphorize, by a deep necessity one cannot escape by a simple decorum, the language it deconstructs.'[33] Derrida concluded that deconstruction is only 'outwith', not outside what it deconstructs. Philosophy as well as bricolage is always within the discourse it criticizes. Any exit outside philosophy is a difficult notion, argued Llewelyn, for we are bogged down in metaphysics by the weight of the discourse we claim to have freed it from.[34] Derrida showed that the simple rejection of philosophies falling within the tradition of the metaphysics of presence is a fall into that which we seek to avoid, finally, because all texts can be read in ambiguous ways, first, as advocating presence, second, as deconstructing presence. And, moreover, what stands under indictment is language itself, not somebody's individual philosophical error.[35] Put another way, misreadings are inevitable, for language, not the reader, accounts for misreading, since it is the nature of language as superabundant that it leads to misreadings.

We can conclude that logocentric discourse contains within itself its own deconstruction, in that the contradictions and inconsistencies it repressed come nevertheless to the surface, as part of its essential structure or logic. Logic, that is to say, is illogical and self-contradictory; it is nonsense familiarized. As with discourse, texts are also self-deconstructing, as Derrida pointed out repeatedly, and the author's knowledge or lack of it is a nonsense question. This self-deconstruction of the text is not a matter of chance, but a structural necessity, since the logocentric language employed does not make complete sense, but disseminates, that is, loses meaning which is not recoverable by analysis. Moreover, the defeat of the theories apparently advocated in the text is in the text itself, in its dissemination of the theories' meanings through inconsistencies and self-contradictory nonsense that only appears to make sense. Derrida used Heidegger's texts as paradigmatic examples of texts as necessarily equivocal, between being logocentric and, on the other hand, criticizing logocentrism. He pointed to the same equivocation in Saussure, Levi-Strauss, and others. He also noted that, like these writers, Hegel and Husserl's texts also equivocated, by founding their philosophies upon two incompatible principles, presence and non-presence. In all texts, Derrida insisted, not merely in those mentioned above, traces of a critique of logocentric thinking occur; that is, traces of non-logocentric writing and difference occur. He pointed, for example, to Plato's *Dialogues*, especially to the *Republic* and the *Sophist*, and showed that there are numerous sections in which speech is seen as not prior, but posterior, to 'writing', and he pointed to sections where a philosophy of differance is suggested. Derrida also noted that his own texts deconstruct themselves, that is, deconstruct the activity of philosophizing, in order to reveal how much 'non-philosophical' discourse, such as metaphor, remains, how much non-logical equivocation inhabits his texts. One aspect of his self-deconstructions was his insistence that there is no knowledge except in the form of *text-écriture*. There is no knowledge outside language, no central truths to which his or anyone's language refers for validations: all knowledge is already textual and in language and in need of interpretation. There is no 'given' that is not already a text.

Thus every deconstruction is itself a text with an *aporia* or inconsistency that is open to deconstruction. De Man approached this singular character through the concept of blindness and insight in critical discourse. One version of 'misreading' is the discrepancy a critic manifests between her explicit themes and her actual interpretations. The practical insights of critics actually disprove the assumptions and theories upon which their insights are based. Thus, the text deconstructs itself, in that it both affirms and at the same time refutes the authenticity of its figurative language and thematics. De Man concluded that texts narrate an allegory of their own misreadings and misunderstandings, and that poetic writing is the most advanced form of a self-deconstructing text. Since texts from the time of Plato onward can be shown to dismantle themselves, there can be no escape outside this tradition. Critics can simply unleash the differences or contradictions inherent in the text. De Man showed that Rousseau's own texts provided the strongest evidence against logocentrism, and he noted Derrida's 'blindness' to Rousseau's 'insights'. He also acknowledged, however, that the problem of the status of knowledge as deliberate and conscious or as passive and unconscious is irresolvable, because the categories of conscious (present) and unconscious (absent) knowledge are inadequate to experience.[36] Derrida bracketed the question of the author's knowledge of the text's ambivalence, as was noted earlier, while de Man likewise insisted that the 'key' to the status of Rousseau's language is not in his consciousness, but only in the knowledge which this language, as language, conveys about itself, asserting thereby the priority of language over presence, self, author, subject, or intention. Language does the talking, not the speaker, to use Heidegger's words, and what it says it simultaneously unsays.

De Man's criticism of Derrida's blindness to Rousseau's insight (that the substantialist notion of language is false), the insistence that Derrida has misread Rousseau, is itself a misreading, however. For de Man thereby unbracketed the question of author's knowledge and intention, and formulated the argument squarely in terms of presence-absence, instead of in terms of language. Derrida's criticism is of Rousseau's language and texts, not of his intention, and hence remains out of the reach of de Man's pseudo-deconstruction of Derrida. De Man thought he was analysing Rousseau's language, when he was analysing his intentions. Hence the disturbing self-contradictions between his claim that Rousseau knew what he was doing (while Derrida failed to see this awareness) and the claim that the question as to whether the author is or is not blinded is irrelevant, since cognitive function lies in language, not in the subject. De Man claimed that Rousseau used the language of metaphysics rhetorically and not declaratively, just as Derrida used it. What de Man could have asserted is that Rousseau's texts can be read rhetorically and not merely declaratively, as they usually have been. This, we have seen, is true of all texts, and de Man's central argument seems to collapse as Derrida was always several steps ahead of him. De Man postulated a pseudo-Rousseau, created by tradition, and then a real Rousseau, who is not blinded and not in need of deconstruction, for the real Rousseau is one of the enlightened authors. If only 'misreading' is possible, and if language is essentially figurative and rhetorical, and if cognitive function resides in language, then the real Rousseau is nothing but a figure of speech that de Man has taken literally. This sort of contradiction runs throughout de Man's work, and illustrates the gap between the American deconstructors and Derrida. De Man's grasp of deconstruction through rhetorical analysis, with little basis in a critique of metaphysics, is no doubt partly responsible for such inconsistencies in his otherwise brilliant practice.

Another way of describing the notion that texts deconstruct themselves is to say that texts are never only, or even, about what they appear to be. The content or subject matter always represses at the same time that it insistently reveals the fact of hidden, concealed content. The hidden, concealed material is not, as the hermeneutic task supposed, meaning or truth waiting to be revealed. This is a version of the decoding notion of structuralism that deconstruction exposed as nonsense, because self-contradictory. Any revealed meaning will conceal another, until the concept of meaning itself is questioned or bracketed at last, and language becomes the subject matter under analysis. Hence, deconstructors like Hillis Miller emphasized the now long-familiar view that poetry and fiction have as their subject matter the writing of poetry and fiction, or, in de Man's terms, writers write figuratively about figuration.[37] Moreover, their language often deconstructs the apparent theories their readers impose upon them. Miller referred to 'linguistic moments' as moments when a text reflects on its own linguistic medium, thereby challenging and exposing the realist illusion of language as a transparent medium of meaning.[38] These linguistic moments are the moments when the text deconstructs itself and language, when it disseminates, by questioning meaning and conceptualization rather than offering meanings. A critical, self-conscious element is inherent in the structure of a text; that is, texts contain their own self-criticism. Words, and language as Novalis argued, become themselves the subject matter of the discourse, the hidden theme, and the text is the action about which it allegorically speaks: its subject matter is also the text itself as reading experience or writing activity.

When language becomes problematic, the forward-moving working of language towards the production of meaning is halted, and – in this bracketing or suspension of meaning – self-reflection as a form of self-deconstruction and self-criticism is enacted. Miller's view is another version of de Man's idea that texts are allegories of misreading, that is, that they tell the story of their misunderstandings, and this is closely related also to Barbara Johnson's description of all narratives as the story of the 'marring' or misreading of their plots.[39] All plots, she concluded, are 'plots' against an authority that creates within itself the scene of its own destruction; or, all plots are plots against authoritative readings that, like their logocentric language, contain within themselves their own deconstruction due to their inherent inconsistency. This inconsistency, this 'undecidable', will be discussed further below, but it should be stressed again that for Derrida every text is said to contain within itself the insight necessary to free readers of their blind misconstructions of it. Or rather, the text is a 'writerly' enactment of potential 'readerly' misreadings of it. All commentaries, all readings, must be put in brackets, then, *sous rature,* under erasure, so that they both state and unstate themselves at the same time. Derrida's commentaries and some of Barthes seem able to do this overtly, and this is one way of characterizing their distinction from American deconstructors.

Miller's insistence that texts are not about their supposed subject matter but rather about language and writing points to the central illusion of logocentric language and thought which Derrida exposed, and which the concept of self-deconstruction raises, namely the question of the referentiality of language to a prior existing self and external world. Reference, according to the logocentric tradition, involves a non-verbal outside to which language refers and by virtue of which it is meaningful. Reference, then, involves the search for a non-verbal ground. It also postulates a subject prior to language who expresses through language her already presencing, experiencing self, while language is a system of signs that are representations of the non-verbal outside, presence, or Being. Derrida revealed this literal or referential notion of language as an illusion born of forgetting the figurative nature of language. Signs are not vessels into which a soul of meaning, the signified, is poured by a presencing 'outside'. Signs are rhetorical figures that are not derived from literal, proper uses, but express the figurative nature of language as opposed to the referential illusion. According to Miller, language is an infinite chain of figurative words with no extralinguistic origin or end. Referentiality is said to be a mere effect of grammar and rhetoric, while the concept of 'outside' is a mere figure of speech.[40] This is not to say that reference is denied; rather, it is problematized, bracketed, suspended, put under erasure, as a self-contradictory notion, as Wittgenstein had done. To deny it is to assume its intelligibility. According to Derrida, it is not even intelligible, and what it appears to be is only an illusion.

Thus, the binary polarities of subject/object, inside/outside, verbal/non-verbal, are challenged, by showing first, that the hierarchical relation between the various pairs can be reversed. Outside is assumed to determine inside as cause determines effect. Cause, however, turns out to be the result of internal effect. For Derrida, as for Nietzsche , the alleged cause is merely an effect of an effect, or, as Nietzsche put it in the *Will to Power:* 'the actual impact of the outside world is never a conscious one. . . . The fragment of outside world of which we are conscious is a correlative of the effect that has reached as from outside and that is then projected, *a posteriori* as its "cause".' And note a further remark from the same publication: 'The whole notion of "an inner experience" enters our consciousness only after it has found a language that the individual understands – i.e., a translation of a situation into a familiar situation: 'to understand', naively put, merely means: to be able to express something old and familiar.'[41]

By exposing the figurative, rhetorical nature of all language of poetry, Nietzsche challenged the notion of a literal language of truth referring to reality (outside), as a mere figure of speech, as is the self. Nietzsche insisted that reality is mere appearance, a result of language, and that the poet must free herself from the constraints of referential truth to face truth squarely as metaphors, as fictions of our own creation, while logic is a scheme posited by ourselves and no criterion of true being (see chapter 1 on Nietzsche).

This exposure and loss of referentiality leads to the absence of a reliable referent or a subject. Such loss of substance can be interpreted as a liberation of the free play of language without the hindrance of referentialist constraints of meaning. Language, whether of poetry or 'ordinary' language, does not appropriate anything, then, not consciousness – as of the poet – nor the object, nor a synthesis of object and consciousness. The effacement of extralinguistic reference is initiated by the act of self-reference, by the 'linguistic moment', when meaning and reference are suspended and language and writing become their own subject matter. As Miller explained, poetry is the transference of things as they are into language, into what they were not, into metaphors.[42] However, there are no 'things as they are', only metaphors of metaphors. The notion of a relation between language and something outside language but represented by it, is broken in poetry and fiction, when the word as such appears, not the word as representation of something, but representation itself, language itself. In this 'suspension of reference', the linguistic moment, language is brought to the fore and shown to be problematic. The reality-reference of literature, as of language, is subordinated to the play of language as figures, metaphors, flowers of speech, and intertextual allusion. Deconstruction shatters the illusion that texts have a direct relation to what they allegedly represent, while the rhetoric of representation is shown to be a sham: reality is exposed as a metonymic charm, a substitution of effect for cause.[43] Being, outside, presence, are 'ghostly effects', produced by words and dispelled by them as well, as texts make their language question its own claims to representation. The linking of a text to an outside is seen to be an illusion, a violation or manhandling of the text. This view led to the notion of textuality, "there is nothing outside the text," as there is no outside to language, no non-verbal ground or substrate to which language refers. Or, as Llewelyn put it, language is nomadic: 'It is everywhere and nowhere. It is spacing.'[44]

This questioning of the meaning of reference is also a philosophical

question about supposed borders and limits between outside and inside
for example, between language and world, mind and nature or matter,
and so on. Derrida suggested that there is an undecidability over thresh-
olds, over what is inside and what is outside, over what is the same and
what is different. He remarked that undecidability is part of the logocentric game and forestalls any clean break with it, presumably because
it perpetuates logocentric arguments. To see how the word undecidable
moves in Derrida's critique of logocentrism, we can relate it to
differance. The latter is said to be not a decided third term or a
reconciliation of opposites, but an undecidable. An undecidable is
an 'insideoutness', a questioning or a transgression of borders, limits,
categorizations, and dualisms. Like dissemination, differance is not a
concept, but an undecidable, in that it cannot be thematized or conceptualized. Undecidables involve a deconceptualization, an overrunning of
borders, not an erection of new ones. They involve a diaspora of meaning, not a making or affirmation of a thesis.[45]

Undecidability can also be related to Derrida's critique of Searle, who
(he said) does not see beyond speech acts as a direct expression of the
speaker's intentions. Derrida, like Wittgenstein, rejected the notion of
speech acts as meaningful and determined by intention; indeed he
denied that locutionary acts are meaningful at all, in the sense of a
determinate, signified concept present to the speaker's mind. He denied, then, determinacy, immediacy, and fullness to the intention of
speech acts (even when the speaker fully intends what she says), through
the concept of 'iterability'. Since any speech act is repeatable and
meaningful within another context, it cannot be dependent on speakers'
intentions, which are absent in the new context. 'Repeatability' detaches
speech acts from present, immediate singular intentions postulated in
the now; it divides and opens up to undecidability the ideal plenitude of
self-presence or the mythical determinacy of intention. Utterances and
intentions are divided by an unbridgeable gap, 'fissiparated' due to
iterability and repeatability. Iterability alters what is said; it shows that we
mean something other than what we mean, and say something other
than what we say. This gap, this otherness is Derrida's 'spacing' or
articulation; it is the 'writing' inscribed in all speech, writing being a
non-concept, the tracing, differance, iteration, that Searle never envis-
aged. Thus, Derrida saw undecidables where others see presence, intention, determinacy. Presence and meaning are for him an 'effect' of
differance, indeterminacy, undecidability, and spacing.

A notable example of Derrida's questioning of borders and insistence
on undecidability is his challenging of the borders between philosophy
and literature, literature and science, and so on. He insisted that we do

not understand these distinctions, pointing out, like Wittgenstein, that there is no mark that distinguishes a text as a member of certain types or classes, and no single property or plurality of properties that allows us to decide. Wittgenstein's concept of family resemblances exposes the inadequacy of the notion of essence or property as class distinction, but, as will be discussed below, he does not seem to go quite the way of Derrida. *Glas*, for example, is not merely a borderline case between philosophy and literature; it questions the very notion of case and border. *Glas* also challenged the style of serious, academic philosophy and criticism, showing that all styles of philosophy are marked by non-seriousness, and it repudiated the border between citation, commentary, and original as simple-minded; philosophy and criticism collapse under the indefinitizing effects of border-erasing. Arnold's dichotomy between creative and critical writing is rejected: criticism is no longer seen merely as the supplement to something superior. Thus, a critical text might be seen as more creative than a 'creative' text, as the German ironists argued. As with Nietzsche's texts, too, the patent literariness of Derrida's writing contrasts with contents and themes usually associated with decorous philosophy rather than literature. Nietzsche and Derrida, however, exposed the literary, rhetorical nature of the philosophical claim to truth: literature is the main (repressed) topic of philosophy and the model for the truth it seeks, yet literature is 'deceitful' too. It is, perhaps, merely more open about its deceitful, figurative properties. As de Man argued, philosophy is an endless reflection on its own destruction (the exposure of its rhetoricity) at the hands of literature.[46]

Derrida offered us not a logic, science, or philosophy of criticism, but only a *bricolage*, borrowing his term from Levi-Strauss. To his 'philosophy', or 'criticism' he gave the status of a kind of literature, called *écriture*, refusing the distinction between them by employing in his texts all the ingrained features of fiction and poetry, from linguistic and rhetorical play to parody and ironic narrative stances. Derrida's criticism is impossible to categorize as such; hence it is rejected as unreadable by the positivist, logocentric philosopher or critic. Since his texts are patently not respectful of traditional boundaries, they can be read with the same attitudes, expectations, and awareness of ambivalence that one brings to the study of literary texts. Commentary is not a subordinate text, as Arnold and the new critics would have it, for the boundary between commentary and original is undecidable, as Coleridge's *Biographia* demonstrated. Criticism, moreover, is not outside literature, but within it, as Samuel Johnson knew, in its linguistic moments, its self-deconstructing texts, and its elaboration of these. We can see Derrida aim not only at a fusion of philosophy and criticism into a philosophical criticism, but also a fusion with literature, to produce a hybrid, composite 'art of criticism', as the German romantics insisted. And, as Hartman put it, the recognition scene for criticism comes when criticism sees itself not as a supplement, but as a creative activity too, both commenting on previous texts (precisely as does literature, both directly and indirectly) and writing texts of its own that require commentary, écriture.[47] Derrida rejected Arnold's and Eliot's notions that criticism must be quite distinct from and even corrosive of creativity, and emphasized what Shelley, Coleridge, Johnson, and others have demonstrated, namely that criticism need not be mere supplementary commentary, but an art form in its own right, in addition to being embedded in all art. Like philosophy, moreover, criticism pretends to a literal language which it cannot sustain.

The theoretical ground so long dreamed of by philosophy, moreover, has been shown by Derrida to be a myth: there is nothing outside writing (écriture), or writerly practice. Philosophy, like criticism and literature, is conceived of by Derrida as intertextual commentary, undeniably literary; unlike traditional philosophy, which has tried to 'deflower' language of its figures of speech, Derrida showed philosophical language to be saturated with figures, and radically metaphoric, as Shelley insisted all language to be. Discourse about texts is not supplementary metalanguage, then; it is simply more textual activity. Like Nietzsche, who also rejected a rational mode of discourse, style, or format in order to prove its illusoriness, Derrida exposed and focused upon the irrational elements which erupt constantly in all discourse before being repressed, and which poetry, for example, draws upon for its richness.

Many of the Derridean themes described above, particularly the critique and deconstruction of western metaphysics, seem to have familiar elements associable with Wittgenstein's project, or the radical indeterminacy of Quine or Peirce's analyses of signs. John Llewelyn cautioned us however that a comparison with Wittgenstein is risky, as is one with Quine or Peirce. For, he argued, 'we have not seen it all before'. Derrida cannot be so easily 'domesticated'. According to Llewelyn, neither Wittgenstein nor Peirce 'break the mould of semiology', even though they break the mould of essentialist analysis.[48] Derrida showed that the mould is already fissured itself, hence he doesn't actually need to break it. Like others (Levi-Strauss, Saussure, Jakobson), Wittgenstein's texts show traces of alterity, though they fall short of Derrida's systematic exposure of the otherness of rational discourse. As for Derrida, for Wittgenstein there is no question about a ground or foundation of language which makes sense or is well-founded or well-formed, since every ground is based on dualistic, contradictory assumptions. The

Socratic scepticism that both Wittgenstein and Derrida seem to face does not claim truth for itself, however; it is simply the Socratic scepticism of not knowing, of undecidability. Yet, Llewelyn insisted, Derrida's texts and scepticism are designed to discomfort us, while Wittgenstein tenders solace. (Here Llewelyn may underestimate Wittgenstein considerably.)

Like Wittgenstein and Peirce, Quine is said to go a certain way in Derrida's direction, but Llewelyn also denied that Quine realized Derrida's project either, and in Quine's and Peirce's cases, he is surely correct. Like Derrida, Wittgenstein, as well as Peirce and Quine, located meaning in practice, while recognizing that practice is itself an inscrutable concept; since it must be interpreted, what it means remains to be seen. Llewelyn insisted that Quine forgot the 'disontological', raising inscrutability to an ontology. All these criticisms of Peirce, Quine, and Wittgenstein could be applied to Dewey and James, and are at the crux of the argument that Derrida's project exceeds that of the pragmatists or Wittgenstein. In one sense, the criticisms are puzzling and unsatisfying, for one could ponder as to why we should read Wittgenstein, Quine, and Peirce in this 'conservative' way. Their texts give an enormous scope for reading them as being as radical as Derrida's in regard to their critiques of metaphysics, at least. Why, for example, should we interpret Wittgenstein's modified conventions and practices, which replace the ideas of Russell and Frege, as nevertheless structures of meaning and logical grammar, so that language games are still naively logocentric? Why not read them rather as, like Derrida, showing that the foundations are already subverted? Likewise, the notion that Peirce's semiotic threatens to remain a semiology is puzzling. In what sense does it threaten, when everything it states seems to deconstruct semiology? Most unconvincing of all is Llewelyn's notion that for Quine, the inscrutable is ontology, and a sign of the forgetting of disontology. If Quine does one thing successfully, it is to deconstruct ontology, however conservative his 'style'.

Llewelyn's criticisms are unconvincing to some extent, much as de Man's of Derrida on Rousseau and of Norris on Rorty. The problem involves an insistence on reading other texts as conservatively as possible, while reading Derrida's as radically as possible. In time, Derrida's texts will also suffer degeneration into dead metaphor and systematization as the texts of other innovative philosophers, however impossible that seems at the moment. Yet Llewelyn is surely correct in his insistence that Derrida has gone further, substantially further, in stylistic respects, which are central to his project. For while in one sense James, Dewey, Peirce, Wittgenstein, and Quine have all thematically deconstructed western metaphysics, and can help us enormously to understand the details of that deconstruction and of Derrida's project, in part, they still remain largely within logocentric language (unlike Blake, Shelley, or Nietzsche, the German ironists, or even Coleridge, in his poetry and *Biographia*). This is what, it seems, Llewelyn is getting at. That is, their language itself traps them, and limits their writings, more than is necessary, while encouraging the reader to read conservatively. Or else the language so readily allows a conservative reading that the radical text is repressed. While all these writers reflected, then, like Derrida, on the status of conceptualization (to put the critique of western metaphysics in the broadest possible terms), Derrida succeeded more thoroughly in deconceptualizing it in practice before our very eyes, in demonstrating, perhaps, rather than in talking about it in conceptual terms.

This is, of course, a radically innovative achievement. Derrida's style liberated him, to a greater extent, from the constraints under which Dewey and the others laboured, and which trapped their texts within logocentric thought, through their almost unrelieved logocentric discourse, however much they sought to put their terms under erasure. In other words, Derrida cannot be said to have escaped logocentric discourse, but he so utterly vitiated it that it no longer presents the undisturbed surface of a reflecting mirror into which we can project our presentness. The narcissistic mirror-language of logocentrism is so cracked, flawed, stained, and scarred in Derrida's texts, that his writing is no longer recognizable as a mirror; no self-image mistaken for reality stares perfectly formed back at us, and we see more of what is behind the mirror surface, namely, the undecidable, the indeterminate, the cracked looking-glass, the nothing which it is.

Derrida's texts are unreadable because he is pressing us to see that we do not know what we are doing when we read. His texts are to some extent incomprehensible because comprehension is at issue. He played with language in absurd and outrageous ways instead of using it to communicate ideas, because he was demonstrating what an inscrutable business communication is. Our ease in all these matters is a mask for the gaping abyss of uncertainty which infects them. All these rational activities supposedly so well-understood and so competently performed, like the rational discourse employed, constantly repress the irrational elements which inhabit them and rupture them, in spite of all our efforts to paper over the cracks. To describe Derrida as a nihilist, however, is to misunderstand him. The effort to undo forces of repression is a creative, positive task of Blakean, Socratic proportions. To confront us with the indeterminacy and undecidability of our experience acquaints us with that which we do not know, and gives us the only knowledge of any value that we ever really possess, namely to know that which we do not know. As Miller wrote: 'the putting in question of transcendent grounds for human values is not necessarily nihilistic or defeatist. It may be a form of exuberant, creative joy'.[49]

Derrida cannot be assimilated to the pragmatism of Peirce, James, Dewey, Wittgenstein, Quine, or Rorty. For while thematic comparsions can be made which may help us to focus on the conceptual issues at stake and to work through the entanglements of dualistic, logocentric thinking, Derrida is exceptional in exposing the tenacity of logocentric language to defuse any criticism of itself couched in that language. All texts using undisrupted logocentric language can so easily be misread, or misinterpreted, that they become cornerstones of logocentric, authoritarian thinking, in spite of clear evidence in the text of criticism of such thinking. Nor however and perhaps more surprisingly, could Derrida be assimilated to deconstruction as practised by Hartman, Miller, de Man, Bloom, Johnson, and others. For with the philosophers above, comparisons can be made about thematic issues, but only Derrida broke out of the decorum of academic discourse to demonstrate his thematics artistically. There is nothing 'wild' about the style of even Hartman, much less anyone else in the group. As Felperin ironically noted, the textual hedonism of the French counterpart of the Americans is too frightening to the Yale puritan.

Felperin further concluded that Derrida's free play turns out to be very hard work for the American deconstructors, whose Puritan work-anxiety prevents them (and most of us) from abandoning themselves and giving up institutional controls of traditional method and system.[50] Yet Felperin was somewhat arbitrary when he accepted Hartman's division of the Americans into hard and soft deconstructors, lumping de Man and Miller with Derrida whilst excluding Bloom and Hartman. Derrida is unarguably in a class by himself, as Felperin virtually admitted elsewhere, when he criticized de Man and Miller for maintaining the distinction between literary and ordinary language, between genuine criticism and institutionalized norms, where for Derrida such distinctions are ephemeral and illusory. There is only *écriture*.[51]

De Man's concentration on rhetoric and language (influenced by Nietzsche's theories) led him to practise close textual analysis without the philosophical deconstruction of the assumptions involved. He never got, arguably, to grammatology, much less graphematics, and hence lacked the self-consciousness that Derrida's stylistics and undecidables made possible. De Man was somewhat trapped in a web of logocentric rhetoricity. For he never practised a deconstructed rhetorical analysis which would put under erasure the referential dimension which an undeconstructive notion of language as metaphorical or figurative keeps intact. Certainly, de Man quoted Nietzsche on the need for such a deconstructed notion of rhetoricity, but he failed (blindly) to practise it in his textual analysis, as becomes evident from his logocentric privileging of literary over ordinary language and literary texts over other texts. Closely related to this hierarchical dualism is de Man's refusal of the interminable interpretive activity celebrated by Derrida (and Barthes) as applicable to all language, not just to literary language. As Vincent Leitch somewhat unfairly put it, de Man set up a new presence, the sacred text, recanonizing great writers and works of tradition, distinguishing, like Arnold, the humble critic as a supplement to the poetic genius.[52] Interpretation is delimited, and the author as source of intentions and meanings is resuscitated. Similarly, writers such as Hartman accepted the idea of free play, and then immediately restricted it within certain acceptable, decorous limits, while the subject – reader – author dichotomy was also retained, in the emphasis on the distinction between strong and weak misreadings. Such a distinction is actually only a veil for the old distinction between better and worse meanings in texts.

Derrida was not obviously interested in judging readings or misreadings as strong or weak; he was patently interested in playing with the text, manhandling, to see what might happen next. No misreading is acontextually stronger or weaker than any other, because they are all equally shot through with logocentric contradictions. Misreading has to some extent become a superficially more acceptable term for making meanings, and it hardly relates to Derrida's concept of free play any more. Misreading implies a summation, reduction, and account, at some point, of the text. Derrida knew that any account at any point would be equally inadequate without a specified context. He never offered misreadings or accounts, whether strong or weak, but only *écriture*. He played, by parodying, by phony etymologies, by grammatical, typographical, or spelling gimmicks, by joking, punning, teasing-out connotations, creating undecidables that are sprinkled throughout his work so that they become its very texture, by mixing themes, genres, producing fragments of wholes that are never completed, thus challenging the very notion of simple, unproblematic language, communication, structure, form, content, unity, reading, and comprehension. For Derrida, as for Stanley Fish, for example, ordinary language was just as riddled with these undecidables and irrationals as is poetic language. There is no question of privileging one over the other. Poetic language seems different, in part because we treat it differently, come to it with different expectations.

Moreover, for Derrida, the 'genius' behind all language is not some individual subject or plurality of subjects, but language itself; that is, the subject-vehicle of language is conscious only of a small portion of what language speaks. The subject is not the origin or determination of what the language that emerges from her can do and mean, as Freud had already reminded us. The language that speaks through the artist can say, do, and mean things that are anathema to her. She is no longer, however, the arbiter of the possible interpretations of her texts, because they are not her own; they belong to language, to textuality, and that alone is the limit of free play. The old idea of the artist as arbiter of meaning has, regrettably, taken a new form as the phallus in Lacan's theorizing. The phallus-genius centres and regulates all interpretation and truth. Texts can be decoded by means of the phallus as an unveiling of the truth.

The greatest difficulty, even for Derrida's closest admirers, is in giving up an authoritative standard that can make possible judgments or discriminations amongst texts. From Marxist critics to Wolfgang Iser and others, something, it is thought, might be found to provide for relatively authoritative interpretation in order to avoid the pluralist dissent that undermines such authority. 'Pluralist' here means 'radically pluralist', that is, not merely allowing of a number of varying points of view within certain limits, but of allowing any and innumerable points of view with no legalistic limits to the possible positions, unless some relative context is openly specified.

This, clearly, constitutes relativistic anarchy at its extreme. How then does one propose to judge texts, for example? The answer may be that we can and do, but provisionally, and, most importantly, contextually: with some aim in view ,as Dewey insisted. Our judgements are, moreover, always subject to revision in the light of new evidence emerging from free play or other textual interaction. Secondly, we redefine the concept of judgement, so that we argue only that some texts in certain contexts stimulate kinds of free play more than others, which encourage repression, though even here we are on shaky ground. One need make no claim that this leads us to truths, meanings, or knowledge – only that play is more akin to life while repression is more akin to closure and death. Repression is in many contexts destructive and is to be distinguished clearly from creative, productive, self-control. One can, then, prefer Coleridge to Southey, for example, for certain purposes, or Wallace Stevens to Ted Hughes for others, not because the former in each case is closer to truth, or produces more truths or meanings or absolutely better poetry. Texts are not better in some vacuum, but are preferable at one stage or another of one's intellectual development, or in certain moods or by virtue of certain specified criteria, because they initiate and liberate certain kinds of responses more readily and intensely in certain contexts for certain people than do others. Texts are rich with a variety of games, not replete with univocal or even limited truth, plural meanings, and knowledge. The word games, as the activity of criticism and description of poetry, is to some readers outrageous, because it suggests frivolity at the expense of seriousness, responsibility, and humaneness.

If we play the games of literature and life with all the imaginativeness available to us, instead of bowing and nodding to repressive traditions and familiar constraints, the results will often be something far more humane than what we now call responsible, serious behaviour, which too often is a facade for the grossest forms of patriarchy, egotism, and the shoring up of entrenched attitudes. Derrida was demonstrating what Socrates and Blake, for example, achieved, and what Nietzsche and Freud (to some extent) encouraged, namely a reversal of our values with, then, a reassessment of them as human conventions, not natural facts or absolutes, and therefore appropriate only within specified contexts and not authoritative. Such conventions must be reassessed constantly, no matter how morally and aesthetically basic they may seem. Like Dewey, Derrida showed that 'criticism' can mean the enlargement of response, the enrichment of experience, and the re-education of perception. It need not be understood in the judgemental sense only or primarily. Derrida has enlarged our perception of what criticism itself can be, or at least reminded us of what German and English Romanticists had shown, in keeping with pragmatists' central commitments to the changing meanings and values of all aspects of human experience.

Conclusion: The 'New' Historicism

Any discussion of new historicism must first acknowledge that there are many different kinds of new historicists and many different practices – as well as theories – which range widely enough virtually to contradict each other. Therefore, one must keep in mind that new historicism is not a monolithic theory or practice – it is varied, diverse, and plural.[1] We can say, however, that such practitioners as Stephen Greenblatt, Louis Montrose, and Catherine Gallagher identified themselves with the movement at its earliest stage;[2] indeed, Greenblatt himself used the term new historicism in 1982.[3] New historicism can be said to be a varied set of attitudes, themes, and preoccupations starting around 1979–80, perhaps even slightly earlier. These themes and shared concerns tend to have been elaborated initially around Renaissance Studies, though they have now spread to every period of literature. Greenblatt now prefers the phrase 'poetics of culture', for a description of this emerging emphasis in literary and cultural studies. Conflicting accounts and practices under the new historicism label show that there is no unified theory or approach, but one can indicate tendencies and themes which recur. For example, new historicism attempts to restore a historical dimension to literary studies; it seeks to replace or to supplement formalist practices, by attending to the historical context in which texts originate. Efforts are made both to situate a text in relation to (so-called) non-discursive practices, and also to reconceptualize or understand in new ways the historical field within which texts are produced. Some New Historicists also allegedly seek a synthesis between formalist practices and historical approaches. Many other new historicists seem simply to reject post-structuralists' textualization of history (textualization constituting a refusal of the dichotomy between history and text; history is text, and is already interpreted material, too).

Such historicists assert a material reality in relation to which texts are secondary. These 'old new historicists', as we will call them, claim that history is not to be seen as a body of texts and a strategy of reading and interpreting these texts, as textualists have argued. History, they argue, can be said to be what actually occurred in the past; and history is also the totality of authoritative texts and documents of other information about the past which has been recorded by reliable historians.[4] This is an affirmation, clearly, that the writing of history can find its foundations in unmediated facts. New historicism, however, can also be described as an effort to discover ways of describing the relation between cultural artifacts and some allegedly distinguishable social context in which these cultural artifacts occur. In this effort to describe the relation between text and context, some new historicists see themselves as trying to decrease the distinction between aesthetic objects *per se* and something called historical background. Most new historicisms admit, then, in spite of their diverse forms, to have an interest in studying the relation of literary works to the socio-economic and historical system in which they were produced. Nearly all new historicists claim to combat 'empty formalisms' by making historical considerations central to literary analyses.[5] Many new historicisms reject 'outmoded' vocabularies of formalism – of irony, allegory, illusion, metaphor, opposition, mimesis – and seek to move outside the text to show how culture and society affect each other. Such an approach almost seems to dissolve literature back into its historical complex, reasserting in some cases, at least, a primacy for history of which literature is the secondary reflection, though some other new historicists explicitly seek to avoid this hierarchy. Indeed, some new historicists say there is no such thing as history in the sense of a referential ground of knowledge.[6]

Historicisms, both old and new, can be said to be reacting against idealism (especially German idealism) – they are anti-idealist, anti-formalist, anti-humanist, and anti-romantic.[7] Both old and new historicisms are committed to the idea of the self as a product of forces over which it can exercise little or no control. The self – as well as all other cultural and social phenomena – is an effect (not an origin as, say, humanists and Romantics might have argued) of monolithic forces – of tradition and institutions, of race, gender, economic and geographical environment, themselves seen as causalities which determine human cultural and social activity. (Greenblatt and others overtly deny this determinism, yet then become trapped within it, by their own assumption of a duality between self and environment.)[8] New historicisms claim to be ideologically less naive than old historicisms – which were allegedly innocent of ideology and political assumptions. New historicists seem overtly, at least, committed to a self-consciousness of their own partiality and emotional blindness, denying any privileged insight. They admit the post-structuralist principle that every critique of art, society, or history uses the very tools it condemns – hence risks falling prey to the practice it criticizes. Many new historicists claim to acknowledge that no discourse gives privileged access to unchanging truths, nor expresses unalterable human nature. They claim also to give up any hopes (unlike old historicists) for a unified history of the past – a master story of large scale elements directing a whole society. They give up the claim to find a single vision or a stable and unified historical story. Old-style totalizing world views are rejected along with grand humanist assumptions of the narrative unity of history.[9] Admissions of rupture and discontinuity in history are part of this rejection. And determinism is allegedly rejected in the insistence, of some new historicists, that art is influenced by society, but also influences it as well, thus reconceptualizing the relations of artistic to other social practices.[10] New historicists claim, then to reject the neat packaging of the history of ideas – of universalizing theories like Marxism, master narratives of the old historians, analysis-*à-clef*, or the study of authorial influences. Such monolithic historiography is rejected as either totalizing or atomizing history. New historicists claim to study history in a new way, by offering a new awareness – a self-consciousness – about how history and culture define each other.

New historicists challenge the traditionalists' notion of the autonomy of literature *vis à vis* history or historical context (the notion that art was somehow above or beyond economic and social influences). For example, Greenblatt has repeatedly argued that the critic should expose the alleged disinterestedness and self-sacrificing character of art – showing how it too operates under economic effects, such as capitalist profit motives. Critics should reveal what is effaced in a text – expose art, for instance, as not above the market place as it (allegedly) claims to be, expose it as involved in symbolic cash value. Indeed, Greenblatt admitted that the critic must expose his own involvement, too – as well as that of texts – and admit the impossibility of extricating oneself as a critic, or one's object of study, texts, from society's dominant ideologies, economies, and social institutions. Frank Lentricchia, however, accused the new historicists like Greenblatt and Montrose of failing precisely to show how such traces of social economy are effaced, either by art or by their own critical writings. Indeed, he argued on numerous occasions that they themselves are the ones primarily to set up art against an inferior realm called the marketplace of ordinary life.[11]

New historicists further challenged the notion of an autonomous self which old historicisms had left unquestioned, in their positing of great individuals who affect the course of history by means of free acts.[12] (Already in 1820 Georg Büchner had rejected what he called this idealist view of history.) Self and text are, according to some new historicists, effects, but not in the sense that post-structuralism understood them, as figures of speech. For these new historicists, self and text are not mere effects, but effects of causes, namely, of monolithic forces or intersecting institutions. Hence, self and text are seen to be not autonomous, because defined by their relation to the 'other', that great force of context which inhibits them from free activity. At this point, one detects a determinism creeping back into historicism: however much it may be denied overtly, there is a tendency for social forces to be seen as stronger than selves or texts, as forces of influence or causality. Though acknowledging the non-autonomy of self and text, most new historicists place both self and text against a monolithic, autonomous complex of causal forces – a reality – some causal notion of context. They thereby reintroduce a pernicious dualism, which post-structuralists had shown to be inconsistent nonsense, and a hypostasization of a dualistic kind of thinking into an expression of the nature of history, reality, society, and context. Dualistic thinking is not revelatory of the nature of reality; it is not a fact, but a product of reflection. Yet this post-structuralist insight has been forgotten by most new historicists.

Other new historicists are less obviously distinguishable from post-structural theorists. Hayden White argued that the conflict between new historicists and their critics is not a conflict between post-structural textualists and 'true' historians, but between different theories of textuality. (Gayatri Spivak, on the other hand, has denounced new historicism as an academic media hype mounted against deconstruction). Louis Montrose is certainly a new-textualist type of new historicist. He argues for the textuality of history, and admits that we have no access to any full and authentic past – some material reality (say, true events that really happened) – unmediated by the surviving textual traces of the society in question. The traces are themselves subject to interpretation or mediation, and are not authoritative grounds. Montrose has also argued for the historicity of texts: all modes of writing are culturally specific and socially imbedded, not autonomous. (No allowance for 'sports of nature' is, however, made.) Hayden White has maintained, however, that many other new historicists have turned to history in the hopes of finding some kind of knowledge that an allegedly specifically historical approach to literature might yield (instead of turning to history for information about the literature they study). Yet there is no such thing, he argued, as a specifically historical approach; there are a whole variety of approaches, as in literature. White noted that, in the same breath, new historicists both deny that they seek such a special historical knowledge, and yet they show a nostalgia for it – a secret hope that their very self-consciousness about their historical context, will somehow give them greater insight than other approaches can give. That is, many such new historicists admit that one 'cannot escape from ideology', and then proceed to try to escape, in claiming that the self-conscious awareness of entrapment in ideology endows one with a special, objective consciousness of the conditions in which we live. To admit that you cannot escape is, allegedly, to gain a more neutral perspective or distance, which purifies and mitigates the effects; this is an echoing of some Marxists' inconsistency.[13]

Indeterminacy, incompleteness, and non-objectivity or non-neutrality of interpretation and of discourse are seen, moreover, nostalgically, as impurities, as less desirable than their opposites. New historicists suggest, Stanley Fish argued, that they are truly sensitive to differences and relativities, to the ways in which orthodox historical narratives try to suppress the economic, social, and other 'realities' which 'unsettle' their texts; they attempt to open up the fissures and ruptures which old, homogenized histories denied. Indeed, materialists accuse many new historicists (the new textualist-type, usually) of aestheticizing critiques of ideology, of being too formalist, too textualist. Yet even the claims of textualist-type new historicists to expose the ideologies of old historicists involves an implied (or often explicit) assertion that they are non-ideological themselves. According to Fish, they show thereby a nostalgia for the very authoritarian perspective which they attempt to deconstruct.[14] In their exhortations to be historically aware, they often assert or imply the possibility of some flexibility, some openness, some more multi-directional mode of discourse and of thinking which escapes the exclusionary discourses that structure our perceptions. In Fish's view, what even textualist new historicists fail to acknowledge is that to be aware of the distortions of ideologies, of the 'violence of received evaluations of fundamental social operators', does not lead to any special approach or some special insight or consciousness. All discourses, all perspectives, are exclusionary. There seems to be a fantasy in some new historicists' writings about such a general faculty of openness, Fish complained, a faculty which leads to an ability to be 'directionless', non-exclusionary, unlimited, non-ideological, non-perspectival. Yet no mode of speech, discourse, or action is ever freed from the entanglements of concrete life situations, of history, of *Dasein*, of time – space, of demarcation. Ironically, what new historicists unconsciously hope to be, it turns out, is ahistorical. They hope to become detached from the very structures of tradition and culture and society to which they pay allegiance, in their often overt call for an absolute indeterminacy of discourse. They hanker after a non-allegorical, non-figurative, non-boundary-drawing way of doing literary criticism through history. This is evident from the very name, 'new historicist': a new historiography is implied, which gives a special view of literature, either never had before, or superior and anterior to other views.[15]

New historicists argue that they are more politically engaged than post-structuralists or other historicists, but this belief does not hold up under scrutiny. They claim to be less constrained by narrow disciplinary boundaries and political ideologies. They think they are able to gain a distance, a purchase, on the larger world of politics, a purchase not, as Richard Rorty would say, just on their small world of the institutional context, but on something large and generalized.[16] Yet, as Fish insisted, you cannot simultaneously stand both within a practice or context and also reflectively survey the supports you stand upon. New historicists engage, then, in a fantasy that contradicts their claims of non-autonomy of the self. They yearn for a freedom of the self which is decadent, in that it is conceived not as the freedom to interact in the context in which the self exists. It is, as critics have argued, a freedom conceived of as a secret recess, a space of aesthetic anarchy. In such a recess of anarchy the private, autonomous self indulges in a holiday from reality, to use Fish's phrase. It engages in an irresponsible passivity, on the grounds that a totalitarian, paternalistic culture determines its being and its acts. Such a self assumes its own incapacity to affect history: human beings are said to be unable to touch the structures of power which deny us our freedom.

One can see that, as a movement, new historicism contains within itself a wide variety of adherents. One strand constitutes what one might risk calling (1) old-style historicism, which rejected post-structuralist ideas. For these historicists, history is posited as anterior reality, with the text as a representation of it. New historicism also contains (2) writers whom we have named textual new historicists, who try to take on board the developments in deconstruction and structuralism, and who seek to create a synthesis of formalism, post-structuralism, and historicism. The latter are rarely able, however, to avoid the inconsistencies and contra-dictions which inhabit historicism as a concept, whether new or old. They adopt aspects of textualism and the relativity of post-structuralism without being able to see these themes through to their logical conclu-sions.[17] The hankering for completeness, determinacy of meaning, and ideology-free perspectives is evident as these are made ideals – unob-tainable, admittedly, due apparently to human limitations, but never-theless ideals to aim for and to guide our thinking and values. What such historicists deny is that these ideals are illusions; rather, they are desirable values which we cannot reach due to the limitations of reason or life. This is merely to return to eighteenth-century scepticisms and limited empiricisms. Such ideals are not goals because, as post-structuralism and pragmatism showed, they are self-contradictory concepts, unreachable because unintelligible. Such new historicists have reverted to the delusions of dualism which romanticists, pragmatists, and post-structuralists exposed as hypostasizations of the reflecting mind: dualisms of art-reality, text-context, text-history, language-world, mind-nature. Once these divisions (as opposed to distinctions) have been established, new historicists, like the traditionalists of philosophy, agonize over how to get them back together again.

These dualities are not facts of reality however, as Dewey, or Derrida, or Coleridge would remind us, but ways of reflecting on reality. Or, in Coleridge's words, these are mere distinctions useful for thought and action, not divisions in the nature of things. One need not agonize over the relations of texts to history or to reality, because this dichotomy is relative and functional, not natural and indicative of two heterogeneous spheres of things. We need not seek to establish the nature of the relation between language and reality, or history either, because we do not need to see experience in terms of such monolithic dualities.[18] One of the outcomes of the 'higher criticism' occurring late in Coleridge's life was the ironic result that history and actuality are no more primary than literature itself is.[19] Both are aspects of what Heidegger called *Dasein*, a being-in-the-world. Texts, literature, art, and the self are not said to be caused by some distinct monolithic complex of forces. No such version of a Kantian manifold exists autonomously, free of textuality. Nor is there some ideology-free discourse we can aspire to by means either of historical or rhetorical awareness. We can aspire to different points of view, but being aware of the fact that every observation is from a point of view, and not neutral or objective, does not lead to some special, superior, historical way of doing literature or history. Privileging history as *the* approach to literature assumes the very dualisms and hierarchies which romanticists, pragmatists, and post-structuralist theorists exposed as merely one possible (albeit self-contradictory) way of ordering experience, not a true, natural account of reality.[20] Even if history is textualized, as some new historicists try to do, the privileging still remains, or new historicisms could not continue to favour history over text and history as the best approach to literature. Otherwise, such historicist textualists would become simply post-structuralists.

New historicism, even at its most imaginative, is self contradictory: it denies the privileging of history while privileging history over literature and texts. It denies ideology-free perspectives while fantasizing that the self-awareness which knowledge of historical limitations gives will lead to special historicist insights about literature. As such, it is inherently unstable: all the historicist can coherently argue for, as Hayden White insisted, is to turn to history for information about that literature in which new historicists are interested, as one mode of approach amongst many, but in no way privileged over formalist or other modes of criticism.[21] This hardly constitutes a new and profound insight; it is just common sense.

Both types of new historicists (old new historicists and textualist new historicists) still fall prey to dualities, and to their resulting hierarchies or privilegings of one element over the other, or one as antecedent to the other. Hence, history is said to be antecedent to the text and to the self, or the historical approach is primary, while formalist and other approaches are secondary. The historically conscious perspective is somehow superior to other kinds of consciousness – such as philosophical consciousness, or literary consciousness, or aesthetic consciousness, or 'ordinary' consciousness. Yet, from Coleridge and Nietzsche through James, Peirce, Dewey, Heidegger, and Derrida, readers have been reminded that there are no privileged perspectives or consciousnesses, but only different ones. Each one has some valuable view to offer us, but none has a privileged access to truth or reality, however much it claims to. Even textual historicists unconsciously assume a dualism between history and literature, in which the latter is unconsciously assumed to be caused somehow by the former. This is a result of the 'outness prejudice', Coleridge would have argued. Derrida too showed that history is a type of text, while texts themselves are events of a contextual kind as well. They too are historical events which occur in a specific time and place, and they are also rhetorical. History likewise is a figure of speech, as Nietzsche and Shelley would say; it is as much a metaphor as is the text, while the discourse of history is as rhetorical as that of literature, though perhaps not so self-consciously rhetorical (or perhaps more, since it often 'pretends' to be factual).

There is no absolute distinction between past events and their linguistic embodiments, to use James's terms, any more than reality occurs 'outside' language as some kind of extra-linguistic Kantian manifold. As Derrida's and Heidegger's texts indicate, language saturates our experience: reality, including nature and mind, comes into conscious existence (as we ourselves do) with the emergence of language. Oppositions are relative functions of each other rather than distinct heterogeneous entities since, as Hegel argued, each element of a duality contains the opposite in its meaning.[22] Oppositions are interdependent notions, not distinct realities, and as such they are reciprocally constitutive for their meanings. Text and history (and context) are not related to each other in some puzzling way, in some hierarchy or primacy of being which we cannot completely grasp due to the limitations of our reason or our historical context. To use Blake's phrase, they are not contraries, but opposites: functions of each other with no meaning independent of each other, as Dewey argued.[23] As such, they are perspectives from which we view and constitute our experience; they are not abstract, independent existences to be interrelated in some mysterious, causal way.

That we cannot gain a definite, correct view of some moment or event of history is not something regrettable to the post-structuralist, pragmatist, or romanticist, as it is to the new historicist. Certainty in any general sense is, for the former, a suspect and inconsistent notion. As Kierkegaard demonstrated, there is no longing after some more accurate view of events, such as the contemporary observer would have had (the first-hand disciple in, for example, *Philosophical Fragments*).[24] Like us, contemporaries viewed their 'present' through a variety of ideological structures. No intelligible notion of 'what really happened', of how things really were, when Socrates needled, or Christ taught, or Shakespeare wrote his plays can be given. The notion of some kind of definite or certain contemporary knowledge – which would improve our understanding of texts in some privileged, valuable way over formalist or other accounts – is a fantasy. Contemporaries of Socrates, Christ, and Shakespeare had very different, even contradictory, views and accounts of how things were. A tentative grasp of the historical context from some perspective may of course give the reader of Shakespeare useful information – and possibly useful disinformation – for reading and responding to the plays. There is, however, no intelligible notion of some objective, true state of affairs to be known, which would clear up ambiguities and uncertainties. History is as much in need of interpretation as texts, whether past or contemporary, and any interpretation is reinterpretable. As Dewey might argue, any interpretation will seem limited and inconclusive from the point of view of other interpretations, which are also inconclusive and limited, but in different respects.

Afterword: Revitalizing the Vocabularies and Genres of Philosophy

In 'A defence of poetry' Shelley achieved a fusion of art and criticism in a genre which defies classification. 'Essay' hardly does justice to his achievement in the 'Defence', any more than Coleridge's *Biographia Literaria* or Kierkegaard's *Philosophical Fragments* fall into conventional disciplines. Derrida's 'Otobiography', or 'Living On: BORDER LINES', or *Glas* may seem more undisciplined than these other three texts, until we look at the reception given them in their own time. Nietzsche's works were, for decades, denied 'philosophical status', while the majority (arguably the best) of Heidegger's writings border on a poetic prose quite unprecedented in 'straight' philosophizing. Berkeley's *Sirus* is ignored almost entirely by the academic establishment, and Plato's *Dialogues* are handled as treatises, with little attention given by academic philosophers to the pervasive literary strategies of extensive framework techniques, resulting indeterminacy of narrative authority, and characterization. Systematic use of figures of speech, from metaphor, simile, and image to irony and rhetorical parody of decorum and formal philosophizing is ignored, in favour of reducing Plato to a system. Philosophy, for Plato's Socrates, was not a profession, with formalities and legalities laid down to distinguish it from other academic disciplines and other forms of life. For Socrates, it was a form of active life – life, that is, lived imaginatively and intelligently, to the highest pitch of intensity. It was intelligence and imaginativeness that distinguished such a life from other kinds of living.

All these writers challenged, by their inventiveness and poetic prose, the absurd and damaging classification of the human spirit into convenient university departments. Both style and genre were challenged in theory and in practice, as a testimony to the 'negative capability' Keats extolled: that ability to hover amongst possibilities and definites, and to accept the hybrid nature of genuinely imaginative thinking. Where intelligent writing disrupts accepted proprieties of boundaries and discourses, there is the place where innovation creates fresh metaphors, new relations, interconnections, and revitalization of old, tired forms. Boundary crossings and disruptions can be the signs of engagement in astute critiques of prevailing regions, laws, and orthodoxies.

Each writer discussed in the present study has written in numerous types of innovative, mixed genres and styles, which defy compartmentalization. Even James and Dewey turned philosophy into intelligent conversation and implicit dialogue, while mixing politics, education, metaphysics, religion, psychology, art, biology, and theory, thereby seeking to locate philosophy in a new realm of contact with human problems, needs, and interests, as Socrates had done. What a world away from the legalistic, strictly logical style, genre, and thematic proprieties of Whitehead, Russell, Frege, Carnap, Husserl, and their other contemporaries.

In the last two hundred years, strait-laced philosophy has been turned on its head systematically and repeatedly, regarding style and genre, but this does not prevent well-intentioned law-makers, usually university professors in philosophy departments, from trying to tell us what is philosophy and what isn't, what is allowed and what isn't, and that reason unenlivened by that dangerous supplement, imagination, is our only hope of a sane world. Science is our main access to objective truth while reality is really mathematical, we are assured. These are the 'psilosophers' whom Coleridge distinguished from the lover of wisdom, in all its variety and forms. Only a studied insensitivity to the imaginative and innovative literariness of philosophical writing from the pre-Socratics, through Bacon, Hume, Descartes, and Hegel, in addition to those already mentioned above, can account for the official university professor's stance. Academic philosophy teachers are distressed by the inevitable, initial incomprehension involved in all innovative art, the disruption of old forms by genuine advances into original modes of expression and the locating of new issues and problems, which causes the discarding of prior traditional obsessions.

Such incomprehension is only initial – not, however, because the faculty of reason eventually analyses and reduces the incomprehension to understandable concepts. Rather, it is overcome by sheer familiarity with the new forms and the (only gradually) dawning awareness of the new experiences that such new forms bring into existence. Patience and geniality are indispensable to aesthetic appreciation, and judgement must be suspended until time allows the initially off-putting and incomprehensible strangeness to give way to acquaintance. Only when the strangeness that breeds fear in many of us gradually eases can we begin to appreciate the extent of the value of any given innovation.

These remarks apply not only to genre innovation, but even more to style, perhaps. Much has been written, both in recent decades and throughout the history of philosophy and letters generally, about the way in which old, unexamined words and vocabulary entrap us in pseudo-problems, unconscious prejudices, and insoluble tangles. No reader of Plato's Socratic dialogues not utterly blinded by traditional interpretations, obtruding dogmas, and systems, can fail to see the challenge to language and vocabulary occurring in each dialogue where Socrates is present. Endlessly, tirelessly, Socrates challenged the young of Athens to ask the meaning of words and phrases. To consolidate this thematic questioning, Plato built into the texture of the Greek lauguage (which even a cursory knowledge of Greek makes evident) endless Heideggerian toyings with words, syntax, verb forms, and figures of speech, from metaphor and irony to imagery, hypotyposis, catachresis, simile, and so on. Readers who ignore these 'literary' devices (actually, they are equally essentially philosophical) will of course read Plato as 'the original university professor', unlike Dewey, who argued:

> Plato still provides my favourite philosophic reading. For I am unable to find in him that all-comprehensive and overriding system which later interpretation has, as it seems to me, conferred upon him as a dubious boon. The ancient sceptics overworked another aspect of Plato's thought when they treated him as their spiritual father, but they were nearer the truth, I think, than those who force him into the frame of a rigidly systematized doctrine. ... Nothing could be more helpful to present philosophizing than a 'Back to Plato' movement; but it would have to be back to the dramatic, restless, co-operatively inquiring Plato of the Dialogues, trying one mode of attack after another to see what it might yield; back to the Plato with a social and practical turn, and not to the artifical Plato constructed by unimaginative commentators who treat him as the original university professor.[1]

Berkeley was as adamant as Socrates, Heidegger, and Derrida about putting words under erasure, or in brackets – a gesture that a 'forgetting' of the history of philosophy makes seem a particular discovery of the twentieth century, though no one steeped in even only the western tradition could sincerely imagine this to be a contemporary discovery. Bishop Berkeley wrote scathingly, both in his published works and only recently published notebooks, of the need to attend to words, and of how little we understand them. First, Berkeley remarked that 'Speech [is] metaphorical more than we imagine.' Then he asked (repeatedly)

'What mean ye' by the words will, God, determine, Reality, thing, matter, spirit, existence, substance, extension, idea, relation, freedom, and so on, and so on (*Philosophical Commentaries* 631, 653, 654, 714, 545, 733, 593, 522, 722, 670, 783, 832, etc.). In *Sirus*, he finally abandoned any genre or theme or style associated with traditional notions of what philosophical texts ought to do, in order to write his most imaginative piece. *Sirus* is scorned by academic philosophers as an incomprehensible, indecorous, non-philosophical aberration. Yet one could argue that it was the imaginative, logical outcome of the essays on vision and the dialogues.

No less than Plato and Berkeley, Coleridge, Hegel, Kierkegaard, Nietzsche, and Wittgenstein struggled with the vocabularies and genres inherited from their predecessors, trying to instil new life into a language which they knew could not simply be jettisoned, but had both to be revitalized and enriched with new metaphors, if they were not to repeat the dogmas their readers had imposed on their predecessors. As Shelley put it:

> language is vitally metaphorical; that is, it marks the before unapprehended relations of things and perpetuates their apprehension, until the words which represent them become, through time, signs for portions and classes of thought instead of pictures of integral thoughts; and then if no new poets should arise to create afresh the associations which have been thus disorganized, language will be dead to all the nobler purposes of human intercourse.[2]

According to Shelley (and, earlier, Coleridge), poets must revitalize language, either by reviving 'dead metaphors' or by creating new metaphors. Every one of the philosophers discussed here showed an acute awareness of the imaginative difficulties of revitalizing language, or of creating new metaphors. This enormously difficult task became a hall-mark of each of their philosophies. It is moribund to ask whether the 'master names' which recurred throughout western philosophy were used naively or in a deconstructive sense. Most readers of philosophy have accused philosophical predecessors of dogmatic and metaphysical and misleading vocabularies. Indeed, most philosophers have themselves later in life criticized their own earlier efforts to revitalize dead metaphors and redefine 'master names' (in order to strip them of their metaphysical connotations) as wholly inadequate. For they watched their readers ignoring their efforts at revitalization, reading the words idea, self-consciousness, *Aufhebung*, the Good, act, God, organic, *Dasein*,

Being, language, certainty, fact, doer, deed, and so on, as if these words had never even been subjected by them to careful scrutiny, erasure, or bracketing.

Yet these philosophers were acutely aware that we cannot escape our language, we cannot obtain some neutral perspective, some 'historical awareness', for example, which will give us a privileged view or a super-sensitive, ideology-free mentality. This is not, of course, a discovery of the twentieth century. Dewey summed up what seems to hold for philosophers and other sorts of writers from Plato to Derrida, when he remarked that the only useful distinction in experience, for the purposes of enquiry or criticism, is not that between objective and subjective, or neutral and ideological, or good art and bad art, or truth and error. He argued for a distinction between experience which has been subjected to and produced by a maximum of imaginative reflection and intelligence, in contrast to experience awash with prejudice, ignorance, and minimal intelligent, imaginative synthesis. This Deweyan insistence on un-reflected, as opposed to reflected, experience is at the heart of his attack on dualism, and is at the heart of Plato, Coleridge, James, and Derrida's endeavours.

To stimulate imaginative reflection and engagement with experience, whether in art, science, or life, is the impetus behind the stylistic, formal, thematic, and generic disruptions, innovations, and vitality of all these writers. The effort to fight the tyranny of an unchecked faculty of analysis ('consecutive reasoning', as Keats was fond of calling it) – suppressing synthesis in the service of decorum and stereotyped convention – constitutes the impetus for apparent 'outrages' in style, language, diction, genre, syntax, theme, and rhetoric. A closer examination (than has been possible here) of the metaphors, general rhetorical strategies, and irony of the writers discussed in this study will reveal to readers the extraordinary degree of sophistication their texts exhibit, about the pitfalls of taking words and language for granted, and about the strengths and achievements which language not thus abused can release for human thought and life.

Notes

1   Plato, *Republic* VII 533b–c in *The Collected Dialogues of Plato, including the Letters*, eds E. Hamilton and H. Cairns, Princeton, 1961; 1969.
2   Plato, *Phaedo* 85c–d, ibid.
3   Plato, *Meno* 86b–c, ibid.

CHAPTER 1   SHELLEY AND NIETZSCHE: 'REALITY' AS RHETORIC

1   'Speculations on metaphysics', in *Selected Poetry and Prose of Percy Bysshe Shelley*, ed. Carlos Baker (New York, 1951), p. 473.
2   See James C. McKusick, *Coleridge's Philosophy of Language* (New Haven and London, 1986), for a thorough account of eighteenth-century language theories and Coleridge's rejection of them, a rejection shared by Shelley.
3   Coleridge, *The Statesman's Manual, Lay Sermons*, p. 36.
4   See especially *The Friend*, Vol. I, essays vi and vii, 'On the communication of truth', and in the final section, essays iv–xi, 'On the principles of method'. And see R. G. Woodman, *The Apocalyptic Vision in the Poetry of Shelley* (Toronto, 1964), for intimations of Shelley's synthetic philosophy. See also E. J. Schulze, *Shelley's Theory of Poetry: a Reappraisal* (The Hague, 1966), for a re-evaluation of Shelley's relation to Berkeley and to empiricism generally.
5   For example, *The Philosophical Lectures*, ed. K. Coburn (London, 1949).
6   As Earl Wasserman and others have supposed; see Wasserman, *The Subtler Language* (Baltimore, 1959), or Carlos Baker, *Shelley's Major Poetry* (Columbia, 1959). Harold Bloom, in *Shelley's Mythmaking* (New Haven, 1959), attends to the 'Defence' and to theories of metaphor in passing.
7   'Speculations on metaphysics', in Baker (ed.), p. 474.
8   'On life,' ibid., p. 460.
9   It also relates them to Derrida; see for example Christopher Johnson, *System and Writing in the Philosophy of Jacques Derrida* (Oxford, forthcoming), for the

role of evolutionary metaphors in Derrida's concept of 'writing' and its meaning for the notion of 'system'. And see John Dewey, *The Influence of Darwin on Philosophy: and other essays in contemporary thought* (New York: 1910; 1938), especially pp. 1–19, where Dewey noted: 'Intellectual progress usually occurs through sheer abandonment of questions together with both of the alternatives they assume – an abandonment that results from their decreasing vitality and a change of urgent interest.' This is a fairly apt description of Derrida's achievement in literary criticism and Dewey's in philosophy, not to mention Richard Rorty's recent challenge to philosophy. See below chapters 4, 5, and 6.

10   Much literature on German romanticism fosters this 'misreading', but for notable exceptions, see, for example, Ingrid Strohschneider-Kohrs, *Die Romantische Ironie in Theorie und Gestaltung, Hermaea*, 6 (Tübingen, 1960), and Oskar Walzel's numerous articles.

11   For example, S. T. Coleridge, *The Philosophical Lectures*, and see chapters 3 and 4 for further discussion.

12   On Neo-platonism see C. A. Patrides, (ed.), *The Cambridge Platonists* (London, 1969), and see W. Schrickx, 'Coleridge and the Cambridge Platonists', *A Review of English Studies*, 7 (1966), pp. 71–90.

13   In 'Kant and philosophic method', originally published in *Journal of Speculative Philosophy*, 18 (April, 1884), pp. 162–74; and see of course the Boydston modern edition, as well as the J. J. McDermott anthology of Dewey: *The Philosophy of John Dewey*, ed. John McDermott (Chicago and London, 1981), 2 vols in 1.

14   In the Coleridge marginalia on Kant, Coleridge's Tennemann marginalia, and in his notebooks and letters; see for example *CN* III 3605 and see below, chapter 7.

15   Especially in its recognition of the role of metaphor in theories and hypotheses generally; see, for example, Colin Turbayne, *The Myth of Metaphor* (New Haven, 1962), and see other philosophers of science such as Mary Hesse, who has written widely on the role of both metaphor and induction in science, as in *Models and Analogies in Science* (Notre Dame, 1966). And see various essays in *Criticism and the Growth of Knowledge*, eds. Imre Lakatos and A. Musgrave (Cambridge, 1970).

16   I. A. Richards was a notable exception; see *Coleridge on Imagination* (London, 1934).

17   'A defence of poetry', in Baker (ed.), p. 502.

18   'On life', in Baker (ed.), pp. 458–9. Compare Dewey, who noted that it is the chief task of philosophers to help get rid of the useless lumber that blocks our highways of thought, in 'From Absolutism to Experimentalism'.

19   See my 'S. T. Coleridge: *Aids to Reflection*. Language and the growth of conscience', in *Literature and Religion*, ed. Solange Dayras (Paris, forthcoming).

20   See Nelson Goodman, *Ways of Worldmaking* (Cambridge and Indianapolis, 1978; 1981). And see Owen Barfield, *Saving the Appearances: A Study in*

Idolatry (New York, 1957).

21 'A defence of poetry', in Baker (ed.), p. 446.

22 On the degeneration of language, truth, and metaphor, see *The Friend* I 110, and related notebook entries.

23 'On life', in Baker (ed.), p. 460.

24 'Speculations on metaphysics', in Baker (ed.), p. 471. Compare Willard van Orman Quine, *From a Logical Point of View* (New York, 1963), who wrote of the 'myth of physical objects' and of 'physical objects [as] conceptually imported into the situation as convenient intermediaries . . . comparable to the gods of Homer', 44. And see his *Ontological Relativity* (New York and London, 1969), for further reflections on the status of physical objects, thoughts, words, and their interrelations.

25 See John W. Wright, *Shelley's Myth of Metaphor* (Athens, Georgia, 1970), for a thorough and elegant elaboration of Shelley's 'Defence', and of its relation to 'Adonais'.

26 On the mind as act, see, for example, *CN* II 2343, and see CL VI 910; and see chapter 7. See also *CN* III 3802 on all reasoning as beginning with an act.

27 In *Experience and Nature*, for example, and see 'Kant and philosophic method', in McDermott (ed.).

28 For Derrida on origins, see for example 'Structure, sign and play', in *The Structuralist Controversy*, eds R. Macksey and E. Donato (Baltimore and London, 1975), pp. 247–65.

29 Willard van Orman Quine, 'Two dogmas of empiricism', in *From a Logical Point of View* (New York, 1963), pp. 42–3.

30 See for example *Rambler*, nos 91, 92, 137, and 158. Not only did Johnson argue that 'criticism has not yet attained the certainty and stability of a science' (158), he also acknowledged that 'the difficulty of attaining knowledge is universally confessed . . . a task which, although undertaken with ardour and pursued with diligence, must at last be left unfinished by the frailty of our nature' (91).

31 'Speculations on metaphysics', in Baker (ed.), p. 474, a remark that anticipates Nietzsche and much modern theory.

32 'A defence of poetry', in Baker (ed.), p. 516.

33 Ibid., p. 516.

34 For example *The Friend* I 429, 513, II 218, and *CN* III 3611 f17, for Coleridge on passion, reading and active engagement.

35 *Daybreak* [or *Morgenröte* (Chemnitz, 1881), Nietzsche's preface], tr. R. J. Hollingdale, intro. M. Tanner (Cambridge, 1982), p. 5.

36 *WP*, 298.

37 For Coleridge on matter as itself vital, see for example his *Theory of Life*, ed. Seth Watson (London, 1848).

38 For Dewey on the resistance of the external world (and his rejection of idealism) see chapter 1 of *Experience and Nature*.

39 See Paul de Man, 'Rhetoric of tropes (Nietzsche)', in *Allegories of Reading* (London and New Haven, 1979). See also 'Rhetoric of persuasion

(Nietzsche)', in the same collection of essays.

40 Martin Heidegger, *On the Way to Language*, tr. P. D. Hertz (New York, 1971), originally *Unterwegs zur Sprache* (Pfullingen, 1959). But for differences between Heidegger and Nietzsche, see Jean-Michel Rey, *L'enjeu des signes: lecture de Nietzsche* (Paris, 1971).

41 From *Will to Power*, as translated and as quoted from Paul de Man, *Allegories of Reading* (London and New Haven, 1979), pp. 105–6.

42 *WP*, 266–7.

43 Plato, *Theaetetus* 190a, and *Sophist* 263e.

44 Compare Nelson Goodman, 'Is a metaphor then, simply a juvenile fact, and a fact simply a senile metaphor?', in *The Languages of Art* (New York, 1968), 68.

45 See Richard Rorty, *Contingency, Irony and Solidarity* (Cambridge, 1989).

46 Immanuel Kant, *Fundamental Principles of the Metaphysics of Morals* (Indianapolis and New York, 1949), first published 1785.

47 See William Blake, *The Book of Urizen*, for example, for Blake's conception of the calculating faculty as tyrannizing over the imagination, and the destructive results of such a tyranny – from dualism in philosophy to sexual repression in life.

48 For further discussion of Nietzsche's rejection of dualism and metaphysics, see Gayatri Spivak's helpful introduction to Derrida's *Of Grammatology* (Baltimore and London, 1974, 1976).

49 *WP*, 266.

50 Norman O. Brown, *Love's Body* (New York, 1966), p. 266, a quotation revealing the close relation of two such apparently different writers as Shelley and Nietzsche.

CHAPTER 2   GERMAN ROMANTIC IRONY AND HEGEL: CREATIVE DESTRUCTION

1 'Monologue', in *German Aesthetic and Literary Criticism: the Romantic ironists and Goethe*, ed. K. M. Wheeler (Cambridge, 1984), pp. 92–3; German version in *Novalis Schriften*, eds P. Kluckhorn and R. Samuel (Stuttgart, 1960–75), II, pp. 672–3.

2 See Heidegger's 'The way to language', in *On the Way to Language*, tr. P. D. Hertz (New York, 1971), for a discussion of Novalis's 'Monolog'.

3 On fragments as seeds, see Novalis, *Miscellaneous Writings*, no. 104, in Wheeler *German Aesthetic*, p. 92.

4 See, for example, *Friedrich Schlegel's Literary Notebooks 1797–1801*, ed. Hans Eichner (Toronto, 1957), for Schlegel on Shakespeare, and see Ludwig Tieck, *Das Buch über Shakespeare*, ed. H. Lüdeke (Halle, 1920). A. E. Lussky's *Tieck's Romantic Irony* (Chapel Hill, 1932) is a basic introduction to Tieck's use of irony in his fiction, poetry, and drama.

5 As in Herder's 'Shakespeare' essay.

6 On irony versus satire, see D. C. Muecke, *The Compass of Irony* (London,

1969), and see Otto Ribbeck, 'Ueber den Begriff des εἴρων', *Rheinisches Museum*, 31 (1876), pp. 381–400. And see J. A. K. Thompson, *Irony: an historical introduction* (London, 1926).

7 Søren Kierkegaard, *The Concept of Irony*, tr. L. M. Capell (London, 1966).

8 See K. M. Wheeler, 'Coleridge's friendship with Ludwig Tieck', in *New Approaches to Coleridge*, ed. D. Sultana (London, 1981), pp. 96–109. And see Max Koch, 'Ludwig Tiecks Stellung zu Shakespeare', in *Shakespeare Jahrbuch*, 32 (1896), pp. 330–47.

9 See note 6 above for historical accounts, but see also Norman Knox, *The Word 'IRONY' and its Context 1500–1755* (Durham, NC, 1961). And see my discussion in chapter 4, *Sources, Processes, and Methods in Coleridge's 'Biographia Literaria'* (Cambridge, 1980), pp. 59–80.

10 Formalist accounts of irony remained, it could be argued, in a conventional realm of characterizing irony as structural-dramatic irony, rather than irony as a radical point of view, cast of mind, and way of life, as Plato's Socrates and the Germans conceived it. See for example Cleanth Brooks, 'Irony as a Principle of Structure', in *Literary Opinion in America*, ed. M. D. Zabel (New York, 1951), pp. 729–41. And see of course Empson's *Seven Types of Ambiguity* (London, 1930; Harmondsworth, 1961), where irony gets very short shrift in its Greek and German sense.

11 *Friedrich Schlegel: Literary Notebooks, 1797–1801*, Eichner (ed.), p. 62; Tieck, *Nachgelassene Schriften*, ed. R. Köpke, 2 vols (Leipzig, 1855), II, p. 238.

12 See Ingrid Strohschneider-Kohrs, *Die Romantische Ironie in Theorie und Gestaltung*, Hermaea, 6 (Tübingen, 1960), for the most thorough and lucid discussion of German irony available. And see Peter Szondi, 'Friedrich Schlegel und die romantische Ironie: mit einem Anhang über Ludwig Tieck', in *Euphorion*, 48 (1954), pp. 397–411. 13 See R. Immerwahr, 'The subjectivity or objectivity of Friedrich Schlegel's poetic irony', in *Germanic Review*, 26 (1951), pp. 173–91.

14 *Literary Notebooks*, Eichner (ed.) pp. 114 and 84, and Strohschneider-Kohrs, *Hermaea*, p. 22. And see Muecke, *The Compass of Irony*, p. 120. See also Kierkegaard, *The Concept of Irony*, p. 272.

15 See for example Schlegel, *Prosaische Jugendschriften*, ed. J. M. Minor, 2 vols (Vienna, 1882) II, p. 186.

16 In, for example, 'Monolog'; see above, Heidegger, 'The way to language'. It would be misleading to interpret *Aufhebung* in a transcendental way. *Aufhebung* was used by the ironists to denote endless play and activity, productivity, and agility, not as denoting a static realm of transcendent being, but as a constant readiness to shift perspectives and take new points of view. See the section below on Hegel for further discussion of a dynamic conception of the word as opposed to a static, transcendentalist interpretation.

17 Friedrich Schlegel, *Gespräch über Poesie* (1800) and numerous fragments, as well as his early essay 'Über das Studium der griechischen Poesie', in 1797, in which he showed uneasiness with Schiller's dualistic aesthetic of naive

and sentimental arts. These essays are collected in J. M. Minor, ed., *Friedrich Schlegel, 1794–1802. Seine prosaischen Jugendschriften,* 2 vols (Vienna, 1882).

18 The connecting link between German romantic ironists and Hegel is Karl Solger, whose *Erwin. Vier Gespräche über das Schöne und die Kunst,* ed. W. Henckmann (Munchen, 1971), and other writings, found favour with Hegel, though he expressed considerable distaste for much of Schlegel's and other ironists' fragments and essays. One could argue that he objected primarily to their style, having a predilection himself for the kind of abstract vocabulary and philsophizing to which Solger was also temperamentally suited; the latter was, however, still able to admire the Derridean pyrotechnics of the ironists. See further, *Tieck and Solger. The Complete Correspondence,* ed. P. Matenko (New York and Berlin, 1933) on Solger's admiration for the ironists and for Hegel.

19 See Schlegel's essay 'Über die Unverständlichkeit' (1800), translated and republished in Wheeler, *German Aesthetic,* pp. 32–40. And see H. Fauteck, 'Die Sprachtheorie Friedrich von Hardenbergs', *Neue Forschungen,* 34 (Berlin, 1940).

20 See the Jean Paul Richter selections in Wheeler, *German Aesthetic* of *School for Aesthetics,* 162 passim, and M. Hale's complete translation (Detroit, 1973).

21 In *Erwin;* see the selections in Wheeler, *German Aesthetic,* pp. 128–50. Coleridge's *Biographia* functions similarly to reach the analogous goal of imaginative and creative 'perceptivity'.

22 See, for example, L. Dieckmann, 'Friedrich Schlegel and the Romantic concept of the symbol', *Germanic Review,* 34 (1959), pp. 276–83, and more generally see Hans Eichner, 'Friedrich Schlegel's Theory of Romantic Poetry', *PMLA,* 71 (1965), pp. 1018–41. And see further G. Wilkending, *Jean Pauls Sprachauffassung in ihrem Verhältnis zu seiner Aesthetik* (Marburg, 1968).

23 'Ideas', Wheeler, *German Aesthetic,* no. 69 (p. 56): 'Irony is the clear consciousness of eternal agility, of an infinitely teeming chaos.'

24 For Solger's systematic and repeated insistence on self-criticism and self-knowledge as essential elements of Socratic irony, see *Erwin,* and for Schlegel see the *Literary Notebooks.*

25 Kierkegaard, *Philosophical Fragments,* tr. D. F. Swenson, intro. N. Thulstrup, revised H. V. Hong (Princeton 1936; 1967). And for Schlegel, see for example 'Ideas', nos 60 and 65, in Wheeler, *German Aesthetic,* p. 56.

26 Jean Paul Richter in *Vorschule (School),* Solger in *Erwin.*

27 *Schriften,* ed. P. Kluckhorn and R. Samuels (Stuttgart, 1960–75), II 470.

28 See the Tieck/Solger letter selections in Wheeler, *German Aesthetic,* pp. 151–61 for Solger and Tieck on audience and reader participation, engagement, and activity.

29 Solger, *Nachgelassene Schriften und Briefwechsel,* eds L. Tieck und F. von Raumer, 2 vols (Leipzig, 1826), II, p. 198.

30 See various essays in the collection, *Consequences of Pragmatism* (Brighton, 1982), such as nos 1, 4 and 6.

31 See especially Solger, in *Erwin,* and in the Tieck/Solger correspondence, Wheeler, *German Aesthetic,* pp. 128–59.

32   As in Friedrich Schlegel, 'On Goethe's Meister' (1798), in Wheeler, *German Aesthetic*, p. 65.

33   *Miscellaneous Writings*, number 27, in Wheeler, *German Aesthetic*, p. 87.

34   Ibid., no. 45 (p. 89).

35   Ibid., no. 26 (p. 87).

36   *School for Aesthetics*, in Wheeler, *German Aesthetic*, p. 197.

37   *Critical Fragments*, no. 108. in Wheeler, *German Aesthetic*, p. 43.

38   *Kritische Schriften*, ed. L. Tieck (Leipzig, 1845–52) I viii, and see also V, p. 81. See further *Nachgelassene Schriften*, ed. R. Köpke, 2 vols (Leipzig, 1855) II, p. 239.

39   Goethe, 'Aphorisms', in Wheeler, *German Aesthetic*, p. 227.

40   'On Goethe's Meister', in Wheeler, *German Aesthetic*, p. 69.

41   *Critical Fragments*, no. 117, in Wheeler, *German Aesthetic*, p. 44.

42   G. W. F. Hegel, 'Über Solgers *Nachgelassene Schriften und Briefwechsel*', *Jahrbücher für wissenschaftliche Kritik*, 51–4 (1828), pp. 105–10; on Solger/Hegel relations, see G. E. Mueller, 'Solger's aesthetics – A key to Hegel', in *Corona: studies in celebration of the eightieth birthday of Samuel Singer*, ed. A. Schirokauer (Durham, 1941), pp. 212–27.

43   On Solger's intermediate position, see Josef Heller, *Solgers Philosophie der ironischen Dialektik* (Berlin, 1928).

44   However much this 'literariness' is conceded, the logical consequences for Hegel's philosophy are generally rejected in most secondary literature, that is, that Hegel's system is not a system; that his *Aufhebung* is not to some notional transcendental reality, but means 'progredibility', to use a romantic ironist's term; and that his dialectic is not designed to lead to a *tertium aliquid*, but to a deferral of identity-in-difference and to dynamic opposition.

45   *Sense and Nonsense* (*Sens et non-sens*), tr. H. and P. Dreyfus (Evanston, Ill., 1964), pp. 109–110.

46   In, for example, *Madness and Civilization* (London, 1967).

47   See Alexandre Kojève, on the relation of reason and unreason, in *Introduction à la lecture de Hegel* (Paris, 1947), or *Introduction to the Reading of Hegel*, tr. J. H. Nicholls Jr, ed. Allan Bloom (New York, 1969), the inspiration for Hyppolite perhaps, in his Nietzschean interpretation of Hegel. And for Derrida on Hegel, see, for example, 'The pit and the pyramid', *Margins of Philosophy*, tr. A. Bass (Hemel Hempstead, 1982), pp. 69–108.

48   Jean Hyppolite, 'The structure of philosophic language according to the "Preface" to Hegel's *Phenomenology of the Mind*', in *The Structuralist Controversy*, eds R. Macksey and E. Donato (Baltimore, 1970; 1972), pp. 157–69.

49   Shelley, 'On life', in *Selected Poetry and Prose of Percy Bysshe Shelley*, ed. Carlos Baker (New York, 1951).

50   See Georges Poulet, 'Discussion', in Macksey and Donato (eds), p. 177.

51   Hyppolite, in Macksey and Donato (eds), pp. 160–1.

52   For further discussion, see below, chapter 5 on John Dewey, and chapter 8, on Dewey's ideas on language, and on reasoning bringing reason into

being. And see Derrida, *Glas* (Paris, 1981), on Hegel and Genet and on deconstructing Reason.

53 *The Phenomenology of Mind*, tr. J. B. Baillie, Intro. G. Lichtheim (New York, 1967), pp. 159–60.

54 *Parmenides*, 142d,e to 143a.

CHAPTER 3   JOHNSON, COLERIDGE, AND METHOD

1 Such as chapter 9, 'Experience, Nature, and Art', which is almost a prolegomena to John Dewey, *Art as Experience* (New York, 1958; first published 1934), along with chapter 10, 'Existence, Value, and Criticism'. The latter constitutes a firm basis for many of Richard Rorty's neo-pragmatist challenges to traditional philosophy's claims, while the former anticipates post-structuralist arguments in such comments as the following: 'the history of human experience is a history of the development of the arts. The history of science in its distinct emergence from religious, ceremonial and poetic arts is the record of the differentiation of the arts, not a record of separation from art'.

2 John W. Wright, 'Samuel Johnson and traditional methodology', *PMLA* 86 (1971), pp. 40–50.

3 Plato, *Republic*, especially Books vi and vii.

4 Compare Dewey, who argued that philosophy is best understood not as revealing the reality behind appearance, or for providing foundations for knowledge. Rather, it is 'intelligent criticism', a mode of interaction best understood as 'the critical method of developing methods of criticism'. Moreover, Dewey also argued that 'all reason which is itself reasoned, is thus method, not substance; operative, not 'end in itself'. To imagine it the latter is to transport it outside the natural world, to convert it into a god', John Dewey, *Experience and Nature*, (New York, 1958, first published 1925), chapter 10.

5 Compare Nietzsche on 'facts', chapter 1 above, and see chapter 1, note 42.

6 As in Dewey, *Art as Experience*.

7 See especially chapter 10 in Dewey, *Experience and Nature* and chapter 13 in Dewey, *Art as Experience*.

8 On Johnson as theoretician, see Jean Hagstrum, *Samuel Johnson's Literary Criticism* (Minneapolis, 1952), and Robert Voitle, *Samuel Johnson the Moralist* (Cambridge, Mass., 1961).

9 See J. R. de J. Jackson, *Method and Imagination in Coleridge's Criticism* (Cambridge, Mass., 1969), for a clear and elegant account of Coleridge's respect for method and the role of imagination in clarifying method. And see M. H. Abrahms, *The Mirror and the Lamp* (Oxford, 1953), for a general account of the romantic aesthetic.

10 J. W. Wright, *PMLA.*, p. 48.

11 The Socratic scepticism of, for example, the *Theaetetus*, or of the *Meno*. And

see the *Sophist* and the *Republic,* especially Books vi and vii.

12 Wright, *PMLA.,* p. 41.

13 Ibid., pp. 44–6 for all quotations in this paragraph.

14 In addition to the *Biographia* and essays in *The Friend,* see also 'On the principles of genial criticism', 'On poesy or art', and 'Fragment of an essay on taste', all found in volume ii of the Shawcross edition of the *Biographia.*

15 See Dewey, 'Existence, value, and criticism', in Dewey, *Experience and Nature,* for his Coleridgean defence of criticism as method, and of intelligent criticism as the definition of aesthetic appreciation. For example, Dewey remarked, 'First and immature experience is content simply to enjoy. . . [but] cultivated taste alone is capable of prolonged appreciation of the same object . . . because it has been trained to a discriminating procedure which constantly uncovers in the object new meanings to be perceived and enjoyed.'

16 See Pamela McCallum, *Literature and Method* (Dublin, 1983) for a lucid analysis not only of Leavis's criticism, but also of Eliot and Richards, and of the critical tradition informing twentieth-century practice.

17 On the distinction between method and arrangement, see *The Friend* I 457, 476, and 497.

18 Dewey, *Art as Experience,* and Coleridge, *The Friend* I 482, on the role of induction as conceived by Plato, for example.

19 See *Biographia Literaria* II, chapter 12.

20 *Biographia* II, 22.

21 See J. R. de J. Jackson, *Method and Imagination,* p. 70, for commentary on this passage from the *Biographia* II, chapter 12.

22 In William James, *Varieties of Religious Experience,* (London, 1967; first published 1902).

23 See for example *CN* II 2672, and see chapter 7. See also *CN* III 3593, 3605, and 4225. And see *Lay Sermons* 9.

24 Dewey remarked on the tendency of 'critical' language to retain idealist and subjectivist overtones even when explicitly seeking to subvert dualism. Specifically in relation to William James's advances in *Principles of Psychology,* Dewey wrote: 'Even when the special tenets of that tradition are radically criticized, an underlying subjectivism is retained, at least in vocabulary – and the difficulty in finding a vocabulary which will intelligibly convey a genuinely new idea is perhaps the obstacle that most retards the easy progress of philosophy.' This was of course one of Derrida's explicit concerns.

Dewey went on to cite James's invention of 'stream of consciousness', a phrase immensely effective for overcoming the atomism of earlier psychology, and he continued by noting that however inadequate other aspects of James's terminology were for progressing out of traditional dualistic problems, his Coleridgean commitment to a 'sense of life as vital' saved his philosophy from its own earlier, dualistic language. This is also the argument one wants to make for Coleridge, and indeed for Heidegger. See

John Dewey, 'From Absolutism to Experimentalism', first published 1930 (republished in the McDermott and in the Boydston editions), a most prescient essay in which Dewey also acknowledged the influence of Hegel's historical sense on evolution and on pragmatism.

25 In, for example, *Shakespearean Criticism, Biographia*, and throughout the marginalia.

26 See my essay 'Coleridge and modern critical theory', in *Coleridge's Theory of Imagination Today*, ed. Christine Gallant (New York, 1989), pp. 83–102.

27 Dewey, *Art as Experience*, chapters 12 and 13.

28 *CL* II 810, dated 1802.

29 Compare Dewey, who criticized static interpretations of organicism in 'From Absolutism to Experimentalism': 'Many philosophers have had much to say about the idea of organicism but they have taken it structurally and hence statically.' Dewey is mistaken to think that 'it was reserved for James to think of life in terms of life in action'. Coleridge and Friedrich Schlegel had explicitly rejected the static conception; see chapters 2 and 3.

30 *Biographia Literaria* II 11, and *CN* I 609. See also *On the Constitution of Church and State*, 24.

31 But see J. R. Barth, *Coleridge and Christian Doctrine* (Cambridge, Mass., 1969), for a sophisticated approach.

32 For example, see introductory aphorisms 5, 7, and 8.

33 *Biographia* I 59, and see *The Friend* I 110 and *CN* II 2535.

34 As the extensive Coleridge marginalia to Kant's works testify; see the *The Marginalia* III. And see the so-called 'Tennemann marginalia' appended to *The Philosophical Lectures*, ed. K. Coburn (London, 1949).

35 Coleridge's references to journey metaphors are numerous; see, for example, *Biographia* II 11 and 121.

36 On substance as opposition of forces, see chapter 7.

37 See *CL* II 698, *CL* VI 630, and *CN* II 2445.

38 See also John Wright, *Shelley's Myth of Metaphor* (Athens, Georgia, 1970), for further discussion of eighteenth-century language theories and Coleridge's and Shelley's rejection of them.

39 Compare John Dewey, 'Ralph Waldo Emerson', originally published in 1903, in *Characters and Events*, ed. J. Ratner (New York: 1929, 1957), I, pp. 69–77: 'I would not make hard and fast lines between philosopher and poet, yet there is some distinction of accent in thought and of rhythm in speech... Looked at in the open, our fences between literature and metaphysics appear petty – signs of an attempt to affix the legalities and formularies of property to the things of the spirit.' Dewey's remark would sum up another central connection between him, Coleridge, and Derrida. See Derrida, 'Before the law', in *Acts of Literature*, ed. D. Attridge (London, 1992), pp. 181–220.

40 See my ' "Kubla Khan" and eighteenth century aesthetic theories', *Wordsworth Circle*, 22 (Winter, 1991), pp. 15–24.

41 *CL* IV 545. Coleridge was fascinated with this image as a metaphor for wisdom in oriental lore; see for example John Beer, *Coleridge the Visionary*

(London and New York, 1959). For further references to the images of snake and serpent as wisdom see *CN* I 609, *Biographia* II 11, and *Church and State* 24.

42 *Lay Sermons* 29.

43 See chapters 4 and 5 for further elaboration of the pragmatist's rejection of any division between the senses and the intellect. And see Ernst Gombrich, *Art and Illusion* (Princeton, 1960) and R. Gregory, *Concepts and Mechanisms of Perception* (London, 1974), on seeing and visual experience as already involving intelligence and judgement.

44 See Blake's letter to Dr Trusler, 23 August 1799: 'To the Eyes of the Man of Imagination, Nature is Imagination itself', and see Coleridge's related comment: 'the very powers which in men reflect and contemplate are in essence the same as those powers which in nature produce the objects contemplated", *Philosophical Lectures*, ed. K. Coburn (London, 1949), 114.

45 From Sanskrit plays such as Bhava's *Rama's Later History* and Kalidasa's *Shakuntala*, to Shakespeare's *Hamlet* and to German romantic ironists' plays, such as Ludwig Tieck's *Der Gestiefelte Kater*, and Friedrich Schlegel's 'novel', *Lucinde*.

46 See *Biographia* I, chapter 13, for the letter. The pun on 'remains' and 'fragments' refers in part to romantic emphases on the fragment form, and relates directly to Shelley's ironic fragments, framing techniques, and journey metaphors, as in 'Ozymandias'. The spiral metaphor of 'winding steps' is akin to Shelley's spiral imagery in 'Adonais' and in 'Alastor', as a symbol of imaginative progression (see note 42, chapter 7 on the spiralling movement of the serpent) as opposed to the less dynamic circle image if unenlivened by radiation metaphors.

47 For further discussion, see chapter 2.

48 J. A. Appleyard, 'Critical theory', *Writers and their Background: S. T. Coleridge*, ed. R. L. Brett (London, 1971), pp. 135–6.

49 John Wilson, 'Some observations on the *Biographia Literaria* of S. T. Coleridge, Esq. – 1817', in *Blackwood's Magazine*, II, pp. 3–18; also in *Critical Heritage*, ed. J. R. de J. Jackson (London, 1970).

50 Hazlitt in the *Edinburgh Review* of 1817, reprinted in *Critical Heritage*, Jackson (ed.), pp. 301 and 303.

51 Wilson, 'Some observations'.

52 Quoted by E. L. Griggs, 'Ludwig Tieck and Samuel Taylor Coleridge', *Journal of English and German Philology*, 54 (April, 1955), p. 267. And see my 'Coleridge's friendship with Ludwig Tieck', in *New Approaches to Coleridge*, ed. D. Sultana (London, 1981), pp. 96–112.

CHAPTER 4 WILLIAM JAMES AND EARLY PRAGMATIST REJECTIONS OF METAPHYSICS

1 'How to make our ideas clear?' *Collected Papers of C. S. Peirce*, eds C. Hartshorne, P. Weiss, and A. W. Burks (Cambridge, Mass., 1931–58), Vol. 5, paragraphs 388–410. This essay originally appeared in 1878, in *The Popular*

Science Monthly.

2 John Dewey, 'From absolutism to experimentalism', in *The Philosophy of John Dewey*, ed. John J. McDermott, 2 vols. in 1 (Chicago and London, 1981), p. 13. Compare this with C. S. Peirce's comment that the 'first rule of reason' must be 'do not block the way of enquiry', Hartshorne *et al.* (eds), *Collected Papers*, I, p. 135.

3 'The need for a recovery of philosophy', in McDermott, (ed.), pp. 59–61.

4 William James, *Pragmatism: A New Name for Some Old Ways of Thinking* and *The Meaning of Truth: A sequel to Pragmatism*, intro. by A. J. Ayer (Cambridge, Mass., 1978), p. 30. See also Israel Scheffler, *Four Pragmatists* (New York, 1974), pp. 58–82, on Peirce's pragmatic method of enquiry.

5 James, *Pragmatism*, p. 28. For a superb and lucid exposition of James's pragmatism, see the introduction by A. J. Ayer.

6 Ibid., p. 28.

7 Ibid., p. 30. See further, R. B. Perry, *The Thought and Character of William James* (Boston, 1935), for a discussion of James's pragmatism in relation to Ferdinand Schiller and its origins in James's own peculiarly flexible and open temperament.

8 Compare Ludwig Wittgenstein's development of these Jamesian ideas, in *Philosophical Investigations*, tr. G. E. M. Anscombe (New York, 1958), into the view that not only our beliefs and theories, but the linguistic expressions of them, are rules for action and rules for 'language games'.

9 James, *Pragmatism*, p. 29.

10 And see Richard Rorty, e.g., *Consequences of Pragmatism* (Minneopolis and Brighton, 1982), for simialr arguments based on Plato's Socrates and the *Dialogues*.

11 James, *Pragmatism*, p. 32.

12 See chapter 6, for Dewey on James's pragmatist influence through his radical reconceptualization of psychology, expecially p. 105. See also H. S. Thayer, *Meaning and Action: a critical history of pragmatism* (New York, 1968).

13 See various essays collected in Rorty, *Consequences of Pragmatism*, especially 7, 8, and 12.

14 James, *Pragmatism*, p. 31.

15 *Ibid.*, p. 32

16 John Dewey, *Characters and Events: popular essays in social and political philosophy*, ed. Joseph Ratner (New York, 1929; 1957), II, p. 440.

17 James, *Pragmatism*, p. 32.

18 Ibid., p. 33.

19 Richard Rorty, see especially, 'The world well lost', *The Journal of Philosophy* 69 (1972), pp. 649–65.

20 See James, *Pragmatism*, pp. 28–34, and see Thomas Kuhn, *The Structure of Scientific Revolutions* (Chicago, 1962), for a relevant, essentially pragmatic, discussion of the nature of scientific truth. The Dewey quotation is from *Experience and Nature* (New York, 1958), p. 219.

21 Rorty, *Consequences of Pragmatism*, xxxix.

22 Ibid., xlvii.

23 James, *Pragmatism*, pp. 193–4.

24 This is a philosophic tenet James shared closely with Dewey and with Nietzsche; see chapters 1 and 5. And see Scheffler, *Four Pragmatists*, pp. 100–117, on James and the truth/interest relation, as well as comments on Peirce's idea of 'truth'. For a discussion of some differences between James and Dewey, see J. B. Pratt, *What is Pragmatism?* (New York, 1909).

25 James, *Pragmatism*, pp. 106–7.

26 Ibid. p. 104.

27 Ibid., p. 104.

28 Ibid., p. 106–7.

29 Ibid., p. 104.

30 For a later development and discussion of this and related views, see Imre Lakatos, 'Falsification and the methodology of scientific research programmes', in *Criticism and the Growth of Knowledge*, eds I. Lakatos and A. Musgrave (Cambridge, 1970), pp. 91–196.

31 'Rearranging' old experience became a central metaphor in Willard van Orman Quine, as it was in Shelley and Coleridge, for describing the effects of new ideas. See, for example, chapter 1 and see Quine, 'Two dogmas of empiricism', in *From a Logical Point of View* (New York, 1963), pp. 20–46, first published 1953.

32 James, *Pragmatism*, p. 42.

33 Ibid., p. 42.

34 Ibid., p. 43. This view becomes in part the basis for James's *Varieties of Religious Experience*, in which he developed another central idea, namely, the relation of character and temperament to the philosophy (or religion) one inclines toward. And see Dewey, 'The development of American pragmatism', in McDermott (ed.), pp. 44–8, for discussion of this aspect of James's and of Peirce's philosophies.

35 See, for example, John Dewey, 'The experimental theory of knowledge', in *The Influence of Darwin on Philosophy: and other essays in contemporary thought* (New York, 1910), pp. 77–111.

36 In the introduction to Rorty, *Consequences of Pragmatism*, one finds repeated assertions of this kind.

37 James, *Pragmatism*, pp. 112, and 216.

38 'Philosophy in America Today', Rorty, *Consequences of Pragmatism*, pp. 211–30.

39 'Philosophical conceptions and practical results', *Collected Essays and Reviews* (London, 1920), p. 412.

40 Quoted in John Dewey, 'The development of American pragmatism', in McDermott, (ed.) p. 42.

41 James, *Pragmatism* p. 97.

42 See chapter 5 on Dewey, who elaborated this theme throughout his philosophy.

43 Dewey, in McDermott (ed.) p. 48.

44 James, *Pragmatism*, p. 97 and Dewey, in McDermott (ed.), p. 49.
45 Dewey, in McDermott (ed.), pp. 49–50, quoting James, and see footnote 8 on the same page, on Russell's misinterpretations of James's metaphors.
46 James, *Pragmatism*, p. 222.
47 Rorty takes a similar position today; see, for example, 'The world well lost', and 'Philosophy in America today', in *Consequences of Pragmatism*.
48 James, *Pragmatism*, p. 117.
49 Ibid., p. 118.
50 Ibid., p. 119.
51 Compare this to Nietzsche's and Shelley's (not to mention Blake's) apocalyptic universe and related composition theories of experience; see chapter 1. It is also a central theme of Dewey's *Experience and Nature*.
52 James, *Pragmatism*, p. 127.
53 Dewey and Rorty both adopted this notion of reality, and it has become a hallmark of pragmatism and of deconstruction, for that matter.
54 For further discussion of this and other related aspects of pragmatism, see L. R. Morris, *William James: the Message of a Modern Mind* (New York, 1950).
55 James, *The Meaning of Truth*, p. 209.
56 Ibid., p. 211.
57 See the related discussion on Coleridge in chapter 7, on the rejection of idealism.
58 A point Dewey argued tirelessly; see for example, 'The practical character of reality', In *Philosophy and Civilization* (New York, 1963), pp. 36–55; originally published 1931.
59 James, *The Meaning of Truth*, p. 173.
60 Ibid., p. 205.
61 John Dewey, 'Experience, knowledge, and value: a rejoinder', in *The Philosophy of John Dewey*, ed. P. A. Schilpp (New York, 1939; 1951; 1971), p. 533, n. 16.
62 For further discussion of Berkeley, see my 'Berkeley's ironic method, in the *Three Dialogues*', *Philosophy and Literature* 4 (Spring, 1980), pp. 18–32. And see Quine, *Word and Object* (Cambridge, 1960) for discussion of what constitutes 'things'.
63 This is a theme of much modernist fiction, such as that of Virginia Woolf, Willa Cather, Dorothy Richardson, and Gertrude Stein. It was, of course, a central plank of realist fiction, but Woolf and others turned it on its head and challenged the notion of the autonomous self, with concretely different results for personal identity from those of the realists.
64 See chapter 7 for Coleridge's tireless insistence on the need for distinction, but not division, in philosophy, and compare Blake's idea of the 'marriage of heaven and hell', and his own rejection of what he called 'contraries' in preference for 'oppositions.' These ideas are not unrelated to Derrida's reconceptualization of 'identity', marked by the neologism, 'differance'.
65 In 'Structure, sign, and play', *The Structuralist Controversy*, eds. R. Macksey and E. Donato (Baltimore, 1975), pp. 247–65. And see Coleridge's denial of

perception as passive below, chapter 7, pp. 168, in his insistence that basic perception is itself highly imaginative, vital, and relational.

66 *Essays in Radical Empiricism* (Cambridge, Mass., 1976), p. 3 (first published 1912).

67 Ibid., 235.

68 See chapter 7 on Berkeley's 'outness prejudice' which Coleridge adopted with enthusiasm. It is central to the latter's attack on dualism and idealism.

69 William James, *Some Problems of Philosophy* (Cambridge, Mass., 1979), p. 46.

70 See above, chapter 1, on Shelley and Nietzsche, but see especially chapter 2, on the German romantic ironists and Hegel, for a discussion of Kojève's reinterpretation of Hegel and the meanings of history, teleology, and idealism in Hegel's philosophy.

71 William James, *Principles of Psychology* (Cambridge, Mass., 1902), II, p. 335; originally published 1890, republished 1983 in a new edition with a fine introduction by G. A. Miller.

72 Ibid., I, p. 284.

73 Ibid., I, p. 284–5.

74 Ibid., I, p. 402.

75 James, *The Meaning of Truth*, p. 222.

76 Ibid., pp. 222–3.

77 James, *Principles of Psychology*, II, p. 333.

78 Ibid., p. 333.

79 Dewey, *Experience and Nature*, p. 40.

80 Ibid., p. 40.

81 For a fuller discussion of pragmatism's relation to twentieth-century American philosophy, see *The Development of American Philosophy*, eds W. G. Muelder and L. Sears (Boston, 1960), and see more specifically, *Pragmatic Philosophy*, ed. Amelie Rorty (Garden City, New York, 1966).

CHAPTER 5   JOHN DEWEY'S CRITIQUE OF TRADITIONAL PHILOSOPHIZING

1 John Dewey, 'The need for a recovery of philosophy', in *Creative Intelligence: essays in the pragmatic attitude* (New York, 1945), pp. 3–69. Reprinted in the modern edition, *John Dewey: The Early, Middle, and Late Works*, ed. Jo Ann Boydston (Carbondale and Edwardsville, 1967–). This article was originally published in 1917. For Dewey on further influences on himself and on pragmatism, see John Dewey, 'Kant and philosophic method', *Journal of Speculative Philosophy*, 18 (1884), pp. 162–74 (reprinted in Boydston), and see John Dewey, 'The Influence of Darwinism on Philosophy', in *The Influence of Darwin on Philosophy: and other essays in contemporary thought* (New York, 1910; 1938), pp. 1–19. John Dewey, 'The development of American pragmatism', in *Philosophy and Civilization* (New York, 1931; 1963), pp. 13–35, was originally published in French in 1922,

and in English only in 1925. This raises interesting questions about rather more direct influences of pragmatism on Derrida than is generally acknowledged.

After some reflection, I have decided to use the John J, McDermott edition, *The Philosophy of John Dewey*, 2 volumes in 1 (Chicago, 1981), as the source for references, in the case of short articles, wherever possible, as this selection of some of Dewey's most incisive and well-known articles is handy and readily available, in both undergraduate and graduate libraries. However, I have nevertheless given the original date of publication and source of each article, as of importance and general interest. All the essays quoted here have now been published as well in the voluminous Jo Ann Boydston edition of the complete works. From here on therefore, I will refer to the McDermott edition, unless otherwise indicated.

2 'The need for a recovery of philosophy', in McDermott (ed.), p. 59.

3 Ibid., p. 89.

4 Ibid., p. 88.

5 Ibid., pp. 64–5. See George Novack, *Pragmatism versus Marxism* (New York, 1975), for discussion of pragmatism as a politically conscious philosophy. But see also H. K. Wells, *Pragmatism: Philosophy of Imperialism* (New York, 1954), for more aggressive criticisms than Novack's.

6 'The Influence of Dawinism on Philosophy', in McDermott (ed.), pp. 31–3.

7 John Dewey, *Experience and Nature* (New York, 1958), p. 40, originally published in 1929.

8 For further discussion, see chapter 9, and see John Dewey, *Art as Experience* (New York, 1934; 1958), for repeated insistence on the shared character of these various disciplines.

9 Dewey, *Experience and Nature*, p. ix; and see Hans Reichenbach, 'Dewey's theory of science', in *The Philosophy of John Dewey*, ed. P. A. Schilpp (La Salle, Illinois, 1939; 1951; 1971), pp. 157–92. See also Novack, *Pragmatism*, chapter 7, 'Dewey's Conceptions of Nature and Science', pp. 85–115.

10 Dewey, 'The development of American pragmatism', in McDermott (ed.), p. 57; and see Martin Hollis, 'The self in action', in *John Dewey Reconsidered*, ed. R. S. Peters (London, 1977), pp. 56–75.

11 Dewey, *Experience and Nature*, p. ix. Compare Joseph Ratner's early essay, 'Dewey's conception of philosophy', in *The Philosophy of John Dewey*, ed. P. A. Schilpp, pp. 47–74. And see the useful collection of essays by Dewey and others, *Dewey and his Critics*, ed. S. Morgenbesser (New York, 1977).

12 Dewey, 'The influence of Darwinism on philosophy', in McDermott (ed.), p. 37.

13 Dewey, *Experience and Nature*, especially pp. 52–60. For further discussion, see Richard Rorty, 'Dewey's metaphysics', in *New Studies in the Philosophy of John Dewey*, ed. S. M. Cahn (Hanover, NH, 1977), pp. 45–74.

14 Dewey, 'The development of American pragmatism', in McDermott (ed.), p. 56. J. E. Tiles, in *Dewey* (London, 1988), pp. 199–203, develops the role

of evolving possibility in Dewey's conception of nature.

15 Ibid., p. 50.

16 Ibid., p. 53.

17 Ibid., p. 48. See William James, *Varieties of Religious Experience* (Cambridge, Mass. and London 1902; 1967), for a thorough application of this view. The 1967 edition is well introduced by R. Niebuhr.

18 Dewey, 'From absolutism to experimentalism', in McDermott (ed.), pp. 12–13. First published in *Contemporary American Philosophers*, eds G. P. Adams and W. P. Montague (New York, 1930), II, pp. 13–27.

19 Ibid., p. 13.

20 Dewey, 'The development of American pragmatism', in McDermott (ed.), pp. 48–9, Dewey quoting William James.

21 Dewey, *Experience and Nature*, p. 47.

22 Ibid., p. 48. See *Essays on Aristotle's Ethics*, ed. A. Rorty (Berkeley, 1980) for pragmatic interpretations of Aristotle.

23 Dewey, 'The need for a recovery of philosophy', in McDermott (ed.), p. 65.

24 Dewey, 'The development of American pragmatism', in McDermott (ed.), p. 46. This is almost a hallmark of much American philosophy; Goodman, Quine, Rorty, and many other contemporary writers describe reality as 'how it all hangs together', rather than as some transcendent or homogeneous being behind appearance. See S. Morgenbesser, *Dewey and His Critics: Essays from The Journal of Philosophy* (New York, 1977), Section II: 'Realism', pp. 77–166, for further discussion.

25 Dewey, 'The need for a recovery of philosophy', in McDermott (ed.), p. 64.

26 The role of the 'absent' and the related role of the symbolic in Dewey's philosophy has hardly been discussed in the secondary literature on Dewey. These images and other such metaphors relate Dewey more closely to Derrida and the romantics than is generally perceived, except perhaps by Rorty. A thorough examination of Dewey's figures of speech would do much to add to the appreciation of his achievement. The purpose of frequent quotation in the present study is in part to draw attention to those rhetorical skills and stylistic richnesses in Dewey's language.

27 Dewey, 'The need for a recovery of philosophy', in McDermott (ed.), p. 70.

28 John Dewey, 'Experience and objective idealism', in *The Influence of Darwin on Philosophy: and other essays in contemporary thought* (New York, 1910), pp. 198–225, and in McDermott (ed.), p. 203. See in addition, W. T. Feldman, *The Philosophy of John Dewey* (Baltimore, 1934) for further reflections on Dewey's critique of empiricism.

29 Dewey, 'The Need for a Recovery of Philosophy', in McDermott (ed.), pp. 65–6. See further, Tiles, op. cit., chapter 4, on relations and connections as occurring in primary sense experience, not superadded by a super-sensual intellect.

30 Ibid., p. 70. On Dewey's criticism of reason as God or Reality, see, for example, Richard Rorty, 'Nineteenth century idealism and twentieth century textualism', *The Monist*, 64 (1981), pp. 155–74.

31 Dewey, 'The need for a recovery of philosophy', in McDermott (ed.), pp. 66–7.

32 Dewey, *Experience and Nature*, p. 1a.

33 Ibid., p. 18.

34 Ibid., pp. 24–5.

35 Ibid., p. 1a.

36 Ibid., p. 34.

37 Ibid., p. 15. Compare Heidegger, *What is Called Thinking?* tr. J. Glenn (New York, 1968), especially lecture 11 of Part II. This distinction between minimal reflection and systematic reflection is at the core of Dewey's rejection of dualism, and is another central shared aspect of his thought with that of Coleridge and Derrida.

38 Note Dewey's insistence, made repeatedly, that he does not mean some 'aboriginal stuff' by the phrase 'immediate experience'. See Dewey, 'The postulate of immediate empiricism', in *The Influence of Darwin on Philosophy: And Other Essays in Contemporary Thought* (New York, 1910), and in McDermott (ed.), pp. 240–8, especially p. 248, note.

39 Dewey, 'The need for a recovery of philosophy', in McDermott (ed.), p. 61. For further discussion, see A. E. Murphy, 'Dewey's epistemology and metaphysics', in P. A. Schilpp, *The Philosophy of John Dewey* (La Sall Ill., 1939; 1951; 1971); pp. 193–226.

40 Ibid., p. 65.

41 Ibid., p. 71. See further, Neil Coughlan, *Young John Dewey* (Chicago, 1973), for accounts of this theme appearing early and pervading Dewey's thought throughout.

42 Ibid., p. 74.

43 Dewey, *Experience and Nature*, p. 4a.

44 Dewey, 'The need for a recovery of philosophy', in McDermott (ed.), p. 78.

45 Ibid., pp. 61–3. On Husserl, Brentano, and other intentionalists, see John Llewelyn, *Derrida on the Threshold of Sense* (New York, 1986), pp. 16–42, and see Gilbert Ryle's classic account in *The Concept of Mind* (London and New York, 1949). See also V. C. Chappell, ed., *The Philosophy of Mind* (Englewood Cliffs, NJ, 1962). For early influences on Dewey's thought see James's *Principles of Psychology*, originally published 1890. Dewey's *Psychology*, first published in 1886), treats extensively of these issues.

46 Dewey, *Experience and Nature*, p. 2a.

47 Dewey, 'The need for a recovery of philosophy', in McDermott (ed.), p. 71. But see Rorty, 'Overcoming the tradition: Heidegger and Dewey', in *The Review of Metaphysics*, 30 (1976), pp. 280–305, a discussion of Heidegger's criticisms of Dewey's vocabulary of metaphysics and the impossibility of overcoming the tradition while using such loaded words as

'experience' and 'nature'. Not that 'Being' and 'Dasein' could be said to have been any better choices. Moreover, Rorty has chastised Derrida for his choice of words such as 'trace', implying something that left the trace. Derrida has other views on the optimism of overcoming the tradition, anyway. (See the conclusion to this book on the vanity of any hopes of escaping the tradition through historical consciousness.)

48   Dewey, 'The need for a recovery of philosophy', in McDermott (ed.), pp. 70–2. For discussion, see Bruce Aune, *Rationalism, Empiricism, Pragmatism: an introduction* (New York, 1970).

49   Ibid., p. 73.

50   On Dewey's concept of experience see, for example, Israel Scheffler, *Four Pragmatists* (New York, 1974), pp. 197–207.

51   Dewey, *Experience and Nature*, p. 21.

52   Ibid., p. 23.

53   See Anthony Quinton, 'Inquiry, thought, and action: John Dewey's theory of knowledge', in *John Dewey Reconsidered*, ed. R. S. Peters (London, 1977), pp. 1–17. And compare this with D. Parodi, 'Knowledge and action in John Dewey's philosophy', in Schilpp, *The Philosophy of John Dewey*, pp. 227–42. See also R. B. Perry, 'A review of pragmatism as a theory of knowledge', in *Dewey and His Critics*, ed. S. Morgenbesser (New York, 1977), pp. 213–22.

54   John Dewey, 'The postulate of immediate empiricism', in *The Influence of Darwin*; McDermott (ed.), pp. 241–4.

55   See J. H. Randall, 'John Dewey's interpretation of the history of philosophy', in Schilpp, *The Philosophy of John Dewey*, pp. 75–102, for this aspect of Dewey's critique of western metaphysics.

56   See Amelie Rorty, ed., *Pragmatic Philosophy* (Garden City, NJ, 1966), chapters 1 and 2 for elaboration.

57   Dewey, 'The need for a recovery of philosophy', in McDermott (ed.), p. 84.

58   Ibid., p. 91. On the spectator theory of knowledge, see W. T. Feldman, *The Philosophy of John Dewey* (Baltimore, 1934).

59   Ibid., p. 91. Compare A. J. Ayer's description with Nietzschean and Shelleyan views (chapter 1): 'If one speaks of the construction of objects out of the flux of experience, it is indeed natural to ask who does the constructing; and then it would appear that whatever self is chosen for this role must stand outside the construction; it would be contradictory to suppose it constructed itself. But the metaphor of construction is here misleading. What is in question is the derivation of concepts, not the fabrication of the things to which the concepts apply. To 'construct' either the material or the spiritual self is to do no more than to pick out the relations within experiences which make it possible for the concept of a self of this kind to be satisfied, and those relations exist whether or not we direct our attention to them', *The Origins of Pragmatism* (London, 1968), p. 261. It is only by ignoring the relation of such analyses as Ayer's to Barthes, Derrida, Rorty, Dewey, and Coleridge, not to mention Nietzsche and

Shelley, that the thematic connections of romanticism, pragmatism, and deconstruction continue to be minimized and poorly understood.

60 Ibid., p. 91. And see above discussion on this distinction as the distinction crucial to Dewey's thought.

61 Dewey, 'The postulate of immediate empiricism', in McDermott (ed.), p. 245.

62 Dewey, 'The need for a recovery of philosophy', in McDermott (ed.), p. 80.

63 Dewey, 'The postulate of immediate empiricism', in McDermott (ed.), p. 246. And on Reality, see Richard Rorty, 'The world well lost', *Journal of Philosophy*, 69 (1972), pp. 649–65.

64 Dewey, *Experience and Nature*, p. 20.

65 Ibid., pp. 2 and 20, as Socrates tirelessly emphasized. See for example the *Meno*, with the slave-boy demonstration, and see the *Theaetetus*.

66 Dewey, *Experience and Nature*, p. 19.

67 Ibid., p. 19.

68 Ibid., p. 2.

69 Dewey, *Experience and Nature*, p. 54.

70 Ibid., p. 50.

71 Ibid., pp. 25–8.

72 Dewey, 'The need for a recovery of philosophy', in McDermott (ed.), pp. 76–7.

73 Dewey, *Experience and Nature*, p. 74.

74 Ibid., p. 74.

75 Dewey, *Experience and Nature*, p. 73. And compare with Coleridge's description of matter as a 'pause by interpenetration of opposite energies.' See chapter 7.

76 Dewey, 'The postulate of immediate empiricism', in McDermott (ed.), p. 248.

77 Ibid., p. 247.

78 Ibid., p. 247.

79 John Dewey, 'The pattern of inquiry', in *Logic: the theory of inquiry* (New York, 1938).

80 William James, *Principles of Psychology* (Cambridge, Mass., 1902), I, 8.

81 Dewey, *Experience and Nature*, p. vi. And see Heidegger, whose concept of 'Dasein' implies similar intimations of mind as a natural event occurring in a natural enviromnent.

82 Dewey, 'The pattern of inquiry'.

83 Dewey, 'The development of American pragmatism', in McDermott (ed.), p. 54.

84 Ibid., p. 54.

85 Dewey, 'The need for a recovery of philosophy', in McDermott (ed.), p. 95.

86 Dewey, *Experience and Nature*, p. 68.

87 Dewey, 'Experience and objective idealism', in McDermott (ed.), p. 200.

88　Dewey, 'The development of American pragmatism', in McDermott (ed.), p. 51.

89　Dewey, 'Experience and objective idealism', in McDermott (ed.), p. 201. See chapter 1 for further detailed discussion of this issue.

90　Ibid., p. 202.

91　Dewey, *Experience and Nature*, p. 15.

92　Ibid., p. 15.

93　Dewey, 'The development of American pragmatism', in McDermott (ed.), p. 52.

94　Dewey, 'The need for a recovery of philosophy', in McDermott (ed.), p. 67, and see Coleridge's marginal note to Kant's *Critique der reinen Vernunft*, in *Marginalia*, III, p. 248.

95　Dewey, *Experience and Nature*, p. 1.

96　See on William James, chapter 4, for detailed discussion.

97　Dewey, 'The development of American pragmatism', in McDermott (ed.), p. 53-4.

98　See 'Dewey's theory of interest', in *John Dewey Reconsidered*, ed. R. S. Peters (London, 1977), 35-55.

99　Dewey, 'The need for a recovery of philosophy', in McDermott (ed.), p. 68.

100　Dewey, 'The development of American pragmatism', in McDermott (ed.), p. 53.

101　Dewey, *Experience and Nature*, p. 19.

CHAPTER 6　JACQUES DERRIDA: DECONSTRUCTING METAPHYSICS

1　Jacques Derrida, 'Differance', in *Speech and Phenomena and Other Essays on Husserl's Theory of Signs*, tr. D. B. Allison (Evanston, 1973), pp. 129–60, originally published in French in 1968. Also in *Margins of Philosophy*, tr. A. Bass (Brighton, 1982), pp. 1–28.

2　Jacques Derrida, 'Structure, sign, and play in the discourse of the human sciences', in *The Structuralist Controversy*, eds R. Mackesy and E. Donato (Baltimore, 1975), pp. 247–65. This essay was also reprinted in *Writing and Difference*, tr. A. Bass (London, 1978). It was originally given as a conference paper in 1966.

3　For Dewey's account, see 'Nature, communication and meaning', in *Experience and Nature* (New York, 1958), pp. 166–207; for Derrida on language see also 'Form and meaning', in *Speech and Phenomena*, pp. 107–128, and reprinted in *Margins of Philosophy*. 'Form and meaning' was originally published in Paris, 1967. And on speech versus writing see also 'Plato's pharmacy', in *Dissemination*, tr. B. Johnson (Chicago, 1981), pp. 61–171.

4　Martin Heidegger, especially *On the Way to Language*, tr. P. D. Hertz (New York, 1971), German title, *Unterwegs zur Sprache* (Pfullingen, 1959), and various essays collected in *Poetry, Language, Thought,* tr. A. Hofstadter (New York, 1971), especially 'Language', pp. 187–210. Dewey used the umage of language as a tool, but not in the dualistic sense. Of course, for Dewey, tools are not 'just' tools, anyway, but the forces that transform our lives. If we wilfully misinterpret Dewey's metaphors, we can read him as just another intentionalist; but given that this is inconsistent with the rest of his remarks about language, it would be foolish to take the tool metaphor literally. Language is a tool, not to express pre-existent private thoughts, but a tool in the sense of a form of life, a social game, a means, like intelligence and reason themselves, for survival in a hostile environment. See also Ian Hacking, *Why Does Language Matter to Philosophy?* (Cambridge, 1975).

5 See H. N. Schneidau, 'The word against the word: Derrida on textuality', *Semeia,* (1977), pp. 5–28, for the relation to higher (Biblical) criticism, and for a lucid early appreciation, generally.

6 For Derrida on the cogito, see 'Cogito and the history of madness', in *Writing and Difference,* pp. 31–63, first published in 1964. Also of interest is *Descartes: a Collection of Critical Essays,* ed. W. Doney (London, 1968).

7 Jacques Derrida, *Of Grammatology,* tr. G. Spivak (Baltimore, 1974; 1976), and see her excellent introduction to this central work, originally published Paris, 1967.

8 'Plato's pharmacy', in *Dissemination.* Johnson's edition of these ground-breaking essays of Derrida's is also accompanied with an erudite and enlightening, if brief, introduction. *Dissemination* was originally published Paris, 1972.

9 Ludwig, Wittgenstein, *Philosophical Investigations,* tr. G. E. M. Anscombe (New York, 1958), especially paragraphs 19, 23, 241. See also Marjorie Grene, 'Life, death, and language: some thoughts on Wittgenstein and Derrida', in her volume, *Philosophy in and out of Europe* (Berkeley, 1976), pp. 142–54.

10 C. S. Peirce, *Elements of Logic,* in *The Collected Papers of C. S. Peirce,* eds C. Hartshorne, P. Weiss and A. W. Burks (Cambridge, Mass., 1931–58), Book II, paragraph 302: 'Symbols grow. They come into being by development out of other signs . . . we think only in signs . . . it is only out of symbols that a new symbol can grow.' This remark is comparable to Shelley's rejection of the literal/metaphorical distinction, and to his insistence that language is essentially metaphorical, littered, of course, with 'dead metaphors' which we pass off as facts, truths, and literalness. Coleridge, like Peirce, preferred the word 'symbol', as did the German romantics. See chapter 1.

11 For a clear discussion of this issue, see John Llewelyn, *Derrida on the Threshold of Sense* (New York, 1986), chapter 3.

12 Richard Rorty, 'Philosophy as a kind of writing', in *Consequences of Pragmatism* (Brighton, 1982), pp. 90–109.

13 Derrida, 'Differance', pp. 139–41; Ferdinand de Saussure, *Course in General Linguistics,* tr. W. Baskin (London, 1974).

14 Quoted in Derrida, 'Differance', p. 140.

15 Roman Jakobson and Morris Halle, *Fundamentals of Language* (The Hague, 1956; 1971).
16 Derrida, 'Differance', p. 145.
17 Derrida, 'Structure, Sign, and Play'. For Derrida, further reflections on origins, see 'The supplement of origins', in *Speech and Phenomena*, pp. 88–104.
18 Rorty, *Consequences of Pragmatism*, pp. 94–5.
19 See the various essays in *Writing and Difference*.
20 Derrida, 'Differance', pp. 158–9.
21 Ibid., p. 135.
22 Heidegger, *On the way to Language*, especially 'Language'.
23 See especially *Speech and Phenomena*, p. xxxix.
24 For C. S. Peirce, see especially 'How to make our ideas clear', in *Collected Papers*, vol. 5. This essay was originally published in 1878. For Dewey, see *Experience and Nature* (originally published in 1925; revised 1929), chapter 5, and see Wittgenstein, *Philosophical Investigations*, G. E. M. Anscombe (Oxford, 1967), especially paragraphs 1–75.
25 *The Archaeology of Knowledge*, tr. A. M. Sheridan Smith (London, 1972; 1977). The American novelist Willa Cather was using powerful archaeological metaphors in such novels as *The Professor's House* (1925), for knowledge, self-discovery, and as an image of the mind, but pre-eminently for language and art themselves, as stratified with meanings, over-determined, and histori-cally 'aware'.
26 Rorty, *Consequences of Pragmatism*, pp. 139–59.
27 Ibid., pp. 90–109.
28 Derrida, 'Structure, sign, and play', p. 249, and see Frank Lentricchia, *After the New Criticism* (London, 1980), chapter 5, for an early recognition of the importance of Derrida's 'decentring' notion.
29 Stanley Fish, 'How ordinary is ordinary language?', *New Literary History* 5 (1973), pp. 41–54.
30 Willard van Orman Quine, 'Two dogmas of empiricism', in *From a Logical Point of View* (New York: 1963; first published 1953), pp. 20–47.
31 See chapter 9 on Dewey's aesthetics, for similar arguments, and see chapter 2, on Coleridge. It was of course the German Romantics who most vociferiously challenged the distinction between literature and criticism, as discussed in chapter 3. Yet the challenge is a perennial one. It arises in Plato; see for example the *Ion* and the *Symposium*. And see Derrida, 'Living on: BORDER LINES', in *Deconstruction and Criticism*, ed. H. Bloom (New York, 1979), pp. 75–176, on breaching discipline boundaries. This is one of Derrida's most sparkling 'essays'.
32 Harold Bloom, *The Anxiety of Influence* (Oxford, 1973).
33 Derrida, 'Differance', p. 149.
34 Derrida, *Of Grammatology*, p. 158. Compare de Man, *Allegories of Reading* (London and New Haven, 1979), and see chapter 11 for further discussion.
35 Schneidau, *Semeia*, pp. 15–17.

36 Rorty, *Consequences of Pragmatism*, pp. 107–9.
37 Derrida, 'Structure, sign, and play', p. 264.
38 Ibid., p. 265.
39 Rorty, *Consequences of Pragmatism*, p. 96.
40 For further discussion see Vincent Leitch, 'The lateral dance: the deconstructive criticism of J. Hillis Miller', in *Critical Inquiry*, 6 (1980), p. 600.
41 Ibid., pp. 604–5.
42 J. Hillis Miller, *The Linguistic Moment: from Wordsworth to Stevens* (Princeton, 1985).
43 Derrida, 'Structure, sign, and play', p. 255.
44 Ibid., 259.
45 Plato, *Dialogues*, eds E. Hamilton and H. Cairns (Princeton, 1961; 1969), 'The seventh letter', pp. 1574–98.

CHAPTER 7   COLERIDGE'S ATTACK ON DUALISM

1 For the finest interpretation of Coleridge's metaphysical 'deconstructions', see Owen Barfield, *What Coleridge Thought* (London, 1971). Barfield's book broke new territory, challenging the orthodoxies of earlier unimaginative accounts of Coleridge's philosophy.

2 I. A. Richards, *Coleridge on Imagination* (London, 1934), paved the way for Barfield's work, but in a more thorough-going aesthetic sphere, where Richards challenged the poverty-stricken orthodoxies about romanticism of Eliot, Leavis, and many other critics. See also R. H. Fogle, *The Idea of Coleridge's Criticism* (Berkeley, 1962).

3 Sound enquiry being, as Dewey repeatedly argued, essentially inductive (not deductive), and therefore wholly reliant on ideas which erupt out of the imagination. In this, Dewey was following Plato's Socrates closely, as in the *Meno*, the *Theaetetus*, and *Republic* vi and vii, to mention only a few dialogues which show a commitment to imaginative reasoning, as opposed to consecutive reasoning.

4 See chapter 9 on the relation of pragmatism, and Dewey's aesthetics specifically, to romanticism; little detailed work has as yet been done, though general remarks abound and influences are generally conceded. Because of preconceptions of metaphysical 'yearnings' in romanticism, the pragmatic origins in romantic thought have been systematically obscured. A reading of *Art as Experience* banishes the obscurity fairly rapidly. And see J. W. Wright, *Shelley's Myth of Metaphor* (Athens, Georgia, 1970), for a thorough refutation of transcendentalism in Shelley and, more implicitly, Coleridge.

5 To use Dewey's phrase in *Art as Experience* (New York, 1958, first published 1934), 34. On the early influences on Coleridge of Plotinus and other neoplatonists, see John Muirhead, *Coleridge as Philosopher* (London, 1930).

6 Letter of Keats to Benjamin Bailey, 22 November, 1817. Dewey's paraphrase of this famous Keats passage is found in *Art as Experience*, chapter 2.

7 See K. M. Wheeler, 'Kant and romanticism', *Philosophy and Literature*, 13 (Summer, 1989), pp. 42–56.
8 *The Philosophical Lectures*, ed. K. Coburn (London, 1949), lecture 2.
9 Ibid., lecture 3, 115.
10 *Biographia* I 177–8.
11 Coburn, (ed.) *The Philosophical Lectures*, lecture 3, 120, and see also lecture 13, 370–2. On that which Descartes, Berkeley, Hume, and Kant have in common, see *CN* III 3605, f120v, dated 1809.
12 See for example *CN* III 4087 (1817), on the errors of materialist philosophers.
13 *CL* III 483, to Cottle, 1814.
14 Coburn (ed.), *The Philosophical Lectures*, lecture 13, 377. According to Coleridge, the ancients had themselves always conceived of nature as vital, animated, and transformative, as Dewey later argued was the strength of William James's philosophy.
15 On matter as the pause by interpenetration of opposites, see *CN* III 3632, 4412, and *Lay Sermons* 81n.
16 *CL* IV 849.
17 *CN* III 3605 f121.
18 Marginal note to Kant, *Metaphysische Anfangsgründe der Naturwissenschaft*. In *Marginalia*, vol. 3. (I am grateful to the late George Whalley and to the late Kathleen Coburn for making the marginalia of Coleridge available to me in the early 1970s.)
19 See Coleridge's *Theory of Life*, ed. Seth Watson (London, 1848).
20 *Biographia* I 182–3.
21 See K. M. Wheeler, 'Berkeley's ironic method', *Philosophy and Literature* 4 (Spring, 1980), pp. 18–32. The problem of terminology made Heidegger reject 'Dasein' later in life, and, as Rorty argued, would have also made Heidegger reject Dewey's efforts to reconceptualize 'experience' and 'nature'. See Rorty, 'Overcoming the tradition', in *Consequences of Pragmatism* (Brighton, 1982). This question of vocabulary has already arisen in chapter 5, n. 47, and will be further explored in the afterword more thoroughly.
22 Discussed further in my *Irony and Metaphor in Plato, Berkeley, and Kierkegaard*, in preparation. And see Derrida, 'White mythology: metaphor in the text of philosophy', *Margins of Philosophy*, tr. A. Bass (Hemil Hembstead, 1982), pp. 207–73.
23 In numerous marginal notes to various of Kant's texts. See *Marginalia*, vol. 3, under Immanuel Kant.
24 Barfield, *What Coleridge Thought*, p. 186 passim.
25 See Coburn (ed.), *The Philosophical Lectures*, for Coleridge's systematic treatment of this subject.
26 *The Friend* I 94.
27 *CN* III 4326.
28 *The Friend* I 94.
29 *CL* IV 808.

30　On the meaning and importance of 'the negative' in Hegel, see John Dewey, 'Kant and philosophic method', in *The Philosophy of John Dewey*, (ed.) John McDermott (Chicago and London, 1981). 'If Reason be synthetic only upon a foreign material, we end in the contradictions of Kant. If there is to be *knowledge*, Reason must include both elements within herself. It is Hegel's thorough recognition of this fact that causes him to lay such emphasis on the negative.'

31　*CL* IV 774.

32　On related interpretations of synthesis, see Dewey, 'From absolutism to experimentalism', in McDermott (ed.), p. 7: 'Hegel's synthesis of subject and object, matter and spirit, the divine and the human, was, however, no mere intellectual formula; it operated as an immense release, a liberation. Hegel's treatment of human culture, of institutions and the arts, involved the same dissolution of hard-and-fast dividing walls, and had a special attraction for me.'

33　*CN* III 4449.

34　Marginal note to Kant, *Metaphysische Anfangsgründe, Marginalia*, vol. 3.

35　*CL* IV 688.

36　*The Friend* I 94.

37　See Coleridge, *Theory of Life*.

38　*Shakespearean Criticism*, ed. T. M. Raysor (New York, London, 1930; republished 1960), I 197–203.

39　Coburn (ed.), *The Philosophical Lectures*, lecture 3, 114. See also *Church and State* 11–16, *The Friend* I 459, and I 467 and 492–3.

40　See Colin Turbayne, *The Myth of Metaphor* (Columbia, SC, 1970).

41　*CN* III 4186.

42　*CN* III 4265.

43　*Biographia* I 184.

44　Blake, letter to Dr Trusler, 23 August, 1799.

45　*CL* IV 885, and see the rest of the letter for a fascinating discussion.

46　*CN* III 4351.

47　Further to these themes, see *CN* II 2330, 3223, III 4319, 4333, *CL* II 864–5, and *Lay Sermons* 31.

48　*Lay Sermons* 29 n. and 72.

49　*CN* III 4265.

50　*Biographia* I 202.

51　*CN* III 4251.

52　Marginal note to Tennemann, *Geschichte der Philosophie* in Coburn (ed.), *The Philosophical Lectures*. And see below the passage quoted from Fichte, note 54.

53　*CN* II 2444.

54　Unpublished notebook entry, British Library *Coleridge Notebooks MS* 36, 2.

55　*The Friend* I 117 nl.

56　*Biographia* II 8.

57　*Biographia* I 88.

58 *CN* III 3802 f 102 n.
59 *Lay Sermons* 72.
60 As in *Aids to Reflection*, ed. Thomas Fenby (Edinburgh, 1905; originally published in 1825).
61 *CL* VI 630.
62 *CL* II 701.
63 Marginal note on Copy G of *The Statesman's Manual* (1816); see *Lay Sermons*, 114 n2 and see *CN* III 4265.
64 *Lay Sermons* 18.
65 *CL* VI 630.
66 *CN* III 4265.
67 Ibid.
68 *Biographia* I 94.
69 *Lay Sermons* 18.
70 *Biographia* I 202.
71 *Biographia* II 12.
72 *Biographia* I 202.
73 *Biographia* I 167.
74 *Biographia* I 202, emphasis added.
75 *Lay Sermons* 29.
76 *Lay sermons* 30.
77 *CN* I 886.
78 *CL* VI 630.
79 *CL* II 698.
80 *CN* II 2445.
81 *CL* IV 850.
82 *CL* IV 689.

CHAPTER 8   JOHN DEWEY: LANGUAGE RECONCEPTUALIZED

1 For some historical-intellectual background, see Ian Hacking, *Why Does Language Matter to Philosophy?* (Cambridge, 1975), and A. J. Ayer, *Logical Positivism* (New York, 1959). On Wittgenstein's influence and general contribution to philosophy of language, see George Pitcher, *The Philosophy of Wittgenstein* (Englewood Cliffs, NJ, 1964) and David Pears, *Wittgenstein* (London, 1981). On Heidegger's position, see Werner Marx, *Heidegger and the Tradition* (Evanston, Ill., 1971), and see Stanley Rosen, *Nihilism* (New Haven, 1969) on Heidegger's relation to Hegel and to his historicism.
2 See for example the essays of Heidegger in *Poetry, Language, Thought*, tr. A. Hofstadter (New York, 1975), which rely pre-eminently on poetic style to communicate, though this fact is obscured by any translation, no matter how finely rendered, especially in a language like German, where 'construction' of words is one of the constant puns and techniques used, as, for example, 'Aufbauen,' 'Umbildung', and 'Entbauen'.

3 Translators of Derrida, such as Alan Bass and Barbara Johnson, have made some very interesting contributions to translation theory in their practice. See the introductions and prefaces to their editions of Derrida for specific comments about translation. And see of course Walter Benjamin's classic, *Illuminations*, ed. Hannah Arendt (London, 1970), on translation.

4 On Husserl and phenomenology, see Derrida, *Speech and Phenomena*, tr. A. Bass (Evanston Ill., 1973), John Llewelyn, *Derrida on the Threshold of Sense* (New York, 1986), and see also Heidegger's dialogue with Husserl in *Sein und Zeit* (1927), and Sartre, *L'Etre et le neánt* (1943), for the attack on the notion of a transcendental ego. And see Merleau-Ponty, *Phénoménologie de la Perception* (1945).

5 But on Ludwig Wittgenstein's pragmatic/Socratic philosophical bent, the *Philosophical Investigations*, tr. G. E. M. Anscombe (New York, 1958; Oxford, 1967), which of course contrast markedly in content and, most notably, in style, with their fragmented, conversational mode, much like that of some of the German Romantics' texts, or Nietzsche.

6 John Dewey, *Experience and Nature* (New York, 1958), p. 168.

7 Coleridge had bemoaned in very similar terms the dualism engendered, he argued, particularly by Descartes; see chapter 7.

For an interesting historical account of the early language theorists, see Noam Chomsky, *Cartesian Linguistics* (New York, 1966), and see his *Language and Mind* (enlarged edition New York, 1968; 1972), for a tendency to submit to the dualistic and essentialist notions rejected by Dewey, Derrida, Wittgenstein, Coleridge, and Shelley.

8 Dewey, *Experience and Nature*, p. 169.

9 Richard Rorty, in *Contingency, Irony, and Solidarity* (Cambridge, 1989), would have seen the falsity of the 'dilemma' upon which his entire theme rests, if he had thoroughly grasped and applied this Deweyan idea of the functional relation between individual and community. In that dualism, Rorty himself has gotten stuck.

10 Dewey, *Experience and Nature*, p. 169.

11 Ibid., 187

12 See Martin Heidegger, *On the Way to Language*, tr. P. D. Hertz (New York, 1971), most notably; but see also *What is called thinking?*, tr. J. Glenn Gray (New York, 1968).

13 Dewey, *Experience and Nature*, p. 170, and compare Coleridge, 'to think is to thingify'; see chapter 7.

14 Ibid., p. 170.

15 Ibid., p. 166.

16 Ibid., pp. 260–1.

17 Ibid., p. 187.

18 Coleridge was equally scathing; the rejection of the empiricists' passive mind theory was another aspect of his own theory of imaginative perception which so deeply influenced Shelley. See 'The struggle with asociationism', the introduction to my *The Creative Mind in Coleridge's Poetry* (Cambridge,

Mass. and London, 1981) for discussion of passive versus active mind theories amongst the empiricists and rationalists.

19 Dewey, *Experience and Nature*, p. 188.
20 Ibid., pp. 170–1.
21 In, for example, *Of Grammatology*, and in numerous others of his texts.
22 This emphasis upon the social and communal was taken up most notably by Stanley First amongst twentieth theorists; see *Is There a Text in This Class?* (Cambridge, Mass., 1980) and see Frank Lentricchia, *Cuticism and Social Change* (Chicago, 1983), for pragmatic-Socratic influences at work (relating to the emphasis upon community as the condition for individuality, and vice versa, in a sense, for the two concepts are indissoluably interdependent for meaning). The Marxist debate with Existentialism was often beset by failures, on both sides, to break out of the dualisms of individual/community, though Sartre was the most successful in addressing himself to this pseudo-dualism.
23 Dewey, *Experience and Nature*, p. 171.
24 Ibid., p. 172.
25 On the history of debates about intentionality, private language, and mentality prior to language, see Jerome A. Shaffer, *Philosophy of Mind* (Englewood Cliffs, NJ, 1968); *The Philosophy of Mind*, ed. V. C. Chappell (Englewood Cliffs, NJ, 1962); and *Body and Mind*, ed. G. M. A. Vesey (London, 1964). See also, *Wittgenstein and the Problem of Other Minds*, ed. H. Morick (New York, 1967).
26 Dewey, *Experience and Nature*, p. 174.
27 Ibid., p. 175.
28 Ibid., p. 178, and see Wittgenstein on pointing, in the early paragraphs of *Philosophical Investigations*, where he insisted that the meaning of pointing is not self-evident, but a communal language-game, learnt at an early age.
29 Compare Richard Rorty, *Philosophy and the Mirror of Nature* (Princeton, 1979; 1980), and also *The Linguistic Turn*, ed. R. Rorty (Chicago, 1967), a collection of papers on language, meaning, and truth, which show profound influences from Dewey.
30 Dewey, *Experience and Nature*, p. 180.
31 Ibid., p. 183.
32 For Wittgenstein on rules and language as a variety of different games appropriate for different social occasions, and on forms of life, see *Philosophical Investigations*, such as paragraphs 3, 7, 21, 22, 23, 31, 35, 37, 49, 50–1, and so on.
33 Dewey, *Experience and Nature*, pp. 187–9.
34 Ibid., pp. 188–9.
35 This is the crux of Dewey's anti-positivist pragmatism, namely, the rejection of mathematics and science as more true or real than art, the physical world, or emotions. The notion amongst rationalists that 'reality is mathematical' was nonsense to Dewey.
36 Dewey, *Experience and Nature*, p. 194.

37 Ibid., p. 185.
38 Ibid., p. 201.

CHAPTER 9   DEWEY'S 'ROMANTIC' AESTHETIC

1 On the importance for Coleridge of 'genial criticism', see the *Biographia Literaria*, Shawcross edition, volume II, 'Principles of genial criticism'. For Coleridge, 'genius' and 'geniality' were both etymologically and conceptually related concepts.

2 *Biographia Literaria* I, chapter 12.

3 See the 'Fragment of an essay on taste', in vol. 2 of the *Biographia*.

4 See above, pages 63–4 and 262, for Coleridge and Dewey on organicism properly understood as vital, not static.

5 See for example Barbara Johnson, *The Critical Difference* (Baltimore: 1981), and chapter ten below for further remarks.

6 John W. Wright, 'Samuel Johnson and traditional methodology', *PMLA* 86 (1971), p. 43.

7 See *Biographia* I, chapters i–iv. And see John Dewey, *Art as Experience* (New York, 1958), pp. 298–99.

8 See Coleridge, *Shakespearean Criticism*, ed. T. M. Raysor, 2 vols (London, 1930 and New York, 1960), 'Introduction', for Raysor's useful account of eighteenth-century neo-classical rules and Coleridge's rejection of them. And see ibid., I 197–203, for Coleridge's own explicit, as opposed to (everywhere) implicit rejection of neo-classicism. See also chapter 2, for brief discussion of Herder and Lessing's related objections. See also Dewey, *Art as Experience*, pp. 301–3.

9 Friedrich Schlegel was always opposed to 'naive', Leavis-type evaluations. For example, in 'Athenäum Fragments', he noted: 'People always talk about how an analysis of the beauty of a work of art supposedly disturbs the pleasure of the art-lover. Well, the real lover just won't let himself be disturbed' (fragment 71). And note Dewey, *Art as Experience*, pp. 306, 308, and 309.

10 See further J. F. Tiles, 'Art, intelligence, and contemplation', *Dewey* (London, 1988), pp. 180–203, for discussion of this and other aspects of Dewey's aesthetics.

11 For further elaboration see Stephen C. Pepper, 'Some questions on Dewey's aesthetics', in *The Philosophy of John Dewey*, ed. P. A. Schilpp (La Salle, Ill., 1939; reprinted 1951; 1971), pp. 369–90. Pepper's objections to Dewey's organicism are the result of taking organicism in a static, structuralist way, which Dewey had explicitly argued against. For him, as for Coleridge, the German Romantics, and for William James, organicism was a concept involving vitality, growth, and transformation (see above pages 63–4 and 262).

12 Dewey *Art as Experience*, p. 310.

13 Ibid., pp. 320, 324–5.

14 Ibid., p. 325. William Blake had argued similarly in his poetry that the primary aim of imagination and art is to cleanse the windows of perception, thereby reunifying the senses and the intellect, and overcoming the tyranny of Reason or the 'calculating faculty'.

15 John Dewey, *Experience and Nature* (New York, 1958), pp. 359 and 360.

16 Dewey, *Experience and Nature*, p. 378, and see p. 360, quoted above. See Heidegger's essays, 'Language', and 'The origin of the work of art', in Martin Heidegger, *On the Way to Language*, tr. P. D. Hertz (New York, 1971). Dewey's own radiation imagery in this passage may have its origins in Shelley's extensive use of radiation (flower, star, song) as an image for imaginative activity. See John Wright, *Shelley's Myth of Metaphor* (Athens, Georgia, 1970), for discussion of the role of radiating and light imagery in, particularly, 'Adonais', but also in 'A defence of poetry'.

17 Dewey, *Experience and Nature*, pp. 381, and 383–4. Implicit everywhere is Dewey's commitment to social change, democracy, and political empowerment. Like Shelley, Blake, and Coleridge, he made no apologies for insisting that art was a pre-eminent means for social and political change, because of its power to disrupt convention, complacency, and prejudice, and because of its power to make us see beyond the immediate status quo, to long-term goals and ideals. This was, for Dewey, the only way of overcoming short-term self-interest and egotism. The pragmatist's definition of the true as 'what is good in the way of belief', stands only if the good is understood as what is perceived by the imagination, namely, long-term good. Hence, Shelley's insistence that 'imagination' is a concept signifying 'prophetic vision'. See further, 'Dewey's aesthetic theory, I and II'. E. A. Shearer, *Journal of Philosophy* 32 (1935), reprinted in S. Morgenbesser (ed.), *Dewey and His Critics: essays from the Journal of Philosophy* (New York, 1977), pp. 404–29. And see further Dewey, *Experience and Nature*, chapter 9.

CHAPTER 10   DERRIDA, TEXTUALITY, AND CRITICISM

1   Vincent Leitch, *Deconstructive Criticism: an Advanced Introduction* (London, 1983), p. 180.

2   Ibid., p. 175.

3   Barbara Johnson, *The Critical Difference* (Baltimore, 1981), p. 14.

4   Ibid., p. 71.

5   John Llewelyn, *Derrida on the Threshold of Sense* (New York, 1986), p. 58.

6   Ibid., p. 85.

7   Howard Felperin, *Beyond Deconstruction* (Oxford, 1985), p. 134.

8   Ibid., p. 115, and Johnson, *The Critical Difference*, p. 196.

9   Paul de Man, *Blindness and Insight* (New York and London, 1971), p. 128.

10 J. Hillis Miller, *The Linguistic Moment: from Wordsworth to Stevens* (Princeton, 1985), p. 49.

11 Johnson, *The Critical Difference*, p. 12.
12 Llewelyn, *Derrida*, pp. 57–8.
13 Ibid., pp. 41, 52, and 46.
14 Ibid., p. 78.
15 Ibid., p. 89.
16 Geoffrey Hartman, *Criticism in the Wilderness* (New Haven, 1980), p. 169.
17 Felperin, *Beyond Deconstruction*, p. 131.
18 Ibid., pp. 118 and 227.
19 Llewelyn, *Derrida*, pp. 55–6.
20 Felperin, *Beyond Deconstruction*, p. 118.
21 Geoffrey Hartman, *Saving the Text* (Baltimore, 1981), p. 121.
22 Johnson, *The Critical Difference*, p. 146.
23 Llewelyn, *Derrida*, p. 46.
24 Leitch, *Deconstructive Criticism*, p. 205.
25 Ibid., pp. 262 and 45.
26 Felperin, *Beyond Deconstruction*, pp. 140 and 145.
27 Ibid., p. 218, and see p. 146.
28 Leitch, *Deconstructive Criticism*, p. 243.
29 Hartman, *Saving the Text*, p. xxiv.
30 Ibid., p. 2.
31 Ibid., p. xxiv.
32 Ibid., p. 121.
33 Llewelyn, *Derrida*, pp. 38 and 39–48.
34 Ibid., p. 50.
35 See further, Paul de Man, *Blindness and Insight*, p. 140.
36 Ibid., p. 118.
37 Paul de Man, *Allegories of Reading* (London and New Haven, 1979), pp. 14 and 20–4.
38 J. Hillis Miller, *The Linguistic Moment*, p. xiv.
39 Johnson, *The Critical Difference*, p. 88.
40 Paul de Man, 'Shelley disfigured', in *Deconstruction and Criticism*, ed. H. Bloom (New York, 1979), pp. 51–3 and see p. 244.
41 *WP*, p. 266; and see p. 319, on the illusion of objects as independent. Compare chapter 1.
42 J. Hillis Miller, *The Linguistic Moment*, p. 9.
43 Hartman, *Saving the Text*, pp. 79, 120–1.
44 Llewelyn, *Derrida*, p. 41.
45 Ibid., pp. 70–90, for full discussion.
46 De Man, *Allegories of Reading*, p. 115.
47 Hartman, *Criticism in the Wilderness*, p. 41.
48 Llewelyn, *Derrida*, p. 69.
49 Miller, *The Linguistic Moment*.
50 Felperin, *Beyond Deconstruction*, pp. 101, 143, 139.
51 Ibid., p. 144.
52 Leitch, *Deconstructive Criticism*, pp. 95–6.

CONCLUSION: THE 'NEW' HISTORICISM

1   For helpful accounts of the central debates and concepts involved in new historicist approaches, see *English Literary Renaissance* 16 (Winter, 1986), especially the essays by J. E. Howard and Louis Montrose.

2   See, for example, Stephen Greenblatt, *Renaissance Self-Fashioning* (Chicago, 1980), and Greenblatt, *Shakespearean Negotiations* (Oxford and Berkeley, 1988); Catherine Gallagher, *The Industrial Reformation of English Fiction* (Chicago, 1985).

3   Though Frank Lentricchia, in *After the New Criticism* (London, 1980), also used the phrase in the chapter, 'History or the abyss: poststructuralism'.

4   See Hayden White, *Metahistory: the historical imagination in nineteenth-century Europe* (Baltimore, 1973), for early, astute discussions of 'history', and see *Tropics of Discourse* (Baltimore, 1978), for further discussion on the various genres of history writing and the discourses of history.

5   Though numerous new historicists recognize the formalism implicit in new historicist theory. See, for example, Alan Liu, 'The power of formalism: the new historicism', in *English Literary History*, 56 (1989), pp. 721–71.

6   See Hayden White for example, *Metahistory* and see further White, 'New historicism: a comment', in the *New Historicism*, ed. H. Aram Veeser (London, 1989), for discussion of such a concept of history.

7   Particularly Jerome J. McGann, *The Romantic Ideology* (Chicago, 1983), who announced that the influence of Romantic theory on criticism either has ended, or ought to end, an ideology almost as convincing as the repeated castigations of Leavis, and the predictions of the 'death of the novel'.

8   For an astute discussion of determinism and history, see Raymond Williams, *Marxism and Literature* (Oxford, 1977).

9   See Frederic Jameson, *The Political Unconscious* (Ithaca, 1981; 1982), for the unconvincing accusation that deconstructionist notions of textuality lead necessarily to 'totalizations'.

10 For an anthropological viewpoint, see Clifford Geertz, *The Interpretation of Culture* (New York, 1973), and his development of the concept of 'thick description'.

11 See Frank Lentricchia, *Ariel and the Police: Michel Foucault, William James, Wallace Stevens* (Hemel Hempstead and Madison, 1988).

12 Yet see Greenblatt, *Renaissance Self-Fashioning*, for an emphasis on great writers as the means of putting us into touch with authentic past events.

13 See Stanley Fish, 'Consequences', *Critical Inquiry* 11 (March, 1985), who refers to this fantasy as the 'antifoundationalist-theory-hope'.

14 'The young and the restless', in Veeser, (ed.), pp. 303–16.

15 Michel Foucault, in, for example, *Discipline and Punish*, tr. A. M. Sheridan Smith (New York, 1977), questions the effects of a consciousness of historical perspective and explores how history can be written.

16 See Richard Rorty, *Contingency, Irony, and Solidarity* (Cambridge, 1989).

17   See W. L. Reed, 'Deconstruction versus the new historicism: recent theories and histories of the novel', paper presented at SAMLA, Atlanta, 1987.

18   Ludwig Wittgenstein was adamant throughout the *Philosophical Investigations*, tr. G. E. M. Anscombe (New York, 1958; Oxford, 1967) about the error of hypostasizing a monolithic structure, language, and then asking how it relates to the monolithic 'other', the external world. Even language/thought dichotomies were rejected. And see above, Coleridge and Shelley, chapters 1 and 3, for rejections of the thought/thing dichotomies, related also to Quine's querying of word/object dichotomies in Willard van Orman Quine, *Word and Object* (Cambridge, Mass., 1960), as well as in later essays on 'ontological relativity' and paradox.

19   See Elinor Shaffer, *'Kubla Khan' and the Fall of Jerusalem: The Mythological School of Biblical Criticism and Secular Literature, 1770–1880* (Cambridge, 1975), on 'higher criticism'.

20   See Thomas Brook, 'The new historicism and the privileging of literature', in *Annals of Scholarship*, 4 (1987), pp. 23–48, where the Deweyan argument is discussed, that the new historicism ignores the specific qualities of literary texts which, while they can be described, do not thereby set up absolute divisions amongst types of writing; hence, Dewey's rejection of the dichotomy between poets and philosophers (see p. 262), while still respecting differences in, for example, 'rhythms of speech'. Coleridge was equally dismissive of the poet/philosopher/historian distinction, while still arguing for qualities characteristic of, but not necessarily specific to, literature, philosophy, and poetry (not to mention science, which Dewey argued was itself an art, both in practice and in discourse).

21   See also Edward Said, 'The problem of textuality: two exemplary positions', *Critical Inquiry*, 4 (1978), in which Said argued for a resistance to reducing literary texts to other texts (such as history). He insisted on the notion that each domain has its own 'impressive' and irreducible characteristics, which should co-exist and be correlated with each other. While one respects Said's effort to avoid reduction, his 'irreducible characteristics' smack of essentialism, and of 'law-making', as Dewey put it.

22   See chapter 2, for further discussion.

23   In John Dewey, *Experience and Nature* (New York, 1958), chapters 9 and 10. And see Dewey on Gottlieb Herder as 'the true historicist', in 'The development of American pragmatism', in *The Philosophy of John Dewey*, ed. John McDermott (Chicago and London, 1981).

24   Søren Kierkegaard *Philosophical Fragments*, tr. D. Swenson, intro. N. Thulstrup, revised H. V. Hong (Princeton, 1936; 1967), provides a most relevant discussion of history, perspective, and the problems associated with contemporaneity (the first hand disciple's knowledge of Christ as no more true than later disciples'?), while being at the same time a demonstration of the overruning of the borders between philosophy, literature, history, and religion. It is also a powerful and eloquent, albeit indirect, exposure of new historicist assumptions, and even of the modified views of Said, discussed

above. And see further Jacques Derrida, 'That Dangerous Supplement', in *Acts of Literature*, ed. D. Attridge (New York and London, 1992), pp. 78–109, where Derrida (like Dewey) rejected the reduction of texts to historical, political, psychological, biographical, or other contexts, origins, or agendas. He urged instead that we read by attending to writing as writing, while avoiding the essentialist arguments that literature has some special, literary qualities which distinguish it as a 'region'.

AFTERWORD: REVITALIZING THE VOCABULARIES AND GENRES OF PHILOSOPHY

1   John Dewey, 'From absolutism to experimentalism', in *Contemporary American Philosophers*, eds G. P. Adams and W. P. Montague (New York, 1930), II, pp. 13–27.
2   P. B. Shelley, 'A defence of poetry', in *Selected Poetry and Prose of Percy Bysshe Shelley*, ed. Carlos Baker (New York, 1951).

Bibliography

Abrahms, M. H., *The Mirror and the Lamp, romantic theory and the critical tradition,* Oxford, 1953.

Appleyard, J. A., 'Critical theory', in *Writers and their Background: S. T. Coleridge,* ed. R. L. Brett, London, 1971, pp. 123–46.

Aune, Bruce, *Rationalism, Empiricism, Pragmatism: an introduction,* New York, 1970.

Austin, J. L., *How to do Things with Words,* Oxford, 1962.

Ayer, A. J., *Logical Positivism,* New York, 1959.

—— *The Origins of Pragmatism: studies in the philosophy of Charles Sanders Peitce and William James,* London, 1968.

Baker, Carlos H., *Shelley's Major Poetry,* New York, 1961.

Barfield, Owen, S*aving the Appearances: a study in idolatry,* New York, 1957.

—— *What Coleridge Thought,* London, 1971.

Barth, J. R., *Coleridge and Christian Doctrine,* Cambridge, Mass., 1969.

Barthes, Roland, *Le Plaisir du texte,* Paris, 1973.

—— *S/Z,* Paris, 1970. *S/Z,* tr. R. Miller, London, 1975.

Beer, John, *Coleridge the Visionary,* London and New York, 1959.

Benjamin, Walter, *Illuminations,* ed. Hannah Arendt, London, 1970.

Berkeley, George, *Works,* eds A. A. Luce and T. E. Jessop, 9 vols, London, 1948–57.

Blake, William, *Blake: complete writings,* ed. G. Keynes, London, 1966; 1969.

Bloom, Harold, *The Anxiety of Influence,* Oxford, 1973.

—— *A Map of Misreading,* Oxford, 1975.

—— *Shelley's Mythmaking,* New Haven, 1959.

Brook, Thomas, 'The new historicism and the privileging of literature', *Annals of Scholarship,* 4 (1987), pp. 23–48.

Brooks, Cleanth, 'Irony as a principle of structure', in *Literary Opinion in America,* ed. M. D. Zabel, revised edition New York, 1951, pp. 729–41.

Brown, Norman O., *Love's Body,* New York, 1966.

Chappell, V. C., ed., *The Philosophy of Mind,* Englewood Cliffs, NJ, 1962.

Chomsky, Noam, *Cartesian Linguistics: a chapter in the history of rationalist thought*, New York, 1966.

—— *Language and Mind*, enlarged edition, New York, 1968; 1972.

Coleridge, S. T., *Aids to Reflection in the Formation of a Manly Character*, ed. Thomas Fenby, Edinburgh, 1905.

—— *Biographia Literaria; or biographical sketches of my literary life and opinions with his aesthetical essays*, ed. J. Shawcross, 2 vols, London, 1907.

—— *The Collected Letters of Samuel Taylor Coleridge*, ed. E. L. Griggs, 6 vols, Oxford, 1956–71.

—— *The Friend. A Series of Essays in Three Volumes. To Aid in the Formation of Fixed Principles in Politics, Morals, and Religion, with Literary Amusements Interspersed*, ed. Barbara E. Rooke, 2 vols. Vol. 4 of *The Collected Coleridge*, London and Princeton, 1969.

—— *Hints towards the Formation of a more Comprehensive Theory of Life*, ed. S. B. Watson, London, 1848.

—— *Lay Sermons*, ed. R. J. White. Vol. 6 of *The Collected Coleridge*, London and Princeton, 1972.

—— *Marginalia. Samuel Taylor Coleridge. The Collected Coleridge*, eds George Whalley and H. J. Jackson (3 vols so far published), Princeton and London, 1980– .

—— *The Notebooks of Samuel Taylor Coleridge*, eds Kathleen Coburn and M. Christensen (4 parts in 8 vols so far published), London and New York, 1957– .

—— *On the Constitution of Church and State according to the Idea of Each with Aids towards a Right Judgement on the late Catholic Bill*, ed. John Colmer. Vol. 10 of *The Collected Coleridge*, London and Princeton, 1977.

—— *The Philosophical Lectures*, ed. K. Coburn, London, 1949.

—— *Shakespearean Criticism*, ed. T. M. Raysor, 2 vols, London, 1930; New York, 1960.

Coughlan, Neil; *Young John Dewey*, Chicago, 1973.

Derrida, Jacques, 'Before the law', in *Acts of Literature*, ed. D. Attridge, London, 1992, pp. 181–220.

——'Differance', in *Speech and Phenomena, and Other Essays on Husserl's Theory of Signs*, tr. D. B. Allison, Evanston, 1973, pp. 129–60.

—— *Dissemination*, tr. Barbara Johnson, Chicago, 1981 (originally published in French in 1972).

—— *The Ear of the Other. Otobiography, Transference, Translation etc.*, ed. Christie McDonald, tr. A. Ronell, P. Kamuf, New York, 1985.

—— 'Form and meaning', in *Speech and Phenomena*, tr. D. B. Allison, Evanston, 1973, pp. 107–28.

—— *Glas*, tr. G. J. P. Leavey, Jr and Richard Rand, Lincoln, 1986.

—— *Of Grammatology*, tr. and introduced by G. Spivak, Baltimore, 1974; 1976.

—— 'Living on: BORDER LINES', in *Deconstruction and Criticism*, ed. H. Bloom, New York, 1979, pp. 75–176.

—— 'Plato's pharmacy', in *Dissemination*, tr. Barbara Johnson, Chicago, 1981,

290   Bibliography

pp. 61–171.

—— 'The pit and the pyramid', in *Margins of Philosophy*, tr. A. Bass, Hemel Hempstead, 1982, pp. 69–108.

—— *Speech and Phenomena*, tr. D. Allison, Evanston, 1973.

—— *Spurs. Nietzsche's Styles*, tr, B. Harlow, Chicago and London, 1979.

—— 'Structure, sign and play in the discourse of the hunan sciences', in *The Structuralist Controversy*, eds R. Macksey and E. Donato, Baltimore and London, 1975, pp. 247–65. (This essay first appeared in 1970.)

—— 'The supplement of origin', *Speech and Phenomena* tr. D. B. Allison, Evanston, 1973, pp. 88–107.

—— '. . . That Dangerous Supplement . . .', in *Acts of Literature*, ed. D. Attridge, New York and London, 1992, pp. 76–109.

—— 'White mythology: metaphor in the text of philosophy', *Margins of Philosophy*, tr. A. Bass, Hemel Hempstead, 1982, pp. 207–71.

—— *Writing and Difference*, tr. A. Bass, London, 1978, 1981.

Descombes, Vincent, *Modern French Philosophy*, tr. L. Scott-Fox and J. M. Harding, Cambridge, 1980.

Dewey, John, *Art as Experience*, New York, 1958 (first published 1934).

—— 'The development of American pragmatism', in *Philosophy and Civilization*, New York, 1931; 1963, pp. 13–35.

—— *Experience and Nature*, New York, 1958 (originally published 1925; revised edition 1929).

—— 'Experience, knowledge and value: a rejoinder', in *The Philosophy of John Dewey*, ed. P. A. Schilpp, La Salle, Ill., 1939; 1951; 1971, pp. 515–608.

—— 'From absolutism to experimentalism', in *Contemporary American Philosophers*, eds E. P. Adams and W. P. Montague, New York, 1930, II, pp. 13–27.

—— *The Influence of Darwinism on Philosophy: and other essays in contemporary thought*, New York, 1910; 1938.

—— *John Dewey: the early, middle, and late works*, ed. Jo Ann Boydston, Carbondale and Edwardsville, 1967–   .

—— 'Kant and philosophic method', *Journal of Speculative phillosophy*, 18 (April, 1884), pp. 162–74.

—— *Logic: the theory of inquiry*, New York, 1938.

—— 'The need for a recovery of philosophy', in *Creative Intelligence: essays in the pragmatic attitude*, New York, 1917; 1945, pp. 3–69.

—— *The Philosophy of John Dewey*, ed. John McDermott, 2 vols in 1, Chicago and London, 1981.

—— 'Ralph Waldo Emerson', in *Popular Essays in Social and Political Philosophy. Characters and Events*, ed. Joseph Ratner, 2 vols, New York, 1929; 1957, I, pp. 69–77.

Dieckmann, L., 'Friedrich Schlegel and the romantic concept of the symbol', *Germanic Review*, 34 (1959), pp. 276–83.

Doney, W. (ed.), *Descartes: a collection of critical essays*, London, 1968.

Eichner, Hans, 'Friedrich Schlegel's theory of romantic poetry', *PMLA*, 71

(1956), pp. 1018–41.

Empson, William, *Seven Types of Ambiguity*, London, 1930, Harmondsworth, 1961.

—— *The Structure of Complex Words*, London, 1951.

Fauteck, H., 'Die Sprachtheorie Friedrich von Hardenbergs', *Neue Forschungen*, 34 (Berlin, 1940).

Feldman, W. T., *The Philosophy of John Dewey*, Baltimore, 1934.

Felperin, Howard, *Beyond Deconstruction*, Oxford, 1985.

Fish, Stanley, 'Commentary: the young and the restless', in *The New Historicism*, ed. H. Aram Veeser, London, 1989, pp. 303–16.

—— 'Consequences', *Critical Inquiry*, 11 (March 1985), pp. 430–41.

—— 'How ordinary is ordinary language?', *New Literary History*, 5 (1973), pp. 41–54.

—— *Is There a Text in this Class? The Authority of Interpretive Communities*, Cambridge, Mass., 1980; 1982.

Fogle, R. H., *The Idea of Coleridge's Criticism*, Berkeley, 1962.

Foucault, Michel, *The Archaeology of Knowledge*, tr. A. M. Sheridan Smith, London, 1972; 1977.

—— *Discipline and Punish*, tr. A. M. Sheridan Smith, New York, 1977.

Gallagher, Catherine, *The Industrial Reformation of English Fiction*, Chicago, 1985.

Geertz, Clifford, *The Interpretation of Culture*, New York, 1973.

Gombrich, Ernst, *Art and Illusion*, Princeton, 1960.

Goodman, Nelson, *The Languages of Art*, New York, 1968; London, 1969.

—— *Ways of Worldmaking*, Cambridge and Indianapolis, 1978; 1981.

Greenblatt, Stephen, *Renaissance Self-Fashioning: from More to Shakespeare*, Chicago, 1980.

—— *Shakespearean Negotiations*, Oxford and Berkeley, 1988.

Gregory, R., *Concepts and Mechanisms of Perception*, London, 1974.

Grene, Marjorie, 'Life, death, and language: some thoughts on Wittgenstein and Derrida', in *Philosophy in and out of Europe*, ed. M. Grene, Berkeley, 1976, pp. 142–54.

Griggs, E. L., 'Ludwig Tieck and Samuel Taylor Coleridge', *Journal of English and German Philology*, 54 (April 1955), pp. 262–8.

Hacking, Ian, *Why Does Language Matter to Philosophy?*, Cambridge, 1975.

Hagstrum, Jean, *Samuel Johnson's Literary Criticism*, Minneapolis, 1952.

Hardenberg, Friedrich von (Novalis), 'Miscellaneous writings', in *German Aesthetic and Literary Criticism: the Romantic ironists and Goethe*, ed. K. M. Wheeler, Cambridge, 1984.

—— *Novalis Schriften*, eds P. Kluckhorn and R. Samuel, 4 vols, Stuttgart, 1960–75.

Hartman, Geoffrey, *Criticism in the Wilderness: the study of literature today*, New Haven, 1980.

—— *Saving the Text. Literature/Derrida/Philosophy*, Baltimore, 1981.

Hegel, G. W. F., *Hegel's Science of Logic*, tr. W. H. Johnston and L. G. Struthers, 2 vols, London and New York, 1929.

—— *The Phenomenology of Mind*, tr. J. B. Baillie, intro. G. Lichtheim, New

292   *Bibliography*

York, 1967.

—— 'Über Solgers *Nachgelassene Schriften und Briefwechsel*', *Janhrbücher für wissenschaftliche Kritik*, 51–4 (1828), pp. 105–10.

Heidegger, Martin, *On the Way to Language*, tr. P. D. Hertz, New York, 1971 (*Unterwegs zur Sprache*, Pfullingen, 1959).

—— *Poetry, Language, Thought*, tr. A. Hofstadter, New York, 1975.

—— *What is called Thinking?*, tr. J. Glenn Gray, New York, 1968. (Was Heisst Denken?, Tübingen, 1954.)

Heller, Josef, *Solgers Philosophie der ironischen Dialektik*, Berlin, 1928.

Hesse, Mary B., *Models and Analogies in Science*, Notre Dame, 1966.

Hollis, Martin, 'The self in action', in *John Dewey Reconsidered*, ed. R. S. Peters, London, 1977, pp. 56–75.

Hyppolite, Jean, *Genesis and Structure in Hegel'sphenomenology*, tr. S. Cherniak and J. Heckman, Evanston, 1974.

—— 'The structure of philosophic language according to the 'Preface' to Hegel's *Phenomenology of the Mind*', in *The Structuralist Controversy*, eds R. Macksey and E. Donato, Baltimore, 1970; 1972, pp. 157–69.

Immerwahr, R., 'The subjectivity or objectivity of Friedrich Schlegel's Poetic Irony', *Germanic Review*, 26 (1951), pp. 173–91.

Jackson, J. R. de J., *Method and Imagination in Coleridge's Criticism*, Cambridge, Mass., 1969.

Jakobson, Roman and Halle, Morris, *Fundamentals of Language*, The Hague, 1956; 1971.

James, William, *Collected Essays and Reviews*, London, 1920.

—— *Essays in Radical Empiricism*. Vol. 3 in *The Works of William James*, eds F. H. Burkhardt, F. Bowers, and I. K. Skrupskelis, Cambridge, Mass., 1976 (first published 1912).

—— *Pragmatism: A New Name for Some Old Ways of Thinking & The Meaning of Truth: A Sequel to Pragmatism*, intro. A. J. Ayer, Cambridge, Mass., 1978.

—— *Principles of Psychology*, 2 vols, Cambridge, Mass., 1902 (first published 1890).

—— *Some Problems of Philosophy*. Vol. 7 in *The Works of William James*, eds F. H. Burkhardt, F. Bowers, and I. K. Skrupskelis, Cambridge, Mass., 1979.

—— *Varieties of Religious Experience*, intro. R. Niebuhr, London, 1967 (first published 1902).

Jameson, Frederic, T*he Political Unconscious: narrative as a socially symbolic act*, Ithaca, 1981.

Johnson, Barbara, *The Critical Difference. Essays in the Contemporary Rhetoric of Reading*, Baltimore, 1981.

Johnson, Christopher, *System and Writing in the Philosophy of Jacques Derrida*, Oxford, forthcoming.

Johnson, Samuel, *The Works of Samuel Johnson*, ed. A. Chalmers, 12 vols, London, 1810.

Kant, Immanuel, *Critique of Pure Reason*, tr. N. Kemp Smith, Toronto and New York, 1965.

Keats, John, *Letters of John Keats, 1814–21*, ed. H. E. Rollins, 2 vols, Cambridge, 1958.

Kierkegaard, Søren, *The Concept of Irony*, tr. L. M. Capell, London, 1966.

—— *Philosophical Fragments*, tr. D. F. Swenson, intro. N. Thulstrup, rev'd. H. V. Hong, Princeton, 1936; 1967.

Knox, Norman, *The Word 'IRONY' and its Context 1500–1755*, Durham, NC, 1961.

Koch, Max, 'Ludwig Tiecks Stellung zu Shakespeare', *Shakespeare Jahrbuch*, 32 (1896), pp. 330–47.

Kojève, Alexandre, *Introduction à la lecture de Hegel*, Paris, 1947. *Introduction to the Reading of Hegel*, tr. J. H. Nicholls Jr, ed. Allan Bloom, New York, 1969.

Kuhn, Thomas, *The Structure of Scientific Revolutions*, Chicago, 1962.

Lakatos, I., 'Falsification and the methodology of scientific research programmes', in *Criticism and the Growth of Knowledge*, ed. I. Lakatos and A. Musgrave, Cambridge, 1970, pp. 91–196.

Leitch, Vincent, *Deconstructive Criticism: an advanced introduction*, London, 1983.

—— 'The lateral dance: the deconstructive criticism of J. Hillis Miller', *Critical Inquiry*, 6 (1980), pp. 593–607.

Lentricchia, Frank, *Ariel and the Police: Michel Foucault, William James, Wallace Stevens*, Hemel Hempstead and Madison, 1988.

—— *After the New Criticism*, London, 1980.

—— *Criticism and Social Change*, Chicago, 1983.

Liu, Alan, 'The power of formalism: the new historicism', *English Literary History*, 56 (1989), pp. 721–71.

Llewelyn, John, *Derrida on the Threshold of Sense*, New York, 1986.

Lussky, A. E., *Tieck's Romantic Irony*, Chapel Hill, 1932.

McCallum, Pamela, *Literature and Method: towards a critique of I. A. Richards, T. S. Eliot and F. R. Leavis*, Dublin, 1983.

McGann, Jerome J., *The Romantic Ideology: a critical investigation*, Chicago, 1983.

McKusick, James C., *Coleridge's Philosophy of Language*, New Haven and London, 1986.

Man, Paul de, *Allegories of Reading: figurative language in Roussean, Nietzsche, Rilke and Proust*, London and New Haven, 1979.

—— *Blindness and Insight: essays in the rhetoric of contemporary criticism*, New York and London, 1971, enlarged and revised, ed. W. Godzich, London, 1983.

—— 'Shelley Disfigured', in *Deconstruction and Criticism*, ed. H. Bloom, New York, 1979, pp. 39–74.

Marx, Werner, *Heidegger and the Tradition*, Evanston, Ill., 1971.

Merleau-Ponty, Maurice, *Sense and Nonsense*, tr. H. and P. Dreyfus, Evanston, Ill., 1964.

Miller, J. Hillis, 'The critic as host', *Deconstruction and Criticism*, ed. H. Bloom, New York, 1979, pp. 217–53.

—— *The Linguistic Moment: from Wordsworth to Stevens*, Princeton, 1985.

Morgenbesser, S. (ed.), *Dewey and his Critics: essays from 'The Journal of Philosophy'*, New York, 1977.

Morick, H., (ed.), *Wittgenstein and the Problem of Other Minds*, New York, 1967.

Morris, L. R., *William James: the message of a modern mind*, New York, 1950.

Muecke, D. C., *The Compass of Irony*, London, 1969.

Muelder, W. G. and L. Sears, *The Development of American Philosophy*, Boston, 1960.

Mueller, G. E., 'Solger's aesthetics – A Key to Hegel', in *Corona: Studies in Celebration of the Eightieth Birthday of Samuel Singer*, ed. A. Schirokauer, Durham, 1941, pp. 212–27.

Murphy, A. E., 'Dewey's epistemology and metaphysics', in *The Philosophy of John Dewey*, ed. P. A. Schilpp, La Salle, Ill., (1939, 1951, 1971), pp. 193–226.

Muirhead, John, *Coleridge as Philosopher*, London, 1930.

Nietzsche, Friedrich, *The Birth of Tragedy*, tr. F. Golffing, New York, 1956.

—— *Daybreak*, tr. R. J. Hollingdale, intro. M. Tanner, Cambridge, 1982 (*Morgenröte*, Chemnitz, 1881).

—— *The Gay Science*, tr. W. Kaufmann, New York, 1974.

—— *Twilight of the Idols and the Anti-Christ*, tr. R. J. Hollingdale, Harmondsworth, 1979 (*Götzen-Dämmerung*, (first published 1889); *Der Antichrist*, 1895).

—— *The Will to Power*, tr. Walter Kaufmann and R. J. Hollingdale, New York, 1968 (*Der Wille zur Macht*. In *Nietzsches Werke*, Leipzig, 1911, vols 15–16).

Norris, Christopher, *The Contest of Faculties*, London and New York, 1985.

Novack, George, *Pragmatism versus Marxism: an appraisal of John Dewey's philosoply*, New York, 1975.

Parodi, D., 'Knowledge and action in John Dewey's philosophy', in *The Philosophy of John Dewey*, ed. P. A. Schilpp, La Salle, Ill., 1939; 1951; 1971, pp. 227–242.

Patrides, C. A. (ed. and intro.), *The Cambridge Platonists*, London, 1969.

Pears, David, *Wittgenstein*, New York and London, 1971.

Peirce, C. S., *Collected Papers of C. S. Peirce*, 8 vols, eds C. Hartshorne, P. Weiss, and A. W. Burks, Cambridge, Mass., 1931–58.

Pepper, Stephen C., 'Some questions on Dewey's aesthetics', in *The Philosophy of John Dewey*, ed. P. A. Schilpp, La Salle, Ill., 1939; 1951; 1971, pp. 369–89.

Perry, R. B., 'A review of pragmatism as a theory of knowledge', in *Dewey and his Critics*, ed. S. Morgenbesser, New York, 1977, pp. 213–22 (first published 1907).

—— *The Thought and Character of William James*, Boston, 1935.

Pitcher, George, *The Philosophy of Wittgenstein*, Englewood Cliffs, NJ, 1964.

Plato, *The Collected Dialogues of Plato, Including the Letters*, eds E. Hamilton and H. Cairns, Princeton, 1961; 1969.

Pratt, J. B., *What is Pragmatism?*, New York, 1909.

Quine, Willard van Orman, *From a Logical Point of View*, New York, 1963 (first published Cambridge, Mass., 1953).

—— *Ontological Relativity and Other Essays*, New York and London, 1969.

—— *Word and Object*, Cambridge, Mass., 1960.

Quinton, Anthony, 'Inquiry, thought, and action: John Dewey's theory of knowledge', in *John Dewey Reconsidered*, ed. R. S. Peters, London, 1977, pp. 1–17.

Randall, Jr, J. M., 'Dewey's interpretation of the history of philosophy', in *The philosophy of John Dewey*, ed. P. A. Schilpp, La Salle, Ill., 1939; 1951; 1971, pp. 75–102.

Ratner, Joseph, 'Dewey's conception of philosophy', in *The Philosophy of John Dewey*, ed. P. A. Schilpp, La Salle, Ill., 1939; 1951; 1971, pp. 47–74.

Reichenbach, Hans, 'Dewey's theory of science', in *The Philosophy of John Dewey*, ed. P. A. Schilpp, La Salle, Ill., 1939; 1951; 1971, pp. 157–92.

Rey, Jean-Michel, *L'enjeu des signes: lecture de Nietzsche*, Paris, 1971.

Ribbeck, Otto, 'Ueber den Begriff des εἴρων', *Rheinisches Museum*, 31 (1876), pp. 381–400.

Richards, I. A., *Coleridge on Imagination*, London, 1934.

Richter, Jean Paul, *Horn of Oberon: Jean Paul's School for Aesthetics*, tr. M. R. Hale, Detroit, 1973.

Ricoeur, Paul, *The Rule of Metaphor*, tr. R. Czerny, London and Henley, 1978.

Riddel, Joseph N., *The Clairvoyant Eye: the Poetry and Poetics of Wallace Stevens*, Louisiana, 1965.

Rorty, Amelie (ed.), *Essays on Aristotle's Ethics*, Berkeley, 1980.

—— (ed.), *Pragmatic Philosophy*, Garden City, NJ, 1966.

Rorty, Richard, *Consequences of Pragmatism*, Minneapolis and Brighton, 1982.

—— 'Dewey's metaphysics', in *New Studies in the Philosophy of John Dewey*, ed. S. M. Cahn, Hanover, NH, 1977, pp. 45–74.

—— *Contingency, Irony, and Solidarity*, Cambridge, 1989.

—— (ed.), *The Linguistic Turn: recent essays in philosophical method*, Chicago, 1967.

—— 'Nineteenth century idealism and twentieth century textualism', *the Monist* 46, (1981), pp. 155–74.

—— 'Overcoming the tradition: Heidegger and Dewey', *The Review of Metaphysics*, 30 (1976), pp. 280–305.

—— *Philosophy and the Mirror of Nature*. Princeton: 1979; 1980.

—— 'The world well lost', *Journal of philosophy*, 69 (1972), pp. 649–65.

Rosen, Stanley, *Nihilism*, New Haven, 1969.

Ryle, Gilbert, *The Concept of Mind*, London and New York, 1949.

Said, Edward, 'The problem of textuality: two exemplary positions', *Critical Inquiry*, 4 (1978), pp. 710–23.

Saussure, Ferdinand de, *Course in General Linguistics*, tr. W. Baskin, London, 1974.

Scheffler, Israel, *Four Pragmatists: a critical introduction to Peirce, James, Mead and Dewey*, New York and London, 1974.

Schlegel, Friedrich, *Friedrich Schlegel's Literary Notebooks 1797–1801*, ed. Hans Eichner, Toronto, 1957.

—— *Friedrich Schlegel, 1794–1802. Seine prosaishen Jugendschriften*, ed. J. M. Minor, 2 vols, Vienna, 1882.

Schneidau, H. N., 'The word against the word: Derrida on textuality', *Semeia* (1977), pp. 5–28.

Schrickx, W., 'Coleridge and the Cambridge Platonists', *A Review of English Studies*, 7 (1966), pp. 71–90.

Schulze, E. J., *Shelley's Theory of Poetry: a Reappraisal*, The Hague, 1966.

Shaffer, Elinor, *'Kubla Khan' and the Fall of Jerusalem: the mythological school of biblical criticism and secular literature, 1770–1880*, Cambridge, 1975.

Shaffer, Jerome A., *Philosophy of Mind*, Englewood Cliffs, NJ, 1968.

Shearer, E. A., 'Dewey's aesthetic theory, I and II', in *Dewey and his Critics*, ed. S. Morgenbesser, New York, 1977, pp. 404–29 (first published 1935).

Shelley, Percy Bysshe, T*he Complete Works of Percy Bysshe Shelley*, ed. R. Ingpen and W. E. Peck, New York and London, 1965.

—— *Selected Poetry and Prose of Percy Bysshe Shelley*, ed. Carlos Baker, New York, 1951.

Solger, Karl, *Erwin. Vier Gespräche über das Schöne und die Kunst*, ed. W. Henckmann, München, 1971 (first published Berlin, 1815).

—— *Nachgelassene Schriften und Briefwechsel*, ed. L. Tieck und F. von Raumer, 2 vols, Leipzig, 1826.

Spivak, Gayatri, 'Translator's preface', *Of Grammatology*, Jacques Derrida, Baltimore and London, 1974; 1976, pp. ix–xc.

Strohschneider-Kohrs, Ingrid, '*Die Romantische Ironie in Theorie und Gestaltung'*, *Hermaea*, 6, Tübingen, 1960.

Szondi, Peter, 'Friedrich Schlegel und die romantische Ironie: mit einem Anhang über Ludwig Tieck', *Euphorion*, 48 (1954), pp. 397–411.

Thayer, H. S., *Meaning and Action: a critical history of pragmatism*, New York, 1968.

Thompson, J. A. K., *Irony: an historical introduction*, London, 1926.

Tieck, Ludwig, *Das Buch über Shakespeare*, ed. H. Lüdeke, Halle 1920.

—— *Kritische Schriften*, 6 vols, Leipzig, 1845–52.

—— *Nachgelassene Schriften*, ed. R. Köpke, 2 vols, Leipzig, 1855.

—— and Solger, Karl, *Tieck and Solger. The Complete Correspondence*, ed. P. Matenko, New York and Berlin, 1933.

Tiles, J. E., *Dewey*, New York and London, 1988.

Turbayne, Colin, *The Myth of Metaphor*, New Haven, 1962.

Veeser, H. Aram. (ed.), *The New Historicism*, London, 1989.

Vesey, G. M. A. (ed.), *Body and Mind*: readings in philosophy, London, 1964.

Voitle, Robert, *Samuel Johnson the Moralist*, Cambridge, Mass., 1961.

Wasserman, Earl, *The Subtler Language*, Baltimore, 1959.

Wells, H. K., *Pragmatism: Philosophy of Imperialism*, New York, 1954.

Wheeler, K. M., 'Berkeley's ironic method', *Philosophy and Literature*, 4 (spring, 1980), pp. 18–32.

—— 'Coleridge and modern critical theory', in *Coleridge's Theory of the Imagination Today*, ed. Christine Gallant, New York, 1989, pp. 83–102.

—— 'Coleridge's friendship with Ludwig Tieck', in *New Approaches to Coleridge*, ed. D. Sultana, London, 1981, pp. 96–112.

—— *The Creative Mind in Coleridge's Poetry*, Cambridge, Mass. and London, 1981.

—— (ed.), *German Aesthetic and Literary Criticism: the Romantic Ironists and Goethe*, Cambridge, 1984.

—— 'Kant and romanticism', *Philosophy and Literature*, 13 (summer, 1989), pp 42–56.

—— 'Kubla khan' and eighteenth century aesthetic theories', *Wordsworth Circle*, 22 (1991), pp. 15–24.

—— 'S. T. Coleridge: *Aids to Reflection*. Language and the growth of conscience', in *Literature and Religion*, ed. Solange Dayras, Paris, forthcoming.

—— *Sources, Processes, and Methods in Coleridge's 'Biographia Literaria'*, Cambridge, 1980.

White, Hayden, *Metahistory: the historical imagination in nineteenth-century Europe*, Baltimore, 1973.

—— 'New historicism: a comment', in *The New Historicism*, ed. A. Veeser, London, 1989.

—— *Tropics of Discourse: essays in cultural criticism*, Baltimore, 1978.

Wilden, Anthony, *System and Structure: essays in communication and exchange*, London, 1977; 1980.

Wilkending, G., *Jean Paul's Sprachauffassung in ihrem Verhältnis zu seiner Aesthetik*, Marburg, 1968.

Williams, Raymond, *Marxism and Literature*, Oxford, 1977.

Wilson, John, 'Some observations on the *Biographia Literaria* of S. T. Coleridge, Esq. – 1817', *Blackwood's Magazine*, 2 (1817), pp. 3–18. Reprinted in *The Critical Heritage*, ed. J. R. de J. Jackson, London, 1970.

Wittgenstein, Ludwig, *Philosophical Investigations*, tr. G. E. M. Anscombe (New York, 1958; Oxford, 1967).

Woodman, R. G., *The Apocalyptic Vision in the Poetry of Shelley*, Toronto, 1964.

Wright, John W., 'Samuel Johnson and traditional methodology', *PMLA*, 86 (1971), pp. 40–50.

—— *Shelley's Myth of Metaphor*, Athens, Georgia, 1970.

Index

LINCOLN CHRISTIAN COLLEGE AND SEMINARY